DIRTY DEEDS

DIRTY DEEDS

 LAND, VIOLENCE, AND THE 1856 SAN FRANCISCO VIGILANCE COMMITTEE

Nancy J. Taniguchi

UNIVERSITY OF OKLAHOMA PRESS : NORMAN

Also by Nancy J. Taniguchi
Necessary Fraud: Progressive Reform and Utah Coal (Norman, Okla., 1996)
Castle Valley America: Hard Land, Hard-Won Home (Logan, Utah, 2004)

Publication of this book is made possible through the generosity of Edith Kinney Gaylord.

Library of Congress Cataloging-in-Publication Data

Names: Taniguchi, Nancy J. (Nancy Jacobus), 1948– author.
Title: Dirty deeds : land, violence, and the 1856 San Francisco Vigilance Committee / Nancy J. Taniguchi.
Other titles: Land, violence, and the 1856 San Francisco Vigilance Committee Description: Norman, OK : University of Oklahoma Press, [2016] | Includes bibliographical references and index.
Identifiers: LCCN 2016011314 | ISBN 978-0-8061-5398-8 (hardcover)
ISBN 978-0-8061-9308-3 (paper) Subjects: LCSH: San Francisco Committee of Vigilance of 1856. | San Francisco (Calif.)—

　　Politics and government—19th century. | Land titles—California—San Francisco—History. | Land tenure—Political aspects—California—San Francisco—History—19th century. | Landowners—Political activity—California—San Francisco—History—19th century. | Vigilance committees—California—San Francisco. | San Francisco (Calif.)—Economic conditions—19th century.
Classification: LCC F869.S3 .T17 2016 | DDC 979.4/6104—dc23
LC record available at http://lccn.loc.gov/2016011314

The paper in this book meets the guidelines for permanence and durability of the Committee on Production Guidelines for Book Longevity of the Council on Library Resources, Inc. ∞

Copyright © 2016 by the University of Oklahoma Press, Norman, Publishing Division of the University. Paperback published 2023. Manufactured in the U.S.A.

All rights reserved. No part of this publication may be reproduced, stored in a retrieval system, or transmitted, in any form or by any means, electronic, mechanical, photocopying, recording, or otherwise—except as permitted under Section 107 or 108 of the United States Copyright Act—without the prior written permission of the University of Oklahoma Press. To request permission to reproduce selections from this book, write to Permissions, University of Oklahoma Press, 2800 Venture Drive, Norman, OK 73069, or email rights.oupress@ou.edu.

To Bob—
who but for World War II
would have been born in California

Contents

List of Illustrations ... ix
Preface and Acknowledgments ... xi

Introduction ... 3

PART I A Contentious Place

1. Unstable Ground ... 15
2. Feisty Editor, Contentious Elections ... 24
3. Land and Newsprint ... 33
4. Under Attack ... 42
5. In Secret Tribunal ... 50
6. The Black List ... 58
7. Arresting Developments ... 66

PART II Vigilantes Rising

8. Escalating Tensions ... 75
9. Rumors and Revelations ... 83
10. Vigilante Blood ... 91
11. Unintended Consequences ... 99
12. Mounting Opposition ... 109
13. Sectional Strife ... 118

PART III Changing Directions

14	A New Agenda	129
15	Trying Times	138
16	Blood Lust	146
17	Release	157
18	A False Finale	166
19	Pirates and Payback	175
20	Politics and Property	184

PART IV A New Era

21	Reputation's Rollercoaster	195
22	Seeking Resolution	205
23	Irreconcilable Differences	214
24	Lasting Transformations	221
25	Secrets	230

Notes	241
Bibliography	279
Index	289

Illustrations

MAP

San Francisco	35

FIGURES

William Tell Coleman	17
San Francisco water lots	19
James King of William	27
Casey shoots King lithograph	39
Casey and Cora taken from jail lithograph	48
King's funeral cortege	55
Execution of Casey and Cora lithograph	56
Print of 1849 Hyer-Sullivan fight	61
Mug shots of Vigilance Committee victims	69
Pro-vigilante depiction of deportations	77
Fort Gunnybags	81
Pro-vigilante depiction of a mass meeting	85
Governor Johnson pushing back "flood" of reform	89
Stabbing of Sterling Hopkins	93
Judge David Terry	95
Cornelia Runnels Terry and baby	105
Bulletin board at Empire Engine House No. 1	114

San Francisco Bay steamer	123
Mounted vigilante battalion	130
Patriotic depiction of hanging	154
More realistic depiction of hanging	155
Final vigilante parade and onlookers	171
Vigilance Committee member certificate	181
Sterling Hopkins with noose	203
David C. Broderick as senator	215
Transcontinental railroad	223
Executive *Minutes* of 1856 Vigilance Committee	235

Preface and Acknowledgments

For years I posed this scenario: "Imagine thirty rich businessmen who commanded an army of six thousand. They kidnapped other men off the streets, gave them secret trials, and either hanged or deported them. When and where did this take place?" Dozens of people leapt to the challenge:

"Sounds like the gangs of New York."

"The Middle East?"

"Cambodia!"

"Texas in the 1990s!"

"Was this in South America?"

"Were they Mormons?"

"That's what they do to Mexicans around here," said my cousin in Phoenix.

"Montana!" cried a western history buff.

"Guantanamo, right? Oh, wait, they don't hang them, do they?"

"Must have been the California gold rush."

The last response was close, but not quite right. The answer is 1856, in San Francisco, where, as the gold rush wound down, the city's leading merchants organized the largest vigilance committee in American history.

History creates memory and, as the cliché goes, tells the story of the winners. Hadn't San Francisco's 1856 Vigilance Committee won, cleaning up the city's politics, thus accomplishing its ultimate purpose of establishing good government? Historians since 1856 have debated the achievement of this laudable objective, yet somehow this extraordinary group has been largely forgotten. Why?

My own pursuit of this question began with the disconsolate Hugh Breen. An unemployed handyman, he spent most of the summer of 1856 in San Francisco, struggling to earn enough money to pay the steamboat fare back to his home in New Orleans. Atypically for a man of his class, he kept a daily diary, in which he recorded the vigilantes' activities, which were roiling the town. As he noted on June 16, "I wish this excitement of Clearing the Blackguards out of Town was finished and Business take a start. If I could only get two or three weeks work it would put me on my feet again." Breen finally managed to return to New Orleans, and to his beloved wife and child. Over time, he and his wife had other children, including a son who inherited Breen's diary and passed it on to his daughter. She, in turn, left her grandfather's diary to her grandson, my friend since college days. In 2005 he handed it to me, saying, "Looks like the Civil War began early in California." Like so many people, he had not heard of San Francisco's 1856 Vigilance Committee. The search for more information about the diarist's life and times eventually led me to write this book.

Every primary source needs a good context, and I spent months trying to find a focus. Given Breen's desperate longing for a ticket home, the rigors of making a trip from California to the eastern states in 1856 seemed like a logical choice. Transit had become easier since the gold rush days, when sea travel meant sailing around the Horn, the southern tip of South America. No American railroad yet linked California to the East, but in 1855 a new line snaked across the Isthmus of Panama, linking Pacific and Atlantic steamships. By 1856, a typical San Francisco newspaper advertisement trumpeted:

> STEAMERS ... [California] Passengers on this line are landed on their arrival at Panama upon the Wharf at the Railroad terminus [on the Pacific Ocean], by the Company's Steam Ferry Boat, and proceed immediately [eastward] BY RAILROAD ACROSS THE ISTHMUS TO ASPINWALL [on the Caribbean Sea], Where there is always a Steamer awaiting their arrival. According to arrangements newly completed, Passengers arriving at Panama in the morning, invariably leave Aspinwall for New York and New Orleans in the afternoon of the same day, thus affording ... A Safe, Pleasant, and Expeditious Transit from Ocean to Ocean.[1]

Working initially with a student assistant, I agreed that she would conduct more research on antebellum New Orleans while I would concentrate on Breen's Central American crossing. We consequently planned a trip to the Sutro branch of the California State Library, which held New Orleans business directories and offered some other tantalizing material.

In teaching California history, I had made several research trips to the California State Library in Sacramento, but I had never been to the Sutro branch in San

Francisco, which holds material on all the states except California—perfect for research on Breen's Louisiana home. In addition, according to a notice inherited from my professional predecessor, the late John Edwards Caswell, professor of California history at California State University, Stanislaus, the Sutro also held an intriguing manuscript. Dr. Caswell had carefully preserved the spring 1957 issue of the *Sutro Library Notes*, which announced the library's acquisition of the Theodore Henry Hittell Collection. According to the anonymous author (Richard Dillon, then Sutro librarian), this collection included "the manuscript of his unpublished book on filibusterer William Walker." This American filibuster had ruled Nicaragua in 1856–57 and controlled that part of the inter-ocean transit where Breen might have crossed. Perhaps Hittell's manuscript could provide me with some useful pointers on Central American events while my student perused the New Orleans business directories. Dillon's article also noted, "Second only to H. H. Bancroft in renown as a California historian is Theodore Henry Hittell" and went on to describe Hittell's background, concluding, "Hittell died in February 1917. On April 19, 1918, his estate deposited forty-one of his manuscripts and typescripts in Sutro Library with the proviso that they be kept confidential for an unspecified time." In 1956, Dillon had contacted the family and received permission to release Hittell's papers for study by qualified researchers. Dillon concluded his announcement by inviting "[a]ficionados of California history ... to have a look at this material," adding that "this collection had remained closed until this moment (after some thirty-nine years) to all researchers."[2] By the time I got interested, it had been almost ninety years since the documents were donated.

Apparently few historians had taken up this invitation by 2006. Sutro librarian Dr. Martha Whittaker proved skeptical but helpful when I asked to see the Hittell collection, wondering if it was still in her custody. A search of the Online Archives of California revealed that this collection was indeed at the Sutro, although when she returned from the locked glassed-in archives room with a sample of Hittell's papers, the unpublished history of Walker was not among them. (It has since been determined to be missing.) However, a strange-looking document was included in the pile: a thick five-by-eight-inch sheaf of papers fastened with two brass grommets at the top, through which was threaded a piece of manila twine. As I gently turned the dry, brown pages, I realized that I was holding the *Minutes* of the Executive Committee of San Francisco's 1856 Vigilance Committee.

These *Minutes* had been generated by the Committee's leaders, who called themselves "Executives." The document recorded in formal language all the motions carried and defeated and identified all the participants by name, whereas to the public and to their own rank and file they were known only by numbers. Unlike its 1851 predecessor, the 1856 Committee never published its records, making these *Minutes* among the most intriguing documents in California history. Other miscellaneous papers from this group can be found in major research libraries, especially the Bancroft Library at the University of California, Berkeley, and the Huntington Library in San Marino, where scholars have long tapped their content. Yet here at the Sutro, along with the rest of his collection, lay Hittell's copy of the Executive *Minutes*, allegedly missing for more than a century. It had been available to researchers since 1957. Did anyone else know that this document existed? Had anyone used it? An exhaustive search of published sources showed that Hubert Howe Bancroft had perused the *Minutes*, but made only airy references to it in his work. Theodore Hittell cited the *Minutes* by date. No one else had ever used them.

Suddenly, my entire research focus shifted. I began making numerous solo trips to the Sutro Library (a round trip of nearly three hundred miles) to copy by hand a document too fragile to photocopy, too faded to photograph, and too valuable to ignore.

Who was the man who created this document? Although Theodore Henry Hittell was a known writer in his day, there was more to him than that. Born in 1830, he had graduated from Yale College with a law degree, and followed his brother to California in 1855. There he pursued newspaper work for a few years, then practiced law. All the while, he wrote. In 1860 he published the popular book *The Adventures of James Capen Adams, Mountaineer and Grizzly Bear Hunter of California*, and in 1865 *Hittell's Digest of the Laws of California*. He produced several other works, both books and articles. A prolific reader, in 1870 Hittell began collecting materials for his magnum opus, the famous *History of California*: a work of more than three thousand total pages, it was published in four volumes between 1885 and 1897. Research revealed that in 1882, at the end of his service as state senator for San Francisco, the police commissioners of San Francisco granted him permission to carry concealed weapons—both a pistol and a knife. Hardly a gunslinger, the bearded, balding, hook-nosed Hittell had probably borrowed the *Minutes*, which thousands of men had promised to guard with their lives. As he furtively made a copy, he may indeed have felt a need to arm himself.

Evidence that Hittell surreptitiously copied the *Minutes* shows in the document itself. The historian squeezed the original 545 pages into 104 five-by-eight-inch pages, tightly written in his cramped, spidery script. Fortunately for the modern researcher, he recorded all the original page numbers. Like so many of us faced with very long documents, he began by copying selectively. He skipped pages, occasionally noting that he had done so, and in places he inserted additional information in brackets. As he got deeper into the work, he may have realized that he needed some of the skipped material, and went back to pick up missing sections, sometimes scrawling them in crabbed, tiny writing on both sides of three-by-five-inch paper. Even he must have found his shrunken, spiky handwriting hard to decipher, for he next resorted to copying some pages out of order, but included the correct page numbers. Given internal evidence, his copy, though not complete, is very close. In all, judging by the recorded original page numbers, ten pages were not copied, although two of the missing pages may simply indicate the lack of numeration. In a few other instances, however, Hittell made no record. Someone put the slips more or less in order and fastened the whole at the top with grommets, obscuring some of the writing.

It is probably a coincidence that Hittell's collection was released for study one hundred years after San Franciscans organized America's largest vigilance committee, but the vigilantes certainly had good reason to preserve their secrecy. Times had changed since 1851: California was more closely connected to the Atlantic states; courts were active, and the Committee's victims knew how to use them. The vigilantes' most ruthless actions were illegal, and their leaders were indictable for kidnapping and murder. Consequently, they passed the *Minutes* from hand to hand for self-protection as demands for this document were later made in one court after another. They struggled against lawsuits for years, even after November 1859, when the *Minutes* dribble to an end.

This record shows the Executives of the 1856 Vigilance Committee to have been both more and less than the classic definition of vigilantism: an exercise of private power through violence by a group claiming to represent "the people" and wishing to create order to meet social needs.[3] They certainly exerted their private power through violent means: kidnappings, secret trials, hangings, and deportations. They also used the press, which they controlled with their considerable economic clout, to extol their role as champions of "the people," thus shaping a favorable history. Their goal, however, was not social needs but economic self-interest.

A series of anomalies pointed to the vigilantes' ultimate objective. Why had their alleged political purification started in 1856, after governmental housecleaning had already begun? The state legislature had passed the San Francisco Consolidation Act in April 1856, a month before the vigilantes reorganized their old 1851 Committee. The act's all-important section 13 mandated new judges of elections, appointed by five of the most respectable men in town for the first election only.[4] These election posts had previously been manned by ward heelers from various political parties, who had miscounted ballots, manipulating the outcome in favor of their cronies. By the time the Committee organized, a state mandate protected the purity of San Francisco's ballot box. A second red flag unfurled as I read the sixth volume of Hubert Howe Bancroft's *History of California*, which covers the years 1848 through

1859. He devoted chapter 25 to assorted California vigilance committees, including San Francisco's of 1856, lauding its traditionally accepted goal of governmental reform. In chapter 26, however, a brief footnote appeared in reference to a plethora of competing land claims to San Francisco stretching back at least to the Mexican era. In tiny print, it noted "the purchase by the vigilance committee of 1856 of documents relating to the Mission lands through A. A. Green."[5] Incredibly, all the while the Committee was in session, no one legally owned the land of San Francisco. As I transcribed the *Minutes*, I discovered that the Committee had kidnapped not only Alfred Green but all his brothers; Alfred had been imprisoned for weeks, and had been released only when he agreed to sell those land documents for a substantial sum at a time when the Committee was running short of money. Finally, there was the saga of Edward McGowan. A former Pennsylvania assemblyman who had moved to San Francisco from Philadelphia, McGowan was relentlessly sought by vigilante "policemen" throughout California and Nevada and into Mexico at great expense. His ostensible offense was loaning a gun that was used in a murder. Everyone agreed that if he was caught by the committee, McGowan would hang. At the same time, the Executives insisted that they only hanged murderers. McGowan was known as a political fixer for Democratic boss David C. Broderick, but the town was full of Broderick men. Why the unrelenting manhunt for this man only? What else had McGowan done? Gradually, the vigilantes' actions started making sense in a way very different from their very carefully cultivated history of political reform. It was actually land they were after.

The word "deed" has two meanings: a feat, exploit, or action, or a document transferring real estate. Both meanings simultaneously applied to San Francisco in the summer of 1856. When the 1856 Vigilance Committee organized, no one owned the land under the city. Many people, however, held claims. As some of these cases approached settlement in federal courts, San Francisco's mercantile elite, who headed the Committee, found their livelihoods in jeopardy. The city's merchants made vast fortunes from goods brought by ships to the waterfront, where ongoing legal disputes threatened their continued access to the all-important wharves. If a hostile claimant were to win ownership of the waterfront, San Francisco's richest men might lose easy access to the very source of their wealth. They felt particularly threatened by the growing power of David Broderick, the city's northern Democratic leader. The old southern Democrats who ran the state had not concerned them, but Broderick went after the jugular through which the lifeblood of the merchants' fortunes flowed: the port of San Francisco. Broderick had connections to myriad land schemes. As one seemed to be defeated, he came back with another. So the solution was twofold: destroy Broderick's political power, and get the waterfront land.

The Executives ruled San Francisco and controlled much of the state for two reasons. First, men of the nineteenth century tended to operate under the concept of deference, deferring to their social superiors. Respectability counted for everything—not just social status, but the ability to do business when a man's wealth depended on his good word. At first, following the template of the brief 1851 Vigilance Committee, success seemed to come easily to the men of 1856. Then a series of unintended consequences prolonged their organization and complicated their lives. While they continued to keep meticulous records in their *Minutes*, they gradually realized that the public approval on which their power rested was slipping away. They were losing their social supremacy. Any hint of self-interest or fraudulent land deals would have destroyed the basis of their hegemony.

Additionally, the Executives were able to engage in questionable legal maneuvers, as well as extreme measures such as hangings and deportations, because in mid-nineteenth-century California, federal retribution was distant and ineffectual. Separated by time and space from the national centers of power, the Executives could act with impunity, as long as they did so quickly. Increasingly, however, the power of the federal government and its ability to strike throughout the country became a reality. Better communications, inimical to vigilante secrecy, crept gradually westward: the pony express, the telegraph, then rumors of a railroad. The walls surrounding the Executives' little empire began to be breached by new people and new ideas.

The only way for the Executives to redeem respectability was through controlling their history. As very young men in 1856, the vigilantes had swelled in importance, decreeing life or death, redemption or banishment. In distant California, no one could contest their power. As time and space shrank throughout the nineteenth century, they could never again exercise the control they had once enjoyed over business and over public perception. National events further undermined their importance as the nation split in a bloody civil war and achieved a modicum of unity with the completion of the transcontinental railroad. The aging Executives increasingly negotiated an economic landscape that shifted beneath them—from an era of individual responsibility to one shaped by national and international forces.

Protecting the Executives' *Minutes* may have saved their reputations, but in the end, it shortchanged their history. The 1856 San Francisco Vigilance Committee has been ignored or forgotten by most of the twenty-first-century public, its narrative considered questionable and ultimately parochial. In preserving the *Minutes*, however, Theodore Hittell ultimately blasted away the old protective screen and revealed the importance of the vigilantes' history. His copy tells a story that is much more complicated than the idealized version, and far more interesting. With the help of digitized newspaper accounts and online legal cases, which enabled me to fill in many of the now-obscure references in the *Minutes*, the full story is revealed.[6] Perhaps now the complete history of America's largest vigilance committee and its objectives will be remembered for what it was.

No one can work on a book for a decade without incurring numerous debts. First, without the generosity of Norman Miller, who shared his great-great-grandfather's diary, this book would never have been written. Second, my thanks to Dr. Martha Whittaker, former librarian of the Sutro branch of the California State Library, who facilitated the long, arduous task of copying Hittell's facsimile of the Executive *Minutes* of the 1856 San Francisco Vigilance Committee. Librarians and archivists all over California have been extremely helpful, including those at the Huntington Library, especially Peter Blodgett; at the California History Room of the California State Archives and at the California State Library, especially Gary Kurutz; at the California Historical Society; at the University of California, San Diego; at Stanford University; at the Haggin Museum and at the University of the Pacific in Stockton; at the University of California, San Francisco; and especially at the Bancroft Library of the University of California, Berkeley, where David Kessler exhibited tremendous patience and professional talent. Librarians at the Boston Public Library also helped track down some difficult materials. My greatest thanks are reserved for the librarians of my former employer, California State University, Stanislaus, including those who provided consistent help with interlibrary loan and computers, particularly Dwayne Machado, who actually read part of the manuscript, and Laura French, for her considerable research skills.

Others also lent a hand. At CSU Stanislaus, aid came from History Department whiz Cathy Lanzon, who typed my transcription of the *Minutes*; colleagues Katherine Royer and Samuel Regalado; conscientious student researcher Stephanie Silcox; student assistants Monica Ruiz and Cristina Aguilar; and the members of the CSU Stanislaus Research, Scholarship, and Creative Activity Policy Committee, who gave me a small stipend to fund some of my travel. Thanks to San Francisco friend Greg Marutani for giving me a personal tour of what remains of the historic city, which helped to orient me in a place so different from its appearance in 1856.

In the ten years I have been working on this manuscript, it has gone through several iterations. Those who assisted along the way by reading and commenting include Gary Bradak (who read two versions), Betty Dawson, Christian Fritz, Randall Ghelardi, Gary Kurutz, Anne Newins, Robert Senkewicz, and several anonymous reviewers, both for Heyday Books (where a previous version won an honorable mention) and at the wonderful University of Oklahoma Press. Particular thanks there go to diligent editors Emily J. Schuster and Jane Lyle, whose good sense and good humor did wonders for this manuscript. Richard Orsi also provided clear-headed advice, and plenty of other friends offered consistent encouragement.

If I forgot someone, please forgive me. It has been a long haul, and my husband, Bob, to whom this book is dedicated, has been with me for all of it. Of course, any mistakes are mine. For the joys of research and writing, and for the flashes of brilliance (if any) in this manuscript, thank you all.

DIRTY DEEDS

Introduction

California meant wealth to the people of mid-nineteenth-century America. Thousands had rushed there in 1848, '49, and '50 to pan gold-bearing streams or to dig nuggets out of the Sierra dirt. By 1855, however, the easy-to-find gold was gone. The lone miner with a burro gave way to the capitalist who could build a huge stamp mill to pound gold-bearing quartz to dust before extracting the metal through a chemical process. Disappointed argonauts increasingly began to settle down and take up land for farming and for commerce instead.

Plenty of people had passed through San Francisco on their way to the Mother Lode. Originally just a shantytown, perched beside a gigantic bay dug by the confluence of three rivers, the village grew into an important city where goods from all over the world flowed in as California gold flowed out. This exchange of goods and gold was managed by ever-wealthier merchants dependent on the wharves. From the beginning, a few far-sighted entrepreneurs had tried to buy the town's real estate, demanding "some kind of a paper from the government officials showing that they had done all they could to obtain a title [ownership], trusting that congress and the courts would not deprive them afterwards of the property . . . made valuable by their labor and enterprise."[1] Desiring to attract American immigration and to provide funds for a new town government, a host of American leaders "granted" San Francisco land without authority to do so. The process started in 1847 with a spurious federal "grant" that allowed San Francisco's American *alcaldes* (mayors) to measure off and sell lots based on the presumption that they were the legal successors to the Mexican officials who had formerly ruled a purported *pueblo* (Mexican town) at San Francisco. Later, a free-wheeling San Francisco justice of the peace used alleged powers to sell lots worth $2,000 to $5,000 for $100. He absconded with the money, leaving his victims to wonder what, if anything, they owned.[2] Other supposed landowners had bought earlier claims deeded by the Spanish and Mexican governments. Unabashed latecomers bought their own claims from the city, the state, or the federal government, including a bayside acreage that was under up to twenty-five feet of water at low tide. An act attempting to regularize titles passed by special city election in May 1855, strengthening the hands of some owners but really resolving nothing.

At the state and federal level, uncertainty also reigned. California statehood had arrived in 1850 with no visible effect on disputed land claims. Consequently, in 1851, California senator William M. Gwin had sponsored the federal Land Act to settle all the land claims in the state. Meeting in San Francisco from January 1852 until March 1856, the U.S. Board of Land Commissioners demanded evidence of ownership from everyone claiming to own land, from Mexican owners who had held unquestioned possession for decades to speculators trying to cash in on recent purchases. A claim denied or conflicting claims for the same land generated appeals to American courts, appeals that dragged on for an average of seventeen years. Sorting out the ownership of San Francisco real estate became so complicated that the federal land commissioners figuratively threw up their hands and approved several claims to valuable territory that each *seemed* legitimate, even though they overlapped. Confusion and competition plagued San Francisco as all sides took to public meetings, to special publications, and to newspapers to broadcast their views.

Readers of the nineteenth century were captivated by the power of words. By the spring of 1856, fifteen local newspapers in several languages competed for the San Francisco readership. Some of these papers were issued weekly, others daily, and some were published purposely to be sent on the mail steamer every two weeks "back to the States," where anxious friends and families waited for the latest news from California. Within the city, San Franciscans regularly passed newspapers from hand to hand, and innkeepers kept them available in several of the city's hotels and reading rooms. Interested citizens plastered noteworthy notices on strategically placed bulletin boards. Objective reporting was foreign to the American press at the time. Editors attracted readers by championing popular causes and espousing a particular political party, even though California editors sometimes had to defend themselves in duels with those they had allegedly wronged.

By the spring of 1856, the dual hot buttons of unstable land titles and newspaper diatribes converged in one acerbic editor: the oddly named James King of William. The editor of San Francisco's *Evening Bulletin*, he had come to San Francisco as a banker, had lost all of his depositors' money in one of the city's vicious economic crashes, and had become an official adviser on land values. In that capacity he had inadvertently misled important investors during a sale of San Francisco's most valuable property: the waterfront. Barred from banking, he had started a newspaper. His potent prose and willingness to skewer—rightfully or not—private citizens as well as politicians spurred increasing public dissatisfaction with the city's municipal government. Local residents felt further disturbed when former county supervisor Alfred A. Green publicly claimed to be in possession of hundreds of Spanish-language documents—the "Pueblo Papers"—showing that the city had once been a Mexican pueblo, thereby legitimizing putative owners who had obtained their titles to land through city officials. Another county supervisor, attacked by King, became so enraged that he shot the editor.

As King lay wounded, a hibernating San Francisco organization awakened. In 1851, in the absence of a smoothly running judicial system, leading city merchants had organized a short-lived Vigilance Committee, which had claimed to reduce crime through secret trials, banishments, and hangings. San Franciscans of 1856, many of whom had arrived after the 1851 Committee's three-month existence, believed in its efficacy. In 1856, the newly reorganized Committee, headed by self-styled "Executives," quickly enrolled thousands of members who mustered to seize their first two victims from the county jail: King's assailant and a Roman Catholic gambler awaiting a second hearing. The Executives conducted their own, secret trial, then hanged the two captives out the windows of their fortified warehouse just after the mail steamer had left, guaranteeing that news of this shocking event would take extra weeks to reach the East. Any federal retaliation would be slow in coming. Belatedly, California governor J. Neely Johnson and the local militia, led by then-banker William Tecumseh Sherman, unsuccessfully tried to discourage the Vigilance Committee and curtail its actions. Their failure to enforce a rule of law became obvious as the Committee continued kidnapping men, trying them in secret, and deporting them while the federal government remained quiescent.

Most vigilante victims were adherents of California's leading northern Democrat, David Broderick, who seemed to be closing in on ownership of the San Francisco waterfront. Avoiding the powerful Broderick, vigilantes continued arresting and deporting his henchmen, more than two dozen in all. They also relentlessly pursued Broderick associate and judge Edward "Ned" McGowan, a former Philadelphia lawyer with influential ties in the East who had allegedly loaned the gun used to shoot King, hardly a hanging offense. However, his other endeavors, long kept secret, spurred vigilante vengeance. All the while, the Executives assured the public, through the press and through mass meetings, that political housecleaning was their only objective.

After nine weeks of activity, the Committee seemed to be phasing out, but a series of events prolonged its existence. The night the Executives were planning to disband, they received word that a government arms shipment was on the way to San Francisco. They sent their men to capture the weapons. A chain of unforeseen events followed, culminating in the stabbing of a vigilante by California Supreme Court justice David S. Terry, a southerner who despised the Committee. The mostly northern Executives took the judge into custody, waiting to see if his victim lived or died. As they had decreed, murderers were hanged. But Terry was as well respected as any Executive, and had been elected to his post by the entire state of California. As Terry remained captive, his accomplished wife sped news of her husband's unlawful captivity eastward, where it eventually reached the U.S. Congress, then enmeshed in increasingly volatile sectional conflict. News of North-South bloodshed in Kansas Territory alarmed San Francisco, where seizure of a southern judge by northern vigilantes seemed to echo the growing national split. Increasing public skepticism about the Executives' high moral purpose weakened their shield of deference. As the Executives' power dwindled, they made a direct grab for the waterfront through the old Pueblo Papers recently proffered by Alfred A. Green. Vigilantes kidnapped Green, and the Executives demanded that he sell them the documents. Insulted, Green refused. Stuck with a high-ranking judge and an intractable former supervisor, the Executives kept prolonging the life of their organization even as their followers grew restive. Trying to quiet them, the Executives decreed two more hangings, which turned much of the city against the Committee.

Although the Executives commanded these actions totally in secret, they kept copious records. Their *Minutes* detail all actions by members—who were publicly known only by number—in an effort to demonstrate that they were not a bloodthirsty mob acting without deliberation. Like the 1851 Committee, they intended eventually to publish this record. Meanwhile, they continued to feed biased stories to the press to shape public opinion in their favor. As their organization prolonged its work and turned more and more to politics, San Franciscans, and some of the Committee members, began to question the decisions of their leaders. After Terry's victim recovered, the Executives reluctantly freed the judge. Rank-and file-objections climaxed. Fearful for their lives, the Executives considered, then rejected, offers to publish their *Minutes*. Instead, they went to great expense to publish the previously closely held transcript of testimony in Terry's trial, doing their best to refurbish a reputation they had earlier tried so hard to destroy in print. Then they permanently dismissed their General Committee.

While exhausted San Franciscans turned away from interest in the Vigilance Committee and fixed their attention on the impending U.S. presidential election, the Executives remained captives of their vigilante past. They watched helplessly as David Broderick won his coveted seat in the Senate. They founded San Francisco's "People's Party," but remained in the background and slowly lost any grip on its actions. They faced a series of lawsuits brought by their deportees and backed numerous legal actions over San Francisco land titles, suits that drained the organization's coffers and sapped its leaders' energy. Some of these issues remained unresolved even after the Executives stopped meeting and the nation lurched into the bloody Civil War.

Only after the war ended in 1865 did many of the events of 1856 come to their final conclusion. Lawsuits dribbled to an end, and San Francisco's land issues were finally resolved in favor of the pueblo, the outcome desired by the Executives. But commerce soon shifted to the new transcontinental railroad, undercutting the value of the city's waterfront and the wealth of the former Executives. Now connected to the rest of the nation, San Francisco blossomed under new entrepreneurs who rose in prominence while the vigilantes faded.

To redeem their youthful prominence, the 1856 Vigilance Committee Executives once again turned to the power of words. Beginning in the 1870s, they enlisted the efforts of two sympathetic historians, starting with Hubert Howe Bancroft, who had been trying to obtain their *Minutes* for years. This flattering publisher-turned-historian, whose main goal was selling books, convinced some of the Committee leaders to provide limited reminiscences of their deeds. Bancroft interviewed only prominent vigilantes, not their opposition, highlighting their successes and ignoring their shortcomings and failures. He asked only about the initial Committee activities, not about lingering lawsuits, and nothing about land. In the second volume of his *Popular Tribunals*, he lauded the vigilantes in language florid even for its day: "The Vigilance Committee did not seek to legitimize their proceedings, did not care whether the fruit of their action was called lawful or bastard. Born of necessity, though out of the legal forms of wedlock, the purpose was as pure as was the virgin's conception, and the offspring of their acts as holy as was her child."[3] In another instance, he added, "I find that nothing but pure patriotism actuated them [the Executives]; but seek not such as this in elections, in legislative halls, in the jumping-jack gyrations of political mountebanks, or in the bladder-blown principles of party or polity."[4] This extravagant language, interspersed with classical allusions, continued for almost 750 pages.

Bancroft's efforts at whitewashing the vigilantes were echoed by those of lawyer Theodore H. Hittell. A specialist in land law, Hittell nonetheless also wrote flatteringly, if more objectively, about the vigilantes in the 981-page third volume of his *History of California*. He refused to use Bancroft's work, instead securing his own primary sources. He somehow obtained the two original Executive *Minutes* books, which he cited extensively. Utilizing organizational techniques to obscure important connections between the 1856 vigilantes and San Francisco land litigation (which he well understood), he, too, extolled the Committee's virtues. "It was in this kind of men...," he explained in an early twentieth-century address, "that the United States excelled, and has continued to excel... from the days of George Washington to those of Abraham Lincoln." During this illustrious period, California had been settled, and its "history as a State is almost a continuous series of acts evincing a greatness unexcelled in any [other] community." Blaming California's early courts and sheriffs for failing "to preserve order or execute justice," Hittell lauded "the great vigilance committees of California" for their "courage,... public spirit, and... devotion to duty, of which it is doubtful whether the history of the world presents a brighter example."[5] His hagiographical view of the vigilantes, together with that of Bancroft, set the canon for the 1856 Committee solely as purveyors of civic political reform. Thus the Executives were enshrined in a sanitized version of history presented by the only two authors who had seen the *Minutes* and who were willing to distort the historical record to support their own inclinations and profits.

Others have since found diverse ways of approaching the Committee. A couple of reminiscences—some unfavorable—were published during the nineteenth century, but decades passed before interpretive historical works appeared.[6] In 1886, Harvard philosopher Josiah Royce—who was not a historian—took a moralistic stand on the 1856 Committee. He identified the lack of civic involvement by the 1856 Executive mercantile elite as a moral failure, while excusing their vigilante behavior as patriotic and well-motivated. Believing that "the Social Order... is divine," he concluded that the vigilantes of 1856 had helped restore that social order, and he admired their restraint in so doing.[7] As historians began professionalizing, in 1921 the conscientious Mary Floyd Williams, who also edited the 1851 Committee's papers, published her dissertation on San Francisco's first Vigilance Committee. She saw that organization as the flowering of the traditional American social compact, "invested with abiding significance... as a demonstration of national life and thought," incubated in the extraordinary events of the California gold rush. However, her painstaking efforts did not extend to the 1856 Committee, though she identified the Executives who served on both committees.[8] Later, as Americans embraced the "great man" view of history, James Scherer, a doctor of divinity, founding president of the California Institute of Technology, and confirmed "Californiac," published a flattering biography of the president of the 1856 Committee, William Tell Coleman, in 1939.[9]

Less complimentary interpretations of the 1856 San Francisco Vigilance Committee resulted from modern contextualization. After the trauma of World War II, historians became increasingly critical of the vigilantes as they approached the subject from unique perspectives. Roger Lotchin, in founding the new urban history, incorporated tales of the 1856 Committee into his 1974 account of San Francisco's rapid growth in the context of governmental challenges and unique ethnic diversity. His focus on geographic locations and close study of rising tensions due to the *Bulletin* newspaper showed the organization in a less favorable light.[10] A year later, Richard Maxwell Brown emphasized violence as he placed the 1856 Committee in a pivotal role between the old rural vigilante organizations stretching back to colonial days and the new urban strife aimed at a host of targets, beginning with the Catholics attacked in 1856 San Francisco and extending later to "Jews, immigrants, blacks, laboring men and labor leaders, radicals, free thinkers, and defenders of civil liberties."[11] While largely objective about the Committee in general, in the absence of the *Minutes*, Brown acclaimed Bancroft as "practically a primary source on the [San Francisco vigilante] movement because of Bancroft's friendship with, and access to, many old vigilante leaders, including the greatest of them all, William T. Coleman."[12] In 1978, Peter Decker identified social instability as the primary impetus for the 1856 Committee, an insecurity particularly affecting San Francisco's mercantile elite. He analyzed mobility—both spatial throughout the city and hierarchical throughout its classes—to contextualize the Committee. In his view, the Executives achieved their goal of restoring fiscal integrity through vigilante violence rather than the democratic process, to which they were unaccustomed, solidifying their gains through the People's Party.[13] Robert Senkewicz, who published his outstanding book on the vigilantes in 1985, acknowledged the "effect of the massive labors of Bancroft and Theodore H. Hittell," which was "to establish almost a dogmatic and standard interpretation of the San Francisco vigilance committee of 1856."[14] Senkewicz departed from this canon by rooting the Committee in the gold rush, and emphasizing religion and politics as the contexts for vigilantism. He ultimately agreed with Decker that commercial failure animated San Francisco's mercantile elite to attempt, "as vigilantes, to remake the entire city in the image of the commercial success that had eluded them."[15] Four years later, retired San Francisco police officer Kevin Mullen analyzed crime statistics to argue that the 1851 (not 1856) San Francisco Committee erupted to benefit the merchant class financially, by now a common refrain. His meticulous study showed that misdeeds were not nearly as common as was asserted by the vigilantes, that courts functioned properly, and that fires (a frequent city scourge) destroyed stockpiles of unsalable goods and won merchants insurance claims for reimbursement.[16] These same insights regarding merchants' self-interest could easily be applied to the 1856 Committee.

The 1990s brought newer perspectives on San Francisco's 1856 Vigilance Committee, studies that did not focus on the mercantile elite. In 1994, historian Philip J. Ethington argued for a political motivation that extended throughout the ranks of the Committee. With persuasive statistics and analysis of political rituals and symbols, he illustrated the role of the working-class membership (skilled and semiskilled) among the rank and file, emphasizing their extreme youth, and explaining the reasons for Irish avoidance of the Committee. He accepted August 18, the date of their final parade, as marking the true end of the Committee, but continued his analysis of the vigilante-sponsored People's Party.[17] In her Ph.D. dissertation of 1998, historian Michelle Jolly took a gendered approach to the 1856 Vigilance Committee, analyzing the *Evening Bulletin* to study the role of women. She found that female roles transitioned from reform leadership, to Committee support, to marginalization as elections loomed in the fall of 1856.[18] After all, women could not vote.

None of these historians connected the 1856 Vigilance Committee to contests over land. This lack of engagement is not surprising. San Francisco's land litigation is incredibly complicated and easy to avoid. Sources are complex and scattered. The standard work on California claims lumps San Francisco together with Los Angeles in a single chapter and discusses the various San Francisco claims individually, giving no sense of chronology, and consequently no indication of the effects of ongoing land suits on anxious San Franciscans.[19] The clearest and most thorough discussion of the entire progress of just one major claim—San Francisco's pueblo land cases—is found in the fine biography of California's federal district judge Ogden Hoffman, written by Christian G. Fritz.[20] A major competing claim—that of José Yves Limantour—is thoroughly explored in a 1961 study by attorney Kenneth M. Johnson. Published in an edition of only two hundred copies, Johnson's book includes the most important pertinent documents, traces the progress of the case, and leaves the reader wondering whether the author truly believed that this claim was a fraud.[21] A third major land claim, the Santillán or Bolton and Barron claim, which was acquired by the San Francisco Land Association of Philadelphia, still awaits a coherent treatment. Yet despite all this litigation that was shaking San Francisco in that difficult summer of 1856, no one has connected these land cases with the 1856 Vigilance Committee.

Consequently, like an intricate, incomplete jigsaw puzzle, the story of the 1856 San Francisco Vigilance Committee has long lacked some key pieces. When those pieces drop into place, the picture changes. This work offers a unique context through which to view the 1856 Committee: control of the city's waterfront. The Executives carefully hid this goal even from their own Committee members, who would not have profited as their leaders did. This work also benefits from three previously untapped primary sources. Two are diaries written by outside observers of the Committee: one an Irish Catholic businessman, the other an unemployed workman who was observing the events around him as he struggled to make enough money to leave San Francisco and rejoin his family in New Orleans. The most important source, however, is Hittell's copy of the Executives' *Minutes*, which for so many years was quietly stored away with the rest of his papers.

Fascinating secrets emerge from the *Minutes*. For example, the careful records of morning, afternoon, and evening meetings set a rhythm to the Executives' work. Their strict attention to the steamship schedule for news control as well as deportations motivated the timing of many of their actions. When it came to discussing the fates of their captives, they were clearly preoccupied with looming meetings of the Committee's Board of Delegates, whose responsibility it was to confirm "all decisions and sentences involving death or banishment."[22] The Delegates' unwillingness to release Judge Terry and their growing resistance to Executive control also strongly suggest the Executives' need to provide an "acceptable" hanging. Perpetual problems with dwindling funds, beginning with Terry's capture, and the Executives' mounting irritation with (and expense of) myriad lawsuits, unmentioned or glossed over in published histories, consistently appear.

Since then, of course, times have changed. Understanding the full story of the 1856 San Francisco Vigilance Committee challenges the imagination of the historian and the reader. Fortunately, carefully kept records from the nineteenth century aid in this version of time travel. Historians in particular cope with interpreting the records that remain, conscious that life was different 150 years ago, trying to be true to them while trapped in our own time. Yet some of those antique events and attitudes still ring true. Today, in the twenty-first century, we again see examples of private vengeance, distrust of the federal government, and political unrest. As I write these words, the Federal Bureau of Investigation has just ousted an armed group of vigilantes from the Malheur National Wildlife Refuge in southeast Oregon—not the first nor probably the last of such challenges. Vigilantism remains a force in America. The 1856 San Francisco Vigilance Committee, while unique, still has a relevant story to tell.

PART I

A Contentious Place

1
Unstable Ground

In 1855, nine savvy businessmen sat down in Philadelphia to create a new company, the San Francisco Land Association of Philadelphia. Their goal: ownership of San Francisco's waterfront, the most valuable property on the west coast of North America. Eight of them, seven capitalists and an attorney, represented the burgeoning industrial growth of the eastern seaboard—steamboats, railroads, and coal mines.[1] Their board of directors also included Joseph C. Palmer, a senior partner at one of San Francisco's largest, most stable banks, which handled all the funds for California's only political party, the Democrats. Two years earlier, in 1853, three of these Philadelphians had spent more than a million dollars for a land claim that, its seller insisted, had originally been granted to an old Mexican priest. Their investment, they thought, had just paid off. Only weeks before their formal organization in 1855, the federal Board of Land Commissioners had confirmed the first controversial California claim, granted to John C. Fremont—not for waterfront land, but for gold-bearing property in the foothills some one hundred miles distant. Interested people had long speculated about whether the land board would be lenient or strict with regard to approving land claims in California. The approval of the questionable Fremont grant indicated to the hardheaded businessmen of the San Francisco Land Association of Philadelphia that their own contested claim would also be approved.[2]

In their prospectus to potential investors, the Philadelphians extolled the value of the grand port of San Francisco. In 1846, the bayside city had existed only to serve the occasional whaling ship and as a depot for East Asian trade. But by the mid-1850s it had mushroomed into a metropolis with tens of thousands of inhabitants, "with an annual export of gold bullion to the amount of upwards of

$50,000,000," which fueled nationwide development. The Philadelphia organizers envisioned a sixfold growth in the western port, and promised a $15 million stock offering once they had secured title through the federal land board, an outcome they felt was certain.³

In broadcasting this glowing promise, the eastern consortium seriously underestimated San Francisco's real estate complications. The city's explosion from tiny Mexican village to gold rush entrepôt had resulted in a transient population, a rapid succession of governments, and leaders who were happy to grant land titles (ownership) to real property that they did not legally own. Basing their decisions on the Land Act of 1851, federal land commissioners had been trying to sort out a myriad of conflicting claims throughout California since January 1852. If a claim was approved, the matter ended. However, if a claim was found to be falsified, or improperly documented, or if there were other, conflicting claims, the various claimants had the right to bring the matter to the American courts. San Francisco, shingled over with land claims, posed particular problems.

To succeed in this land litigation, it very much mattered who came first, much as with shoppers who line up for Christmas sales today. Therefore, grants awarded by California's Mexican regime, which predated any American government, appeared most valid. The Philadelphia group had purchased an old Mexican claim allegedly granted to the priest of San Francisco's Mission Dolores, Father José Prudencio Santillán, in February 1846, before the American takeover of California. However, two problems plagued this claim. First, competing contestants questioned whether a priest could legally hold and grant land. Second, other men alleged that they held earlier grants from the Mexican regime. Just before the land board stopped accepting any more documents in February 1853, José Yves Limantour, a French merchant operating from Mexico, submitted paperwork supporting two massive claims to San Francisco and its environs dated 1843.⁴ If Limantour's assertions were legitimate, they would predate the Santillán claim held by the Philadelphia group. Another faction clung to much the same land based on the purported existence of an official Mexican "pueblo" at San Francisco, supposedly founded in 1835. The governor of the pueblo had arguably had the power to grant land, which power had been transferred to his successors in the American regime.⁵ Therefore, the pueblo claimants, if successful, came first.

Ownership was further complicated by other considerations. The U.S. government held claims to the city's forts, the Post Office, the San Francisco Mint, and the U.S. Customhouse. The state of California had other claims. In addition, during the years of American governance, the city, on the basis of disputed powers, had repeatedly sold underwater "water lots" or "tide lots," which were unquestionably excluded

One of the richest men in San Francisco, William Tell Coleman inspired confidence in his leadership among his peers due in large part to his wealth and his practiced organizational skills.
Courtesy of the Bancroft Library.

from any Mexican grants. San Francisco's shoreline had been continually filled in, bringing many water lots to the surface, and much of that land now constituted the San Francisco waterfront. Under these circumstances, who really owned the port?

Even the accomplished lawyers who staffed the federal Board of Land Commissioners could not figure it out. Until the land board's demise in March 1856, the commissioners approved all claims presented that *appeared* to be properly documented, regardless of obvious conflicts over the actual property. Therefore, the most important contests moved to the courts, creating another problem. The first claim approved by the courts would probably moot all others. Under these circumstances, it would be many years before anyone knew who actually owned San Francisco.

Among the men who were competing for San Francisco ownership, two titans took opposite sides with the 1856 Vigilance Committee. The first, native Kentuckian William Tell Coleman, later the Committee's president, had been exceptional since birth—in a leap year, on February 29, 1824. Despite his baby-blue eyes and choirboy face, he quickly became known as "the terror of all the small boys in the neighborhood." As a child, he had formed his playmates into a Roman-style military company and drilled them daily. At twenty-three, he had gone into the Wisconsin woods to collect two years' worth of overdue payments for a St. Louis lumber company. Using falsified legal papers and his own strongmen, whom he had sworn to allegiance, he seized 800,000 board feet of milled lumber and floated it more than three hundred miles down the Mississippi to his overjoyed employers. In 1849 he came overland in the California gold rush, encountering a successful miner who flaunted his leather bag full of gold dust and nuggets because "people don't steal here now. They used to, but we strung a lot of 'em up over at old Dry Diggings—they call the place Hangtown, now."[6] Coleman never forgot the coercive power of hanging.

Realizing that the way to make money from the gold rush was not to pan for gold but rather to supply the miners who did, Coleman eventually settled in San Francisco, where he became a leading commission merchant. He thus joined a select group of men who bought up entire shiploads of goods, sight unseen, to auction off to the highest bidder. For six years Coleman had been auctioning off lots of sperm candles, manila rope, cloth, tobacco, butter, whiskey, codfish, prunes, turpentine, and other assorted items, all necessities in a land that at the time produced virtually nothing but gold.[7] Understanding the value of timing, Coleman paid the city's marine reporter fifty dollars a month "to report to me privately one hour before he did to any one else" exactly which ships were coming in, and with what cargo on board. When a ship arrived in the outer bay at noon with "goods that were very high, and very sensitive," Coleman would make sure that by 3:00 p.m. "my entire stock of that article would be loaded on the Sacramento, Marysville, Stockton, and other interior boats, with instructions to interior correspondents" to dispose of the goods immediately "before the vessel came to anchor." The next day, when the ship unloaded, the price of these goods plummeted. "But," Coleman rationalized, "the interior people heard of it later, and felt it less keenly; nor would the interior buyers be likely to suffer so much relatively, as they in turn shipped" the goods to more distant towns.[8]

Given his need for waterfront access, Coleman joined the city's confusing land rush. In 1851 and 1852 he "bought, filled in at great expense, and reclaimed the tide-lots at the corner of California and Front streets, and built the large, fireproof warehouse which he long occupied" on what was now waterfront property.[9] These lots had been bought from the city even though some were originally under twenty-five feet of the sea at low tide. Selim E. Woodworth, the first man to buy a chunk of water-covered land and build his warehouse on stilts above it, faced plenty of ridicule from other citizens, since so much dry land was still available. However, when he started monopolizing San Francisco's lighterage (barging goods from ships out on the bay to the sandy beach that was then San Francisco's port of Yerba Buena), the laughter stopped.[10] Sales of water lots boomed, as did myriad other land transfers: "Alcalde's grants and the Prefect's grants . . . the first city sales by auction, under the Town Council," and many, many more. In reality, none had proper authorization.[11]

Eager San Franciscans claimed and fenced underwater land in hopes of present opportunity and future wealth as the city's shoreline extended ever outward. *Courtesy of the Bancroft Library.*

Even dry land offered questionable promise. "Very little, if any... was level or suitable for building on without some change, either of excavation or filling up," remembered an early writer.[12] Sand hills reared up to eighty feet high.[13] Residents graded and filled all over San Francisco. In the process, sand was dumped into the bay, and previously submerged water lots became prime waterfront property. Other landowners lost access to the bay. "In 1851, we established ourselves at the corner of Sacramento and Sansome Street," recalled another merchant. "The water came up there at that time," but by 1856 their lot was some six blocks from the water.[14]

As the city expanded, so did the role of William Tell Coleman. He took an active part in San Francisco's first Vigilance Committee of 1851, a seven-hundred-man body that was organized after five major fires struck the city in the sixteen months from late December 1849 to early May 1851. Local newspapers blamed former convicts from the Australian penal colony in Sydney, who had allegedly set the fires to promote looting. Committee members captured a Sydney man seen stealing a small safe, gave him a "trial" in a locked warehouse where only their own sympathizers could attend, then dragged him to death on the way to their makeshift gallows.

Coleman and other leaders, calling themselves "Executives," subsequently kept careful minutes of their secret meetings, which they later published together with their papers to show that they were not a lawless mob.[15] However, a contemporary noted, "The warehouses of San Francisco were glutted to the roofs; but the precious commission merchants of San Francisco could not make returns to their Atlantic shippers; and then came the terrible conflagrations which gave them a clear balance sheet.... [N]obody benefited [from the fires] but the merchants of San Francisco," who also got reimbursed for their losses by eastern insurance companies.[16] But the vigilantes claimed that they had cleaned up crime.[17]

Coleman soon solidified his position among San Francisco's moneyed elite. After the Committee's short three-month duration, he returned east in 1852 to marry Carrie Page, the daughter of St. Louis banker Daniel D. Page of the well-established bank of Page and Bacon.[18] With his in-laws' support, by 1856 Coleman owned his own San Francisco bank, shipping tens of thousands of dollars in gold to New York every two weeks. For example, in early May 1856, his bank shipped almost $55,000, the eighth-largest shipment in a total of more than $2 million sent out by some forty institutions and individuals on the mail steamer.[19]

Coleman thus flourished in the maritime commerce that inflated the value of the city's wharves. For example, the Pacific Mail Steamship Company, which delivered the U.S. mail, originally paid the owners of the Central Street Wharf $10,000 to secure the use of their dock, and later had to pay Cunningham's Wharf $1,500 a month for docking privileges.[20] Those who controlled San Francisco's waterfront made fortunes.

Another man who understood this fact very well was David Colbert Broderick, a former stonemason born in Washington, D.C., to Irish immigrant parents. Broderick had also arrived in California in 1849, eager to overcome his working-class background and to claw his way up the social ladder. His progress so far had been amazing. Left fatherless in New York at fourteen, Broderick soon also lost his mother and younger brother. He turned to a mentor, George Wilkes, editor of the *National Police Gazette*, whom a contemporary historian called "the Jonathan to this David, loving him with a devotion passing the love of woman," and who got credit for smoothing out his rough edges.[21] Broderick joined a fire engine company, a time-tested route to political prominence in New York's Democratic Tammany Hall. His method proved successful when in 1846, at the age of twenty-six, he was nominated for Congress by the young men of New York's Democratic Party—an extraordinary honor for someone so young. The older elite Democrats, repulsed by Broderick's Irish Catholic working-class background and hard-edged qualities, backed a more refined politician, splitting the Democratic vote between "the classes" and "the masses." The

Democrats lost the election, and Broderick left for California, stung by the elite's rejection and facing a social barrier that would haunt him for the rest of his life.[22]

Broderick made no secret of his desire to be elected U.S. senator when California became a state, and began rising in a society that put less emphasis on background than New Yorkers had done. He partnered in a private mint and founded San Francisco's Empire Engine Company, emulating the method he had used to enter Tammany Hall. In the first state elections of 1850, Broderick won a seat in the assembly. In 1851 he rose to the senate, where he served as president and de facto lieutenant governor.[23] As a sympathetic biographer later noted, "There was no party system in the town [of San Francisco], and he constructed one."[24] Broderick had found an unoccupied political niche that opened as national unity crumbled.

San Francisco, like the nation at large, was quietly tearing apart over sectional issues. A local businessman later gave his view of the city's growing divide: "When the State of California was added to the Union [in 1850], the great emigration that came here was composed of two distinct classes. The Northerners went into business,—trade, mechanics, mining, and had no time to attend to politics. The politics of the State was entirely in the hands of people from the South, almost all the offices were filled with Southern people, who had before held offices in their own states."[25] While the elite merchants indeed avoided any political participation, by the early 1850s an increasing number of northern-leaning Democrats were becoming fed up with the statewide power of southern Democrats (known as "Chivs," for "chivalrous"). These politically active newcomers welcomed the brash New Yorker who was willing to challenge the status quo.

Accepting the leadership of the northern Democrats, Broderick consistently pushed toward his ultimate goal. He particularly supported "legislative candidates who would be favorable to his well known and openly avowed candidacy for the senate" in those days when state legislatures elected U.S. senators. Understanding how politics worked, he allegedly used some of his wealth to pay his followers "a regular stipend, like employees in a merchandise establishment, when he could find for them no permanent [political] appointment."[26] He also "possessed a personal magnetism so great that he gathered around him a large mass of adherents, whom no person could entice away from him."[27]

Broderick soon directly confronted San Francisco's merchant elite. In 1851, he had harangued the members of the first Vigilance Committee from the back of a cart while they dragged their first captive to death on the way to the gallows.[28] Understanding land as the route to wealth, Broderick also went after the disputed waterfront lands. He managed to purchase almost twenty of the waterside "Peter Smith" lots, sold by the city in a disputed transaction to pay off thousands of dollars in debts owed to Dr. Peter Smith for caring for the city's indigent sick in 1850 and 1851. City fathers claimed the power to make this sale based on the city's dubious former status as a Mexican pueblo, despite objections from state authorities, who also claimed ownership. State-authorized commissioners of the funded debt got the backing of prominent lawyer David O. Shattuck, and published a proclamation saying that the "Peter Smith" land sales would not carry title. Consequently, the lots sold cheaply (although many of them soon changed hands again at greatly inflated prices).[29] The city realized little income from these sales, so another city land sale followed, then another, all with contested titles. As a result, the "Peter Smith" men, virtually all Democrats, now claimed to own significant (though disputed) commercial and waterfront property.

Using his political skills, Broderick began to manipulate his new "ownership" of San Francisco's waterfront to his own advantage. In 1852, the state legislature, under Broderick's influence, considered an "Extension Bill" that would add a strip six hundred feet wide to San Francisco's "permanent" waterfront. The sale of this land was expected to raise an estimated $6 million to meet those lingering city debts. One-third of the profit would accrue to the state, the rest (some $4 million) to the Peter Smith contingent, including Broderick.[30] The bill was defeated in the legislature in 1852, but it was reintroduced in 1853. During the assembly vote, Broderick sat in attendance, despite the fact that he was not an assembly member. When the senate vote split evenly, the lieutenant governor was forced to decide. He voted no.[31] For a moment, the opposing claimants took a deep breath. But the controversy returned in 1853, when the California Supreme Court, now including *Justice* David O. Shattuck, *confirmed* the original Peter Smith titles as legally valid. Broderick and his cronies had gained the upper hand, for now. The possibility of a new Extension Bill, or a later incarnation, the Bulkhead Bill, continued to threaten the access of San Francisco's merchant elite to the all-important waterfront.

The local economy was also teetering precariously because of legislative finagling and uncertain weather. When the cash-strapped 1853 state legislature passed a Revenue Act imposing new taxes on San Francisco businesses and property, the wealthy commission merchants refused to pay. They brought lawsuits, and when the California Supreme Court upheld the law, they threatened to appeal the decision to the U.S. Supreme Court. The 1854 legislature modified the act, but the merchants still refused to pay what they considered an unjust portion of the tax, and the law was never enforced.[32] At the same time, a lack of rain in the winter of 1853–54 drove jobless miners and other transients into the city, which collapsed into its first major financial panic. Squatters settled on San Francisco's many empty lots, and embraced rumors that as "settlers" they would be first in line to get clear title when the Board of Land Commissioners made its long-awaited declaration about San Francisco land ownership, then expected at any minute. Frightened elite claimants and squatters clashed with pistols, knives, and clubs. A few men died.[33] On June 6, 1854, an estimated one thousand prominent San Franciscans formalized a new voluntary association with the same structure as the 1851 Vigilance Committee to act as "special police to aid the authorities" in removing interlopers.[34] Within days, they were calling themselves the "People's Organization." They soon persuaded city officials to hire forty-eight additional policemen to calm the squatter threat.[35] They were successful in protecting their alleged property rights while official land deliberations continued on and on and on, without resolution.

2
Feisty Editor, Contentious Elections

The swirling events of the mid-nineteenth century had spat out a man as distinct as his name. James King of William had always been "a drove by himself," in the words of his father, William, whose name his son had added to enable him to stand out from the other local "James Kings" in his native Washington, D.C. For example, after finishing his religious studies to join his parents' church, the young King had ridiculed another member of the congregation for painting himself as "'a great sinner, one of the vilest of the vile.' Now, I don't believe that, nor do I believe that he thinks so himself," declared King, "and if a man were to come in here from the street, and say [that] of him . . . he would hit him." King insisted that people should "tell nothing but the truth, and be consistent. I thank the Lord that I am not a vile sinner," he added. "I don't intend to sin any more." The congregation immediately complained to the minister. King left the church shortly thereafter. He never joined another.[1]

The forceful, dark-haired King arrived in California in 1848, and by December 1849 he had opened his own private Bank of James King of William (a viable profession in a state that, by its original constitution, allowed no public banks). Known for his honest dealings, King attracted numerous depositors and was soon worth a staggering $250,000. He made friends, sent for his family, and joined the Masonic Order. In 1851, he lost his bank building in one of the fires that ravaged the wooden city, so he enrolled in the first Vigilance Committee and handled some of its funds.[2] In mid-September 1851, during the Committee's reorganization, he was elected to its Executive Committee.[3] Given his prominence, he became a commissioner of the funded debt, and declared to the world the worthlessness of the

Peter Smith land titles. When the state supreme court declared them legal, furious San Franciscans blamed the commissioners of the funded debt for misleading them. King found his integrity questioned and his motives impugned.

King's fortunes sank even further in the destabilizing city. The winter of 1853–54 was unusually dry. Discouraged miners, needing snowmelt to pan out their "pile," left the mountains empty-handed and drifted into San Francisco, needing something to do. With little gold to coin, private mints began to close, although the U.S. Mint stayed open. More than two hundred San Francisco businesses declared voluntary bankruptcy, leaving three hundred commercial buildings vacant in a city with some forty thousand inhabitants.[4] Much of the dwindling gold flowed through Adams and Company, which by 1853 had become "the leading business house in the state, dealing with more people, . . . handling more money, and probably making more profit than any other establishment."[5]

In this atmosphere, King suffered through a season of bad investments, misplaced confidence, and the looming ruin of his bank. As the bank faltered, other bankers offered loans to carry him through, but the proud King refused to accept their help. Instead, he took his depositors with him to Adams and Company, where he accepted a position at a generous monthly salary of $1,000, and became a manager.[6] His situation continued to improve until "Black Friday," February 17, 1855, when the eastern mail steamer arrived with the news that California's leading bank, Page and Bacon, had failed in the East.[7] A bank partner, sent by senior partner Daniel Page (Coleman's father-in-law), had already rushed to California and shipped out all the gold dust and nuggets he could collect on two successive outbound steamships to prop up the St. Louis parent bank. Thus almost $1 million that could have gone to local banks departed California, resulting in a complete "crash that smote San Francisco on the twenty-third of February."[8]

Bank manager William Tecumseh Sherman (still years away from his Civil War fame) explained events in detail to his own parent branch of Lucas, Turner, and Company. "On Saturday arrived the *Oregon* and quick as lightning flew the intelligence that Page & Bacon of St. Louis was bankrupt." Panic ensued, and a run started. "I was thunderstruck to see the crowd and tumult. Adams & Co. closed, Wells, Fargo & Co. afraid to open, Robinson & Wright's Savings Banks closed before a dollar could be called for and the assertion in every man's mouth that all must break. . . . We knew where we stood and were determined not to break." Sherman's bank called on every possible source of money; $40,000 was raised on his word alone that every penny would be repaid by March 1. His bank endured. A few days later, after the panic ended, Sherman reflected, "California is hereby thrown back three years—but the mines are still here. . . . We have a city with its wharves, warehouses and stores and dwellings . . . although individuals must be ruined."[9]

One of those ruined individuals was James King of William. King had continued to receive deposits until noon on Black Friday, assuring clients that Adams and Company would not fail. Those who took his word for it lost everything. The firm descended into prolonged bankruptcy litigation, its remaining assets transferred to the Democrat-connected bank of Palmer, Cook and Company (PC&C), headed by Joseph Palmer, who had quietly taken up a directorship at the San Francisco Land Association of Philadelphia. This bank remained solid during the panic and bank run because its depositors all left their money in place, knowing that PC&C handled all the city, county, and state taxes funneled into it by Democratic politicians. As the Adams and Company bankruptcy proceedings unfolded, King "demanded $20,000 as his share" of its assets for business he had brought to the bank. The bank officers refused. A war of words began in print, in which King "was held up for public condemnation as a dishonest man, guilty of faithlessness and fraud." The public believed those accusations.[10] An Adams and Company broker even challenged King to a duel, a common rejoinder to insults in 1850s San Francisco. King replied by published letter that he objected to dueling on moral grounds, but he would definitely defend himself if assaulted.[11]

Permanently shut out of banking because of public distrust, James King of William listened to the praise for his published diatribes against Adams and Company and decided to start his own newspaper. Turning to R. H. Sinton of the real estate house of Selover and Sinton, he borrowed $250 to found the *Daily Evening Bulletin*.[12] From its beginning in October 1855, King used the paper to vent his own uncompromising moral judgments, particularly attacking institutions and individuals he had come to know well as a banker. In his eyes, respectable married fathers (like himself) held the most honorable positions, supported by wives whose purity was absolutely beyond reproach. His opponents, however, reveled in vices such as gambling, harlotry, and political corruption. They remained bachelors, like the hard-eyed, increasingly wealthy politician David Broderick. King's editorial job was to reveal their failings. He demanded, and got, "absolute control of [the paper's] columns so that . . . bad men whose influence he had determined to overthrow" could not buy controlling interest from the publisher and silence his voice.[13] As King spewed vitriol, one observer commented, "Many of his attacks upon individuals were not sustained by any proof, or even plausible testimony, and others were unjust, and even inexcusable; but these mistakes were overlooked by the people generally for the sake of the good motives attributed to Mr. King."[14] Others disagreed with this tolerant view, criticizing King's practice of publishing "personal assaults upon

James King of William, a failed banker, used his *Evening Bulletin* newspaper to illuminate the "sins" of San Franciscans, both real and imagined. *Courtesy of the Bancroft Library.*

the reputation of private citizens as well as upon public men," thus converting his paper "into a vehicle for private vengeance."[15] King also initiated a "Fireside" column with moralistic stories for women and children, alternating muckraking with pious homilies.[16] This titillating juxtaposition fascinated locals, and the "paper was read most extensively; the whole community was profoundly agitated by its disclosures."[17] The *Evening Bulletin* soon enjoyed the largest circulation of the city's fifteen newspapers.

The papers had plenty of exciting news to report. Politics offered a constant fount of juicy material. Like its national counterpart, California's single party, the Democrats, had split over slavery. California's pro-slavery southern or Chivalry wing (the "Chivs") followed Senator William M. Gwin, who had authored the 1851 Land Act that initiated decisions on the disposition of the state's real estate. In 1850, the forty-four-year-old Tennessee native had won one of California's first U.S. Senate positions and luckily drew the long straw, ensuring a term that would last until 1855.[18] In sharp opposition, in 1854, northern-leaning David Broderick, still nursing his own senatorial ambitions, had tried for the third time to get California's legislature to elect him to the U.S. Senate, as state legislatures were required to do until the twentieth century. He openly contended for Gwin's seat, which would not become vacant until March 1855. Horrified citizens realized that if Broderick succeeded a year before the vacancy occurred, nothing could stop any given legislature from electing U.S. senators well into the future. Even a sizable bribe allegedly offered by staunch Democrat Joseph Palmer of Palmer, Cook and Company could not win Broderick his Senate seat. The legislature soon passed a bill preventing any future such manipulations.[19]

In this context, Democratic Party conventions had been anything but cordial. The July 1854 meeting floundered through two competing chairmen, pushing, shoving, and an accidental gunshot that sent delegates leaping out through shattering windows. The only substantive remarks came in a keynote speech by pro-Broderick filibuster William Walker. The calm, charismatic Walker—a future inspiration to the vigilantes—delivered such a vivid anti-slavery speech that a Chiv delegate swore "that no freesoil or abolition men should be permitted to sit in democratic councils." Late at night, the two competing chairmen—one of them Broderick's man, Edward McGowan—left the aborted meeting arm in arm to reconvene separate conventions the following day.[20]

Given these ugly public clashes, a new national party began to take hold in California: the Know-Nothings, or American Party. It had begun in the East in 1853 as a conservative reform party, holding its first national council in June 1854. In New York, the port of departure for most northern emigrants to California, the Know-Nothing Council No. 1 organized as the "Committee of Thirteen"—a name attractive to San Franciscans seeking political reform.[21] That same year in New Orleans, a city closely linked to San Francisco by steamboat connections, an election in which 1,400 votes were cast by only 932 registered voters led to riotous attacks on polling places and on the Irish who allegedly controlled them. Again, Californians took note.[22]

In 1854, San Francisco's electoral politics became more confused than ever. Although the Know-Nothings waited until the morning of the election to publish their ticket, the city elected a Know-Nothing mayor, treasurer, recorder, and five other officials. Leading San Franciscans, increasingly from the North, had flocked to the Know-Nothings out of expediency and a desire simultaneously to break with land-hungry Democrat Broderick and to disassociate themselves from the southern taint of the state's Democratic Party. Most, however, repudiated the anti-foreign, anti-Catholic views of their eastern brothers. Meanwhile, California's state legislature had also muddied San Francisco's electoral waters. It had recently passed a change in the city's charter, mandating that these new officials would serve only until the following June 30. Consequently, San Franciscans had to hold a special municipal charter election on May 28, 1855, well prior to the usual September election day.

San Francisco's tangled land contests also intruded into this special charter election. James Van Ness, a trained attorney from Vermont and a candidate for San Francisco mayor, obliged some of the city's largest landholders by crafting a clever ordinance just before the election. According to this document, which Van Ness portrayed as an attempt to quiet conflicting land claims, the city of San Francisco would relinquish its titles to persons "in actual possession ... on or before the 1st of January 1855." How could this possession be established? First, the Van Ness Ordinance declared, the courts had to decree that San Francisco had been a genuine Mexican pueblo, thus supporting grants made by pueblo (and city) officials rather than claims derived from Santillán or Limantour, among others. However, in a clever maneuver, the ordinance also specifically approved "any Conveyance duly made by the Commissioners of the Funded Debt of the City." These commissioners, as noted, had loudly disputed the legitimacy of the Peter Smith sales resulting in Broderick's alleged ownership. Under the Van Ness Ordinance, Broderick's ownership would be invalidated and completing claims legitimized. This biased document concluded, "Nothing contained in this ordinance shall be construed to prevent the city from continuing to prosecute ... her claim ... for [Mexican] pueblo lands," the legal requirement for its own validity. Specifically, the controversial Van Ness Ordinance required state legislative approval, and also stipulated that the United States must agree to relinquish its own San Francisco land claims. If the alleged pueblo was established in law, and the state and federal governments acted quickly (which in those days sometimes happened), San Francisco's mayor would be able to grant lands. After the election of May 1855, that person might be James Van Ness. However, before full approval could be gained, the original document was lost.[23]

In San Francisco's charter election, certain men took a sudden interest in voting. On May 28, around every polling place gathered the usual "dyed-in-the-wool politician ... [the] vaunting worker, paid by one or the other of the parties ... [and] voters drummed up from among the boarding houses and drinking saloons of the city." Surprisingly, however, as a local paper noted, "the merchants and other respectable portions of the community" could be seen "mingling ... *for once* in the strife."[24] Ten days before his departure from office on June 20, 1855, the outgoing mayor signed the recently passed Van Ness Ordinance into law. His successor, winning the mayor's office by only 65 out of more than 11,600 total votes, was James Van Ness.[25]

Conflicting claimants did not simply roll over and play dead. Just after the election, there was another problematic sale of San Francisco water lots. The city's leading auction firm, Selover and Sinton, conducted the sale "by rapidly skipping from one part of the catalogue to another and accepting bids of persons instructed in the scheme before others could be heard. . . . [The auctioneer thereby enabled a] combination to buy lots worth thousands at eight dollars apiece." Most of the successful bidders were Broderick's friends.[26] Even if the "Peter Smith" claimants, of whom Broderick was one, were denied ownership of earlier purchases by the provisions of the Van Ness Ordinance, Broderick and his followers would still own some of San Francisco's highly lucrative waterfront.

Political disputes continued to stew in the contested city, where the Democratic state primary of August 1855 spawned more than the usual hostility. Irish American New Yorker James P. Casey, the foreman of Crescent Engine Company No. 10, had recently abandoned Broderick for the Know-Nothings. On the day of the primary election, five Broderick men attacked Casey as he left the polls. When a shot grazed Casey's temple, he snatched up a knife and plunged it into an assailant's side, severing a rib and puncturing a lung. A bystander helped scoop up the injured man's entrails and ease them into his body cavity while a doctor stitched him up. Although all of the participants were arrested, no one appeared the next day to prosecute Casey, so he was freed after a night in jail.[27] A vigilante—no friend of Casey's—later called this "one of the most desperate fights on record against great odds."[28] Even one of his worst enemies regarded the scrappy, 130-pound Casey as "a man of considerable intelligence . . . possessed of a good deal of brilliancy, activity, and smartness."[29] Another called him "a man of considerable character, of strong will."[30] That assertion was about to be tested.

The regular September election shook up California politically. At the state level, the Know-Nothings elected their entire ticket. A former Chiv Democrat, thirty-three-year-old David S. Terry, was elected associate justice of the supreme court, and Senator Gwin's protégé, thirty-year-old J. Neely Johnson, became governor.[31] When the legislature, which had to elect the U.S. senator, met the following January, Chiv dominance ensured that Broderick again could not be elected as Gwin's term expired. However, Broderick used his influence to ensure that no one else would be chosen, either, leaving California with but a single U.S. senator.[32]

At the municipal level, the fall election had brought San Francisco some unusual results. For example, the First Ward election judges quietly tallied twenty-six more votes for scrappy James P. Casey than there were voters in the district, despite the absence of Casey's name on their ballot and his residence in the Sixth Ward. The county court judge refused to overturn the election results. Over the protests of two prominent Democrats, the Know-Nothings muscled Casey onto the San Francisco County Board of Supervisors.[33] The Fifth Ward inspectors (all Know-Nothings) behaved no better. Together with the election judges and tally clerks from their same party, they were preparing to count the ballots when Democrats intervened and found four tightly wrapped packages, each containing some twenty Know-Nothing tickets, printed on fine tissue paper. These spurious additions amounted to seventy-nine bogus ballots, which matched fictitious names on a fake poll list. The election judges reluctantly had to reject them. A newspaper sneered that "the *purifiers* have boldly charged fraud upon the Democratic Party only to lull suspicion and thus conceal their own schemes."[34] Incredibly, these actions were not illegal, so no one was arrested. "It is no offense, under our election law, to stuff votes into a ballot box, or to steal or change the same," another article added.[35]

Shortly after the elections, a new scandal rocked San Francisco. In November 1855, an Italian Catholic gambler named Charles Cora shot and killed U.S. Marshal William H. Richardson under murky circumstances. The original report said that the tall, brooding Richardson, who always carried two derringers, had taken unreasonable offense to some lighthearted remarks of Cora's and, while in his cups, had sought out the man who had supposedly insulted him. Backed against a wall, the Italian gambler allegedly had no choice but to shoot or be shot. Later that evening, someone tapped the Monumental Engine Company bell, the traditional signal for the 1851 vigilantes. Remnants of that Committee gathered, but they soon dispersed. Given the unequal statuses of the two participants, Cora was accused of "cold blooded murder," although the coroner's inquest proved indecisive.[36] Three days after Richardson's death, the press put the blame for the whole affair on Belle Cora (née Arrabella Ryan), Cora's beautiful paramour and the madam of the fanciest "house" in San Francisco. Cora's mistress had supposedly caused an insult to Richardson's wife at a theater a day or two earlier by sitting too close to the respectable lady and attracting unwanted attention.[37]

In reporting this fracas, James King of William strove for major impact, even if it meant twisting the facts. Less than a week after Richardson's death, a young out-of-town visitor stupidly tried to bribe the county jailer, William Mulligan, to release Cora, mistakenly believing both that Mulligan was Cora's friend and that bribery would set Cora free. Mulligan arrested the fellow.[38] Knowing that Mulligan and the San Francisco sheriff were both Broderick Democrats, King editorialized, "If the jury which tries Cora is packed, either *hang the sheriff* or drive him out of town and make him resign." Trivializing Mulligan, King added, "If Billy Mulligan lets his friend Cora escape, *hang Billy Mulligan* or drive him into banishment."[39]

Cora's trial generated more ink for King's pointed pen. Wealthy Belle Cora had hired distinguished attorney Edward Dickenson Baker, San Francisco's most celebrated orator, to defend her lover. Baker was reluctant to serve, but the money was good, and in the end he gave a sterling defense. At Cora's January 1856 trial,

Baker celebrated Belle for her devotion to Cora when the prosecution tried to blacken his name with their association. "Who in God's name, gentlemen, would be his friend if she wasn't?" he asked. He stressed his own admiration for a woman who, "abandoned by the world, and pointed at in derision, could yet give her all" for the man she loved.[40] Baker's emotional closing speech helped hang the jury, but it infuriated King, because no "fallen woman" deserved such praise. Cora was returned to the county jail, awaiting a second trial. King promptly demanded a new Vigilance Committee, "to give a fair trial without the technicalities of the law."[41] While stragglers tried to reunite the 1851 vigilantes, the elite stayed aloof. The time for a new Committee had not yet come.

3
Land and Newsprint

Under these uncertain circumstances, Alfred A. Green may have unknowingly catalyzed the 1856 Vigilance Committee. A native of Canada, Green had arrived in California in 1847 to fight in the U.S.-Mexican War. The army had temporarily sent him to Mexico, where he became fluent in Spanish, enabling him to woo and wed a local California woman. Eventually, his mother and five brothers joined him on the San Francisco Peninsula. Green strongly believed that San Francisco was a former Mexican pueblo, and as such was entitled to four square leagues (some sixteen thousand acres) of contested lands, including some of his own. In the spring of 1856, he was shocked to learn that the city, in negotiations with the U.S. attorney, had recently agreed to reduce its claim to three square leagues, thus excluding his property west of the city and weakening his claim to ownership. Green marched up and down Montgomery Street, San Francisco's leading commercial thoroughfare, informing "several leading citizens of what was doing." He also claimed that he had obtained San Francisco's old Pueblo Papers from the last Mexican administrator. For years, he said, he had presented them to a series of officials, but the men he approached had declined to take action because they held land under other, competing grants. Now he wanted to share the documents with the city. The word spread. Before sundown, Green was asked to give a public lecture about San Francisco's pueblo lands.[1]

Green was well aware that two other, overlapping land claims were the pueblo's main competitors for San Francisco's most valuable real estate. Most San Franciscans had largely forgotten about these colossal tracts, which had recently been approved by the federal land board. One of the largest under consideration, some 10,186 acres, had allegedly been granted on February 14, 1846, by the Mexican government to Father

José Prudencio Santillán, the former parish priest of San Francisco's Mission Dolores.[2] In 1853, as soon as the federal land board approved the very first claim in line, chances that the Santillán claim would also be approved seemed rosy. Consequently, Mexican business partners James R. Bolton and Eustace Barron acquired Santillán's claim. Within weeks they sold what was now also called the "Bolton and Barron claim" for $200,000 to a trusted employee of the bank of Palmer, Cook and Company, who sold it again a month later to the San Francisco Land Association of Philadelphia for $1.3 million. The midwife for this slick deal was apparently native Philadelphian Edward McGowan, a sharp lawyer and Broderick adherent who had co-chaired the abortive 1854 Democratic Convention. In 1855, when the Philadelphia association reorganized, Joseph Palmer, PC&C's senior partner, a Broderick supporter, and a friend of McGowan's, sat on its board of directors. The association then issued a promotional circular in order to sell $15 million worth of stock in San Francisco real estate it allegedly owned.[3] On June 5, 1855, the federal land board approved the Santillán (Bolton and Barron) claim, now the property of the Philadelphia group. Federal attorneys (representing the U.S. interest in the Customhouse, several forts, the Post Office, and the Mint) decided to mount an appeal.[4]

The competing Limantour claim posed an even greater threat to other San Francisco claimants. On February 3, 1853, just one month before the land board's submission period ended, José Yves Limantour had submitted two massive claims to tracts of land in San Francisco and environs, totaling some sixteen thousand acres, or roughly one-half of the then-occupied city plus some neighboring islands. Limantour, a Frenchman who had fought for Chile in the wars of Latin American independence, had allegedly sailed up to San Francisco, befriended California's Mexican governor, and lent him money at a crucial time. The grateful governor then supposedly gave Limantour seven grants. The Frenchman abandoned all but the two he later brought forward. While American suspicion discounted the testimony of Mexican Californians, Captain William A. Richardson, San Francisco's earliest Anglo resident (since 1835), had been the lead witness in favor of Limantour. The former Mexican governor who had signed Limantour's documents, and who might have clarified matters, had died in September 1853. Richardson's testimony grew in importance. On January 22, 1856, the Board of Land Commissioners confirmed Limantour's claim to thousands of acres of Bay Area real estate, worth an estimated $14 million. Appalled federal attorneys decided to contest his claim in the federal Court for the Northern District of California. On February 28, one of Limantour's associates published a letter promising to share proof of Limantour's fraud if he could be compensated with $50,000. When no such sum was forthcoming, the associate sailed for the East. He returned in April 1856 and gave a deposition to a

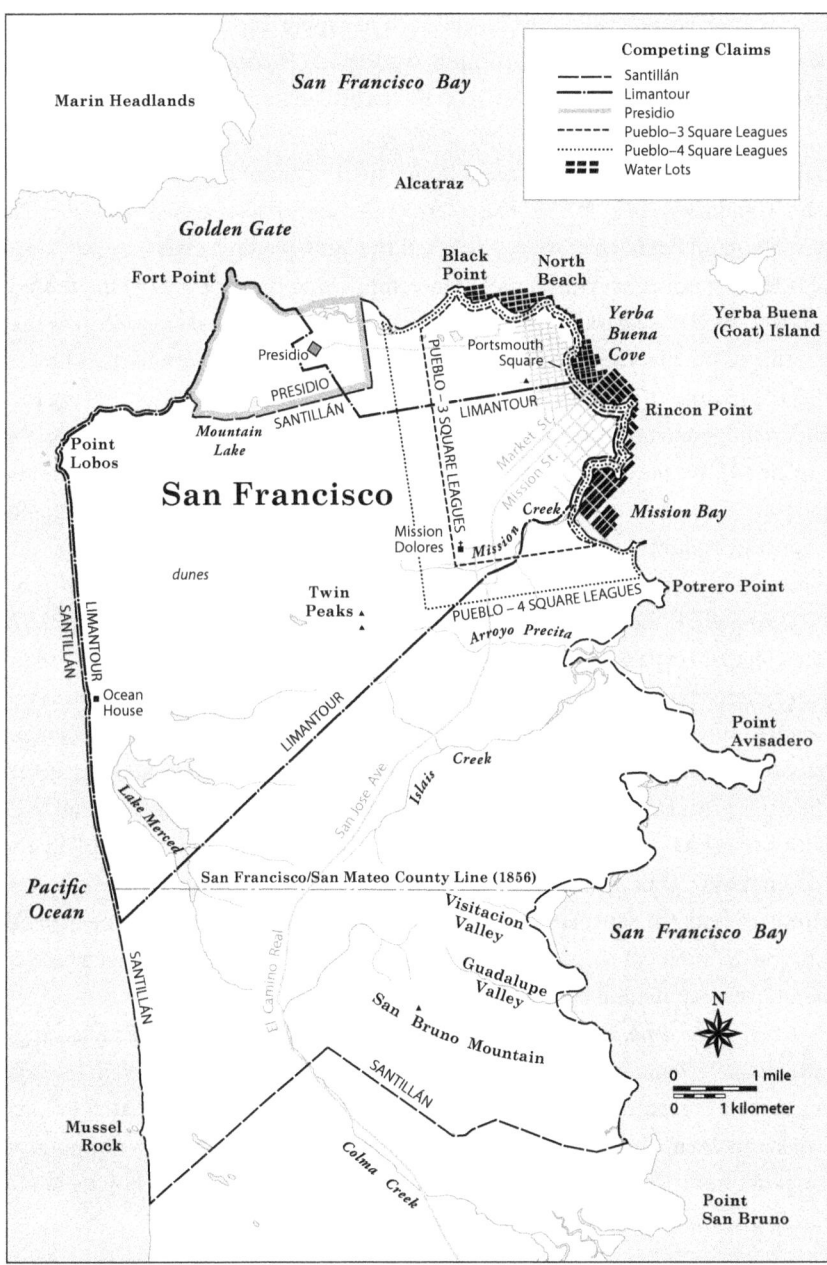

Map of San Francisco. The confused record of claims to San Francisco does not precisely agree on the city's boundaries, which were in litigation for decades. At least five ranchos also lay within this area, as well as the United States' claims to small plots including the Mint, the Customhouse, and the Post Office. *Map by Ben Pease. Copyright © 2016, University of Oklahoma Press.*

federal attorney describing the falsification of supporting documents in Mexico, actions that included the collusion of William A. Richardson.[5] Before further testimony could be taken, on April 20 Richardson died.[6]

In the meantime, Limantour had made good money off his claims. He offered a quitclaim deed (conveying the *presumption* of ownership) to anyone on "his" land who would pay him a "tax" of 10 percent of the property's assessed valuation. The new claimant could then more easily sell the land, passing what is called "color of title," but not conveying actual ownership. Limantour apparently made some $200,000 to $250,000 from these transactions.[7] Some of these weary contributors "had purchased their lots several times over, being covered over by various titles besides that of Limantour."[8] Others ignored the ongoing land cases entirely, believing they had been "gotten up mainly for levying blackmail."[9] As one wealthy Executive later explained, "We purchased all the titles we could get. We bought the City's title and the State's title and then somebody claimed a little interest in it which we fought for some time and cost us considerable money, but finally compromised for $2,500.... I found the title as good there as in any place in the city," which was not saying much.[10]

On April 21, the same day the papers reported Richardson's death, Alfred A. Green spoke to a packed crowd on "The Title of San Francisco to Her Pueblo Lands." He proffered the original papers from the old Mexican pueblo, asking that they be examined and verified. The crowd shouted its approval and backed three recognized experts. On May 5, after perusing 395 documents and ten books (all in Spanish), the experts declared the Pueblo Papers to be genuine.[11] If San Francisco had truly been a Mexican pueblo, then the city's rights predated the grants to Santillán and to Limantour, Thus, those who bought land from city officials had first right to it. However, both the Santillán and Limantour claims were already crawling through the courts. If one of them were to get legal approval, any other claims would be moot. Anxiety about local real estate mushroomed.

At the same time, James King of William intensified his attacks. He increasingly lambasted Democrats, Roman Catholics, and the Irish (who were often one and the same). For example, he repeatedly denounced Democrat-affiliated Palmer, Cook and Company "as a political institution . . . [using] deposits . . . for political purposes to further their own interests," which may have included buying land.[12] In his *Evening Bulletin*, King also critiqued the morning papers:

> The *Town Talk* thinks that the [recent] Selover [land] sale swindle should be set aside for fraud or irregularity. . . . The *Chronicle* thinks [filibuster William] Walker will either sink or swim in Nicaragua, but don't [sic] decide which. The *Alta* gets off something about the [proposed transcontinental] Railroad. . . . Who the deuce edits the

Sun now? It has certainly improved of late.... The *Herald* mourns over heavy taxes, but ignores the fact that by its silent acquiescing in the schemes of Palmer, Cook & Co., it helps increase the evils complained of.[13]

King also turned on local Catholics. He published two anti-Catholic editorials, one specifically blaming local priest "Father Gallagher ... [for] brutality at the Hospital ... [with the connivance of] Sisters of Mercy (?) with Jesuit fathers."[14] This unfounded personal attack on a beloved priest horrified local Catholics. One respectable Catholic lady believed that King's Know-Nothing backing allowed him to write "outrageously against men of education and standing in the city, venting his personal spite in a blackguard manner and calling it zeal for the public good."[15] Wealthy Irish merchant Denis Oliver recorded in his daily diary that he had met with other Catholic elites, who agreed that the only way to deal with King was "to write a card [personal ad] signed by some of the best men in the Congregation denying the Charges."[16] Twenty-six of the city's most prominent Catholics published a letter asserting that Father Joseph Gallagher "has not now, and never had any control of the Hospital" and blamed King's "animosity to him personally, or to the denomination of which he and we are members" for the malicious editorial. King printed this card, and in the same article harrumphed:

> The cowardly attempt of this Committee of twenty-six ... to draw us into a controversy with the church ... is too apparent.... Father Gallagher's friends show us that it is their fault, they will see that we do not shrink from our duty. The same remarks apply to the whole Catholic community.[17]

King would not let up. In his editorial of April 18, 1856, ignoring the continuing local recession, he thundered:

> Fourteen hundred souls left our wharves on steamer day!... The women and children—aye, *native born* California children, too ... [are] eastward bound. [Why?] ... our public men, our representatives, our office holders ... are of the *most notorious scoundrels in the community*!... Look at the Board of Supervisors running this county in debt at railroad speed.... Look at your Mayor, imbecile for any good.... Look at your public offices, filled, not by honest merchants or mechanics ... but by gamblers, and thieves, and shoulder strikers.[18]

In those days, readers expected newspapers to be partisan, and San Francisco editors did not disappoint. It seemed that everyone with a political or personal vendetta was starting one. The *Advertiser*, a pro-Democratic paper, backed David Broderick. James P. Casey, that strangely elected San Francisco supervisor, launched his *Weekly Sunday Times* on December 24, 1855. William Mulligan, Cora's jailer, started an illustrated weekly paper, "a decidedly disreputable sheet," in March 1856. More serious figures also had their newspaper associations: John S. Hittell, later the author of a history of San Francisco, became associate editor of the *California Chronicle* in fall 1855, eventually switching to the *Daily Alta California*, which became strongly pro-vigilante in 1856. His brother Theodore worked at the inflammatory *Evening Bulletin* of James King of William. Catholic John Nugent of the *Herald* (also vilified by King for his religion) maintained his independent views, although he had to fight two duels over material he published. San Francisco also sported papers in German, Spanish, even Italian, with varying life spans.[19] Given the local popularity of solving problems with weapons, one man remarked that King "was a doomed man, and he would not live long."[20] Understanding this, King claimed to carry a weapon, in case any of his victims sought revenge.[21]

Sometimes editorials descended to the level of personal vendettas. Casey and King began to skirmish in print over the Customhouse, known locally as the "Virginia poor house" because of the many southerners who had been granted patronage positions there. King's muckraking articles had attacked many of its employees, but had been strangely silent regarding its superintendent, who had provided the editor's brother, Thomas Sim King, with a comfortable job. In his own paper, Casey not only sneeringly noted this oversight, but published a typically anonymous letter under the pen name "Caliban," claiming that Thomas King had wanted the marshal's post made vacant when Cora shot Richardson. Thomas King had been denied, and Richardson's replacement was now constantly ridiculed by James King of William. In response, Thomas King threatened to duel with the anonymous Caliban, whom Casey refused to name.[22]

Casey also took potshots at Alfred A. Green. Casey discounted the "great emergency . . . [and threat to] the city's claim to the pueblo lands, and a danger to the homes of our citizens generally," Green later claimed. Within days, Casey, whose *Sunday Times* was allegedly more friendly to "other claimants who held lands adverse to the [pueblo] title of the city," wrote that Green "ought to have his head shaved and be sent to the lunatic asylum." Green consequently started looking into Casey's background. "I had ascertained," Green said, "that he had been convicted of felony in New York, and had been in the State Prison there, and I thought it my duty to give these facts to James King of William."[23]

Matters between King and Casey came to a head on May 14, 1856. Returning to his Customhouse exposé, King pilloried U.S. Customs employee John W. Bagley,

ASSASSINATION OF JAMES KING OF WILLIAM.

In this era of difficult photography, engravings or lithographs served to illustrate dramatic events of the day. One of several different renditions of this scene stressed the "assassination" of King by Casey, leaving no doubt as to who was in the wrong. *Courtesy of the Bancroft Library.*

who had fiercely attacked Casey at the polls the previous year. King wrote: "Our impression ... was that in the Casey fight Bagley was the aggressor. It does not matter how bad a man Casey had been.... The fact that Casey has been an inmate of Sing Sing prison in New York, is no offense against the laws of this state; nor is the fact of him having stuffed himself through the ballot-box, as elected to the board of supervisors ... [no matter how] richly the latter [Casey] may deserve to have his neck stretched for such fraud on the people."[24] Of all these insults, the one that truly stung Casey was the revelation of his New York prison term, possibly uncovered by Green. Rushing to the *Bulletin* office, Casey angrily demanded that King divulge the name of his informant. King refused. Casey threatened revenge. That evening, as the editor strode out on his customary route homeward, Casey was waiting. A contemporary reported, "Casey stepped right up, and immediately said, 'Protect yourself,' and ... shot him on the spot."[25]

The news of King's shooting electrified San Francisco. For his own protection, Casey turned himself in at the city jail. As a mob surged around, crying, "Hang him! Hang him!" the county sheriff and city marshal crammed Casey into a carriage and raced to the stronger county jail, which was already occupied by several criminals, including gambler Charles Cora, still awaiting a second trial. The mob followed.²⁶ The two-story stone and brick county jail sat in an excavation at the side of Telegraph Hill, which loomed over the building's rear wall. In front, the lowering of Broadway had left an earthen embankment about eight feet high and ten feet wide, surmounted by a flight of heavy wooden steps up to the jail's front door. As deputies rushed Casey up the steps, armed members of the local militia held back a growing crowd of thousands yelling, "Hang him! Kill him!"²⁷ Thomas Sim King, brother of the wounded editor, fought his way through the throng, climbed on a nearby balcony, and promised to "lead a party to tear down the Jail, take possession of it, kill the officers, and shoot down every gambler in the city, and hang the prisoner."²⁸

James Van Ness, who had tried so hard to become mayor with his merchant-friendly ordinance, found himself with a mess on his hands. Thanks to the close election, he now headed a city of some fifty thousand inhabitants, most of whom were young men, many of them unemployed, bored, and seeking excitement. The shooting had unleashed tensions bubbling just below the surface. Trying to head off any confrontation, Mayor Van Ness stepped out from the crowd and asked for calm. The seething throng retorted, "Hang him! Hang him!"²⁹ It was hard to tell which of the two men the crowd wanted to hang.

As the rabble yelled for a rope, more elite residents quietly gathered in other parts of town. The time had come to reorganize the vigilantes. Some local businessmen assembled at Pioneer Hall, opposite the Plaza, where they signed a petition "calling for a Committee of Safety." George Frink, who had arrived in 1852, too late for the first Committee, eagerly signed. The group then trooped up to North Beach, to the warehouse of merchant Gabriel B. Post. Frink later remembered the "second story filled with people, all wanting to talk at once. Among those who got a word in edgewise were . . . Wm. T. Coleman, and G. B. Post, who was considerably tight. He insisted on going right to the jail, and taking the men and hanging them, and some of the others agreed with him. He said he had arms enough to blow the jail down." Others counseled patience. As the meeting dissolved, Frink and Coleman left together. They noticed two ship's cannons loaded on carts out in the street, which they quietly appropriated. Then they went to the Bank Exchange Saloon for a drink, and decided "to call a meeting of the Vigilance Committee at the Know Nothing rooms" the next day.³⁰ Coleman wrote out a notice for publication inviting "Members of the Vigilance Committee in good standing" to an organizational meeting, signed by the "Committee of Thirteen."³¹ Locals well knew that another "Committee of Thirteen" had met in New York a few years earlier to inaugurate the American Party, or Know-Nothing Party.³² Coleman also claimed that this title was the name "under which . . . the [vigilante] organization of 1851 had disbanded."³³

Within twenty-four hours, a group of well-heeled young men had gathered at San Francisco's Know-Nothing Hall. They included Coleman, who at the age of thirty-two was a successful merchant, auctioneer, and banker, the son-in-law of Daniel Page and brother-in-law of Henry D. Bacon of the bank of Page and Bacon. Those in attendance urged Coleman to take the lead.[34] He declined at first (as was expected in that day), but then demanded "absolute control." He would organize the Committee only if "what I said and did was accepted as authority and unquestioned." The others agreed. Together they drew up a sacred binding oath, "pledging everything, life limb, property, honor, all they had."[35] Coleman insisted that "there will be no names used, but every man will take his number, and be known by his number only." The city's first Vigilance Committee had established the practices of identifying men only by their numbers, holding secret trials, and keeping their formal minutes hidden from the public, although they later released their papers for publication. Following their lead, Coleman took the number 1 and swore in the first group of vigilantes from among his elite friends.[36] One of them was James D. Farwell, a former steamboat captain who had first met Coleman in 1850 during negotiations over a shipload of imported goods. Twenty years later, Farwell claimed, "I put my name down, and was No. 17."[37] "I joined the Committee of '56 among the first, my number being 33," boasted Isaac Bluxome Jr., soon the permanent secretary.[38] (He had been "67 Secretary" in the Committee of 1851 and had since led the dashing "Bluxome's Battery" of the California Guards, and served as secretary of the secretive Odd Fellows organization, to which many Executives belonged.)[39] Twenty-eight-year-old Bluxome proposed the admission of Clancey Dempster, "a cool, calculating, brave man, not a bit nervous, the pluckiest little fellow in the world and you can't frighten him. He made a first rate member."[40] At twenty-seven, Dempster, the son of foreign missionaries, was the youngest of the new leaders. The oldest was "old" James Dows, age forty-six.[41] Each of these, and dozens more men familiar to the elite leaders, took their numbers and solemnly swore their binding oath. From the beginning, San Francisco's 1856 Vigilance Committee was cloaked in secrecy.

4
Under Attack

The men of antebellum California loved secret societies. *Colville's San Francisco Directory* for 1856 listed myriad statewide organizations that were represented in the city, including 105 lodges of ritualistic Free and Accepted Masons, 15 lodges of Royal Arch Masons, 62 lodges of the Independent Order of Odd Fellows, 2 encampments of Knights Templar, and assorted other groups such as the teetotaling Sons of Temperance and the Temple of Honor.[1] The avid acceptance of these and other secret societies mirrored activities that had continued for centuries throughout Europe and the United States. Fraternal organizations, artificial "brotherhoods," had long united men across sectional and class lines, providing social capital that could be used to address mutual concerns.[2]

In California, this highly masculine land of gold, men used familiar rituals to forge the bonds of brotherhood in a place otherwise strange and far from home, and to exclude other, different sorts of men who had also been drawn by supposedly easy riches. The vigilantes' Executive Committee was no exception. Its members decided that they would "act on their own responsibility without consulting the general committee who had nothing to do but obey orders," later recalled the vigilante Chief of Police. This was "a very fortunate arrangement," since infiltrators—and there were several—were frustrated "by the secrecy with which the Executive Committee conducted all their meetings and all their business."[3]

Over the next two days, hundreds of men lined up quietly to be grilled by the Examining Committee, who checked their "answers and references."[4] Once admitted to the vigilantes' rooms, each put his hand on a Bible and declared, "I do solemnly swear to act with the Vigilance Committee and second in full all their actions as expressed through their executive Committee." Then each signed the roll sheet next to his number, adopting the only identification he would use inside and outside the highly secretive Committee.[5] By the end of the first day, "We had probably about 1500 [members] enrolled," Coleman recalled, most from the North and West, but also dozens of foreigners. Mounting a table, Coleman sorted them into Roman-style divisions, as he had done in childhood, this time each of one hundred men. Most foreigners spoke adequate English, but the French spoke only their own language. Coleman therefore "said in French, 'Les Français se metter au centre.'" The French promptly gathered in the middle of the room and became the 25th Division or "French Legion" (later to be augmented by the 28th). Each new member was informed of the daily password needed for future admittance.[6] Other wealthy Executives quietly rented vacant rooms throughout the depression-wracked city so that each hundred could have its own "armory," or headquarters.[7]

Meeting in secret, the Executives introduced formal motions, which were duly recorded in their closely held *Minutes* by "33 Secretary," Isaac Bluxome Jr. After they had chosen officers and located permanent quarters, their next resolutions read:

> Resolved: That full power be given to Executive Committee to act for General Committee upon all matters and to report at future meetings of this body;
> Resolved: That members withdraw their support from the Herald newspaper and use their influence with their friends for that purpose[;]
> Resolved: That this committee as a body visit the County jail at such time as the Executive Committee may direct and take James P. Casey and Charles Cora; give them a fair trial before our members or a committee thereof and mete out such punishments as justice may require.[8]

In line with the second resolution, the vigilantes took control of San Francisco's press. They particularly targeted the *Herald*, edited by Catholic lawyer and journalist John Nugent, who had immediately editorialized against a new Vigilance Committee.[9] His paper instantly lost 212 subscribers and most of the merchants' advertisements. When an Executive suggested that Nugent should be called in to defend himself, "a dozen voices spoke up and said that it [the editorial] was bad enough, that the *Herald* had always been on the wrong side."[10] Rowdies seized all the copies of his paper, piled them up on Front Street, and burned them.[11] With one exception, the other papers all quickly fell into line. The *Bulletin* willingly published the documents generated by Casey's New York trial and incarceration.[12] The *Chronicle*, which had first cautioned against hasty action and urged "due process of law" rather than mob rule, recanted when its subscribers and advertisers turned to the *Daily Alta California*, where the *Herald*'s former advertisers also appeared, making the *Alta* the premier journal in the city. Other editors took note and leapt to support the new Vigilance Committee. Only the *Sun*, after wavering a day or two, also condemned the vigilantes, to its own detriment, some days publishing whole or half blank columns under regular advertising heads, making light of its own loss of business.[13]

In his diary, Catholic merchant Denis Oliver branded the assault on the *Herald* "contemptible tyranny. I and my friends ordered extra copies." Oliver also noted that large incendiary placards had been "posted up round the City."[14] These signs bugled "EMERGENCY OF THE MOMENT!—TO THE PEOPLE!" Calling the law a "MOCKERY," they demanded that men defy it with "RESISTANCE." Let "the majority of the people TRY THE PRESUMED MURDERER, and then, if he be guilty, EXECUTE!" they shrieked.[15]

In fact, King was not dead. One of his friends, twenty-six-year-old Dr. Richard Beverly Cole, still recuperating from his own stomach wound (accidentally self-inflicted two years earlier), had stayed by the editor's bedside since the shooting, bringing care and comfort. Some twenty other physicians had gathered, and one of the senior men suggested that a white surgical sponge be inserted in King's wound to stanch the bleeding. All the medical men agreed. The following morning, Dr. Cole suggested that the sponge be removed before King was moved to more comfortable quarters in the Montgomery Block. The others refused, so Cole stalked out and joined the vigilantes, becoming number 253.[16]

Other men flocked from all over, eager to join. Future vigilante police chief Robert B. Wallace, who at the time resided more than two hundred miles away in Nevada City, later noted that "when King was shot . . . the news was telegraphed all over the State. I knew what would follow & the same night found me on my way to San Francisco."[17] Businessman and West Point graduate Francis Pinto, soon to be captain of the 5th Division, remembered, "I had dissolved my partnership on May 1st with the expectation of going home to New York, but I became so much interested in this campaign against vice that I could not leave until the war was over."[18]

The busy Executives quietly expanded their grasp. They demanded an alarm bell to alert their followers to emergencies and selected a permanent secretary to keep a precise record of their actions in the *Minutes*. They moved and carried a motion to capture and deport those whom they considered "notoriously undesirable and universally obnoxious . . . and dangerous to the lives and persons and property." If these exiles returned, the Vigilance Committee would apply "decisive action . . . to relieve the community of their presence." That meant death.[19]

Meanwhile, the vigilantes' opposition had also organized. San Francisco sheriff David Scannell called his own meeting to try to prevent Casey's lynching, attracting only fifty-four men, including a one-armed judge. This group called themselves the "Law and Order Party," and elected West Point graduate and banker William Tecumseh Sherman as their leader. Sherman immediately declined.[20] He had already accepted the governor's appointment as commander of the 2nd Division of the California State Militia (including San Francisco) on May 10, "simply for the purpose of organization."[21] Four days later, Casey shot King. Nonetheless, Sherman went with the Law and Order Party simply to give his military assessment of the county jail where Casey was imprisoned. As Sherman reported to his banking partner, the jail was "open to the rear, overlooked on all sides by brick houses with parapet walls, no part of the interior of the jail safe from shots but the cells, which are full of prisoners. . . . [I]f I were forced to meet an armed mob, I would rather be in an open prairie than in that jail."[22]

Mayor Van Ness, after facing the mob at the jail, also tried to assemble antivigilante forces. He first called out the local militia. Those responding included "the Volunteer Companies, three of infantry, amounting to some sixty men . . . , a few straggling mounted men," and about a dozen others with two small six-pound cannons, reported Sherman.[23] But most militiamen had gone over to the vigilantes, taking their weapons with them.[24] As an Executive later noted, they added "the new *Independent* to their old titles," calling themselves the Independent City Guard, the Independent National Guard, and so on.[25] Concerned, Van Ness telegraphed Governor J. Neely Johnson, requesting that he come down from Sacramento on the next steamboat. Arriving that night, the thirty-year-old governor ducked away in the crowd on the Pacific Street Wharf and went to find his close friend, William Tell Coleman. In private conversation, the two men appeared to agree that the vigilantes would simply drive away "notoriously bad characters; . . . purify the atmosphere morally and politically, and then . . . disband," recalled Coleman. The governor would not interfere.[26] The two men split up before Sherman and the others arrived. They knew nothing about this meeting.

More meetings ensued. Now united, the governor's party went out to find the Executives, stopping in to see James King of William on the way. Despite King's loss of blood, reports posted on bulletin boards around town said that he should recover. When the governor and his companions located the Executive Committee, Coleman came down and, after a brief, stilted exchange with Governor Johnson, entered into a general conversation about the vigilantes' aims of political purification. The sticking point became who should have custody of Casey. At first, Coleman intimated that Casey should be given up to the vigilantes, which Johnson flatly refused to do. But the governor, negotiating an oral treaty with the vigilantes, naïvely permitted "a few men of their number" into the jail, as "an assistant guard, but under the control of the Sheriff."[27] Ten vigilantes shortly piled in among the regular jail guards. "From that hour I knew that the fate of Casey was sealed," recalled Broderick's friend, former Philadelphian Edward McGowan. "Several of us threw down our arms in disgust and left."[28] Clapping on his signature white stovepipe hat, McGowan stepped out into a city he would soon have to flee for his life.

While the trusting governor let vigilantes into the jail, the Executives hunkered down in an imposing two-story brick warehouse about a block from the waterfront on land recently reclaimed from the bay. The property of merchant-auctioneer Executive Miers Truett and his brother, it connected with the two neighboring buildings, fronted on a large burned-out lot, and had a highly unusual back alley, allowing easy access to the rear. There were two front entrances: the main one on Sacramento Street and the Executives' private entrance around the corner on Front Street, through the store of Truett and Jones. The Executives commandeered the whole second floor, where carpenters were kept busy "making alterations, cutting doors, and building stairs to connect the several buildings" on the block.[29] On the second floor emerged the "Executive Committee Court hall and rooms, the rooms of the officers, the rooms for the guards, and the small, close, crimped cells for the prisoners," recalled a witness.[30]

Security remained tight in this makeshift fortification. To enter, each vigilante had to give his number to the armed sentries on guard at each door, midway up each staircase, at the top of the stairs, and in front of each room.[31] "The number referred to a certain page on the books which contained a description of the person," recalled the vigilantes' Chief of Police, Martin Burke, whose four-hundred-man force had access to all of the buildings and received regular pay, unlike other members.[32] At the rear, carpenters soon built stables for the fifteen to twenty horses used by the vigilante cavalry, leaving room for the storage of artillery.[33] Outside the fort, sentries remained on duty to prevent attacks or dynamiting.[34] Everyone initially called this complex "Fort Vigilance."

Arms flowed in. The Executives elected merchant Charles Doane as Grand Marshal, giving him command of all the Committee's military forces. A local arms dealer offered to lend them all the muskets they would need. Known as "George Law" muskets, these ancient single-shot weapons with bayonets were government surplus, bought at a discount by New York entrepreneur George Law, who had intended to sell them in Europe during the Revolutions of 1848. Rejected by the Europeans, these out-of-date weapons had literally been floating around the world for eight years. The Executives agreed to pay $5,000 to rent them for seventy days.³⁵ In the room below the Executives' chamber, men drilled incessantly, using loaded guns. "The French Legion ordered arms with a great deal of vim," Executive Oliver Crary remembered. "The muskets had flint locks and some of them were a little loose, and sometimes the bullets came up into our rooms."³⁶ "Once or twice balls came up through the floor and through the chairs where we were sitting. Fortunately no one was injured," remembered another Executive.³⁷ However, when a bullet lodged in the chair of James Dows, the Executives decided to move to another part of the complex. They had already armed themselves with "pistols, generally [held] under the coat. We had a stand of arms in the committee rooms, right behind the president's chair, all shotguns, loaded with wire cartridges."³⁸

After making their preparations, the Executives resolved to "notify Gov. Johnson that we maintain the treaty made with him last night," but they offered "no [other] pledges . . . except that we would make no attack on the jail while our guard remained within it."³⁹ The next day, they formed their War Committee.⁴⁰

Sunday morning, May 18, dawned as one of those rare warm spring days with "brilliant sunshine, cloudless skies, a soft breeze & the stillness of Sabbath," one Executive remembered.⁴¹ James King of William remained in danger, the putrid sponge still embedded in his wound. At Fort Vigilance, Grand Marshal Doane told Francis Pinto, a Mexican American war veteran and captain of the 5th Division or Coleman Guards, "to time my watch with his," and keep his men close to headquarters. Around 11:30 a.m., Pinto received a sealed package containing three messages: "the plan of the Jail and surrounding streets," directions to march to his assigned position "at precisely five minutes after 12 o'clock," and a "General Order: No man shall fire a shot or use his bayonet without the order of his commanding officer under penalty of military discipline. All cheering and noise forbidden." He also got three ball cartridges for each soldier, one to be loaded in his gun and two to carry in his pocket.⁴² With fixed bayonets glinting in the sun, the silent army began to move.

Pinto's command marched down Kearney Street, taking no notice as "hundreds of men came out of the gambling dens, and saloons," joined by residents heading home from church, many of whom had heard the Protestant clergy sermonize in favor of the Committee.⁴³ (The Catholics opposed it.) Two crack American companies marched by, then a company of French soldiers and one of Germans, followed by the rest of the troops in formation. Twenty-four companies converged on the jail in almost perfect order, each at about half-complement (or fifty men).⁴⁴

Decades later, men remembered the scene. "I recall I stood right in front of the jail door," said a vigilante, "and behind us was a brass cannon, loaded. . . . [The] Captain of the California Guards . . . had it shotted [with a fully prepared charge]

SURRENDER OF JAS. P. CASEY AND CHARLES CORA

Although the artist gives some idea of the staircase to the jail (too short) and the crowds watching (too few), the main idea of vigilante justice went out to readers in both San Francisco and abroad. *Courtesy of the Bancroft Library.*

and had a slow match lighted all ready to fire. If they had refused us we would have stepped aside and they would have shot the door down."[45] Next to them "was stationed the company of Frenchmen," some of whom had fought in the Napoleonic Wars.[46] One old sea captain, lacking a gun, brought his whale harpoon. Soon the jail door opened, and the vigilante leaders ordered their Committee members inside to vacate. They did.

Everyone understood that removing the vigilante guard from the jail signaled an attack. Impotently watching this scene, William T. Sherman had joined Governor Johnson, Mayor Van Ness, and a growing throng on the roof of the International Hotel across the street. From a prearranged perch, Coleman, too, watched the maneuvers. "[T]o me it was very charming to see every single command arriving at its respective objective point almost within a half minute of each other," he later recalled.[47] Soon, an estimated twenty thousand onlookers blackened the hills around the jail.[48] The helpless sheriff could not protect his prisoners. James Casey, knowing what the vigilantes wanted, agreed to come quietly. The Executives promised that "he be not tried this day," but that was all.[49] Soon the handcuffed Casey was brought out, shoved into a carriage with his friend Marshal Hampton North and Executives William T. Coleman and Miers Truett, and taken down to Fort Vigilance. There, guards removed a knife from Casey's boot and took him to a small cell, where two men with crossed bayonets remained constantly on guard.[50]

The vigilantes then went back to get Charles Cora. Startled, Sheriff Scannell refused. The Committee gave Scannell one hour to reconsider, while the vigilante troops began "marching and counter-marching, forming in line and other military maneuvers," recalled a participant.[51] Inside the jail, Executive Truett of the War Committee spoke personally with Cora, pledging that "he should have a trial, that it should not be immediate, that he may see Belle Cora and that in case of conviction he shall be permitted to see friends."[52] In the end, the Committee got Cora, too.

Yet the vigilantes ignored another convicted killer, Rodman Backus, who had fatally shot a German in the back over a woman.[53] Sherman's Catholic wife soon wrote to her parents that "for political purposes the ringleaders of the Know Nothing mob [the Executives] have influenced the populace against Casey and Cora under pretense that the law is incompetent to punish crime." They ignored Backus, she wrote, "because his relatives are rich—are influential—are Know Nothings."[54] Backus immediately abandoned his pending judicial appeal and headed for San Quentin, where he was soon released from his cell. Made chief clerk, he dined "in a black coat and fine linen" with the prison administrator.[55]

As vigilante troops marched away from the jail, an agitated crowd followed Cora's carriage down to Fort Vigilance and milled about, waiting for a hanging. They saw vigilante companies tramp "down to the ends of the wharves and discharge their musketry into the water," the easiest way to unload the ancient weapons.[56] Three hundred armed vigilantes remained on guard around the building, but the rest dispersed into the throng.[57] After an hour or two, Executive Dows came to the second-story window and announced in his nasal voice that there would be no execution that day. If one were to come later, they would be notified.[58] The multitude slowly melted away.

5

In Secret Tribunal

Men were temporarily distracted from vigilante activities by the pressures of "Steamer Day." In that pre-railroad era, California stayed connected to the East mainly by federally funded mail steamers that left every two weeks, on the 5th and 20th of the month (unless that date fell on a Sunday). The day before the sailing was universally known as Steamer Day, when merchants collected outstanding bills, residents wrote letters home, and travelers purchased last-minute tickets. The largest newspapers printed "Steamer Editions," with summaries of the last fortnight's news to go out on the ship. Gold bullion—usually some $2 million worth—also went out on the steamer, which docked at the Isthmus of Panama, where passengers and cargo were transferred by railroad to Atlantic steamships bound for eastern ports. As one vigilante later noted, "There was no telegraph in those days to the eastern states, and the time for communication was from twenty-two to twenty-eight days [one way]; and therefore the Committee could have accomplished a vast deal before the national government could have known anything about it."[1] On May 20, however, it was mechanical problems that delayed the steamer.

As other San Franciscans busied themselves with steamer preparations, the Executives refined their operations. Claiming to represent a wide swath of San Francisco society, they admitted Calvin Nutting, a forty-three-year-old blacksmith, into their group. He represented the "mechanics" or workingmen of the city, but was among the most distinguished, having established a flourishing business after his arrival in 1849, even constructing the ornate iron fence around the Plaza (or Portsmouth Square), San Francisco's civic center.[2] The Executives then passed the following motion: "That here forward no gentleman shall be added to Executive

Committee without the consent of two thirds of present Committee." The Executives also developed a system for their secret "trials," deciding, "Each of the prisoners shall have the privilege of choosing one member from this body as attorney to assist him in his defense," as they nicely put it in their *Minutes*.[3] The accused had to face all the Executives seated in a semicircle. Forty-three-year-old John Manrow, one of the oldest Executives, "accepted the chair in all the murder cases. The chair put all the questions. . . . The whole Executive Committee acted as a jury or a senate. The testimony was all taken down in writing, and the suit was conducted the same as in any other court."[4] Except, of course, that all of the participants, including the "defense attorneys," were vigilantes. Manrow later explained that "most of the trouble had come from the lawyers, and we could do better without them. . . . There were no lawyers in the Executive [Committee]."[5] President Coleman acted as foreman of the jury, which consisted of all the remaining Executives.[6]

Then the secret trials began. Cora asked to be able to call witnesses, which the Executives allowed. Just as his trial got underway, Grand Marshal Doane entered with an announcement: James King of William was dead.[7] That afternoon, by a bare majority, the Executives found Cora guilty of the murder of Marshal Richardson, announced to the public as a unanimous vote.[8] That evening, the Executives reconvened and tried James Casey for the murder of James King of William. "Every point was discussed thoroughly," remembered a vigilante policeman. Casey offered "no reason . . . what he said was chiefly with regard to his former services . . . in the service of his country, in which he said he had been wounded, I think in the Navy, and was simply a plea for life."[9] Casey's case lasted into the night, yielding a unanimous verdict: guilty. Both men were sentenced to hang by the neck until dead. Then the Executives swore: "We hereby pledge our sacred honor to God and ourselves not to divulge the votes both in our verdicts rendered in the trials of Cora and Casey to any living [being] outside these rooms. So help us God."[10] The vigilantes' Surveillance Committee watched while Casey wrote a last letter to his mother in New York.[11]

Outside the fort, others also penned last-minute notes for the delayed steamship. Before the bell tolled to warn of the boat's imminent departure, Sherman wrote to his banking partner:

> The Vigilance Committee are now in full possession of San Francisco and in a free American country where we pay taxes of four per cent on full valuation, we now are at the mercy of irresponsible masses. To be sure, the heads and guiders of this business are deemed some of our worthiest and best men, who profess to improve on the law and its administration. They may succeed. . . .

> There are [also] vast numbers of men here, desperate, too lazy to work in the mines, unable to go away, strong for mischief and powerless for good. . . . At all events, I am not implicated with it and though it may be impossible, I will endeavor not to provoke the special enmity of our new rulers.[12]

On Wednesday, May 21—one week since King had been shot—the mail steamer chugged slowly away from the dock in a thinning rain. Inside Fort Vigilance, the vigilantes' Board of Delegates had assembled, three men elected from each of twenty-eight military companies as representatives of the General Committee. They took their own sacred oath of secrecy and agreed that a majority vote would be declared unanimous. After they heard the transcripts of both trials read aloud (which took hours), they "unanimously" upheld both verdicts. The Executives then permitted the Delegates to schedule the hanging. Everyone knew that each departed steamship spent the first night inside "the heads" at the Golden Gate, where it was potentially reachable by a fast boat. In two days, the steamer would be well at sea. The Delegates chose to hang the men at noon on May 23.[13]

Just as the Delegates concluded their work, the sheriff and a deputy arrived at the fort with a writ of habeas corpus "and demanded [the] person of James P. Casey." They were barred from entering and told that "the Committee was satisfied that . . . [they] had performed their duties according to law, and that the Committee had no further communication to make."[14] City government had been proved powerless against the vigilantes.

Throughout the city, rain fell all night. King's demise had been "known instantly upon the street," remembered an observer. "By telegraph the event was known before night throughout the State." Black crape went up all along the main thoroughfares, men wore crape armbands, and "the bell-handles of many houses were trimmed with crape. A stranger would have thought a plague was raging."[15] The next morning, the early papers announced that the funeral for James King of William would "take place to-day (Thursday) at 12 o'clock, from the Unitarian Church."[16] Meeting at 6:00 a.m., the Executives decided to disregard the Delegates' decision and instead scheduled the execution of Casey and Cora to coincide with the passing of King's funeral cortege. They planned to hang the men out the windows of Fort Vigilance, and directed "the Committee on Execution . . . to take such steps in handing the bodies over to the coroner [afterward] as shall be least likely to implicate any member of this body."[17]

As the Executives met, waves of excitement surged over the city. Word had come by telegraph to the Merchants' Exchange that the steamship *Golden Age*, a week late and carrying badly overdue news thirty-one days out of New York, was on the horizon. As the mail steamer docked, San Franciscans learned that its delay had been caused by "an accident to the Panama Railroad cars by which 53 persons were killed and 100 wounded."[18] People feverishly sought to discover if their own friends and relatives had survived.

Inside Fort Vigilance, Casey and Cora prepared for death. The Executives admitted Bishop Allemany, Casey's confessor, who had already appeared at Fort Vigilance right after Casey's capture but had been denied admittance. The bishop gave Casey absolution, but he refused to do the same for Charles Cora, who, though unmarried, had long lived publicly with the madam who called herself Belle Cora. For Cora to receive absolution, the two had to marry. Cora sent for Belle. She came at once.[19]

Ten years earlier, the polished thirty-year-old Cora had rescued nineteen-year-old Belle from the life of a common whore. At the age of seventeen, she had been seduced and become pregnant. Her preacher father had thrown her out on the streets of Baltimore, where she miscarried the baby. Completely abandoned, she was passed from man to man down to New Orleans, selling her body to survive. In 1846, the dapper Cora won the pretty teenager in a coin toss and took her as his mistress. Together they had come to California during the gold rush and soon settled in San Francisco. Belle ran a fancy brothel and Cora worked the gaming tables, amassing an estimated $400,000.[20] He had rescued her from the worst of the sex trade. Now she could save him from perdition.

The increasing activity around Fort Vigilance had drawn a solid, expectant mob. Belle Cora's vigilante escort had to part the crowds around the building so she could get through. Armed vigilantes were lining up across the street from the fort. Others wheeled cannons to face west and east, flanked by a line of cavalry to contain the crowds and repulse a possible attack. Inside, carpenters could be heard hard at work. Belle was hustled through the rear entrance and up to the second floor, where she had to step "over the very beam that Cora was afterward hung on, as the men were engaged in hoisting it up in making the arrangements for the execution," recalled a vigilante. With hammering and sawing going on all around her, Belle encountered some of the Executives, who escorted her into Cora's cell. After the marriage ceremony, which was witnessed by two Executives, "she was returned to her home, and did not see Cora again until after the execution," remembered a guard.[21] But Cora had earned absolution.

In a nearby four-by-eight-foot cell, Casey held a last meeting with his executor, Charles Gallagher, leaving instructions to dispose of some $30,000 to $40,000 worth of property. A vigilante monitored their entire conversation. When Gallagher left, the Executives allowed him to take Casey's private papers (which the vigilantes had seized), Casey's money, and a daguerreotype of Casey and Marshal North, a gift for the marshal. The bishop also withdrew, but two priests stayed with the condemned men.[22]

Preparations for the hanging continued. The fort's second floor, "which contained hundreds of men, was cleared by order of the Executive Committee, the guard stationed, and everything made ready," recalled a vigilante policeman. But no one wanted to be the hangman. A prominent merchant, given special permission to stay and watch the execution, stated, "I do know of a man but you cannot get him, as he is in the ranks." A written order was immediately sent to the appropriate Division Captain. Shortly thereafter, "Sterling A. Hopkins . . . [arrived], who was entirely willing to perform the office of executioner," the vigilante reported.[23] Hopkins, "a notorious character," had once "had a difficulty" with Casey, and it was claimed that he had "begged the Committee to officiate in the event of Casey's condemnation to death by the rope."[24]

In another part of the city, King's funeral began. Throngs packed the Unitarian Church, listening as three ministers eulogized the late James King of William. Approximately five thousand people had viewed his body the night before, despite gloomy weather and fitful showers. By morning, all city flags dripped at half-mast above windows draped in black. Toward 1:00 p.m., the massive funeral procession left the church as bells tolled all over the city. First, on foot, came King's fellow Masons wearing regalia and carrying flags. Behind them were the clergy in a carriage; two attending physicians; the hearse with King's remains drawn by four white horses and accompanied by fourteen pallbearers; ten coaches containing King's friends and relatives; employees of the *Evening Bulletin* on foot (probably including the paper's legal editor, Theodore Hittell, who would later immortalize the vigilantes); and the uniformed Sacramento Guard, down from the state capital. They were followed by hundreds of others in uniforms or mourning apparel, ending with eight African Americans with badges, and thirty-one carriages of miscellaneous mourning citizens. The mile-long procession took forty minutes to pass through the muddy streets.[25] One observer remarked, " I did not know there were so many horses in the county before."[26]

King's tolling funeral bells meant death for Casey and Cora. By prearrangement, as the bells' deep tones rang over the city, the Executives led their victims to the second-floor windows and onto the drops. With the Executives' permission, Casey proclaimed in his full, sonorous voice, "I am guilty of no crime. I only acted as I was taught—according to my early education—to avenge an insult. Let not the *Alta*, the *Chronicle*, and the *Globe*, persecute my memory; let them no more proclaim

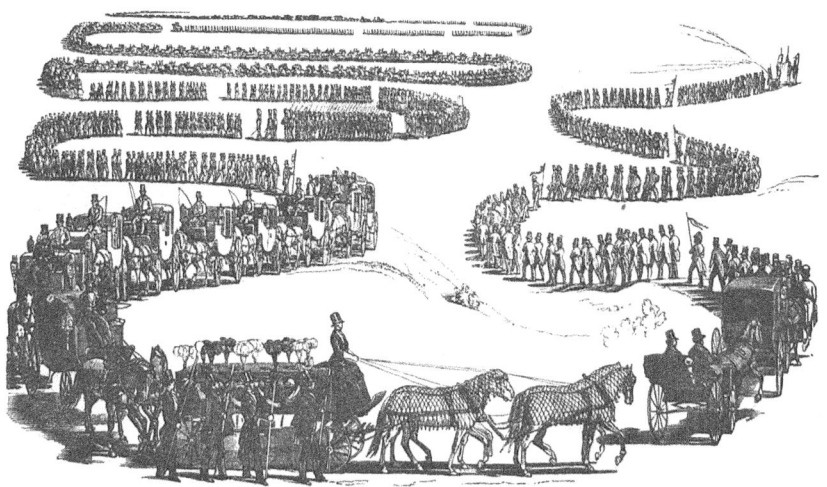

The *Wide West* newspaper treated readers to this meticulous rendering of King's funeral cortege. The hearse fills the foreground, followed by ten coaches. Directly above them can be seen the Sacramento Guard with their shakos on their heads and their muskets shouldered. *Wide West*, June 8, 1856. *Courtesy of the California History Room, California State Library, Sacramento.*

me a murderer to the world. I have an aged mother in the Atlantic States, and I hope that she will never hear how I died."[27] Cora remained silent. Both men kissed the crucifix. The executioners placed the ropes around their necks and drew white hoods over their heads.[28] As Sterling Hopkins hooded Casey, he hissed something that made the prisoner start "as if to break the bands which held his arms."[29] An Executive clapped his hands twice. "[T]he word cut was immediately called" by a chain of vigilantes leading to the one with the knife on the roof, "and the drop instantly fell."[30]

At that moment, King's funeral procession had "stopped . . . [overlooking] the place of execution," reported a mourner. "Thousands instantly quitted the funeral pageant. . . . Like an ocean wave, propelled by the dread fury of the elements, came these mighty masses of human beings, rushing, struggling and clamoring to the scaffold."[31] Another onlooker wrote that "by long battling and edging and crowding, I got a chance to see Casey and Cora hanging by their necks, in front of the building. They had been hanging nearly half an hour when I saw them."[32] The next day, a card appeared in a local paper thanking the captain of a Redwood City sailing bark for a speedy trip across the bay and "the attention and interest he displayed to forward our passage in season to witness the execution of Casey and Cora."[33] After being ogled by the public, the bodies were withdrawn into

The bodies of the Vigilance Committee's victims swung from the second story of its improvised fort, as a public display and as a warning to others. *Courtesy of the Bancroft Library.*

Fort Vigilance, where the coroner went through the formality of an inquest. The Vigilance Committee's surgeon, Dr. R. Beverly Cole, identified the cause of death as strangulation. No one remembered who had put the ropes around the necks of the deceased.[34]

Repercussions rippled outward. When the new foreman of Casey's Crescent Engine Company publicly complained about the hanging, some half-dozen men muscled him down to Fort Vigilance and locked him up. He was soon released, "as there was nothing against him," but with a warning that "it would not be well for him to speak his mind again in the streets, as these were exciting times."[35] At the same time, someone crept into Casey's Crescent Engine house and cut the fire hoses.[36]

Mourning permeated San Francisco. The day after the hanging, large crowds lined up to view the dead men's remains. Casey lay in state at his fire company headquarters under glowing candelabras in a solid mahogany coffin attended by a sobbing female cousin. He had "almost a smile upon the lips. . . . The neck, from a slight sinking of the head in the cushions, appeared to have been broken." At a friend's home, Belle Cora had laid out her husband in a "magnificent coffin . . . neatly dressed in black cloth garments and a white cravat." His face "looked natural," contrasting with the "agony depicted on the countenance of Mrs. Cora, as she sat at the head of the coffin."[37] The next day, Cora's funeral cortege with a hearse and seven carriages proceeded solemnly to the mission, where he received a Catholic burial at his young widow's expense.[38] Casey's funeral procession set out a day later from Crescent Engine Company No. 10, of which he had been chief. Eighty-three carriages and seventy-seven horsemen—approximately eight hundred mourners in all—formed a cortege half a mile long to escort the deceased to the mission past the surrounding squares, which were packed with onlookers.[39] James King of William's *Evening Bulletin*, now edited by his brother, the volatile, acerbic Thomas Sim King, identified Casey's mourners: "Charles Gallagher, Chas. P. Duane, . . . William Mulligan, James [Yankee] Sullivan," and others. The writer concluded, "There were, so far as we could observe and learn from others, not over a dozen American born citizens (besides the members of No. 10) in the procession."[40] By implication, the rest were Irish. It was an accusation. After Casey's coffin was lowered into the earth at the mission, grieving ladies threw in so many "floral offerings" that some of the firemen had to jump into the grave and mash down the flowers "to make room for the dirt." Then a priest read the service for the dead.[41] Later, Engine Company No. 10 erected a massive sandstone monument with bas-reliefs of fire caps, inverted torches, and a "hook and ladder, the latter of which was broken," representing not only Casey's membership in the company, "but his fate." On the worn tombstone, the faded epitaph can still be read: "God forgive my persecutors."[42]

These hangings prompted vigilante reconsiderations and realignments. As Cora's cortege rolled through the city, the Executives tried to establish their own legitimacy by crafting bylaws and a constitution based on those of the popular Vigilance Committee of 1851. With these documents in hand, the 1856 Executives could claim that they were not a mob.[43] President Coleman sat on this committee, although it was chaired by the youngest Executive, twenty-seven-year-old Clancey Dempster, later called by Coleman "the Jefferson of our little republic."[44] One member of the General Committee wrote to the Executives, "The object for which I joined your Association having been accomplished, I now resign."[45] The rest of the men stayed put, expectantly awaiting other duties.

6

The Black List

For the Executives, hanging Casey and Cora was only the beginning. They settled down to work, deciding to pay for their own cigars and liquor so as not to waste donors' money. They reorganized their subcommittees. They sent a directive to each of their military companies, demanding that the members elect a captain and vice captain with military experience, and choose a third man who would serve with the elected officers as Delegates. They directed Executive Calvin Nutting, the blacksmith, to procure a large alarm triangle, which they installed on the roof. Then they started their Black List, targeting specific Democratic operatives.[1] As Clancey Dempster, the youngest Executive, admitted years later, the Executive Committee had "received innumerable letters asking for redress of grievances."[2] But they had no intention of rounding up every thief, fighter, seducer, drunk, and abortionist (yes, there was one complained of) in San Francisco.[3] They only went after the Irish, particularly those who held land. Those first on their blacklist were William Mulligan, Bill Lewis, Daniel Aldrich, John W. Bagley, Martin Gallagher, and James "Yankee" Sullivan. Casey had probably mentioned these Broderick Democrats, with whom he had recently split, when on May 20, before his trial, the Executives had sent a "Committee of five ... to confer with Casey and obtain information about his abettors, accomplices, etc."[4]

What had these men done? As a contemporary related, county jailer William Mulligan, known as a fighter and Democratic enforcer at elections, had "served as collector of moneys for the County Treasurer two years, and fully accounted for every dollar that he had received." Martin Gallagher, who had worked as a boatman, was "active in the party manipulations in the interest of Mr. Broderick in the First Ward," the all-important waterfront. A "tough man to handle in a fight," Gallagher often sat as a delegate "in city, county and State conventions." James "Yankee" Sullivan "had helped Mulligan and Casey in some of their election operations. There was no charge of any other nature than this and his fighting quality," a contemporary wrote.[5] Yet they were all good fighters, whose duties had included protecting less muscular politicians and the polls. As one vigilante later asserted, "Casey, Woolly Kearney, Yankee Sullivan, Billy Mulligan, . . . and others had attempted to rule the city . . . to assume all political power."[6] In these contentious times, when the entire city itself was up for grabs, it very much mattered who ruled in San Francisco.

The Executives positioned themselves to take full advantage of San Francisco's changing government. In less than six weeks, city powers would be disappearing, thanks to the Consolidation Act, passed by the California legislature on April 19, 1856. This bill stipulated that as of July 1, 1856, only the county government would rule the coterminous city and county of San Francisco. In their secret meeting on May 25, three days after Casey and Cora swung, fireball George Ward, not over five feet tall, announced the Executives' ultimate agenda. He was preparing a motion for the May 27 meeting, "to invite . . . [the county judges] to resign their official positions, preparatory to extending this invitation to Sheriff Scannell, Thos. Hayes, County Clerk; H. H. Byrne, District Attorney; the assessor and other county officers who may be deemed objectionable." If these county officers could be forced to resign, only the vigilantes would be left to govern the contested city.

Already knowing what they planned to do with those they captured, the Executives that day also established the Committee on Foreign Relations "to furnish transportation to those persons, who may be required to leave the State by the Committee of Vigilance."[7] Vigilantes soon spread out through the city to "arrest" men unaware of the fact that they were wanted. On May 26, they kidnapped Mulligan, Gallagher, and Sullivan and hustled them to their fort. Sullivan, a British citizen, "placed himself under the protection of the British Consul."[8] Little good it did him. The consul had been cooperating with the vigilantes, and had earlier recommended a special investigator, Henry Johnson, to them. "Johnson came as a detective from Australia," remembered a vigilante. "He got so well known by the thieves there that he was compelled to leave the country. We took him as a detective."[9]

The Executives went through the motions of legal process to maintain their honor and respectability. A day after the capture, deep within Fort Vigilance, they staged the secret trials of Gallagher, Mulligan, and Sullivan, who remained locked in their small, dark cells, unable to confront their accusers. Sullivan was assigned a particularly oppressive room under the stairs to the roof.[10] After reviewing the evidence, the Executives convicted all three as "disturbers of the peace of our City, destroyers of the purity of our elections, active members and leaders of the organized gang who have invaded the sanctity of our ballot boxes and perfect pests to society," and sentenced their captives to be "transported out of the territory of the United States . . . [and] be warned never to return to California under penalty of death."[11] Their Committee on Foreign Relations, assigned to "furnish transportation," had already reported that "Capt. Wakeman of Ship Adelaide"—also a member of the 1851 Committee—was "willing to take any number of prisoners we may have to deport."[12]

The sentence hit Sullivan particularly hard. He had been transported before. The man who became James "Yankee" Sullivan had been born in Ireland around 1813 under another name. He had been convicted of a crime less than murder (a hanging offense) and sent to Australia in 1838. After four months on a rocking ship plagued by crowding, vermin, and cruelty, he was put ashore and forced to work on a chain gang in thirty-pound irons under the broiling sun. He rebelled and faced a litany of punishments. Men were flogged for minor offenses, usually bleeding after the fifth blow. Those who suffered two hundred blows or more—and there were many—had the flesh stripped in chunks from their backs and buttocks, to be scavenged by dogs and ants. Normal conditions meant freezing nights, with men and boys huddled together in twos and threes under one threadbare blanket, where the young and weak became ready prey for sexual assault. Sullivan must have defended himself with his fists, for he was later allowed a few organized fights against other convicts.[13]

Somehow Sullivan escaped; even more incredibly, he survived. He stowed away on an American whaler and wound up safely on Long Island, New York, in mid-July 1840.[14] Perhaps it was this experience that led to his desire to be known as "Yankee," for he thereafter wore the American flag on a scarf in some of his fights. From New York, Sullivan sailed to England, where he quickly gained fame as a bare-knuckle boxer. He immigrated back to New York in 1841.[15] There he took up tavern-keeping, but he kept on fighting as well, defeating an English prizefighter in September 1841, which heartened his ragged Irish patrons who had been forced out of Ireland by the intensifying potato famine. A year later, Sullivan helped arrange a prizefight in which Christopher Lilly killed his opponent in the 119th round, the first fatality in American boxing. Lilly fled, eventually ending up in San Francisco; Sullivan spent two years in jail for his part in the illegal fight. Pardoned when he promised to give up boxing, Sullivan immersed himself in New York's ward politics, but he kept hearing the call of the ring. In February 1849 he took on native-born Tom Hyer, the darling of the Know-Nothings, who was seven years younger and thirty pounds heavier than his Irish opponent. In a snow-dusted corner of rural Maryland, eager spectators wagered some $300,000 on the illegal fight. After sixteen rounds in

One of the Executives later claimed that the vigilantes had not kidnapped the "real" prizefighter, Yankee Sullivan, but rather an unrelated tough, despite all the facts to the contrary. The boxer's popularity remained undimmed, as indicated by this print of the 1849 Hyer-Sullivan fight published in the *New York Illustrated Times* in 1884. From the author's collection.

less than eighteen minutes, Sullivan reeled into the ropes, insensible. Hyer earned the title "America's first heavyweight champion" when results of their match were telegraphed all over the country. Prints of the Hyer-Sullivan fight by the artistic giants Currier and Ives bedecked saloons and barbershops for a generation. Despite this loss, Sullivan remained a hero, particularly to the Irish.[16]

Thereafter, Sullivan bounced back and forth between New York and San Francisco until 1853, when he finally settled in the West and got involved in ward politics. A year later, he ran off to Hawaii with Mrs. Emily McElroy, but 1856 found them both back in San Francisco. Not long after, Sullivan was in vigilante hands.[17]

After Sullivan learned of his conviction and sentence of banishment to Australia, his spirits sank. Various Executives ascribed his sudden mood change to a lack of liquor or a sluggish constitution.[18] While Clancey Dempster later described banishment as "little more than allowing the criminal to select the city to wh[ich] he should make a pleasant voyage & the com[mittee] defrayed the expense of the trip generally," this dewy-eyed view hardly reflected Sullivan's reality.[19] During the boxer's prison term, recaptured Australian convicts had been sent to the penal settlement on Norfolk Island, a lump of ocean-beaten rock a thousand miles east of Australia and four hundred miles north of New Zealand. Its sadistic commander lashed laboring convicts, or ordered solitary confinement in a completely dark prison with solid walls some four feet thick, where the air grew fouler and fouler with the stench of their own waste. Some men poisoned themselves, or got a friend to cut off their toes with a hoe, or even gouged out their own eyes. The blind could not work. No one ever escaped Norfolk Island. It is debatable whether Sullivan knew that Norfolk Island had been closed, but even in 1856, recaptured convicts were shipped to broiling, barren western Australia, where many still slaved in chains in the heat, goaded by the lash. Or they were hanged.[20] Making his rounds of inspection of the prisoners, the vigilantes' chief physician, Dr. Cole, had tried to comfort the despondent Sullivan. Cole assured the boxer that he would not be hanged; "the most that would be likely to befall him was exportation."[21]

Outside the fort, vigilante actions spawned speculations about the seizures, searches, rumors, and innuendos infecting the city. Catholic merchant Denis Oliver observed in his diary, "The VC made more arrests today . . . everything is done so secret."[22] Vigilantes had succeeded in capturing William "Billy" Carr and William "Wooley" Kearney, two more of Broderick's strongmen. At Kearney's home, vigilantes found a ballot box, "about fourteen inches broad and high, twenty inches long," with two sliding panels, still stuffed with votes for two different candidates from the 7th Ward Democratic primary election in 1854. The Executives surmised that whoever paid the larger bribe would see his votes added to the official pile.[23] Overlooking the obvious conclusion that the seized ballot box had not had any extra ballots released during the 1854 election, nor had it been used since, the Executives promptly put the "patent ballot box" on public display as evidence of ongoing election fraud.[24]

In cold, foggy San Francisco, vigilante squads kept marching through the muddy streets, their muskets on their shoulders, their bayonets fixed. The Executives knew that arming and drilling would keep their followers busy and protect the Executive Committee from unwanted questions and advice.[25] Mayor Van Ness, furious at this affront to his power, called a public meeting, where the attendees agreed that the city of San Francisco was "in a state of open, flagrant insurrection." Leading citizens went to call on the governor to urge his support for this statement, which would become, by law, a declaration of war against the vigilantes.[26]

When the city's petition for aid reached thirty-year-old Governor Johnson, he asked militia commander William Tecumseh Sherman to develop a military strategy. At his superior's command, the reluctant Sherman suggested procuring federal arms to be shipped to San Francisco by the navy, calling out and arming volunteers, and taking "possession of a thirty-two pound-gun battery at the Marine Hospital on Rincon Point," from which soldiers could pound Fort Vigilance should the vigilantes fail to disband.[27] Considering that a thirty-two-pound cannon fired a ball of that weight, Sherman envisioned a formidable threat to the merchant-heavy Executives, who had just been identified by name and occupation in the *Herald* in a largely accurate list.[28] Sherman, Governor Johnson, and California's secretary of state then went to the city of Benecia to requisition federal armaments in person from General John Ellis Wool, commander of the Pacific Department of the Army, who had been exiled to Benecia, far from San Francisco, due to sectional differences with his superior, Jefferson Davis, the U.S. secretary of war.[29]

The split between Wool and Davis represented difficulties that had been incubated in distant lands. Actions on the part of former San Franciscan William Walker, who soon earned the nickname "the grey-eyed man of destiny," had catalyzed their split. After his stirring anti-slavery speech at California's 1854 Democratic Convention, Walker had sought greater worlds to conquer—quite literally. The brilliant thirty-one-year-old Tennessee native had become one of America's youngest formally trained physicians at age nineteen when he graduated from the University of Pennsylvania Medical School. After a discouraging sojourn in Europe, he had practiced law in New Orleans with close friend Edmund Randolph, but he soon turned to journalism. The death of his fiancée drove Walker to seek a new life in California, where he wrote for the papers, including a stint as associate editor at John Nugent's *Herald*. In print, he claimed that a couple of hundred "regulators" (or vigilantes) could clean up government—the first to suggest such a solution. Walker next organized an illegal filibustering expedition (a privately funded military effort) to invade Mexico in 1853. Northern sympathizer General Wool, fully familiar with America's Neutrality Laws and dreading the extension of southern slaveholding into conquered Mexican territory, had requested permission to prevent Walker's departure. However, Wool's superior, Secretary Davis of Mississippi (later president of the Confederacy), seeking new lands for slavery's expansion, had responded that the Neutrality Laws still lacked "full judicial consideration," so Wool had had to let Walker leave. The breach between the two men never healed. Davis stationed Wool at distant Benecia, and Walker instituted Central American actions that would have strong subsequent impacts on troubled San Francisco.[30]

In events that would inspire the vigilantes, Walker soon ruled his own country. Although his Mexican expedition ended badly, his efforts caught the attention of Nicaraguan Patricio Rivas, who in 1855 invited Walker to take his side in an ongoing civil war.[31] By fall 1855, the conquering Walker had assumed the position of commander in chief behind puppet president Rivas. Most important to California, Walker decided to shift official control of the Nicaraguan trans-isthmus steamboat company away from New York titan Cornelius Vanderbilt and into the hands of men who could aid him by bringing more filibusters to Nicaragua. Walker contacted Edmund Randolph, his former law partner, who negotiated with former San Francisco mayor Cornelius Garrison to shift company ownership. In a complicated plot officially authorized in February 1856, President Rivas revoked the charter of Vanderbilt's Accessory Transit Company; Walker seized its property and transferred its holdings to Randolph, then later to Garrison and his eastern partner.[32] Since anyone traveling by steamship from San Francisco to Atlantic ports (including the vigilantes' exiles) had to cross the isthmus at either Panama or Nicaragua, this shift in control would later have major repercussions.

While seemingly unrelated events transformed Nicaragua, the governor's arms acquisition meeting at Benecia seemed to go well. Touring the armory, Sherman spotted gun boxes containing four thousand muskets that had come around Cape Horn in 1846, when California had won its independence from Mexico. To ship them to San Francisco, Wool requested that the men speak with Commodore David Glasgow Farragut, the ranking Pacific naval officer, who had been elevated to the rank of captain just one year earlier. The fifty-five-year-old Farragut had served in the navy since 1811, when, at the age of ten, he had sailed out of New Orleans under his adoptive father. In 1854 he had been detailed to California to establish the naval yard on Mare Island, where the sloop-of-war *John Adams*, Captain Edward B. Boutwell commanding, had just arrived for refitting. Learning of San Francisco's situation, Farragut cautioned that he could act in civil disturbances only with direct orders from the Navy Department. Having solely the *John Adams* available, Farragut could not offer it for arms transportation, but would allow it to "drop down abreast of the city after certain repairs, to lie off there for *moral effect*."[33] Before returning to San Francisco, Sherman asked Governor Johnson to get a clear statement from Wool of his intentions. The general answered, "I understand, Governor, that in the first place a writ of *habeas corpus* will be issued . . . [for] one of the prisoners." When it was, of course, ignored (as it had been for Casey), "you [will] then issue your proclamation commanding [the vigilantes] to disperse." When they refused, "you will call out the militia, and command General Sherman with it to suppress the Vigilance Committee as an unlawful body," Wool concluded.[34] With that oral understanding, the men parted.

In San Francisco, Quartermaster General William Kibbe of the California Militia did what he could to augment the Law and Order arms. Acting on the governor's instructions, he appeared at Fort Vigilance and demanded two cannons that had been taken by the vigilantes. He was ignored.[35]

Sherman, with his West Point education, knew all too well the carnage of war. He did not want to fight. The day after the visit to Benecia, he published an open letter in the morning papers, stressing that the state legislature had already chosen new "Inspectors of Elections" for San Francisco. Reminding readers that "no Vigilance Committee can eradicate these evils unless by their private examples," he called on the aloof Executives to take a more active role in politics. "Moreover," he concluded, "if one-tenth the money had been expended, or one-tenth the effort had been exerted, to sustain the Courts as have been to overthrow them, our city would be as well governed as any in America."[36]

As early-rising San Franciscans mulled over Sherman's thoughtful letter, inside the fort Dr. Cole made his daily inspection of the vigilantes' prisoners. Entering Sullivan's dark cell under the stairs, Cole stepped into a pool of blood. He found the prizefighter "dead and cold, lying on his bed, with an ordinary dinner knife lying by his side, partially clenched by his right hand." With all the force of his fight-hardened right arm, Sullivan had severed his left bronchial artery.[37]

7

Arresting Developments

News of the bloody cell alarmed an already jittery San Francisco. Diarist Oliver recorded "a great excitement round town and all kinds of rumors afloat."[1] While the Executives insisted that the death was suicide, there was a rumor that Sullivan had been murdered by "a noted French thief... on guard over him in his cell." The Executives supposedly then "spirited [the killer] out of the State, where he later told of the perpetration of the act."[2] Convinced, the Catholic Church gave Sullivan a sanctified burial right next to the walls of San Francisco's Mission Dolores.

Tales of Sullivan's bloody end and fighting prowess mesmerized San Francisco. Before the funeral, some ten thousand curious people filed past his pale, mangled corpse laid out in the coroner's office.[3] The coroner's hearing soon revealed that Sullivan's wife, after days of pleading, had been allowed to see her husband.[4] At the hearing, she testified, "[H]e looked at the wedding ring on my finger and stated that it was the first present he had given me, and then took a diamond ring out of his pocket and handed [it to] me, saying that it would be the last.... He did not seem to be much depressed in spirits... he was always afraid of committing suicide... if he did he would not obtain the rites of his Church, he being a Catholic." Sullivan had asked for a priest the night before he died, which was refused him as unnecessary, since he was not to be hanged. His wife also testified to their legal marriage, and that they had a five-month-old daughter. She added, "Mr. Sullivan intended to go away from the country at the time he was arrested by the Vigilance Committee; the day of his arrest he gave me directions to pack up all his clothes, also my own, as he was going to leave the country for good."[5] Upon reading this published testimony, the Executives astutely realized that they might be able to scare their targets into leaving the city, saving the expense of board and steamer tickets.

While the Executives pondered this realization, a new figure entered the fray against them. In the midst of the turmoil over Sullivan's demise, California Supreme Court justice David S. Terry disembarked at the Pacific Street Wharf to carry out the task agreed upon between Governor Johnson and General Wool: serving the Executives with a writ of habeas corpus for captive William Mulligan. Even in the recent election that had carried the tall, dignified Terry into office on the Know-Nothing ticket, the new judge's reputation had remained unsullied. In an unpublished letter received by James King of William just before his death, the writer noted, "Before proceeding further in the subject of land titles in San Francisco, I wish to make a disclaimer as regards [newly elected] Judge D. S. Terry ... whatsoever charges may be made against him, I have yet to learn that veniality and corruption are among them."[6] Terry indeed clung staunchly to his lawyer's oath, taken years earlier back in Texas, to uphold the U.S. Constitution and the law. He consequently despised the vigilantes, who worked in secret, ignoring established legal procedures. He was willing to confront them.

The service of the writ did not go well. When a San Francisco deputy sheriff arrived at Fort Vigilance, the vigilantes repulsed him. The Executives were preoccupied, fascinated by captured correspondence. As the *Minutes* report, just before the writ was presented, "[Executive] Truett reported that he and Arrington had secured possession of the private papers of Ed McGowan. A box and champagne basket were brought out."[7] The young Executives ignored news of the deputy's arrival as they eagerly perused stolen letters addressed to one of Broderick's leading assistants, the debonair man-about-town and alleged election fixer, former county judge Edward McGowan. They read acknowledgments of fixed elections, warnings of a near-duel, and regards from acclaimed actress Matilda Heron, who wrote from Paris "of all the grateful remembrances" of McGowan's generosity.[8] Soon realizing their mistake in ignoring a legal demand, the Executives transferred all their prisoners to adjoining buildings and sent permission for the deputy sheriff to "search the premises for Billy Mulligan in order to comply with the writ of *habeas corpus*." It was too late. The deputy had already returned the writ to Terry with the news that he had been "prevented from serving it by a body of armed men."[9] That single action would have fearful repercussions.

The Executives' long preoccupation with McGowan deserves further explanation. The brilliant Irish Catholic lawyer later noted in his memoirs that he had entered political life in his native Pennsylvania in 1838. He was elected a district clerk, "and was re-elected *five years consecutively* to the same position." After holding a couple of clerking positions, in 1842 he won election to the Pennsylvania legislature, then served two years as a governor's appointee before he was "elected

Superintendent of Police for one of the Districts of Philadelphia, and held this position for several years." In these various positions, he became acquainted with some of Pennsylvania's leading men: the mayor of Philadelphia, a couple of members of Congress, the U.S. postmaster general under President Pierce, and other lawyers and judges. Then the "California excitement" lured him westward in 1849.[10]

McGowan's career had flowered in California. The white-hatted bon vivant had served as judge of San Francisco's Court of Sessions (the county court). He became fellow Catholic David Broderick's most prominent lieutenant, chairing Broderick's side of the contentious 1854 Democratic Convention.[11] McGowan allegedly managed the city elections in 1853 and 1854, handling Democratic money and sitting in his office at the back of Palmer, Cook and Company, offering payola to those who were willing to exchange Broderick tickets for Citizens Reform tickets already placed in the ballot box.[12]

The Executives' interest in McGowan had developed gradually. They had ignored him at the jail on May 17 when he threw down his rifle and left as vigilantes marched in, although they began hunting him shortly thereafter.[13] As McGowan repeatedly dodged from room to room throughout San Francisco, on May 21 the Executives had succeeded before the grand jury (at least half of whose members were vigilantes) in indicting him as an accessory to King's murder for lending Casey his pistol.[14] Although city police now had cause to arrest McGowan, the vigilantes wanted to get him first.

Ranging through the uneasy city, some eight to ten pistol-packing vigilante police soon created a sensation. They invaded the room of California's former state treasurer, a practicing lawyer. They briefly detained the protesting attorney while he unsuccessfully demanded a search warrant.[15] Public protest prompted the Executives to pass a motion that "searches or arrests shall only be made under a written order." They warned their chief of police not to enter any building forcibly. At the same time, they offered "rewards for arrest and detaining of Ned McGowan ... to any member or members of City Police."[16] A predawn raid on the Washington Restaurant and Saloon woke the proprietress, who screamed for help from her bedroom window. An invader clapped his hand over her mouth. She fainted, and was revived by "a quantity of water over her person." The departing intruders informed her "that they had made the visit by the authority of the Vigilance Committee in search of Edward McGowan."[17]

After more public outcry, the Executives instituted a range of damage control while intensifying their search. The *Bulletin* published a card from the Executives stating that the vigilantes had no intention of "searching private residences or rooms for the purpose of arresting criminals, without receiving permission from

JAMES P. CASEY,	CHARLES CORA	YANKEE SULLIVAN,	EDW. M'COWAN,
According to his own account, was born in New York City, in 1827, and at the time of his death was twenty-nine years old; but by the Sing Sing Prison certificate and description of his person, he is said to be at that time (1849) thirty-two years old, which would make him thirty-nine at the time of his death and, as his description is very accurate in other respects, we are inclined to believe it most reliable in this.	Was born in Genoa, in the year 1819, and was forty-three years old at the time of his death. Of his early history little is known—the first we hear of him was at Natchez, Mississippi, about the year 1850. He was then quite a young man, leading a dissolute life, associating with abandoned characters, and gambling for a livelihood. From there he went to New Orleans, where he took up with Bella Cora, with whom, in 1849 or '50, he came to California.	The subject of this sketch was born in Ireland, and at the time of his death was about forty-nine years of age. His vocation is too well known to require mention here. He came to California in 1850, and soon left for New York, from which place he returned to San Francisco in 1854. He was arrested by the Vigilance Committee, and terminated his career by suicide, for fear of being sent to Sydney, where he had been transported for felony, and escaped to the United States in 1860.	Who was indicted as an accomplice of Casey in the murder of JAMES KING of WM., and who is now a fugitive from justice, has been a prominent politician in San Francisco, and held a responsible office under Gov. Bigler. He has been more or less connected with the leading political events of this city for the last four years. He has thus far eluded the vigilance of the Committee.

Vigilante sympathizers published a letter sheet with mug shots of the Committee's victims and biased descriptions of men no longer able to defend themselves. The writers added ten years to Casey's life, undercutting his pleas of youthful indiscretion; stressed Cora's "dissolute life"; and ignored Sullivan's pugilistic career, calling him only a convicted felon and a suicide. Included in this rogues' gallery was Edward McGowan, branded as "a fugitive from justice," in the hope that someone would turn him in to the vigilantes, who wanted to hang him. *Courtesy of the Bancroft Library.*

the proprietors," unless they carried a warrant from city authorities, which they were unable to get. It also warned the General Committee "against participation in any search ... without the authority above referred to."[18] Privately, vigilantes began buying breakfasts, suppers, dinners, even eight gallons of coffee at a time from the assaulted proprietress of the Washington Restaurant. In less than two weeks, she had earned more than $140 (the equivalent of nearly $4,000 in twenty-first-century dollars).[19] Turning to their captive, William Mulligan, the Executives promised him his liberty if he would assist in capturing McGowan. Mulligan indignantly refused to cooperate.[20] Then, on May 30, a "secret service fund of $450.00" that the Executives had appropriated led to the seizure of McGowan's papers.[21]

Given McGowan's reputation, as an Executive later noted, as "a man who, without being absolutely wicked, yet gloried in a reputation for vice," why this concentrated manhunt?[22] The loan of his pistol was only a flimsy excuse for competition over land. Thanks to his bicoastal connections, McGowan had helped unite Philadelphia capitalists with his friend Joseph Palmer. The San Francisco banker, a senior partner of the Democrat-connected bank of Palmer, Cook and Company, had loaned $5,000—possibly San Francisco's tax dollars—to the Philadelphians, who began selling stock in 1854 to formalize the organization of the San Francisco Land Association of Philadelphia to contend for the western city's most valuable real estate.[23]

Targeting Palmer himself backfired. Within days, vigilante police attempted to enter Palmer's home, allegedly seeking McGowan. The elite banker indignantly refused them admittance and filed a complaint with the Executives, who promptly tabled it.[24] In reporting the incident, the *Evening Bulletin* claimed that men "unauthorized by the Vigilance Committee, obtained a warrant to search the house," a fiction unsupported by any other records.[25] Public outrage prompted the reorganization of the vigilante Police Committee. After shuffling three men, one of whom lasted only one week, William E. B. Andrews, who had been involved in the raid on Palmer's house, became head of the vigilantes' police forces.[26] In the meantime, disguised as a Mexican, the portly forty-three-year-old McGowan had sneaked out of town and begun riding south.[27]

While the fruitless hunt for McGowan continued, the vigilantes successfully rounded up others on their Black List. Drawing on the knowledge that Yankee Sullivan had been preparing to leave when he was arrested, the Executives issued warnings to eleven more Democrats to "leave this state" and told a twelfth "to reform as the eyes of the Committee were upon him."[28] They had previously arrested timorous Edward Bulger, who was still locked in his cell awaiting deportation and would later cause them a major headache.[29]

But the Executives could not scare away Charles Duane, one of the most powerful men in the city and a special target of the French. French Executive Jules David had moved Duane's arrest, knowing that Duane had very nearly killed his countryman Amédée Fayolle, described as an actor/theater manager, by shooting him in the back in a barroom scuffle. The heavy-set, dark-haired Duane, a known brawler, had claimed self-defense and was freed by a hung jury. When the case came up for trial a second time, Fayolle had left town, supposedly forever. Despite the portrayal of Fayolle as an effete man attacked by a bully, the Frenchman was more likely a hardened fighter. Buried evidence shows that Fayolle later returned to San Francisco long enough to become one of four commanders who were handpicked to accompany a French filibuster who was then attacking Mexico, and that he was killed in battle there in 1852. Meanwhile, Duane had been released for lack of evidence. Duane's popularity soared on the basis of his strength and bravery in fighting fires, the scourge of San Francisco. In 1853 and again in 1854, he had been elected head of all of San Francisco's fire engine companies in two fraud-free contests. As the *Herald* pointed out, Duane had "done more for the protection of life and property in San Francisco than the entire Committee together, [yet he] was arrested in midday and kidnapped."[30]

Duane's kidnapping had not been easy. As a crowd of captors muscled the struggling former fire chief four blocks to the Committee rooms, a raucous throng gathered around them, alarming the vigilantes. While guards hustled their popular prisoner into a windowless upstairs cell at the fort, vigilante militia formed up outside, and those on the roof pointed their loaded muskets at the crowd. All afternoon and evening, vigilante cavalry patrolled the streets.[31] As Denis Oliver wrote in his diary, "There is a great am[oun]t [of] indignation felt about the arrest of C. Duane, he was the best Fireman in the City."[32]

Varied reactions tumbled out in quick succession. The *Herald* published a call for a "mass meeting" to rouse public support "in favor of maintaining the supremacy of the Constitution and Laws of the State."[33] Inside the vigilantes' fort, President Coleman made the surprising report "that he had failed to make arrangements with ship Adelaide," whose captain had previously agreed to deport all the vigilantes' prisoners, which would have easily rid them of Duane.[34] Meanwhile, the Committee's mouthpiece, the *Evening Bulletin*, published two pro-vigilance articles, one reporting arms arriving for war against the vigilantes, the second containing four- and five-year-old extracts from county trial records against Charles Duane and William Mulligan, respectively. The *Bulletin* assured its readers that the judge and the district attorney involved in these trials were "never legally elected to the offices they now fill," and were criminal participants because of "the aid and protection they give these shameless villains who stuffed them into office."[35]

Fearful of further difficulties, the vigilantes quickly dealt with their remaining prisoners. An Executive summoned them to hear the "Resolution of Conviction and Sentence" that had resulted from their secret trials—the first the captives knew of the entire procedure. Almost as an afterthought, the Executives then called their Delegates into session and read them the trial testimony. The Delegates unanimously upheld the Executives' decisions to deport William Mulligan, Martin Gallagher, William Carr, and William "Wooley" Kearney.[36] Meanwhile, a heavier guard mustered around the vigilantes' makeshift fort. Inside, the Executives prepared a published statement for the *Bulletin* to calm adverse reactions to their treatment of the late Sullivan. The "Confession of Frances Murray, alias Yankee Sullivan" stretched down the middle of its entire front page on June 3, heavily redacted, allegedly because "several of the parties implicated are not yet arrested." In part, the article read, "____ rode out to the Presidio House . . . and offered me four or five hundred dollars . . . to change the returns and throw out ____ and ____ and bring in a large majority for ____ and ____," all under the seal of "33 Secretary."[37] This potholed article would go east on the June 5 steamer along with the news of the famous Sullivan's death.

While the Executives used the press to burnish their standing, their opposition continued organizing. On June 2, 1856, William Tecumseh Sherman attended the *Herald*'s touted Law and Order mass meeting in the Plaza along with some three thousand other interested citizens, but left early to correspond with state quartermaster Kibbe. "Civil war is so horrible to contemplate," he wrote, that he would do all he could to avoid it. He held out hope that the ongoing "public meeting ... [would be a] safety valve to the passions that now blind many who are otherwise good people."[38] But Sherman had left before rowdy participants began yelling insults and banging tin pots and pans to drown out the Law and Order speakers. At the edge of the crowd, men held up large posters reading "MEMBERS AND FRIENDS OF THE VIGILANCE COMMITTEE COME OUT" and "MEMBERS OF THE VIGILANCE COMMITTEE: ORDER MUST BE MAINTAINED." In the deafening racket, the meeting folded. The next day, the *Herald* pegged the heckling as "not the result of any orders issued by the Committee," but concluded, "the Executive Committee have not the power to control their armed minions."[39]

That same evening, not far from the noisy Plaza, the Executives were giving Charles Duane his own quick secret trial. Serving as attorneys, judge, and jury, they heard affidavits read both for and against him. The next day, they decided that Duane had "for years been a disturber of the peace of this community by repeated assaults, often with deadly weapons, upon unoffending citizens and by his interference with our elections; resolved, that he be sentenced to leave this state ... and warned never to return under penalty of death. Order transported. Board of Delegates approved sentence."[40] Locked in his guarded cell, Duane had refused to eat anything except two boiled eggs delivered in the shell for fear of being poisoned. He knew nothing of the vigilantes' proceedings.[41]

In Sacramento, news of San Francisco's relentless turmoil had finally spurred Governor Johnson to action. He sent a telegram to Sheriff David Scannell in San Francisco: "Do you require a military force to aid you in executing any process, civil or criminal?"[42] Scannell shot back with the sorry tale of Terry's aborted writ for Mulligan, his own lack of firepower, and the assertion that the Committee "cannot be put down without exercising the Military power of the State."[43] Later that day, Governor Johnson telegraphed Sherman with orders to call up the California Militia.[44] This correspondence was promptly reported in the *Evening Bulletin*.[45] Someone had read their private telegrams.

On June 3, Governor Johnson issued an official proclamation, demanding that the vigilantes disband. If they did not, he declared that San Francisco would be in a state of insurrection.[46] Everyone understood that this document was a declaration of war.

PART II
Vigilantes Rising

8
Escalating Tensions

The chance of war escalated as both sides sought more men and more weapons. The vigilantes had no intention of disbanding. Their opponents, the Law and Order Party, wanted to prevent any illegal deportations, indicative of official powerlessness. In a published address, Sherman called on all male San Franciscans "between the ages of eighteen and forty-five years, not members of the regularly enrolled Volunteer or Fire Companies" to join established military units.[1] Soon, Law and Order enlistments totaled 1,135 men.[2] From Sacramento, Governor Johnson wrote to Sherman, ordering him to inventory San Francisco's available arms and ammunition and to secure one or more steamships to be used to prevent the forcible deportation of the vigilantes' captives.[3] Once again, the substance of the governor's private letter was reported in the *Bulletin*.[4] Hundreds of other men rushed to join the vigilantes, who quickly acquired about four thousand small arms and twenty-seven cannons to arm their followers.[5] To summon their ballooning membership, the Executives replaced their hundred-pound triangle on the roof with the seven-hundred-pound bell from the Monumental Engine Company, which had also been used for the Committee of 1851. Its tones rang clearly throughout the city.[6]

On the night of Steamer Day, June 4, the Executives prepared their captives for deportation. Three men appeared at the cell of Charles Duane and read him the sentence of exile, which threatened death should he return. Immediately thereafter, armed vigilantes marched him down to the night-black wharf and left him in the care of French vigilantes. For a moment, Duane feared he would be murdered. He was shortly joined by five other handcuffed captives marched in out of the fog: William Mulligan, Edward Bulger, Martin Gallagher, William Carr, and William

"Wooley" Kearney. Before they boarded a steam tug that appeared out of the foggy blackness, "the Committee of Surveillance . . . [took] steps to procure from the prisoners such revelations and disclosures as may lead to the arrests of others and make record of their names," reported the Executive's *Minutes*.[7]

As dawn broke, San Franciscans awoke to the sight of large shipments of gold flowing out of the struggling city. Banks wanted to send their money to less contentious ports. Earlier, on May 21, the *John L. Stephens* had hauled away more than $2 million worth of bullion from more than fifty private San Francisco banks.[8] On June 5, the day scheduled for the first vigilante deportations, another $2,657,000 was loaded on the mail steamer. Wells Fargo contributed almost $390,000; Sherman's Lucas, Turner and Company sent out $160,000; and W. T. Coleman and Company's $46,000 more than doubled its previous shipment.[9]

A curious crowd milled around the docks, unaware that the vigilantes' exiles had already departed. Before dawn, a tug carrying the deportees had tied up to a clipper bound toward the open sea. By 6:00 a.m. both boats were about eight miles outside the heads in violent ocean swells. Boatmen Gallagher and Carr easily found their sea legs; the vigilante landlubbers grew more and more seasick as the tug pitched and rolled. The clipper then cast off and sailed away, leaving the rocking tug behind. Soon, the bark *Yankee* of G. B. Post and Company sailed up, headed for Hawaii. Protesting their forced departure, Gallagher, Bulger, and Carr were unmanacled and put on board. Bulger immediately lurched up to the bow, far away from his captors. *Yankee* captain James Smith informed the men that he had been a member of the 1851 Vigilance Committee, and that the current Executives had arranged for their passage. Back on the pitching tug, the other three captives waited until 4:00 p.m., when the mail steamer *Golden Age* puffed alongside with its golden cargo. Seasick vigilantes removed the handcuffs from Mulligan, Kearney, and Duane and transferred them to a small boat and then to the steamer, bound for Panama.[10] The vigilantes had outwitted the Law and Order Party, whose members continued patrolling San Francisco's docks, still seeking to save the vigilantes' victims.

After these first successful extraditions, the Executives turned their attention to the threat posed by William Tecumseh Sherman. As Executive Alfred L. Tubbs later explained, "If Sherman had come in with his will and force we would have had blood-shed."[11] Sherman had originally pledged money to support the Committee, but after the vigilantes had captured and hanged Casey and Cora, Sherman refused to pay, growling that "this Committee had violated their pledges to the Governor of the State and to himself," referring to their meeting while James King of William was still alive.[12] Sparse evidence suggests that Sherman attempted to negotiate

The vigilantes' prisoners can be identified by their handcuffs as they are marched down to the dock in the dark of night, their captors demonstrating orderly behavior in this pro-vigilante illustration. *Courtesy of the Bancroft Library.*

with the vigilantes, who rejected his pleas to disband. One of their emissaries reminded him that his "banking house would be destroyed and the money lost" if he continued in his opposition.[13]

Both sides turned for armaments to seventy-two-year-old General Wool, the highest-ranking army general on the Pacific, who controlled federal weapons. Sherman wanted the arms he had been promised; the Executives feared that he would get them. Subsequent discussions led a "Committee of Citizens," who had secretly met with the Executives, to accompany Sherman on the steamboat up to Benecia, supposedly by chance.[14] Just before their departure, a new story began leaking through San Francisco. A client at Sherman's bank told him, "If you expect to get arms of General Wool, you will be mistaken, for I was at Benecia yesterday, and heard him say he would not give them." Unbeknownst to Sherman, Governor Johnson had already received a written refusal from Wool and was making arrangements to confront the general in person. While the governor prepared a message to Sherman to join him, Sherman wrote to General Wool that "any hesitation on his part would compromise me as a man of truth and honor."[15] With trepidation, he boarded the upriver steamer.

As the steamboat bearing Sherman and the Committee of Citizens chugged inland, clouds were gathering in Benecia. Furious at the general's change of heart, Governor Johnson refused to call on Wool, who was old enough to be his grandfather. Sherman went to the governor's hotel room and found him surrounded by an eight-man entourage, including Volney Howard, head of the Sacramento Militia, and Justice David Terry, whose writ of habeas corpus the Executives had earlier refused to accept. When the members of San Francisco's Committee of Citizens were finally admitted, they had to remain standing, while Terry, who had already denounced Wool as a "damned liar" and the Citizens' Committee as "no better than 'Vigilantes,'" sat sullenly, "his hat on, drawn over his eyes, and with his feet on the table."[16] No settlement resulted, and, after the Citizens' Committee's departure, the frustrated Sherman scrawled a letter of resignation for the governor and left the room. Two days later, a more coolheaded Sherman wrote the governor a private letter, citing his own "false position, and . . . the extreme ideas of Judge Terry, General Howard and others." He regretfully noted that the discourteous treatment of the Citizens' Committee had alienated "several gentlemen who have been zealous on our side from the first," and recommended a couple of military men as his possible replacement.[17] Unbeknownst to Sherman, as soon as he had stalked out, Johnson had turned to forty-seven-year-old Volney Howard, asking him to take Sherman's place. Howard, a college-trained lawyer who had already served as a U.S. representative from two southern states, had accepted.[18]

Within days, Sherman made his resignation public. He published a letter explaining his withdrawal, citing his own "moderation and forbearance" in the face of "the high and chivalrous [meaning southern] sense of duty which has actuated the Governor."[19] As soon as the Executives learned that he had resigned, they rescinded their previous proposal to honor writs of habeas corpus earlier negotiated with Sherman, claiming that their offers had been "misconstrued as weakness or timidity and . . . were not responded to."[20] There would be no reconciliation.

All the while negotiations were underway, the Executives had continued preparing for war. The vigilantes obtained their own thirty-two-pound cannon from the Russia American Ice Company and dragged it into place, pointing it up Sacramento Street.[21] Workmen reinforced the roof of Fort Vigilance after the Executives learned that an unfriendly Irishman was "an active man on the 'law and order' side" with experience in dumping "sulphuric or other strong acids . . . from the tops of houses upon the soldiers." They also heard that another man had "enquired after rockets lately, which shod with iron tops would no doubt be a fearful 'infernal machine' on our crowd."[22] The Executives had authorized their "Committee on Arms . . . to procure certain sabres and muskets said to be in the market on sale" and had inventoried weapons already in their possession: 1,209 guns and rifles, more than 1,000 with bayonets; 13 cannons; 9 cutlasses; 30 swords; and about 60 sashes. Vigilante Grand Marshal Doane had reported the readiness of his field officers and staff, and agreed to find ways to disarm the Law and Order Party. Given the weaponry being assembled, the Executives had identified five doctors in their ranks. Next, an Executive left to procure "all the wire cartridges in this City." An arms dealer offered "his short guns . . . without charge, provided the committee guarantee to him their safe return in good order," a promise that was not forthcoming.[23] Within days, the Executives staged the Committee's largest recruiting drive, reorganizing their troops and providing for a new election of military officers.[24] Two independent militia companies, the Marion Rifles and the Scottish-clad Wallace Guards, publicly went over to the Committee.[25] Doane increased patrols, while the Executives decided that three of their own number would remain on guard at their fort every night.[26] As one of them later observed, "I have seen at one time not less than five men, members of the Vigilance Committee, with muskets in their hands, taking turns at guard, not one of whom was worth less than half a million dollars."[27]

The Executives also recruited foreign veterans of European conflicts. They contacted "one or two Bombers" who would "aid in case of attack" and promised them "protection in writing."[28] After all, the bombers were Irish. An experienced French engineer offered his services, and President Coleman proposed the construction of "twelve portable barricades . . . but that two only be first constructed and submitted for inspection and approval."[29] The prototypes arrived a few days later, each consisting of "a sort of frame work, with wheels attached, so . . . it can be used, as required, for a barricade, a scaling ladder or a litter." Each also came with a bullet-proof mattress. For the first two, the Executives paid $95.37 (about $2,300 in twenty-first-century dollars).[30] No more were constructed. Finally, the Executives invited the distinguished Hungarian count Samu [Samuel] Wass, supporter of Hungarian freedom fighter Louis Kossuth (then being lionized throughout America), to join the General Committee, although a second Executive visit was needed to convince him.[31] Wass's position as the head of a private San Francisco mint also meant that, if necessary, he could coin money for the vigilantes.[32]

Despite these precautions, the Executives remained anxious. They realized that their fort was indefensible and considered moving, but opted instead to fill up the underground sewers with stones to prevent ingress. They explicitly took responsibility "for damage to all horses used for removal of pieces of artillery which may occur while in use." Their Military Committee identified emergency rendezvous sites and dispersed armaments to merchants' stores in other parts of the city.[33] Finally, the Executives delivered a note to the businessmen next door, offering to pay "their expenses should they think it proper to move their goods from the store now occupied by them." The neighbors did so.[34]

West Point graduate Francis J. Lippitt, newly elected colonel of the vigilantes' 4th Division, devised the most memorable change of all.[35] In addition to fortifying their warehouse with $46.74 worth of lumber (worth almost $1,300 in twenty-first-century dollars), he arranged a novel defense.[36] In the middle of the night, James Curtis, one of the vigilantes' military leaders, went to the drill room in Fort Vigilance and called out, "'Two hundred men with side arms for special duty required.' The whole boodle of them rushed forward," thinking "there was fighting on hand." The two hundred volunteers were marched out to the sand hills on Second Street, where bales of gunnybags and dozens of shovels had been stored. As soon as they "could just discern the carts and gunnybags and shovels . . . [they] called out 'Sold! Sold! Sold!'"[37] But they worked all night, filling and stacking sandbags at the fort's front and rear entrances, areas further fortified "with artillery bristling on every side," remembered Francis Pinto. "After this our quarters were known as Fort Gunny Bags."[38]

Simultaneously, the Executives began a blacklisting bonanza. They had fill-in-the-blank indictments printed that read:

> In view of the notorious and public bad character of _____ we hereby find him guilty of being a bad person, a disturber of the peace, dangerous to the community and guilty of interference in the purity and integrity of the ballot box, hereby sentence him to banishment from this state.
>
> Resolved, that notice be given _____ to leave this state on or before the 20th inst. and never to return under the severest penalties

Utilizing these, they blacklisted ten more men.[39] In later years, vigilante president Coleman explained that "our rule of action" sprang from the knowledge that "delays are dangerous and the results thereof pernicious," so they had to move quickly on "the arrest of these notorious characters."[40]

Conflict intensified in print. To maintain their moral pose, the Executives promulgated their "Proclamation" and address "To the People of California," stressing their own high-mindedness and assuring readers that as soon as their reform was complete, they would return their power to "the people, from whom it was received."[41] A thousand printed copies were soon circulating through the state.[42] About the same time, vigilante William H. Rhodes, who had been fired as the governor's private secretary for his public anti–Know Nothing letters, published a

Artistically emphasizing the Monument Engine bell and the respectability of the vigilantes (all in top hats), the pro-vigilante *Wide West* newspaper caption emphasized the "impregnability" of Fort Gunnybags and "the courage of its defenders." "View of Fort Vigilance," *Wide West*, July 13, 1856. *Courtesy of the California History Room, California State Library, Sacramento.*

provocative editorial in his San Francisco newspaper, the *True Californian*. Pushing the Executives' reasoning in their "Proclamation" to its logical conclusion, Rhodes argued that if the Vigilance Committee truly represented the will of the people, it should rule California. He consequently called for "the formation of Vigilance Committees throughout the State" and demanded "a Convention on the Fourth of July next to form a new Constitution for the State and turn out all present officials."[43] Offers of support arrived from vigilance committees in Centerville and Alameda County.[44] Thomas Sim King, now editor of his late brother's *Evening Bulletin*, volunteered to use his paper to call a state constitutional convention.[45]

Feeling the pressure, Governor Johnson privately dashed off three plaintive notes: a brief reprimand to Sherman for his wording in his published resignation letter; a demand to Quartermaster Kibbe for additional arms; and a note to Justice Terry, who was still in San Francisco. To Terry, he urged "caution in provoking a conflict" and requested "organizing and arming such forces as can be relied on for the emergency." He asked Terry, in the absence of arms from General Wool, "Can't we buy any muskets in San Francisco from the same sources" used by the vigilantes?[46]

Six days later, Governor Johnson formally authorized Terry and three others "to negotiate a loan of not exceeding (for the present) twenty five thousand dollars to be used as a fund to suppress the existing insurrection."[47] In a letter that crossed the governor's on the upriver steamer, new militia commander Volney Howard informed Johnson that Terry had already purchased some guns in Sacramento. But the wealthy Terry had not bought ancient muzzle-loading muskets like the ones the vigilantes held. Instead, he had personally purchased the latest available small arms: Sharps rifles. Costing about twenty-five dollars each, these rapid-fire breech-loading weapons had rifled bores, which caused bullets, primed by an automatically fed ribbon, to travel much straighter than they did from the mouth of a musket.[48] Howard planned to ship these new rifles to Benecia, where the federal ordnance was stored, in the hope of getting the state's weapon allocation from the reluctant General Wool. Then all the guns could be shipped together to San Francisco.[49]

9
Rumors and Revelations

Attempting to cultivate more public support, the Executives incited a series of pro-vigilante mass meetings. The first, on June 11, featured Judge David O. Shattuck, who had upheld the Peter Smith titles on the bench after assuring the commissioners of the funded debt that the sheriff's sales would not convey title. He had recently lost the election for supreme court justice to David S. Terry and now extolled the vigilantes' political and moral "purification" goals to fellow "property owners." After other speeches, the attendees could not agree on "resolutions expressive of the sense of the meeting," so they called another gathering for the following evening.[1] The second mass meeting fostered even more pro-vigilante enthusiasm and a call for a third assembly two days later.[2]

The expanding furor deeply affected Hugh Breen, an unemployed Irish American handyman who had earlier come to San Francisco with his in-laws. As the economy faltered, Breen's wife and daughter had gone back to New Orleans. All he wanted now was enough money to join them. On June 13 he began to keep a diary, noting, "everything dull in the Business department," but "the Vigilants are still adding to their armament in the shape of Cannon—Grape Shot and Balls. . . . There will be a great Mass Meeting held in front of the Oriental Hotel at 12 Oclock tomorrow noon for the purpose of endorsing the acts of the Vigilance Committee." From opinions he had already heard, he expected "twill be unanimous."[3]

Breen was almost right. On June 14, some seven to ten thousand men gathered to listen to another series of pro-Committee speakers, including city attorney Bailie Peyton, a secret vigilante, and one of the supposedly "disinterested citizens" who had called on Governor Johnson at Benecia. Peyton railed loudly against ballot-box stuffing and political corruption, then called for an endorsement of the

Vigilance Committee. "Let us be ready to fight for them if necessary!" he shouted. Instantly "such a thundering 'Aye' went up as seemed sufficient to rent the sky," remembered a participant. A call for nays brought two brave responses of "No" from men who were immediately seized by the vigilantes. After other speeches, one man called for the resignation of all San Francisco county and city officers. The crowd cheered. Then Peyton took up the infamous "patent ballot box," no longer stuffed with unused ballots from the 1854 Democratic primary election, which the Executives had explicitly permitted him to display.[4] Holding it aloft, Peyton jokingly regretted that he could not also produce fugitive Edward McGowan, still being hunted throughout California and Nevada, who had allegedly operated it so deftly. An assistant demonstrated the use of its sliding panels, which could release additional ballots into the box. Peyton's suggestion that the box be sent to the National Archives for preservation roused the crowd to tumultuous cheering as the meeting closed.[5]

In contrast to the tumult outside, the sequestered Executives quietly pursued their own political goals. First they considered the Bulkhead Bill, the latest manifestation of Broderick's recurring attempt to control the city's waterfront. Merchant-auctioneer Thomas J. L. Smiley privately reported to his fellow Executives that the bill was unlikely to pass, but he would continue to monitor its fate.[6] They all realized that if the bill could be stalled until July 1, it would die with the Common Council itself, because on that day only county officials would remain, thanks to the Consolidation Act.

Second, the Executives prepared for outright rule of San Francisco. If after July 1 the county officials could be ousted, the Vigilance Committee would become the only power in the city. Therefore, right after the June 14 mass meeting, President Coleman moved that an Executive subcommittee be formed to "inquire into and report upon those County Officers who should be invited to resign."[7] The next day he sought to clarify "who and what power would fill those vacancies [caused by resignations] until next election." His main concern was to determine if the detested Democratic Committee, Broderick's adherents, could "lawfully act as a Board of Supervisors until the election in November."[8]

Regardless of legal procedures, if Broderick's men were gone, they could not rule. Consequently, the Executives sent two men to find evidence against selected targets. Executive Charles V. Gillespie, a searcher of records (private investigator), went "to investigate the records of the Governor and other [sic] county officers," but found nothing useful.[9] San Francisco policeman John Durkee, now a vigilante, went to abstract the Records of the Court.[10] Specifically disregarding Chinese and Mexicans, Durkee searched the records back to 1853 for the names of "notorious

In this biased illustration, the waving flags and crowds of listeners, not only in the plaza but all the way up the hill in the background, served to indicate the Vigilance Committee's widespread popularity. *Courtesy of the Bancroft Library.*

characters" with a Broderick taint. One active Democrat, discharged a single time for fighting in 1855, made their Black List. Another man who had been arrested eight times beginning in January 1853 (for assault, battery, disorderly conduct, and receiving stolen property) had not been politically active and was ignored.[11] Adding several Broderick operatives to the list, the Executives themselves took responsibility for obtaining damning testimonies and turned to their Delegates for approval to convict and deport everyone they had blacklisted.[12] As Executive James Dows later sneered, that "'sort' was not entitled to a trial."[13]

This haphazard method of secretly convicting in absentia, getting Delegate approval, and then finding evidence to convict led to increasingly arbitrary captures. For example, the Executives secretly blacklisted Thomas Cunningham, who had joined the Law and Order militia less than two weeks earlier.[14] On June 16, unbeknownst to Cunningham, the Executives heard evidence against him and found him guilty of counterfeiting. Then they consulted the district attorney to see if a case against Cunningham could be proven in court. He informed them that it could not.[15] So a group of vigilantes arrived at the Cunningham residence a little after midnight on June 17, demanding that Cunningham accompany them to Fort Gunnybags "as a witness." When he refused, the vigilantes returned in greater strength and rushed in to seize him, wildly firing a couple of shots. A German vigilante was shot in the buttocks, and Mrs. Cunningham, clinging to her husband, "received . . . a blow in the face." A shocked Cunningham agreed to go quietly.[16] The next day, the Board of Delegates met and upheld Cunningham's sentence of guilty of passing slugs, and confirmed the Executives' decision not to hand him over to the legal authorities. While Cunningham was in custody, the Executives agreed to pay the expenses of the wounded vigilante, and allowed Cunningham's wife and a friend to see him in the presence of one of their number. Before the departure of the June 20 mail steamer, a photographer took the prisoner's picture so he could be recognized upon his return, if need be. Then the Executives informed Cunningham of his sentence: deportation, and death if he returned.[17] He would have to leave his wife behind.

As the Executives pursued their goals in secret, rumors surged through the city. The pro-vigilante *Wide West* promptly editorialized against converting the Committee "into a political body," calling such a shift "suicidal" and a clear indication of vigilante abuse of power. The editor added that a few men "have for a long time been plotting the formation of a Pacific Republic," but so far, no justifications for this move existed, "and we trust will not."[18] Certainly, former Mississippi senator and governor Henry Foote, who had come to California with ambitions to be reelected to the U.S. Senate, had recently written an address to the people of San Francisco suggesting secession, and wished to see it published in the *Bulletin*. Informed of Foote's proposed article, the Executives told the *Bulletin*'s editor that "the Committee of Vigilance could not in their organized capacity either approve or disapprove of such an address," but indirectly they discouraged its publication.[19]

The Executives could hardly squelch secessionist ideas outright, for they themselves had discussed the possibility. Hearing rumors to this effect, both General Wool and Captain Farragut had spoken with President Coleman. Wool had particularly questioned whether the Committee "was a political organization" and delicately asked if "there was nothing of secession nor of Pacific independence . . . as part of our work," Coleman later recalled.[20] Although the president guaranteed that there was not, he later acknowledged that Committee members had "quietly argued that California was geographically, and should be politically, separated from the Atlantic States, that it was a natural location for a great Pacific Empire, and that now was the most fitting time to take the initiative, if not indeed the bold step towards separation."[21] Executive Clancey Dempster later reported that some Committee members "were dazzled by the prospective glory of . . . [creating] an empire destined to rank among earth's proudest." California's secession "might almost by a single effort relieve them [the Executives] from both the personal & pecuniary peril wh[ich] all felt to be menacing."²² Isolated from the eastern states by a vast continent, a pestilential isthmus, and raging oceans, California had actually been a republic from 1846 to 1848, and had remained politically independent for the last eight years. Thoughtful men reasoned that in the midst of the current power shift, the state might indeed break free. "If the project of secession and an independent Pacific confederacy were adopted and carried out in California," a New York paper later expansively speculated, "California could easily raise a body of [military] volunteers which . . . could overrun and conquer . . . Mexico, and . . . carry their line of annexation to a junction with General Walker in Nicaragua."²³

Former San Franciscan William Walker's latest achievement indeed seemed to point the way. In mid-June 1856, the latest bimonthly news of the outside world had brought a report summarized in Denis Oliver's diary: "Walker's Government in Nicaragua was recognized by the United States, [which has led to] a prospect of war with England" over competing Nicaragua claims.²⁴ Walker had conquered Nicaragua in the fall of 1855, subsequently serving as commander in chief behind a puppet president. As the true power in Nicaragua, he had taken transit rights across the isthmus away from powerful New York steamboat magnate Cornelius Vanderbilt, perhaps America's richest man. Walker had transferred Vanderbilt's Accessory Transit Company to the New Yorker's former employee, Cornelius K. Garrison, also a former San Francisco mayor. Enraged at Walker, Vanderbilt had funded a coordinated invasion by Costa Rica and Honduras during Nicaragua's ongoing civil war, which fizzled during a virulent cholera outbreak. Thereafter, Walker ruled Nicaragua outright.²⁵ If former San Franciscan Walker could face down all these challenges and rule his own county, why could the Executives not rule California?

These power plays by two well-known former San Franciscans, Walker and Garrison, also seemed to offer a solution to the Executives' most immediate practical dilemma: the cost of deportation. The Executives gave their Committee on Evidence "discretion to allow [the] accused power of leaving before sentence," in a continuing attempt to scare their targets away.²⁶ When most targets refused to leave at their own expense, the Executives contacted Garrison, requesting free passage for their exiles. To their surprise, he refused. Consequently, the Executives decided that they had better find "means of compliance" for passage out before they made any more arrests.²⁷

Concurrently, others bought steamboat tickets for the East. At the last minute, Governor Johnson decided to send two emissaries on the June 20 steamer with a letter for President Franklin Pierce outlining the whole vigilante story, beginning with the Committee's formation, its arrests and subsequent hanging of Casey and Cora, its unwarranted searches of private residences, its spying and rejection of Terry's writ of habeas corpus, the spate of kidnappings and deportations, Sullivan's death, and the so far unsuccessful request for arms from Wool. Without federal arms, Johnson concluded, the state could not protect its citizens, and the Committee's "acts of aggression and disobedience" would lead to the "entire destruction" of state government.[28] Guessing his envoys' mission, the *Sacramento Daily Union* ranted against "the first application ever to the President by a State Governor for assistance against the people who elected him," and warned that a federal attack would prompt secession.[29] On the same outgoing steamer traveled the vigilantes' own messenger, determined to present their side of the story.[30]

The governor also kept pressing for weapons. He itemized the only federal arms still due the state: "113 more muskets . . . one horse artillery sabre and two bullet molds," the last two articles included "to make up the value of a faction of a musket."[31] Even these were hard to get. General Wool stalled, demanding additional paperwork. Confused directives finally determined that the armaments would be sent to the state prison, where convicts could clean up the aged weapons. Then they could be shipped to San Francisco on the night of June 20, when the commotion of the departing steamer might mask their arrival. Given that the new guns bought by Terry in Sacramento were now on the water headed to San Francisco, this plan "would concentrate all these articles at the same place, from whence their removal might be made promptly and quietly," wrote Johnson's agent.[32] Consequently, Law and Order men boxed up Wool's muskets, addressed them to Governor Johnson, and placed them aboard the schooner *Julia* under the direction of James Roby (or Reuben) Molony, known locally as "Reub." Molony belonged to the Constitution Guard of the Law and Order Party, under the command of Dr. Richard Porter Ashe, David S. Terry's best friend from their youthful days in Texas. Soon, two boatloads of guns were on the water from different ports, both on their way to San Francisco.[33]

With the wide appeal of the Vigilance Committee, it was hard to keep these maneuvers secret. On June 20, as the boat for the East built up steam, the Executives received a letter from the captain of the schooner *Bianca* announcing the location of the load from Benecia and volunteering "to go in my schooner and try to bring the same to the Committee of Vigilance rooms." The Executives accepted his offer and authorized a force of vigilantes to assist.[34] A Vallejo merchant also reported another launch with "arms on board . . . either procured from friends of the Law & Order party or stolen from the U.S. arsenal." In this second letter of June 20, addressed to "S.A. Hopkins, Esq. of the Vigilante Police," the new informant noted

Reflecting the popular tale of Mrs. Partington trying to turn back the stormy Atlantic with a broom, a pro-vigilante paper portrayed a feminized Governor J. Neely Johnson in the fruitless attempt to sweep back the "reform flood" of vigilance with the broom of his proclamation, while standing on the "Chair of State." Below him flounder miniaturized Law and Order members, while the scrawny *Herald* and *Sun* urge him on. *Wide West*, July 6, 1856. *Courtesy of the California History Room, California State Library, Sacramento.*

that the guns were headed to the state prison, but "the tide will not turn for three hours," and therefore "they cannot leave for that time."[35]

In the meantime, men gathered at the docks for the excitement of the steamer's departure. Hugh Breen, waiting in frustration for a $100 loan from his brother to pay his passage home, noted in his diary, "I wish this excitement of Clearing the Blackguards out of Town was finished and Business take a start. If I could only get two or three weeks work it would put me on my feet again." The next night: "Don't know what to do with myself. Can't sleep, can't settle down to read . . . can't get no work at anything. . . . Oh! If my Brother had sent that money three months ago I would have been Home and happy." On June 20, Breen reported, "There has been some excitement and anxiety to witness the departure of the prisoners in the hands of the Committee. The mail steamer left about four o'clock and the *Sierra Nevada* started at the same time but after going out a little way down the Bay she dropped anchor." Those who tried to spot prisoners being loaded on board were disappointed. "We waited to near 11 o'clock but no signs so we went home." He noted the "squads parading and drilling in different sections around the city for the purpose of attracting the attention of the people that they may conduct the prisoners without fear of a rescue aboard the steamer. I only wish the[y] would conduct me aboard—but I am not rascal enough."[36]

While vigilantes wheeled and marched throughout the city on June 20 and idle men gathered at the docks, the Executives remained in session all night to plan for adjournment. Fearful of conflict, they set their quorum at eleven in case of "the need for prompt action." They agreed to accept only "extreme cases" after June 24, in order to deport stragglers on the July 5th steamer. After a grand parade on the 4th of July, the General Committee would disband. But the Executives and Delegates would "still continue to meet and the General Committee shall hold themselves ready at all times to respond to their regular orders," since the threat of death would continue to hang over returning exiles. Finally, the Executives agreed to inform the Delegates of these decisions.[37]

As the Executives crafted these finishing touches inside their fort, excited vigilante police led by John Durkee slipped down to the docks, boarded waiting craft, and sailed out toward Benecia, "to intercept a vessel supposed to have arms in her belonging to the law and order party."[38] Traveling in the opposite direction, the schooner *Julia*, facing a headwind, anchored for the night at San Pablo Point, about thirty miles out from San Francisco. In the hold lay six boxes addressed to Governor Johnson containing 113 muskets, a saber, and two bullet molds.

10
Vigilante Blood

On the *Julia*, unarmed Law and Order men awoke in the blackness between 2:00 and 3:00 a.m. on June 21 to Colt's revolvers pointed at their faces. The attackers tore off the ship's hatches and broke open one of six innocuous-looking boxes. It contained muskets. They seized two Law and Order men and the guns and "took them on board the ship . . . on which they came," the *Julia*'s captain later testified. They "said they were the Vigilance Committee."[1] Returning to San Francisco, the vigilantes carted the arms and their two captives, J. R. Molony and John Phillips, to Fort Gunnybags. Deciding to keep only the guns, the Executives released the men, but had them followed.[2]

Later that day, the Executives changed their minds. As they finalized plans for their closing parade, they got word that the two men from the *Julia* had headed for a meeting with Law and Order leaders. They sent vigilante policeman Sterling Hopkins out to make an arrest. The Executives also learned that the other Law and Order arms shipment was approaching San Francisco on the *Mariposa*, and sent out other vessels in pursuit.[3]

Raids climaxed in different parts of the bay. When vigilantes boarded the *Mariposa* and dug under its load of bricks, they discovered "twelve cases of Sharp's rifles and a large number of swords and sabers."[4] The vigilantes now had cutting-edge arms, secretly bought by Justice Terry. Second, Molony and Phillips had split up, and Phillips had disappeared. Unbeknownst to the others, he was a vigilante, number 3569.[5] The Executives soon canceled orders for his arrest.[6]

Molony's report of the arms heist from the *Julia* unsettled the Law and Order partisans. The newly released Molony had found four or five other anti-vigilante men with his commander, Dr. Richard Porter Ashe, in the doctor's combined residence and office. Among the group was state supreme court justice David S. Terry, who always stayed with his best friend Ashe when he was in San Francisco. Given this devastating theft, the Law and Order group decided that they had to inform militia commander in chief Volney Howard, who had arrived the night before on the daily boat from Sacramento. They never got the chance. Suddenly, someone knocked on the door.

"Come in," said Ashe, knowing the door was unlocked. Hopkins entered and demanded Phillip Roach (confusing him with John Phillips). Molony told him Roach was not there.

"Step outside," said Hopkins to Molony. "We need to talk."

"If you want anything of me, I am here; we can do it here," replied Molony.

"No, you need to come with me, to the rooms of the Vigilance Committee," insisted Hopkins.

Molony resisted, asking if the stranger had a warrant. Hopkins had none, but tried to force Molony outside. Molony's companions shoved Hopkins out the door.[7] As an angry Hopkins left to get reinforcements, the Law and Order group knew what was coming next. The Vigilance Committee never accepted a refusal to "come to headquarters." Ashe's rooms were indefensible. The nearest safe haven was at the old post office, now the armory of the still-loyal California Blues, only three blocks away, up on the rising outskirts of Telegraph Hill.[8] The small group armed themselves and headed out at a quick march, with Molony in the lead, while Terry and Ashe protected the rear.

Meanwhile, Hopkins quickly got reinforcements. Unexpectedly encountering vigilante physician R. Beverly Cole, Hopkins borrowed his horse, making short work of the seven-block distance to vigilante headquarters. There he demanded that recruits "arrest a person." Vigilante James Bovee joined him. "Mr. Hopkins came along from toward Commercial street and . . . then turned around and walked to one of the drinking saloons and took a drink," recalled Bovee. Losing sight of Hopkins, Bovee continued up the street, as a curious crowd gathered behind him. When Bovee saw Hopkins again, "he was running a sort of slow run; and just about this time I saw a party of five or six men with guns in their hands . . . running along slowly, fifteen or twenty steps ahead of us." As they closed in, Bovee asked, "Are we going to arrest a man out of that party?"

"Yes," replied Hopkins.

"At all hazards?" asked Bovee.

"Yes."[9]

Catching up with the fleeing Law and Order group, Hopkins yelled for more vigilantes. Men broke away from the crowd and raced after the small armed band

Although this workmanlike print captures the essence of the dramatic stabbing of Sterling Hopkins, like all of its contemporaries it fails to show the hill on which the men stood, the second man who had hold of Judge Terry's gun, and the surging crowd of surrounding vigilantes. *Courtesy of the California History Room, California State Library, Sacramento.*

hustling up the hill, with Molony still in the lead and Ashe and Terry at the rear, holding their rifles out horizontally. The vigilantes caught up and began surrounding their enemies as Molony sprinted for the Blues Armory. One of the vigilantes grasped Ashe's gun and put a pistol to his head, yelling, "Let go that gun, you son of a b____." Ashe dropped his rifle. At that same moment, Hopkins grabbed the muzzle of Terry's rifle; another vigilante grasped the stock. A cap snapped—a dry shot. A vigilante behind Terry fired his pistol, and the ball passed between Terry and one of his assailants. Ashe stumbled. Terry let go of his rifle, pulled out his sheath knife, and plunged it into Hopkins's neck.[10]

Spurting blood from a four-inch gash, Hopkins doggedly held on to Terry's gun while the second vigilante released his grasp and melted into the swirling crowd. Hopkins "passed his left hand to his neck," recalled another vigilante. "I could see the blood run down between his fingers. . . . Judge Terry started up the street about five or six steps; he stopped by a lamp-post and faced around. . . . The way he looked frightened me."

"Somebody up the street halloed 'Come to the Armory.'"

"'Come up Ashe,' said Terry," addressing his best friend from their old Texas days. Pursued by twenty or thirty vigilantes, the fleeing men dashed to safety.[11]

Direct confrontation could no longer be avoided. While Terry and Hopkins were struggling, Molony had dashed uphill and up the stairs to the armory of the California Blues, one of San Francisco's few independent militia companies still loyal to the state. The other hunted Law and Order men rushed in as word of the stabbing flew to Fort Gunnybags. The Executives demanded Terry's capture.[12] Francis Pinto, the new colonel of the 2nd Division, was commanded "to take a hundred men and make the arrest. Before I could get the men armed and in readiness," Pinto remembered, "word came that Hopkins had been killed."[13] The deep-throated Monumental Engine Company bell on the roof of vigilante headquarters began tolling.[14] Three taps on the bell, a pause, then three more, over and over, prompting a rolling echo "like the firing of a volley" as hundreds of "iron doors and shutters of the warehouses and stores" slammed shut. Thousands of armed vigilantes poured into the streets, as men "dropped business, seized . . . arms, and hurried to the muster," ready to serve their leaders' commands.[15] Within three minutes, "every passageway to our quarters was blocked with the excited members rushing in to get their arms," remembered Pinto. "It was impossible for me and my men to get out; the tide was so strong.[16] "The streets were literally alive with people," one of the Executives remembered later. "Men were coming from the [Vigilance Committee] rooms, with their arms full of muskets and sabers, with instructions to form in wherever they could. The drays loaded with freight for Sacramento were abandoned, the harness thrown off the horses, the headstall left on, and the men jumped on them, formed into line, and very soon hundreds of armed men, on foot and horseback, were marching in regular line to the place where Terry had taken refuge in the armory."[17] "In less than fifteen minutes there were not less than three thousand armed men on the double quick marching" through the streets of San Francisco, Pinto concluded.[18] A vigilante who fell in running with the first troop he saw remembered that each had to wear a white ribbon in the buttonhole of the left lapel of his coat to identify his status as a Committee member and avoid being attacked for being a Law and Order man. He ripped off a piece of his shirt and stuck it in his lapel. Many vigilantes locked arms as they strode from their fort to the stronghold of the Blues.

A dramatic scene unfolded. "As we reached the armory, I saw Dick Ashe, on the second story balcony, declaiming violently," reported a vigilante. "All I heard was, 'I am glad I did it. I would do it again,' as he stepped inside and slammed the iron shutters behind him."[19] From his spot on the balcony, Ashe had spied his commander, Volney Howard, in the throng below and shouted out their situation. Howard ordered the men inside to "stand to their position until further orders were transmitted."[20] Almost immediately, vigilantes roughly seized Howard, perhaps

The distinguished Judge David Terry, like many other men of his high social class, sat for this formal portrait by William M. Shew, one of the most famous photographers in San Francisco. *Courtesy of the Haggin Museum, Stockton, Calif.*

under the impression that he was Terry (or possibly with malicious intent). When they discovered his identity, they released him.[21] Escaping the encircling mob, Howard marched off to confront the Executives. He met with President Coleman and two other Executives at a neutral spot. Howard called the vigilantes "outlaws," promised that he would put them down "in sixty days (if not before)" with government aid, and sought "to address the Executive Committee.[22] He immediately pressed for Terry's freedom, sending the convened Executives a pointed letter demanding the release of Judge Terry to "officers of the law." He added, "This is the only course which will avoid an immediate collision of arms."[23] Although "Mr. Coleman spoke of moderation," Howard later reported, the Executives refused to meet with him and sent "a verbal answer that there was no reply."[24] The Executives knew they had all the federal arms from the *Julia*, and that the *Mariposa* was probably being boarded at that very minute. Howard had no idea.

Caged in the Blues Armory, Terry, Ashe, Molony, and the others took stock of their situation. They noted the weapons on hand: rifles, cartridges, body belts, percussion caps, and swords—but there were only sixteen men to wield them.[25] Terry wondered whom he had stabbed, hoping "that the wound would not prove fatal." To his best friend he added, "Ashe, I saw you reel, and thought they had killed you." As vigilantes outside bayed for Terry's blood, Ashe told Terry he would die there with him, "selling my life as dearly as possible." At this promise, Terry wept. Fully aware that he had acted in self-defense, Terry rejected Ashe's offer and hoped out loud that some Committee members would be "gentlemen" and would not, "under the circumstances, see me sacrificed."[26] Who were these Executives? Would it matter to them that Terry was a supreme court justice, a family man of impeccable reputation, a Protestant, and a Mason who had been elected by all of California's voters on the recent reform ticket? The tiny band gathered in the armory knew that the vigilantes had already kidnapped at least a dozen men, deported several, and hanged two of them. But the Committee's earlier victims had been members of San Francisco's underclass: ruffians, gamblers, ballot-box stuffers, and Roman Catholics—all the antithesis of Terry. Nonetheless, Terry was a southerner in a predominantly northern town. Would the vigilantes hang him?

Swelling crowds responded to the rumor that Terry had killed Hopkins. Excited "men ran calling 'Hang him, hang him!'" reported banker Sherman to his distant partner. "All kinds of stories flew about that Terry had shot Hopkins dead, and indeed it was hours before the truth was known. All stores were closed; so wild was the tumult that I had the money put in the vault and locked, and commanded all the clerks to stand by. Crowds of people with muskets and swords and pistols poured by up Jackson Street [past Sherman's office], and a dense mass of men filled the street from Montgomery to Stockton. Knowing Terry and Ashe to be desperate men," Sherman added, "I took it for granted that blood would be shed."[27]

Negotiations began between the Executives and the caged Law and Order men. Two Executives arrived at the Blues Armory to negotiate arrests as notes flew back and forth. Finally, Terry, Ashe, and Molony agreed to capitulate "if the Executive Committee will give us protection from violence." The response came that if the hunted men would surrender "together with their arms and ammunition in your possession . . . we will give you and the building in which you remain our protection. . . . By order of the Executive Committee of which we are members no. 12, no. 13, no. 50, no. 645, no. 332."[28]

"We then surrendered," Ashe tersely reported.[29]

Just as this agreement was concluded, other messengers arrived demanding the arrest of the entire Law and Order Party.[30] Escorted by vigilante troops, the three prominent captives—Terry, Ashe, and Molony—got into waiting carriages and rolled off to Fort Gunnybags. As the heavily guarded three-carriage procession wound through throngs of idle San Franciscans, the group passed another Law and Order stronghold. The vigilantes massing there presented arms, prompting a large detachment to quit the carriage escort and, with their cannon, strengthen the force surrounding the next armory.[31] Back at the Blues Armory, the rest of the Law and Order men—who had relinquished their arms—were imprisoned, too.

"We had a barrel of handcuffs," recalled a captor, so they led out the militiamen in irons and paraded them like convicted felons through the noisy, jeering crowd down to the fort.[32] Other vigilante companies combed the city for Law and Order weapons, with orders to capture any man "who might be found bearing arms against the Committee."[33]

Pressing their advantage, the Executives sent other forces out on attack. Three state armories quickly capitulated, but Captain Joseph R. West, head of the First Infantry Battalion, stood fast. Two months earlier, West had been overwhelmingly elected lieutenant colonel of infantry by all the San Francisco military companies, including men now serving with the vigilantes. His major was the governor's brother.[34] Inside his armory were about seventy men with four rounds of cartridges apiece. General Volney Howard forced his way into West's armory through the heckling crowd, again narrowly avoiding capture, and inspected the loyal troops. Howard ordered West "not to order his men to fire except in case of an attack."[35] After Howard left, West's troops stationed themselves at the most advantageous spots in the besieged building. As they peered out the Kearney Street door, they spied a cannon being wheeled up by some of the fifteen hundred to two thousand vigilantes outside. West sent a courier to seek instructions from Howard, while the vigilantes gave him five minutes to surrender or the cannon would be fired into the building. Howard sent a written reply that West should surrender if there was no reasonable hope of successful resistance, since all the Committee was demanding was their weapons.[36] West, surrounded by his men, waited until the last minute and then handed his sword to Grand Marshal Doane, who entered with his aides. As the captive troops passed over their own arms, some three hundred to four hundred vigilantes, including Executive Smiley, crowded inside to inspect West's muster rolls for "enemies of the public weal in his ranks."[37] They selected one man as a disreputable character, a groundless accusation that nonetheless blasted his reputation.[38] Then, in a shock to the captive men, the vigilantes demanded that the unarmed prisoners surrender.

Smiley, characterized by a fellow Executive as "very active and useful, though not of very good judgment," made the callous demand.[39] The tall, dark-eyed auctioneer later recalled, "I had been at the head of a gang of men, scouring the town, and I felt like a man in battle with no sense of danger, all excitement, all idea of danger being lost in the courage of animal excitement."[40] At West's armory, Smiley insisted that the largely Catholic members take the following oath: "I do solemnly promise and swear, in the presence of Almighty God and these witnesses present—by the hope of a future state—by the blessed Virgin Mary and all the Saints in the calendar, that I will not bear arms against the Vigilance Committee of San Francisco. So help me God and the blessed Virgin."[41] If they refused to take his oath, he said, they would be banished. A stone-faced West protested that his men had been mustered into service under an oath to uphold the Constitution and the laws, the direct opposite of Smiley's sectarian pledge. Nonetheless, West "asked the men if any of them would take it. A dead silence prevailed along the ranks, and the moment he got through . . . , all answered as one man, 'No.'"[42] Then they spontaneously gave three cheers for their commander, for their battalion, and for the Constitution and the laws, and three groans for the Committee. The startled Smiley, his blood still racing from the electrifying events of the day, angrily snapped that any future moves against the Committee would meet "with the severest punishment," meaning death. Smiley then had the unarmed men clapped in irons in pairs before parading them through the heckling crowds that lined the streets all the way to Fort Gunnybags.[43]

That evening, another vigilante detachment captured all the weapons belonging to Captain Thomas Hayes's Law and Order cavalry corps, stored at the mission.[44] President William Tell Coleman cheered his men's "clean sweep . . . [of] men, arms, and munitions."[45] An Executive later proudly recalled, "That ended the militia of the State of California."[46]

More than twenty years later, Coleman recalled that day. "The state forces on every side undertook resistance; but, they quickly saw how futile it was. . . . The whole city was amazed at the completeness of our movement. Of all the field days of the whole campaign . . . this day probably excelled." The vigilantes now completely controlled San Francisco. But with the icy clarity of hindsight, Coleman also noted, "On the 21st [of June, 1856] we had precipitated upon us the most unexpected and the severest trial which fell to our lot during the year. . . . It was indeed a calamity."[47] The Executives now could not disband. Events they could not control propelled them onward.

11
Unintended Consequences

Throughout California, reactions to Terry's capture exploded. Reported an observer, "All over the State, the feeling for Judge Terry was very strong.... Harm to him would have ... extended into the interior, and raged there in bloodshed and devastation."[1] That night, Hugh Breen wrote in his diary:

> I think this is a death blow to the Governor[']s forces but I suppose if this man dies from his wound there will be another excitement. Where it will end tis rather a hard matter to determine but I hope twill soon be all over. Business this afternoon was completely suspended. All the stores was closed. Two thirds of the people was out either bearing arms or lookers on—no work nor sign of any. Truly we have fallen on evil times.[2]

The Executives began damage control, sending two colleagues "to telegraph throughout the state a true statement of ... [what] occurred this day."[3] Newspapers snapped up the cable. The anti-vigilante *Herald* reminded readers that Terry had actively prevented "an act of forcible abduction and kidnapping of a free citizen [Molony]." Recalling the vigilantes' usual accusations of election fraud against their captives, the article continued, "Judge Terry had no sin to answer for in the way of ballot-box stuffing.... [I]f frauds were committed in this city at the last election, they were committed against him."[4] In contrast, a pro-vigilante editor emphasized the quick muster of the vigilantes' troops and burnished Hopkins's reputation as an everyman who "had fallen a martyr to the cause [for] which they [the vigilantes] all had pledged their lives, their property and sacred honors."[5]

What had happened to Sterling Hopkins? Right after the stabbing, Dr. R. Beverly Cole had rushed to the Pennsylvania Engine Company and found Hopkins "sitting on a chair, bleeding profusely from the wound, and also from the mouth and nose." Suddenly, Hopkins fainted. The vigilante surgeon laid him on the floor and administered a stimulant, bringing the patient back to consciousness but restarting his bleeding. Cole pressed his bare hand over the wound, while other physicians, recently arrived, urged him to operate. One of them kept a finger on Hopkins's pulse while Cole took out the only instruments he had, basic equipment he carried in a pocket case. By now it was evening, and the light was failing. Cole gingerly eased his unwashed fingers into the four-inch gash in Hopkins's neck and felt his way as he drew a string-like ligature around the artery, trying to avoid catching the major nerve as well, which would have killed the patient. Suddenly, Hopkins's pulse stopped. The other doctors gave him more drugs as Cole tied off the surgical thread. Hopkins's heart started beating; the bleeding stopped. Hopkins was still alive, for now.[6] Reporting later to the Executives, Cole pinpointed the "critical period . . . from three days hence until the twelfth day. Hopkins' situation now is precarious," he emphasized.[7] Executive Smiley hired a nurse to tend Hopkins. All the food and water she gave him dribbled out through the cut in his neck.[8]

State officials also reacted. Quartermaster General William Kibbe, officially responsible for state arms, immediately sought a writ of habeas corpus from a Stockton judge, in the faint hope of bringing Terry under the official legal system.[9] Kibbe also asked Governor Johnson to raise, if possible, up to $100,000 "in cash on the credit of the State. . . . [Then] we shall find little trouble in raising the men" to oppose the vigilantes.[10] The money proved impossible to get. Kibbe wrote to the Vigilance Committee detailing the arms stolen. "Believing that no act of this nature could be sanctioned by any order of your committee," he disingenuously added, he requested an investigation into the robbery and the immediate return of all "arms & accoutrements."[11] Kibbe went to Fort Gunnybags in person to secure the weapons. One of the division colonels showed him the state arms, "very nicely arranged at our rooms in Sacramento St. Those that were in constant use, quite a large quantity, were nicely put up in racks. . . . All the arms in the hands of the military companies at that time belonged to the state." Kibbe spotted the six-pound cannons of the California Guard, and "said he would give us credit for one thing . . . that we kept them in splendid condition." The vigilantes promised to return the weapons when they were no longer needed, which would not be any time soon.[12]

Public pressure on the Executives intensified. Lacking weapons, Law and Order adherents attacked with the law, securing a federal indictment against vigilante

John Durkee and others for piracy for the attack on the *Julia*. Convicted pirates were hanged.

Durkee's indictment created new chaos. When the news arrived at Fort Gunnybags, an angry vigilante struck the Monumental bell on the roof. Armed Committee members rushed to the streets, wondering whom to attack. Immediately, the Executives ordered commanders to quiet the troops and "prevent their attempting the rescue of John Durkee now in charge of the U.S. Marshal."[13] Although contemptuous of state officials, the Executives wanted to avoid conflict with federal authorities at all costs.

Federal authorities were indeed concerned, especially native Virginian Captain Edward B. Boutwell of the U.S. Navy's sloop-of-war *John Adams*. The thirty-year career naval officer sent the Executives a note "desiring to know how long Dr. Ashe [the U.S. naval agent] would be retained by the Committee."[14] Boutwell strongly disapproved of the vigilantes. He had already joined San Francisco's social circle on the dinner invitation of Ellen Ewing Sherman, the wife of banker William Tecumseh Sherman, renewing a friendship begun years earlier in Washington, D.C. Those present no doubt commiserated about the treatment the vigilantes dealt to Roman Catholics, a religion Boutwell shared with Mrs. Sherman (as well as Casey, Cora, Sullivan, Broderick, and most of the vigilantes' deportees to date).[15]

The Executive Committee, fearful of federal intervention, noted that "the arrest of Ashe would involve us in a difficulty with the U. S. Government." Thus, they felt great relief when the naval agent offered to go on parole. Ashe promised "as a man of honor ... [to be] neutral in word and action." The Executives first required his sworn affidavit describing the Terry-Hopkins clash to compare with later oral testimony, allowing a lieutenant from Boutwell's sloop to be present during his deposition. Then vigilantes escorted Ashe beyond Committee lines and, at his request, all the way home.[16] As a later historian noted, "if Ashe had known what trouble his presence caused, he would not have acted as he did." His parole, and the silence it commanded, solved two problems for the Executives.[17]

The Executives also faced criticism for imprisoning some six dozen other Law and Order partisans who had clearly committed no crime. Unexpectedly, a "large and eminently respectable body of citizens" arrived at Fort Gunnybags, requesting the release of the captive militia. Somewhat embarrassed, the Executives agreed to release the bulk of them later that day, retaining only "those against whom there were specific and serious charges for crimes."[18]

Keeping the militia captive posed a host of problems for the Executives. To forestall any attack on Fort Gunnybags, they suggested to the visiting committee "in as delicate a manner as possible ... [that the citizens be] vigilant in guarding against fire." From inside his own vigilante cell, Colonel West asked to see his command. He was refused.[19] Given the perceptible public hostility toward their holding so many respectable citizens, the Executives delegated guard duty to French vigilantes, who could not understand English and thus could not be influenced to free the captives. But this choice posed other problems. Why were foreigners imprisoning American citizens in a major American city? Later, Executive Smiley recalled, "The Bloody Reds and Communes [the French] were for hanging and quartering [the captives]; some proposed lashing, others to keep them on bread and water for thirty days." Other vigilantes suggested that the prisoners should "run the gauntlet, and be paraded through the town."[20] Instead, Smiley ordered the militia's handcuffs removed and sent all but seven out of the fort through a double line of some two thousand jeering vigilantes.[21]

The *Bulletin* made political hay of this situation. It published a sneering anonymous letter taunting the conspicuously absent would-be senator David Broderick, concluding, "David, most of the leaders . . . of your party are gone, [and] those that are left looked wofully [sic] chop-fallen as they marched single file from the Committee rooms on Sunday last. With them your occupation and your political aspirations are gone forever."[22]

Inside the vigilantes' fort, Terry became the center of attention. The Executives decided to try the judge under the same rules they had used for Casey and Cora, allowing witnesses for the defense to be heard as well as those for the prosecution, a courtesy previously extended to no one else. They also agreed that "no vote of the Executive Committee inflicting the death penalty shall be binding unless passed by two thirds of those present, provided that the trial jury shall not be composed of less than twenty six members or two thirds of this body." Members of the Committee on Evidence therefore entered Terry's cell and asked him for a list of defense witnesses.[23] The Executives also allowed Terry to receive two important colleagues from San Francisco's legal community. However, three Executives accompanied them into his cell to monitor their conversation. Immediately thereafter, the Executives forged a bill of indictment against Terry, charging him with resisting arrest by the officers of the Vigilance Committee; "committing an assault with a deadly weapon with the intent to kill Sterling A. Hopkins a police officer of the Committee of Vigilance"; carrying out assorted "attacks on [four] citizens when in discharge of their duties"; and defrauding some former clients, the "infant heirs of the Sanchez family." They also decided to allow "Mrs. Terry . . . to see her husband at any hour she may demand admittance."[24]

Cornelia Runnels Terry came that night, putting the Executives at a distinct disadvantage. Despite their fortified warehouse, stacks of arms, and six-thousand-man militia, the vigilante leaders had no idea how to combat a respectable woman. In fact, many of them admired her. One called her a "lion-hearted lady . . . [who] buoyed him [David Terry] up."[25] By contrast, Cornelia Terry, an elite southern beauty, had long known how to deal with men. In fact, it was her feminine imperiousness that had originally driven David Smith Terry to California.

David Terry and Cornelia Runnels had grown up in the same southern society. Although not blood relations, they had been raised as cousins, since her uncle's wife was his aunt.[26] But David was a rugged frontier fighter, Cornelia a true southern aristocrat. Her grandfather had been the governor of Mississippi; her uncle was soon to be the governor of Texas (and the only man ever to defeat Sam Houston for office).[27] David, on the other hand, had led a rougher life. Born in Kentucky on March 8, 1823, he had moved with his family to Mississippi, where his parents divorced when his father opened a saloon. His devoutly Christian mother took her four sons to Texas (then part of Mexico) to be near her own mother. When Terry was thirteen, his mother died, and he escaped the control of her strict elder brother by joining the fight for a Republic of Texas. His formal education therefore ended at age twelve.[28] At age eighteen, when his guardian uncle died, Terry helped his recently married older brother Frank tend the two younger boys and manage the two-thousand-acre family plantation along the Brazos River, worked by eighteen slaves. A couple of years later, Terry left the plantation, read law, and at age twenty-two was admitted to the Galveston bar, taking an oath to uphold the U.S. Constitution and the constitution of the new state of Texas. When war broke out between the U.S. and Mexico, he joined his best friend, Dr. Richard Porter Ashe, as a private in renowned Colonel John Coffee Hays's First Regiment of Texas Mounted Riflemen. When their company marched deep into Mexico, Terry "particularly distinguished himself at the storming of Monterey, being among the foremost in the brilliant attack made upon the Bishop's Palace and Independence Hill," another participant later recalled. A gangly six-foot-three, with thick, sandy hair, Terry must have been an imposing figure charging through the smoke and dust over the palace walls. When the war ended, Terry went back to Houston to practice law and grew closer than ever to the dark-haired, dark-eyed teenager Cornelia Runnels.[29] His courtship abruptly ended when, in 1849, nineteen-year-old Cornelia spurned his proposal of marriage.

Like so many men escaping woes at home, Terry headed for California. With only two days of preparation, he joined his older brother Frank, who had already planned to go. As the party rode out of town, David stopped at Cornelia's home, intending "to request as a last favor that you would write to me occasionally," he later confessed. But "the fear of a refusal . . . and the presence of others" left his request unspoken.[30] The Terry brothers joined a company of 120 others pioneering the Gila River route to California that April—David not caring where they went as long as he could leave the place "in which I had lived whilst indulging dreams from which the waking was so terribly bitter."[31] The company reached California safely. David had intended to write to Cornelia in hopes of a reply, but letters from home informed him that she "had spoken unkindly & disparagingly of me after my departure."[32] He kept his peace. For a short time the Terry brothers tried mining, then Frank returned to his family and ranch in Texas.[33] Shortly thereafter, David heard a rumor that Cornelia was engaged. Hope died.

For two and a half difficult years, Terry diligently built his legal practice, keeping to himself or visiting with a few other southerners. Unlike most other young men, he avoided saloons, gambling dens, and bawdy houses. Then, in October 1851, he opened a letter from an old Texas friend and found a note from Cornelia enclosed. Not knowing what to think, he replied, "It is my wish that we shall meet as friends if we ever meet again and if there is anything in our past . . . which would be unpleasant to either that it may be forgotten."[34]

Their correspondence blossomed. A month later, upon arriving home after a fifty-mile journey to attend court, Terry found another unexpected letter from Cornelia. He sat down to answer it at once, spurred "by the fact that I was entirely unprepared for its receipt or the expression of the sentiment it contained." After hearing of her engagement, he explained, "I presumed, of course, that I was forgotten . . . by one whom I had loved with all the devotedness of which my nature was capable." In her letter, Cornelia had asked, "Have you proved the truth of the assertion you once made me, [that] time & distance would not effect [sic] your love for me?"

David wasn't sure how to respond. "It is said that love however devoted cannot exist without hope. For more than two years and a half I have striven to entirely eradicate from my mind all thoughts of love for you because I felt assured the feeling was utterly hopeless. . . . But why this question? Though you once confessed that I was dearer to you than any other, yet you said that you feared the sentiment you felt for me was not love. . . . You [now] wish me to write you that I forgive and will love you as I once did. If you desire my forgiveness most readily and fully I grant it. For my love, I have ever loved you Cornelia." After five long pages, David turned to news of himself. "I have a large practice & enjoy the confidence of the public . . .—but for the feeling of loneliness which often comes over me and a frequent yearning for the society of the loved ones at home, I could be contented to live in California." In closing, he made the request he had wanted to voice almost three years earlier: "That you will continue to write me until the period of my con[templated] visit to

Like many Californians, the Terrys strove to maintain family connections through photographs. Here, Cornelia Runnels Terry holds their baby for the camera, possibly their third son, David, born in January 1856. *Courtesy of the Haggin Museum, Stockton, Calif.*

Texas and that when we meet I will find you cherishing for me those sentiments of affection the expression of which has caused me so much happiness? Good bye my Dear Cousin. Believe me—Ever yours, David S. Terry."[35]

Cornelia responded, and they began to exchange regular letters. Some five months later, she voiced concerns that David's brother Frank and their local friends were opposed to her. David soothed her: "My brother . . . is well aware that I always rebelled against any appearance of controll [sic] or dictation . . . he will not seriously seek to thwart me in so important a pursuit."[36] Two weeks later, without waiting for her next letter, David formally proposed. "As to the opinions . . . of my want of pride & independence," he added, "[i]f you approve, . . . believe me, I will care little for the opinions of others. . . . [I] esteemed you for your frankness and sincerity, your independence of character and perfect freedom from affectation or dissembling before I learned to love you." Although friends then visiting in California had reported that Cornelia was "somewhat changed from what I knew but . . . much improved," he concluded, "I would not have you changed."[37]

This time, Cornelia accepted his proposal. In the fall of 1852 Terry returned to Texas, and on November 25, Cornelia Runnels married David Smith Terry. After a trip to visit family throughout the South, Terry took his bride to California. Late in 1853, Cornelia's cousin reminisced about the wedding in a letter from home, asking "about the boy—he will soon be two months old. . . . Does he favor you or cousin Dave?"[38] The following May, however, a distraught little group gathered around a tiny grave, the first in the Terry family plot in Stockton, California. The tombstone reads: "Frank D. Terry, May 6, 1854, in his first year."[39]

Cornelia delivered a second son, Samuel L. Terry, in February 1855, and a third, named after his father, in January 1856. But by melancholy southern tradition, a baby was not counted a full member of the family until he had survived his first year. Cornelia had turned twenty-seven the day that Casey and Cora were hanged.[40] She knew that her husband's life might also be over.

Even in captivity, David Terry maintained his role in his family and society. He had the support of a distinguished group of lawyers and judges, who appealed to the Executives on his behalf, wishing to speak to him on items "strictly of a business character."[41] The Executives probed them for the possibility of future clemency from the governor should they disband. The attorneys were in no position to say. After two days of debate, the Executives finally agreed that "in no case shall the said Terry be surrendered."[42] They further denied the men future entrance.

When the Executives cut off his visits from local members of the legal community, even withholding a letter to him "until a statement of the circumstance of the stabbing of Mr. Hopkins be received," Terry sat down and wrote his own letter to the Executives.[43] He explained that he wished a lawyer's help in handling his family's financial affairs, to "settle with all creditors and ensure to them a modest competency" in case he was sentenced to death. He also wanted the "opportunity of vindicating my fair name which is dearer far than life." Therefore, he requested a public jury trial, offering not to apply "for a change of venue or for Bail and [I] will object to no person [on the jury] because he is a member of your body." Finally, should Hopkins die, Terry agreed to resign his elected position on the state supreme court and "if acquitted [in the jury trial] will at once leave the State should you require it." His motivation, he stressed, was that "I do not wish to leave my family dependent on the charity of others[.] For myself I have sufficient fortitude to endure without flinching any fate which providence may have in store for me." If, however, the Executives refused, Terry needed at least two more days to procure "witnesses—as well as the most respectable gentlemen of Stockton from all sections of the Union to refute the aspersions upon my character."[44] As citizens were increasingly aware, the southern judge had fallen into the hands of a northern-heavy vigilance committee.

The Executives flatly refused Terry's request for a public trial and sent Executive Clancey Dempster to tell him so. Thus, Dempster was in Terry's cell and could prevent conversation when a deputy U.S. marshal wandered in with a writ of habeas corpus for J. R. Molony. Molony, meanwhile, had been spirited out of the building.[45] Nonetheless, the marshal "went about in a careless way asking no questions, traveling all over our buildings. There were several of them connected by doors and stairways," remembered a vigilante. "I do not think he expected to find his man, and did not appear as if he was disappointed."[46] In fact, the deputy had just obtained firsthand knowledge of the intricacies of the vigilantes' stronghold.

Agreeing to one part of Terry's proposal, the Executives interviewed a stream of defense witnesses arriving at Fort Gunnybags. Quartermaster Kibbe debriefed them afterward, and was able to write the governor that "[t]he affidavits go to prove that Judge Terry acted purely in self defense." But "the masses outside are clamorous for blood. The question is, if Terry is acquitted of murder, can the Vigilance forces be controlled if Hopkins dies? If he is acquitted the Ex[ecutive] committee fear danger; if he is hung danger to them is certain. This committee would give their fortunes to be extricated from their present difficulties."[47]

Support for vigilantism had definitely dwindled. Two days after Terry's arrest, for the first time, the Executives' cash on hand dropped to only half of the amount of the audited bills unpaid, $872.30 and $1,662.37, respectively. Treasurer James Dows promptly moved that "an order be drawn on the Treasurer of Citizens Committee for $5000."[48] These well-heeled men, including banker William Ralston and merchant Thomas O. Larkin, financially supported the Vigilance Committee but avoided public identification with it. This time, Dows secured only $1,000.[49] In a local barroom, a vigilante revealed the day's secret password, claiming that he was a vigilante in good standing but felt that "the VC should not hang Judge Terry." If they did, "more than one half of the members of the V.C. would revolt and take up arms in his favor."[50] Quartermaster Kibbe received a practical suggestion from the state militia commander in the Mother Lode, who also noted dwindling support for the vigilantes. Observing that the Committee was headed by "merchants, traders and clerks," he advised that "the almighty dollar must be affected. Shut up trade and you break up the Insurgents."[51] However, his practical suggestion to blockade the port of San Francisco was impossible to achieve. Even the Executives' enthusiasm for vigilantism faltered. On June 26, only twenty-three Executives—too few for a quorum—appeared for their meeting. They tabled the idea of hiring a stenographer for the Terry trial when the cost was estimated at from $250 to $1,000.[52]

In the meantime, Cornelia Terry had been allowed to spend as much time as she pleased with her husband.[53] She was present when a Committee of Citizens arrived to persuade Terry to resign from the bench in return for his freedom. The Executives offered the group this final proposal: first, Terry and Chief Justice Hugh Murray must resign and leave the state, their places to be "filled by such parties as shall be satisfactory to the people" (meaning the vigilante Executives). Second, all of San Francisco's county officers must vacate their official positions. Third, "all the prisoners in our possession and such characters in this county as we desire ... [must be] compelled to leave, never to return." Finally, the Executives must be allowed to execute any returning exiles. The Committee of Citizens flatly rejected these stipulations.[54] Cornelia heard these proposals. As a vigilante later reported, while "the Executive Committee were endeavoring to induce him [Terry] to resign, ... Mrs. Terry raised her voice and said, 'Judge Terry, I would rather see you hanged from one of those windows than to recognize that you were compelled to resign your official position.'"[55] And that was that.

12
Mounting Opposition

Stuck with Terry, the Executives now had to look to their own security as well as the security of their newest prisoner. Borrowing the horse-drawn fire engine from the Monumental Engine Company, vigilantes thoroughly soaked the sandbags surrounding their fort to prevent the sand from leaking. Within days, they extended this fortification farther down Sacramento Street and added a row to the top of the old wall.[1] The Executives detailed "not less than 75 men" to stand guard at various points leading to their rooms.[2] Heeding a rumor that Law and Order stalwarts had "arranged to take the prisoners on a certain night," they mandated a "strong guard, two or three thousand men."[3] The Executives extracted Terry's promise "not to communicate by shout or otherwise his whereabouts." At his captors' urging, Terry also wrote a letter for publication "desiring that no writ of habeas corpus be issued" on his behalf, or it would, as he put it, "prejudice his comfort and safety."[4] A vigilante policeman took up residence in Terry's cell. Cornelia was no longer admitted, and could communicate with her husband only in writing. Terry was then removed to a smaller cell over the office of the sergeant at arms.[5]

Everything depended on the fate of Terry's victim. Although Hopkins's condition was "extremely grave," the Executives even arranged to take his deposition at his bedside.[6] As Hugh Breen summarized in his diary on June 27,

> Hopkins is still in a critical situation [and] if he dies I would not be at all astonished at having a brush of some kind here. Terry has a great number of friends and they will move Heaven and earth for Judge Terry's acquittal. Then on the other hand he is an American and the foreign population will say you hung Casey because he was

an Irishman and a Catholic also Cora because he was an Italian and also a Roman Catholic but Judge D. S. Terry is an American and a Protestant and they [sic] may be a split on that peculiar point—but I hope for Judge Terry, the people at large, and the Family of Hopkins that he may recover.[7]

Unknown to outsiders, that day, in secret, the Executives had begun Terry's trial.[8] They could wait no longer. The *Minutes* report that on Friday morning, June 27, "Prisoner David S. Terry [was] brought before the Executive Committee at 15 minutes of 11 o'clock and placed on trial for the murder or attempted murder of ____ Hopkins."[9] Executive Farwell vividly remembered the moment. "When Terry was brought in by our Sergeant at Arms to the Executives' room for the first time, to stand in his trial, we were all sitting round in a semi-circle, and all eyes of course were turned upon the prisoner. He was the only person who ever came before us who did not break down."[10] The prosecutor, Executive T. J. L. Smiley, read the charges. Terry refused to plead either guilty or not guilty "until he was assured that there was no outside pressure bearing upon this Committee," then "pled not guilty of any offense whatever."[11]

The vigilante version of a trial began. Terry, forbidden to hear testimony, was returned to his cell. In his absence, prosecution witnesses began testifying as an expensive stenographer took down every word.[12] One described a confused scuffle between Terry's best friend, Richard Porter Ashe, and vigilante James Bovee. "Ashe put his gun cocked to Bovee's breast. Ashe asked Bovee if he was a friend. Bovee said yes, and knocked the gun on one side, drew his revolver, and put it at Ashe's ear. Ashe turned very pale, and said, 'Don't shoot.'" Another vigilante continued the tale. "Bovee had hold of the gun, the shot-gun that was in the hands of Dr. Ashe. I saw a pistol sticking out of the holster of Dr. Ashe, and I took hold of it with my left hand and pulled it out." He loosed his own pistol "for the purpose of striking Dr. Ashe across the arm, if he wouldn't let go of the gun. At this time, John Nugent, a police officer [not the *Herald* editor of the same name], jumped in and caught hold of the gun also; at the same time he struck my elbow that held my pistol, and caused the pistol to discharge." Vigilante Bovee himself explained further. As the vigilantes closed in on the fleeing Law and Order group, the two men at the rear, Ashe and Terry, presented their guns. "They turned round, and as Hopkins attempted to rush past, Terry's gun was presented at him. Hopkins then took hold of the barrel of Terry's gun." Joseph Capprise seized the breech. Bovee continued, "I let go of my pistol in my pocket, and brought the gun in my left hand up to my shoulder ready to fire, and pointed it in the direction of Terry, when John Nugent rushed up and said, 'For God's sake, don't fire, Bovee.' ... With that, as Nugent caught hold of the gun, I looked and saw the knife go down."[13]

With the trial begun, the Executives decided to readmit Cornelia Terry. Her husband met with a colleague who later escorted her into his presence.[14] That evening, when they left, Cornelia secreted a letter from Terry to Commander Boutwell of the sloop-of-war *John Adams*. In it, the judge described the events that had led to his imprisonment, the previous illegal activities of the vigilantes, and his ignominious treatment. "I have suffered the indignity of being *handcuffed* by the rebels, my friends are denied all access to me, and all kinds of terrorism are resorted to compel me to resign my office," he wrote. He therefore invoked "the protection of the *flag of my country*" and asked Boutwell for help.[15]

Simultaneously, Governor Johnson wrote to Commander Boutwell seeking armed protection for Terry.[16] Realistically, the only guns not in vigilante hands were floating on the ships in the harbor. Given Boutwell's known anti-vigilante attitude, the guns of the *John Adams* constituted a threat. Boutwell, while sympathetic to the governor's view, responded that unsuccessfully demanding Terry's release would compel him to "batter the town down or render myself ridiculous in the eyes of the world." All he could offer was, "If Hopkins dies and the Committee condemn Judge Terry to death I will make an effort to save Judge Terry's life in such a manner as not to be offensive to my fellow Citizens."[17]

Boutwell's armed proximity deeply concerned the Executives. Five days before Terry's arrest, Boutwell had cruised in from Mare Island to anchor off North Beach at Farragut's command. There he remained.[18] To improve their own safety, the Executives decided to have five of their number spend every night in their chambers, starting immediately. Anyone who shirked this duty would "be considered guilty of gross neglect and subject to such punishment as may be awarded hereafter." They immediately put their personal guns in order and commanded their Military Committee to "buy a portcullis drawbridge." They even shelved plans for marching out en masse to celebrate the Fourth of July, which would leave their fort undefended.[19]

Others recognized the importance of navy clout. Former U.S. senator from California William Gwin attempted mediation, inviting senior naval officer Captain David Glasgow Farragut and two others from the Law and Order Party to meet in secret with four Executives in an upper room at the Customhouse, a southern stronghold. They discussed removing Terry from San Francisco for six months, a proposal Terry had already suggested. Executive James Dows, attending, announced in his nasal voice that the Executives had been considering this proposition, but had to see whether Hopkins would live or die. "[B]ecause of the intense feeling against Terry among the larger proportion of the Committee troops," stronger measures might be necessary, he intimated. Speaking much more directly, young Executive James D. Farwell, a former sea captain himself, haughtily announced that the vigilantes recognized no authority higher than themselves. "'We have,' he continued, '. . . proved ourselves the superiors of the City and County government, and of the State government; and if the Federal government dares'—He got no further. Commodore Farragut sprang to his feet, his eyes flashing fire. . . . 'Stop, sir!' he thundered." Stunned, Farwell sunk into his seat. The fifty-five-year-old Farragut—later America's first admiral—delivered a forceful five-minute lecture to the Executives on the patriotic duties of American citizens. With that, the meeting dissolved.[20]

After this aborted meeting, Farwell, the head of the vigilantes' Marine Committee, developed an attack strategy. He later recalled that he had planned "to take two tug boats, and place them alongside of an old hulk of a vessel that was lying there [in the harbor], and put a couple of sharpshooters into the hulk." When Boutwell began shelling San Francisco, vigilantes would lay the hulk "alongside of his ship, opening fire upon him as soon as we could get within range."[21] The Deputy Grand Marshal got directions to take charge of "a boarding party, get on board with the [vigilante] riflemen, and prevent the [navy] men from working the guns, to take the frigate, seize the guns, and have the riflemen shoot down the men who attempted to work the guns, if necessary." In addition to deploying these commandos, the Executives planned to launch "some combustibles . . . attached with chains, to bring round with the tide and consume the frigate." A steamer had already been secured "to take the riflemen on board."[22] Farwell was determined to "blow her [the *John Adams*] up, feeling she would be forever after a disgrace to the Navy, if she fired upon a defenseless town."[23] This dangerous vigilante assault, claimed another Executive, appealed to "a great many Frenchmen . . . [who] wanted to take the ship. They had it all arranged . . . had the barges and lighters all ready to throw one or two thousand men on the ship. We had so many [Frenchmen] we could afford to have as many killed as they [could in order to] . . . take the ship."[24] In addition, according to Executive Charles V. Gillespie, Farwell "made plans to capture the commander [Boutwell]," and "went to the Navy Yard, in charge of Farragut, and brought him [Farragut] down here" to meet with vigilantes in San Francisco.[25] The vigilantes also gave Farragut a duplicate of Boutwell's letter to the governor regarding Terry, a letter they had stolen from the U.S. mails, copied, and then reposted.[26] "I never told him what our preparations were in regard to the sloop of war," Farwell concluded, but told him "our operations were local, and we should do our best to fight shy of coming in contact with the federal or state authorities."[27] However, if they had to take on the local members of the United States Navy, the vigilantes, both American and French, were ready.

Right after he parted from the Executives, the justly concerned Farragut wrote several letters. He reported to Secretary of the Navy James C. Dobbin, a young southerner thirteen years his junior, describing the Committee's activities to date and assuring his superior that he had refused Governor Johnson's request to interfere. Captain Boutwell, he added somewhat disingenuously, had also "declined all interference in the matter."[28] Despite this assertion, the next day Farragut wrote to Boutwell, revealing that the Executives had shared Boutwell's note and stating, "I cannot agree that you have any right to interfere in the matter." Farragut cautioned Boutwell to wait "until we receive instructions from the Government."[29] Increasingly, San Franciscans wondered, when would word come?

This frightening uncertainty prompted the vigilantes to clean house. Executive attendance dwindled from more than thirty the day that Terry's trial began to only seventeen two days later.[30] Shortly thereafter, one often-absent Executive received an "invitation" to resign; those remaining had to round up "absent members" to get a quorum for their meeting of July 1.[31] The 3rd Division captain, whom the Executives had refused to release on June 14, was now reported as disloyal, possibly even a spy for the Law and Order forces. "I don't know whether he is a Mason or not, it may be so & I hear daily that more or less of the Masons & their fraternity are arrayed against the Committee on the Terry case, and are moving to release him," wrote a vigilante.[32] After secret testimony, the captain was expelled from the Committee.[33] Within days, an estimated 165 other suspected disloyal vigilantes were denied the password and ejected.[34]

Even David O. Shattuck, the Superior Court judge who had supported the Vigilance Committee at the June 11 mass meeting, now reversed his stance. When the Executives spurned Shattuck's personal letter appealing for Terry's release, the judge posted a public broadside throughout the city and saw it published in the *Herald*. Shattuck reasoned that neither Terry nor Hopkins was a criminal; they simply served different masters: "Terry was obeying the law of the State, and Hopkins the law of the Vigilance Committee." Furthermore, since the governor's insurrection proclamation had created a legal state of war in San Francisco, Hopkins was a fallen warrior, and Terry a prisoner of war. Terry's situation paralleled that of vigilante John Durkee, who, when he took government arms from the *Julia*, was not really a pirate. Shattuck extolled the Committee's "brilliant exploit" in capturing the state arms and militia, which, he claimed, did not really constitute robbery and kidnapping. People should consider the times, he wrote, and should

News traveled fast around San Francisco, in part through the use of established bulletin boards like this one to the left of the entrance to Broderick's Empire Engine House No. 1, with the eagle of the Union grandly displayed on top. *Courtesy of the California Historical Society.*

realize "that those opposed to us [the anti-vigilantes] may be governed by motives as pure as our own"—a position the Executives could never accept.[35]

Shattuck's published broadside helped Commander Boutwell respond to Terry's smuggled letter.[36] Boutwell wrote to the Executives, "If you occupy the position assigned to you by Judge Shattuck . . . [I] request that you will deal with Judge Terry as a prisoner of War and place him on board my ship." On the other hand, if the Executives considered themselves "a party of Citizens," he urged them to follow "the Constitution . . . [and] surrender Judge Terry to the lawful authorities of the State."[37] The Executives authorized a noncommittal, "courteous reply."[38]

Shattuck was also one of the few who paid attention to Durkee. The accused pirate had appeared before the U.S. Circuit Court for Northern California on June 28 for a bail hearing. Judge Ogden Hoffman sat alone, since his newly appointed colleague, Judge Matthew Hall McAllister, was still in transit from the eastern states. Hoffman reviewed the facts of the arms seized from the *Julia* and then heard one of Durkee's attorneys insist that his client had acted only as "the servant of a large and respectable body of men, who, though they might be political offenders, were not criminals." The prosecuting attorney disagreed, calling Durkee and his colleagues pirates in every sense of the word: "the arms had been taken by force; the invaders were armed to the teeth, and displayed their weapons." Although state courts could apply only light punishment for such activity, "before the United States Court, the punishment provided was death." After noting that the vigilantes "had trampled upon the authority of the Government," Hoffman set Durkee's bail at $25,000. Four vigilante leaders promptly paid, and Durkee was discharged, pending the convening of the trial court some two months hence.[39]

While this legalistic parrying continued, San Francisco was treated to "a great Newspaper War," in the words of diarist Denis Oliver.[40] The *Bulletin* headed the anti-Terry campaign, first painting Hopkins as "a true-hearted, courageous patriot . . . [motivated by] the righteousness of the cause." Terry, by contrast, was libeled as "by nature, a street-brawler, and a rowdy . . . [who] excited the passions and appetites of bad men simply to gratify a morbid taste for riot and bloodshed."[41] In contrast, the anti-vigilante *Herald* published a signed card by popular John Coffee Hays, now the federal surveyor, who joined a colleague in describing Terry as they had known him from boyhood: "a good citizen, of *peaceable* demeanor, and also as a young man peculiarly exempt from the too common vices of gaming and drinking."[42]

Terry's sympathizers took practical steps, as well. Some decided to open a saloon next door to Fort Gunnybags.[43] There, a Law and Order man was reportedly hidden for "some weeks, during Terry's trial, . . . armed with a rifle," later recalled a vigilante. If "Terry was hung, he was going to cut the rope with his rifle ball and let him drop."[44] Others exerted their personal influence. As prosecutor Smiley later complained, "[T]here was every kind of pressure, Masonic, social, political and legal, brought to bear on his behalf."[45] Executive Farwell later complained, "The women were the fiercest in this town."[46] "The wives of members of the Ex[ecutive] Com[mittee] were called upon by ladies, evidently acting in concert, who under cover of a friendly visit would enlarge on the equities of Terry's case," reported Executive Dempster. "Social efforts of every kind were repeatedly made to work in the minds of the Ex. Com. who were his judges. Day after day gentlemen used to come into my office," he added, "as they went to those of others, some of whom were friends, some mere passing acquaintances and even others whom I met for the first time—and either at once began to speak of Terry or by degrees led the conversation to that point. I have never known or heard of a case where a man's friends worked so hard in his behalf." Determined to put a stop to these entreaties,

Dempster told his callers that "should Hopkins die and every other member of the Vig. Com. fail to do justice, I would myself inflict upon Judge Terry the penalty wh[ich] I considered to be his due" even if this moment "would also be my last. After that I was troubled no more."[47]

Law and Order correspondence suggested other remedies. Quartermaster Kibbe wrote to Governor Johnson inquiring about the governor's willingness to pardon the vigilantes—a possible inducement to get them to release Terry.[48] Kibbe's letter crossed one from Johnson, commanding Kibbe to dismiss the now unarmed state forces, and urging his quartermaster to communicate exclusively by mail, as the telegraph and the local express company were "unreliable."[49] (In fact, so was the mail.) Simultaneously, Colonel Joseph R. West, head of the San Francisco Militia, wrote an unprecedented letter to the governor about the probable vigilante response should the Executives themselves pardon Terry. "I believe that a fair proportion of the Committee will uphold the decision of their regularly constituted authorities," he wrote, but others, particularly the foreigners, would stop at nothing short of hanging. Therefore, West offered his own forces to support the Executives—the very people who had ordered him handcuffed and imprisoned—"should they decide that Judge Terry should not be hung." But the governor must "provide the necessary arms," since all the weapons from West's command were still in vigilante hands.[50]

Cornelia Terry also continued fighting for her husband's freedom. She called on Quartermaster Kibbe and was "very firm in the position which the Judge & herself have taken i.e. that the Judge shall never disgrace himself by any compromise with the committee; that he shall hang first," Kibbe soon informed Governor Johnson. "She is certainly a woman of a thousand. She says they will not hurt him. She is cool, calculating and has every means of information, and thinks they will liberate the Judge." Kibbe added, "Mrs. Terry was denied admission to the Committee Rooms this morning and . . . while in the carriage some 8 or 10 of the Executive[s] came to see her and urged her to induce him [Terry] to resign. Whereupon she told them emphatically that she would not, and to do their worst with him."[51]

Cornelia Terry had indeed faced the Executives in person. As she later reported to the papers, "Up to last Saturday morning [June 28] I had been allowed to visit my husband at intervals in his confinement. Since then I have been refused admittance." She had tried to gain access to him a day later, with no success. "I then begged that my husband might be allowed to write to me, and inform me of his welfare," she wrote. She went down on Monday and again on Tuesday, always refused admittance. On the second attempt, she sent the Executives a letter: "His private interests are already suffering for want of attention, and as I do not ask a private interview, but that I may see him if you require it in the presence of the whole Committee. Hoping that this reasonable request will not be denied, Yours, &c [etc.], Cornelia Terry."[52] They turned her down. As she told the press, she herself had to choose to "become a close prisoner [in Fort Gunnybags, deserting her children] or else be denied the privilege of seeing her husband."[53] Although the Executives knew that separating a dependent wife from her husband was widely considered a dishonorable act, they would not let her in.

The Committee's public approval sank. In response, the pro-vigilante press stepped up its anti-Terry campaign. In a flurry of anonymous letters, the *Bulletin* published a missive from "A Member of the General Committee" who insisted that the judge had come to San Francisco "with a deadly determination and fiendish malice resolve[d] to murder the Executive[s] of the Committee with his own hand." The writer concluded, "It is, I know, a terrible thought to realize that a Judge must die an untimely death, but justice demands—confidence [of the public in the Executive Committee] requires it; and I now . . . [wonder] whether there is meaning in the glorious motto of the Committee that 'JUSTICE MUST BE DONE THOUGH THE HEAVENS SHOULD FALL.'"[54]

Letters like these—and there were many—deeply shook Cornelia Terry. She privately confided her deepest fears to her mother, then visiting in Stockton from Texas, who replied: "My Dear suffering Child, . . . My opinion is changed with regard to his being in San Francisco. If our Gov'r would not vindicate the Constitution of his State I feel proud to think that your husband" did. She stressed rumors of "a 'mighty' reaction up in the mountains in favor of Law and Order" but agreed that, thanks to vigilante power in San Francisco, "things there are more gloomy." She promised that the day was growing close when the vigilante "rebels will meet with their dues. Don't look at a vigilance Paper. They will only make you uneasy with their lies."[55]

13
Sectional Strife

As both sides struggled for public support, San Francisco learned that the mail steamer *John L. Stephens* was in sight, possibly with federal directives. Thanks to some quick action, however, it did *not* bring Charles Duane. For weeks, the fearless and feisty firefighter had been trying to come back to San Francisco. Deported by the vigilantes in the first cohort on June 5, Duane had jumped ship when the outbound steamer stopped at Acapulco, Mexico. He contracted yellow fever but survived, and almost a month later he boarded the northbound steamer *John L. Stephens* under Captain Robert Pearson, "determined to return to San Francisco at all hazards." Of course, Duane had no money, having been forced out of town in the middle of the night, so he was denied passage. He hid on board, and by the time he was discovered, the steamship was well underway.[1]

Passengers on the *Stephens* included prominent federal judge Matthew Hall McAllister, on his way to take up duty on the U.S. Circuit Court for Northern California alongside Ogden Hoffman to decide Durkee's piracy case. The portly Georgian had previously lived in California with two of his sons and was returning for a second time.[2] On board, the voluble Duane buttonholed McAllister, describing the situation in San Francisco and insisting that he "could not live and hold up his head in any other place," having been deported like a common thief. He intended to "deliver himself up to the Vigilance Committee, to be disposed of as the Committee pleased, but not to be sent out of the country."[3] Moved by Duane's account, McAllister offered to pay the stowaway's fare, which the purser refused to accept—an action that would later have legal ramifications.

Conditions hardened en route. Captain Pearson received the surprising news from another passing ship that the Vigilance Committee had not yet disbanded.

Fearing the consequences if he dropped Duane off in San Francisco, he forced Duane onto the outbound mail steamer at sea three days later. Duane "surrendered without any resistance... [since] Judge McAllister... [had] advised Duane not to leave the ship unless they used force to put him off, and if they did then to go. The old Judge was in high dudgeon, considering that an outrage had been committed on the high seas; for which the officers of the ship and the Company ought to be made responsible and punished. That was all that saved Duane's life," the ship's surgeon asserted, given that he would have returned "at the height of the excitement about Terry."[4] This action had two lasting effects. First, Duane knew that he had a right to sue, and would not forget. Second, his removal also freed the vigilantes from having to hang a widely popular man, or revealing their weakness if they did not. As the *Bulletin* scoffed at the time, there "would probably have been no great disturbance had Duane returned, as the Committee would soon have had him in custody, but a great excitement at least has been prevented" by his forced continuing exile.[5]

On July 1, the *John L. Stephens* docked in San Francisco, a city almost without government thanks to the Consolidation Act. Coming into effect the same day, this law eliminated all city officials in the coterminous city and county. Mayor James Van Ness, author of that problematic land ordinance, was demoted by law to police judge, forced to hear complaints involving the lowest kinds of criminals in the city. Interim county supervisors were appointed until the November 4 election; they would have to select one of their own as interim mayor, but had not yet met. Some former incumbents refused to leave office, insisting that their terms ran until October 1 under earlier provisions. In addition, the new county board of supervisors was forbidden to contract any debt not authorized by the act.[6] Since they had not been elected, they owed nothing to any man; they also consequently lacked supporters.

Of more immediate concern to the Executives was the anticipated action of the federal government. Fortunately for the vigilantes, however, no governmental directives arrived on the *Stephens*. U.S. officials in Washington had instead become preoccupied with the sectional slaughter in Kansas. There, remarked one San Francisco paper, "two classes of our fellow citizens... [are] arrayed against each other in deadly conflict" over attempts to convert Kansas Territory into a slave state to balance the more northerly free state of Nebraska.[7] On May 21, the same day James King of William died in San Francisco, privately organized guard units had attacked Lawrence, Kansas, sacking and burning free-soilers' buildings. In response to this bloodless "Sack of Lawrence," the fanatical John Brown (later famed for his assault at Harper's Ferry) and six followers dragged five pro-slavery men and boys, none of whom actually owned slaves, to the banks of Pottawatomie Creek. They hacked and shot their victims to death, then left their mutilated bodies on the public road. Armed men on both sides retaliated. Killings increased. On the July 1 steamer, San Francisco got its first news of "Bleeding Kansas."[8]

An accompanying article further upset the skittish city. In response to the Kansas bloodshed, Senator Charles Sumner of Massachusetts had delivered a ringing speech, "The Crime against Kansas," in the U.S. Congress. The tall, scholarly, egotistical Sumner described "the rape of a virgin Territory, . . . a depraved longing for a new slave State, the hideous offspring of such a crime." He specifically insulted three fellow senators, including Andrew P. Butler of South Carolina, accusing the aging legislator, who was absent that day, of choosing a "mistress . . . the harlot, Slavery," and of promoting secession.[9] Sumner arrogantly refused to retract his statements when confronted by Representative Preston Brooks, Senator Butler's second cousin. On May 22, the day Casey and Cora were hanged, Brooks strode over from the House to where Sumner was seated at his Senate desk, busily franking copies of his printed speech to mail to his supporters. Brooks began beating Sumner over the head with his heavy cane. Only the intervention of fellow senators prevented the senator's assassination.[10]

San Franciscans immediately reacted to this unsettling national news. One paper called Brooks's attack a "gross and cowardly outrage" and rebuked "the manner in which it is seized by politicians North and South."[11] Another editor wrote that if the Kansas controversy "should result in a dissolution of these United States, freedom will have received a blow from which she cannot recover for centuries."[12] In a country cursed with growing sectionalism, the northern-leaning vigilantes who were holding a staunchly southern judge realized that San Francisco could soon mimic "Bleeding Kansas" and "Bleeding Sumner." Later, this view crystallized as a leading vigilante opined, "There is no doubt in my mind but that [Terry's attack] was the first hostility between the North and the South."[13]

More than ever, Terry became a lightning rod. Despite his so-called "secret" trial, on July 1 the *Herald* published a long biography of Terry, explicitly rebutting the vigilantes' confidential indictments against him.[14] In private, some leading vigilantes still tried to push Terry's removal from the bench as preliminary to their own secession objectives. On July 3, Oscar Shafter, the partner of Trenor Park, legal adviser to the Vigilance Committee, confided in his diary: "The popular outbreak here has taken on the impress of a Revolution. . . . There are many minds here that have cherished the project of an independent 'Pacific Empire,' and they will avail themselves of the present state of things . . . if there is a fair show of success." Shafter mentioned Terry's ongoing trial, then added: "An effort has been made to compromise on terms that he [Terry] should resign and quit the state, and . . . it was proposed that I should be his successor." Shafter promptly refused. "The office is one which I would not accept under any circumstances, least of all would I step into it as a successor of a man who had been driven from it by popular violence, and for no crime but for having forcibly resisted it."[15]

In the city's sectionally tainted atmosphere, the previously circumspect Farragut hardened his stance. He informed the Executives that he agreed with Boutwell in favoring "the release of Judge Terry, in accordance with the Constitution of the United States." He added his view that the Vigilance Committee was completely unconstitutional: "The society is secret, and all its acts are conducted with secrecy." He reminded them that the Constitution mandated that "the United States shall guarantee to each State a republican form of Government," which the vigilantes emphatically were not. Farragut nonetheless planned to proceed peaceably "rather than . . . add to the chances of the horrors of civil war." He also agreed to contact Boutwell, who was still feared by the Executives.[16]

The result was an exchange of notes between the two aging naval officers who stood on opposite sides of the national sectional divide. On July 2, Boutwell responded to Farragut's recent command that he not "augment the very great excitement in this distressed community" by pointing out that Farragut had agreed to serve on a mediating committee between the state authorities and the vigilantes when he had met with Gwin and the Executives at the Customhouse. Was this not a form of involvement? Boutwell continued, "I am a State rights man myself," and therefore opposed to those who "overturn the laws of the State, hang men without trial by jury, and imprison a judge of the Supreme Court." He also relayed that he had been contacted by "the Governor of the State, Judge Terry, the prisoner himself, the Collector of the Port, and the United States Marshal of this district, and appealed to by the distressed wife of the Judge." If he had misread Farragut's instructions, he was "prepared to meet the consequences."[17] Responding, Farragut claimed that his own "willingness to act as a peace-making agent" with the Committee—which action he took, he claimed, as an individual, not as a naval commander—did not constitute interference. "That you are besought by the Government party to blow the town down, I am well aware," he continued, without mentioning Boutwell's copied letter given to him by the Executives. All the more, Farragut urged Boutwell to exercise "unbiased judgment . . . [as the] people on both sides are violent."[18]

Farragut also penned a second letter to the secretary of the navy (a southerner) for the July 5 steamer. Farragut decided to include Boutwell's correspondence, together with a more complete summary of events, in which he noted that after the raid on the Law and Order armories, everyone was released except "our old naval storekeeper Maloney [Molony] and Judge Terry, of the Supreme Court." Given the mounting tensions, "There is very little doubt that the Committee are anxious that Hopkins may live, and that they regret the whole affair," he added. "[U]p to the time of Terry's arrest, the Committee were sanctioned by an overwhelming majority" of local citizens, but now there was "a division in public opinion, and people are beginning to come to their sober senses." Farragut believed that San Franciscans were no longer willing "to be governed by they know not whom."[19]

Farragut's mention of Molony indicated a man more respectable than the vigilantes' tarring brush of "Irish Catholics" would allow. Molony's arrest had also disturbed several elite San Franciscans. On July 2, a group of nine highly respected citizens, including a former appointee to the United States Board of Land Commissioners and Henry B. Truett, brother of Executive Miers Truett and part owner of Fort Gunnybags, wrote a letter to the Executives on behalf of Molony. They testified to Molony's sterling reputation, having known him for "many years when [he was] a resident in the Atlantic States." Due to vigilante secrecy, they had no knowledge of "the particular charges which may have been brought against him," but they considered it unbelievable that "he has by criminal practice forfeited his good name and character and brought disgrace upon his respectable relations upon the other side whose honor and good name are intimately bound up with his." The Molony testimonial concluded, "as a mere matter of justice to one many of us have known from boyhood . . . [this letter should be given] weight and consideration" by the Executives.[20]

For their own reasons, the Executives would not acknowledge Molony's respectability. Although one of the Executives described Molony as an "active and influential man," who had committed no crime against the ballot box or against any other man, he was slated for deportation for unrevealed reasons. Later, Executive James Dows, stating that they "must treat the influential and all others alike," noted that Molony "had been mingled up with that Terry affair and the State arms."[21] The consequences of that "affair" of the state arms would later mature in the piracy trial of vigilante John Durkee in a federal court.

Further complicating matters, Molony's relatives were indeed distinguished. They included a brother, Richard Sheppard Molony, who was elected as an Illinois Democrat to the House of Representatives in the same congressional delegation as the "little giant," Senator Stephen Douglas, Abraham Lincoln's chief opponent. Senator Douglas had recently championed "popular sovereignty" to resolve matters of slave or free in Kansas—a topic that would increasingly come to haunt Californians.[22] Incidents in isolated San Francisco were becoming more and more entangled in national strife.

Giant side-wheel steamers plied the waters on both sides of the Isthmus of Panama, transporting cargo, passengers, and accounts of the turmoil in San Francisco to the East, and bringing reactions back to the City by the Bay, where citizens waited eagerly for the latest news. *Courtesy of the Bancroft Library.*

Given this anxiety-charged atmosphere, July 4 came and went without the usual festivities. The Executives continued meeting throughout the holiday, readying six more deportees for the next day's steamer.[23] Cornelia Terry made sure that news of her husband's captivity would go out in the July 5 steamer mail. In her recent fruitless attempts to enter Fort Gunnybags, she had learned that the Executives, who now allowed her to communicate with David Terry only by letter, were reading their mail. She therefore summoned her feminine weapons, turning to the *Herald* and the *Sun* to publish an exchange of notes between herself and her husband. In her letter, Cornelia repeated that only conviction in a public trial would prompt the judge to resign, reminding readers that as an honorable man, he would never yield "to the violence of the majority of a town" when he had been elected "by a whole State." With true feminine respectability, she ended by imploring forgiveness for anything "unwomanly" in her actions, since "an unheard of proceeding has deprived me of access to my protector and adviser."[24]

SECTIONAL STRIFE

Cornelia included David's response for publication. He reported "taking down the testimony of the witnesses against me," which he found "very conflicting." Knowing that any normal jury would acquit, David acknowledged that he was being tried by men "who are at once my judges and accusers." He denied any malice toward Hopkins, and felt that the Constitution demanded that he protect Molony, even though he was "a bad man." David followed with a brief autobiography, beginning with the Revolutionary War service of both his grandfathers, to indicate that he was as good an American as anybody, not some kind of foreigner. He ended with his election by all Californians to the state supreme court due to his "unblemished reputation for honor and integrity." He closed by urging Cornelia to keep up her spirits, and to thank his friends for "their devotion . . . it is not possible that a bad man should have such friends."[25]

The steamer readied for a pivotal sailing, bringing fresh news of San Francisco to the agitated East. Papers carrying the full texts of both of the Terrys' letters were stuffed into huge canvas mailbags ready for shipment. As the mail steamer's boilers chugged to life, well-armed vigilantes escorted their six latest exiles to the dock in broad daylight, no longer afraid of opposition from the unarmed Law and Order contingent. The new deportees included former Sydney convict Thomas Mulloy, who had served as "Mayor Garrison's Body Guard and right hand man during his Election in 1854—he then obtained a lot of land."[26] Mulloy was shipped out without his "woman," Sophie McInness, the only female ever blacklisted by the Executives. Nine days out of port, he threw himself overboard.[27]

The last forced to board was thirty-two-year-old J. R. Molony, caught in the *Julia* raid. As he boarded, Executives Miers Truett, T. J. L. Smiley, and Charles Case demanded his signature on a document stating that he was "desirous of leaving San Francisco for Panama." Molony was neither desirous nor ready. He had a wife, was given no chance to get either clothing or money, and had several thousand dollars owed to him from his wholesale liquor business and purchased letters of credit, which he had to collect within a stipulated period or forfeit the money. His Executive escort threatened that if he persisted in his refusal, he "would be taken back to the Committee rooms, and after being secreted there awhile, shipped on a sailing vessel to some distant island in the South or North Pacific," the same plan being incubated for Terry and California's chief justice, Hugh Murray.[28] The Executives finally pressured Molony into signing despite the fact that he had never committed a crime. To some San Franciscans, Molony was a "compound character" who favored strong drink and was "'brave'—with his mouth."[29] He was loyal to his friends, as he had demonstrated in captivity when the Executives encouraged him to turn on those "the Committee sought to ruin," particularly Terry and Ashe.

They pointed out that Terry had called Molony "a bad man" in his published letter, calling the judge's words "very unkind, unfair, and even cruel." Molony, whom vigilantes had twice handcuffed and once put in leg irons, had nothing negative to report about the judge and the naval agent. "From that moment on," Molony added, the Executives "never again visited me" until the day before his deportation. "No trial—no charges—no, not even a word of justification of the sentence" until an Executive "intimated to me—cause: Witness v. Durkee."[30]

As the steamer churned away from the dock, the Executives, meeting in secret, took stock of their draining coffers. They owed almost twice as much money as they had on hand: more than $1,400 and $799, respectively. Over the next week, their balance worsened. They instructed their commissary to slash the salaries of police, messengers, armorers, and the marshal's clerk, and "to discharge each person not absolutely necessary on the score of economy."[31] Despite a new $500 donation from "a Committee of Citizens," by July 19 the Executives had only $210 on hand and outstanding debts of more than $1,500.[32] A few days later, they decided to ask the always vulnerable Chinese for a loan until August 1. They also tapped the Board of Delegates for voluntary loans, "to be refunded when all our debts are paid."[33] Since Terry's lengthening captivity had dried up other sources, they had nowhere else to turn.

PART III
Changing Directions

14
A New Agenda

The Executives' ambition grew apace with the Committee's lengthening duration. With Hopkins's condition still unresolved, Terry remained a captive, his trial dragging on for weeks as some sixty witnesses successively arrived. The Committee knew its military strength: it held virtually all the guns in San Francisco, and General Wool would not be providing any more. Throughout the city, twenty-odd vigilante divisions practiced maneuvers, presented arms, and marched in time to regimental music. Invited to review a company of militia, President Coleman and Executive Oliver Crary passed along the column of troops. On seeing the two Executives, "the band struck up 'Hail to the Chief,' and Coleman said, 'Crary, do you hear that ? That's me. Hail to the Chief.'" Crary later characterized the youthful Coleman as "a capital merchant, but extremely vain."[1] Francis Pinto, however, shared Coleman's pride. The Committee, he said, was "probably the most perfect organization of its kind that had ever been formed in the world's history. There was the Military Department, consisting of infantry, artillery, and cavalry. The Police Department and Detective squad, and Executive, all working in perfect harmony; then we had a stable full of horses ready for any emergency." They had members by the thousands, which could be summoned day or night. "The City was truly under martial law."[2]

Politically and legally, San Francisco was in chaos. The Consolidation Act eliminating city governance had guaranteed confusion in local government. All the major land claims remained unsettled. A July 1 *Bulletin* editorial, probably penned by legal editor Theodore Hittell (later a pro-vigilante historian), mixed grumbles about politicians with complaints over land. Calling San Francisco "the worst governed and best plundered city," the editorial expressed "supreme contempt ... [for] your

MOUNTED BATTALION IN MOTION,
CORNER OF MONTGOMERY AND WASHINGTON STS.

A pro-vigilante print emphasized the Committee's popularity as onlookers cheered its passing cavalry, drilling in the streets of San Francisco. *Courtesy of the Bancroft Library.*

genuine wire-working San Francisco politician." The writer particularly pilloried those connected with "Palmer, Cook & Company[, who] are the owners or agents of the Bolton & Barron [Santillán] claim, which pretends to cover a large portion of our city and county."³ A week later, the *Bulletin* again attempted to stir public animosity against the Philadelphia association. It published an article accusing an agent funded by the bank of Palmer, Cook and Company—the Democrats' bank—of "splurging in Washington on the money pilfered from the collectors of Adams & Company [James King of William's former employer], to perfect a plan for the fraudulent Bolton & Barron claim."⁴

In this context, the Executives intensified their hunt for Edward McGowan, broker of the San Francisco Land Association of Philadelphia, which now owned the Santillán claim. Nine days after extending their gratitude to a group of the American elite in southern California "for horses and other services to expedition for Ned

McGowan," the Executives definitively learned that he was in Santa Barbara.[5] The hunted bon vivant, who had dropped from 182 pounds to about 140, had been hiding in canyons, foraging for food (even punching holes in his famous white hat to make a net to catch fish), and depending on sympathetic locals for sustenance.[6] Back on his trail, the vigilantes boarded their recently purchased schooner *Exact* and headed south. Executive Farwell, the former sea captain, had outfitted the ship, obtaining everything from nails to tablecloths, washbowls to sails, from himself. (He cleared more than $420—more than $11,500 in twenty-first-century dollars.)[7] Arriving in Santa Barbara, the vigilantes displayed a copy of the San Francisco bench warrant naming McGowan as an accessory to the murder of James King of William and promised locals that they would hand him over to the legal authorities. No one believed them. After scattering handbills offering $300 for McGowan dead or alive, the thwarted vigilantes sailed south, all the way into Mexican waters.[8] McGowan went into hiding at the ranch of a prominent Santa Barbara Catholic, Dr. Nicholas Den. The vigilantes returned to San Francisco empty-handed.[9]

Frustrated, the Executives returned to an idea proposed in the first days of the Committee: an outright political takeover of the disputed city. They passed a secret motion proposing that a host of county officers—the only ones remaining—be "invited to resign their official positions."[10] To legitimize their efforts, the Executives turned to the closest thing they had to a democratic process: on July 11, they called a Delegates' meeting. Two Executives took turns reading the unflattering "Report of Committee appointed to investigate actions of the County officers" to persuade their followers to back their plans. The Delegates, three from each military company, noncommittally accepted the report with their thanks.[11] Unaware of the Executives' growing absorption in attempts at landownership, many of the rank and file still could not stomach the idea that the Vigilance Committee itself might replace elective government.

The Executives consequently took other steps to further weaken their opposition. They blacklisted eight additional Broderick men, several of whom were involved with real estate, and began kidnapping them. A Broderick supporter who had a long-running dispute with the second in command of the vigilantes' 7th Division over some specific property was slated for deportation.[12] A former Democratic county supervisor was captured and "ordered to leave on steamer for Panama tomorrow and his passage to be paid by Committee on condition that same be refunded from proceeds of his property." He also had to sign the usual admission of guilt (for what, was not specified) "and appeal for permission to leave this state with a pledge never to return."[13] Another target was former prizefighter Christopher Lilly, a "man of some property" who owned a house called "The Abbey" on the San

Jose road. This structure had been used to define the "official" boundaries of San Francisco under the Consolidation Act.[14] Arrested in early July, Lilly was bailed out by two friends within two days after he promised that he would leave to fight for Walker in Nicaragua on July 20.[15]

Not all arrests sent so smoothly. Former Democratic county supervisor John D. Musgrove had first been placed on the "Doubtful List" on May 23, and had been officially blacklisted on June 9. Ten days after his blacklisting, the Executives had received a letter in which the writer denounced Musgrove for receiving kickbacks on a $6,500 road contract, insisting, "Road is impassable except on horseback."[16] Another, undated letter alleged that as supervisor, Musgrove had been guilty of shortchanging bridge builders by paying them in severely discounted city scrip.[17] Most importantly, he had drawn a city map for which he had allegedly been paid some $10,000 of $75,000 supposedly swindled from the city. Maps often held the key to San Francisco's tortuous ongoing land litigation. However, the pro-vigilante *Alta* deemed Musgrove's map "incorrect and unreliable."[18] Unfortunately, the map has not survived. The hunted former supervisor had gone into hiding, so on July 9, President Coleman issued a duplicate arrest order to a Sacramento merchant for his capture.[19] Musgrove could not be found.

This new round of arrests started closing in on those at the top of San Francisco's political pyramid. On July 11, Denis Oliver noted, "Chas Gallagher a prominent politician and friend of J. Casey[']s was arrested."[20] When a respectable merchant appeared to pay Gallagher's bail, the Executives refused to accept the money.[21] Ignoring Gallagher's respectability, the Executives kept him imprisoned to extract his testimony. Revealing their ultimate mark, while Gallagher remained in custody, two Executives sallied forth to seek other "testimony . . . in the matter of the People v. Charles Gallagher and D. C. Broderick."[22] They had decided to attack their greatest political opponent directly. When Gallagher himself provided no damning evidence against Broderick, and could not be found to have committed any criminal offense, he was finally released on July 15.[23]

During Gallagher's captivity, the Executives had been furthering their own governmental ambitions in orchestrated events, again relying on mass meetings to court public approval. As Oliver reported on July 12, the vigilantes called "a large meeting . . . to get the County officers to resign. There was a committee appointed to wait on them and report at a meeting to be held at the same place" two days hence.[24] Although the first meeting did not really provide an Executive mandate—an estimated one-third of those present voted against the proposed resignations—"the other resolutions carried without venturing to consult the meeting, notwithstanding that repeated demands were made for the question," reported another observer.[25]

The next day, pro-vigilance papers headlined "Official Corruption" dating back to 1851, taken from the "report of the Committee on County Records" previously read to the Delegates.[26] Although local citizens looked forward with interest to the next mass meeting, no popular call for vigilante rule arose.

If the Executives could not easily replace San Francisco's elected officials, they could at least attempt to secure the city's land. As William Tell Coleman explained some twenty years later, "At the same time that this work [of political reform] was going on, the Committee were induced to enter upon an undertaking which proved very laborious, very expensive, and for a time ungrateful [sic], viz.—obtaining and restoring to the city the archives of the old Pueblo of San Francisco, which had fallen into the hands of former San Francisco supervisor Alfred A. Green and his brothers." Coleman branded these documents of "incalculable value to the city and the community," because they would prove that San Francisco really had been a Mexican pueblo. He added, "If the city, or those claiming under the city, could get possession of them [the Pueblo Papers], it would establish the right of the city and others to all the old Mexican Pueblo grant [of four leagues]. If they were lost, or concealed, or suppressed, the city and those claiming under them would probably be defeated by claimants under forged titles, of which there were many."[27] Coleman did not explain two points. First, he and many other Executives held grants from the city as opposed to other sources of title. Second, as astute lawyers understood, there was no guarantee that *any* of the competing claims were genuine.

The Executives plunged heedlessly into a legal morass. As sympathetic *Bulletin* journalist, lawyer, and historian Theodore Hittell later wrote, "The question, as to whether there had ever been a pueblo at San Francisco or not, was an intricate legal one, which the vigilance committee was not competent to pass upon; and it seems that none of their lawyers, who acted as its advisers in the matter, were in any better condition."[28] That lack of understanding did not stop the Executives, as they moved decisively on what they thought they knew. On July 13, in the interim between mass meetings to unseat the county officials, the Executives secretly decided to arrest Alfred Green for unspecified "high crimes" and seize the Pueblo Papers.[29]

Chosen vigilantes went on the attack. A day later, between 2:00 and 3:00 a.m., a sleeping Green was jolted awake by barking dogs and stamping horses. He heard foul language, pounding feet in the portico, and the sound of the house's door being broken open, startling both him and his pregnant wife. "I sprang from my bed, and attempted to hold the door of my room, calling out, 'Who's there? What do you want?' The only answer was, 'Seize the damned villain! Seize the scoundrel!'" With his wife and mother watching fearfully, Green was handcuffed, thrown into a wagon, and taken to Fort Gunnybags.[30] The remaining vigilantes flung open trunks and ladies' workboxes, broke locks and emptied desks, and insulted the women who tried to stop them. As they left, unrewarded, they rode their horses through Green's grain field.[31]

Green was brought before the Executive Committee to explain how he came into possession of the Pueblo Papers.[32] He later described the scene: The Executives were seated "in a kind of semi-circle round their Chairman or President, Wm. T. Coleman." Unsure why he had been seized, Green, who while supervisor had served alongside Casey, assured them that he had properly handled election monies entrusted to him "by the Central Democratic Committee of this city. . . . I have never had anything to do with ballot box stuffing, directly or indirectly." He did, however, recall one instance of ballot-box stuffing back in 1849, which had led to the election of a a man who was now an Executive. Startled Executives cried, "'Point him out.' 'Name him!'" Green pointed to Charles V. Gillespie. As the commotion died down, President Coleman brought up Green's recent lecture on the pueblo lands. "You produced these original Spanish documents," he noted. "We have nothing against you; bring them to us, and you may have your liberty."[33]

Green had no intention of yielding the Pueblo Papers. He told the Executives that he had been trying for years to interest a spectrum of authorities in pursuing the pueblo title against other litigants for San Francisco property, with no success. Although Green was opposed to the Committee, he assured them that, "had you sent for me, and said to me, 'Mr. Green, bring us in those papers,' . . . in a peaceable, respectable manner, I would have jumped with joy to think that I had at last found some powerful body . . . to help me in this unequal contest. But, gentlemen," he continued, "you have not done this. You have dragged me from the side of my wife and family and brought me here as a felon; you have degraded me, and . . . I am now a blasted and doomed man."

Coleman interrupted his rant, sharply questioning, "Will you give us those papers, sir?"

Green answered that he might previously have handed them over, but "since you have brought me here forcibly, against my will, and degraded me, I shall not give them up unless you pay for them; I must have money enough to take me and my family away from this ill-fated city."[34]

The mood in San Francisco was indeed shifting. Doubts about the wisdom of vigilante omnipotence had begun spreading to the Executive Committee itself. Just prior to the second mass meeting, in anticipation of the imminent removal of all of San Francisco's officials, the executive treasurer had moved that "no members of the Executive Committee or other permanent officers of the Committee of Vigilance shall . . . accept any appointment to public offices."[35]

The treasurer need not have worried. Outside Fort Gunnybags, approximately two thousand agitated men learned that there would be no easy political switch. The superintendent of schools was the only one who had agreed to quit, but only as part of a general resignation. The rest—the county judge, sheriff, recorder, clerk, coroner, assessor, treasurer, district attorney, mayor, surveyor, and justices of the peace—had flatly refused.[36] As the emotional crowd listened to the results, some cheered wildly for the Constitution of the United States; others cheered the Vigilance Committee.[37] Captain Farragut reported to the secretary of the navy, "[I]t was difficult to decide, on the passage of certain resolutions, which (the ayes or nays) had the majority, [until] the Vigilance Committee . . . made a number of arrests of Law-and-Order men, and sent them to prison." After that, he noted, "the resignation of city and county officials . . . carried in the affirmative." He added that he had "detained the John Adams until I see the result" of Terry's trial. Still awaiting federal directives, he also requisitioned another ship, as "absolutely necessary to the faithful carrying out of any system of coercion that the Government may see fit to adopt."[38] Likewise, Quartermaster Kibbe reported to the governor that the "meeting was very unsatisfactory to the parties who induced it." Without the dampening effect of arrests by vigilante police, he assessed, "the meeting would have turned out a complete failure."[39]

These results did not discourage Executive deliberations. The next day, President Coleman proposed that "a committee of five be appointed to report . . . as to the best mode of summoning the County officers and then conducting the government thereafter." The motion passed. Coleman himself would head this new committee.[40]

During this discussion, national politics had erupted on the local scene. The mail steamer *Golden Age* had swung into its berth on July 14 with news from the East of presidential nominations.[41] Tar barrels had been ignited on Telegraph Hill, where the newly organized Republican Party was boosting California's former senator John C. Fremont, the head of the "black Republicans," who espoused the abolition of slavery. Fremont's candidacy threatened the South. If he won, that section's social structure, economy, and political system would be ruined. Other candidates offered alternatives. James Buchanan, the darling of San Francisco Democrats, was a "doughface," or northerner with southern sympathies, who might be able to avoid war between the sections. The old Know-Nothings stayed above the sectional fray by championing former president Millard Fillmore, who was abroad and had never attended any of their gatherings. (The virtually moribund Whig Party also backed Fillmore.)[42] Many people believed that America was teetering on the edge of a civil conflict that would split the nation. Some consequently cast their fortunes with local connections, a more secure bet if war came in the East.

Operating as if they had blinders on, the Executives bore down on the local regime, attacking San Francisco kingpin David Broderick personally for the very first time. Recognizing that they had been deporting the politician's henchmen since June 5, the Executives heatedly discussed the merits of Broderick's arrest. Finally, a motion carried to continue the debate on "Monday at 2 o'clock PM and not then without there are twenty six members present."[43] The records for that meeting are missing.[44] Soon, Broderick was "invited" down to Fort Gunnybags to meet with the Executives. Journalist James O'Meara described what may have been that unrecorded meeting. Also "invited" to the Committee rooms from the home of some friends, O'Meara was led into Fort Gunnybags by the back door through two lines of sentries who insisted on the password from his vigilante escort. They mounted a narrow flight of stairs past several other armed guards, each time giving the password, even to one Executive whom O'Meara had known for years. O'Meara was then locked alone in a room for an hour until Broderick was likewise brought in. Joseph McKinnon, later a member of the U.S. House of Representatives from California, joined them shortly. They passed an hour joking about their situation until "Old Jim" Dows—the only gray-haired Executive—entered. Apparently surprised to see the three of them, he exchanged pleasantries with them, until O'Meara said that he "wished the Executive Committee would hasten whatever business they had in my case and let me go, as I was eager to return to the house I had been visiting." Dows exited, returning ten minutes later, and took O'Meara to the head of the stairs, announcing to the first guard there that "it was all right." Alone, O'Meara passed out through a series of wary guards, each of whom kept requesting the password. The cry of "all right" was shouted down, until one of the last interior guards took O'Meara by the arm and escorted him through the outside lines all the way to the street.[45] Dows later commented that Broderick "was opposed to us at first, but subsequently not very openly. He was summoned before the Committee to answer questions in regard to ballot box stuffing, but nothing was proved against him to found any serious charges upon."[46]

In the meantime, word of Broderick's detention by the vigilantes had spread throughout the city. Members of his Empire Engine Company, suspecting that their leader was imprisoned, apparently passed a resolution to kill Executive John Manrow, known to chair the vigilantes' trials. "I knew at that stage of the game [that] they would go after any one of the Committee," Manrow later declared, fearing that he would be attacked on his way home. But his groom called for him, and he arrived home safely.[47] Rumors of Broderick's confinement also reached Gerritt Ryckman, a much-respected leader of the 1851 Vigilance Committee who had refused to join in 1856. Noting that Broderick had committed no crime, and aware that imprisonment by the vigilantes would destroy Broderick's senatorial aspirations, an angry Ryckman visited the Executives and accused them of turning their committee into "a political engine." He threatened, "If you don't countermand that order for the arrest of Broderick, I will tap the bell, and order an opposition, and arrest every damned man of you."[48] The Executives backed down. Broderick was released, and left San Francisco for the mountain counties to drum up support for state legislators likely to back him for U.S. senator.[49]

15

Trying Times

Trying to solidify their shriveling power, the Executives redoubled their attempts to coerce the Pueblo Papers out of Alfred A. Green. When they brought him before them, he assured them that he had obtained the papers honestly. In an attempt to force Green to relinquish the documents, the vigilante guards brought in Tiburcio Vasquez, the native Californian whom he had allegedly cheated out of them. As the *Minutes* record, "after having his [Green's] affidavit read in Spanish and English [Vasquez] stated that it was true."[1] Vasquez departed, and Green was returned to his cramped, dark cell. Next, the Executives captured and interrogated Green's brother Daniel. By that evening, all the other Green brothers—Henry, Benjamin, Robert, and John—had also been detained at Fort Gunnybags. In their searches of Alfred Green's residence, vigilantes had turned up "a package of miscellaneous papers twenty three (23) in number," which they brought to the Executives. But the three-hundred-plus Pueblo Papers were still missing. Within a few days, all the brothers were discharged "on parole" except Alfred. After recording another statement from him, the Executives sent him back to his cell. Then the cash-strapped Executives directed "Smiley and Coleman [to] use such means *other than purchase* as may seem to them advisable to obtain from Mr. Green the papers in question."[2]

The Executives had another bit of unfinished business. Almost forgotten in the brouhaha over Terry and Green, another man still languished in a vigilante cell. Philander Brace, always described in the *Minutes* as "the murderer," had originally been blacklisted at the beginning of June, when an Executive had proposed that he be arrested on the basis of "sufficient circumstantial evidence . . . that Brace was concerned in the murder of Capt. West."[3]

Almost a year earlier, all of San Francisco had read the shocking story of the death of Joseph B. West, who had made the magnificent stained glass windows at Trinity Church. Acting as deputy sheriff, West had joined a posse trying to capture thieves operating near the mission, including Brace and his companion, John Marion. When the posse closed in on the thieves, they shot West, who died, leaving behind two children and a wife then disabled by paralysis. His assailants escaped across the bay, pursued by the posse.[4] Brace escaped, but Marion was found dead with a gunshot wound to the head. The paper originally reported that he had killed himself, "placing the muzzle in the centre of his forehead." Later, many of those who viewed the body remarked on the absence of powder burns on Marion's face and blamed the pursuers for his death.[5] The blame soon fell on Brace, who had allegedly killed West and then slaughtered his partner to hide his crime. The grand jury, however, failed to indict Brace due to a lack of evidence.[6]

Then the Vigilance Committee was born. West's brother, who drove a freight wagon for vigilante policeman Francis Pinto, knew that his boss was actively involved with the Committee and had approached him about Brace's capture. "I put him in touch with the Executive Committee," Pinto later recalled, and they took the case.[7] But when vigilante John Durkee searched San Francisco's criminal records for evidence to convict "notorious characters," he turned up only two entries for Brace: the grand jury investigation, and an entry for May 5, when he was sentenced to thirty days in jail for petty larceny. Nonetheless, Durkee had scrawled across the bottom of his notes, "The above named Brace I consider one of the worst men in California."[8]

When Brace was released from jail shortly thereafter, vigilantes tried unsuccessfully to capture him. A few days later, another vigilante revived Brace's story after reconnoitering an abandoned Law and Order encampment near Mission Dolores. There he encountered West's widow, who tearfully described how she had been left without support for herself and her children. Brace, said the vigilante, had "since made his boast that he could always . . . get clear."[9]

The hunt for Brace intensified. A week later, cooperative police officer Isaiah W. Lees (Durkee's close friend) spotted Brace in San Francisco. Afraid to attempt an arrest by himself, Lees asked the vigilantes to help with the capture. Committee members tracked Brace to the south end of San Francisco Bay, where he was finally caught. Lees earned the Executives' thanks for the information, and Brace was hustled into a dark cell in Fort Gunnybags.[10]

The busy Executives kept Brace in solitary confinement for more than a month while trying to solicit his "confession or testimony in regard to others." When they finally began his trial, they atypically allowed the twenty-one-year-old New

Yorker to be present to hear the list of charges against him.[11] He stood accused of two armed robbery attempts (one unsuccessful) in 1855, aiding and abetting a gang of robbers, and the murders of West and then of his own accomplice. Brace admitted that he had been "one of the party [of thieves] but did not fire the pistol" on the first count of armed robbery, and pled not guilty to the rest. Only one witness had been heard before the Executives suspended Brace's hearing, caught up in the trial of Terry.[12]

The Executives could do nothing with Terry as long as Hopkins's fate remained in doubt. On July 11, Executive Smiley had "reported that Hopkins' case presented new and alarming features."[13] His wound had become infected. Hopkins's mother, waiting by his bed, recalled "some twenty-five or thirty thousand dollars [raised] for King of Williams' family after his death." Turning to her daughter-in-law, she opined that the younger woman could soon be "'a rich widow, for the Vigilance Committee will raise twenty-five or thirty thousand dollars for you.' Hopkins turned over and mumbled, 'Don't speculate on my life. I am not going to die.'"[14] Yet in mid-July, his survival was still uncertain.

Trapped by circumstances, the Executives continued taking Terry's "trial" testimony, getting to know both Hopkins and Terry better and better. As James Dows later recalled, "Terry was a very intelligent man, a rank Southerner, a regular Texan . . . and showed it in every way. He took an active part against the Committee . . . [but] he was a man of courage." In contrast, Hopkins was one of those men "who belonged to the Committee who were not very worthy citizens, but yet who were not openly so bad that they could be charged with anything wrong. Hopkins was . . . [also] a very impulsive and very indiscreet man, and probably not much of a man anyway."[15] The emerging contrast increasingly disturbed the Executives. Consequently, on July 16, witnesses' testimony regarding Hopkins became limited to "Do you know S. A. Hopkins? How long have you known him? What is his general reputation for honesty? From what you know of him and his general reputation would you believe him under oath?"[16] As the Executives repeatedly learned, although a few would believe in Hopkins's honesty, a wide spectrum of men did not trust him.

With the Committee's prolonged existence and change of direction, many vigilantes found their work increasingly onerous. Executives who had been meeting two or three times a day for two solid months began dropping away. On July 18, only fourteen Executives, less than half the usual complement, arrived to continue Terry's trial. The sergeant at arms had to round up others to ensure a quorum. Fines for non-attendance still brought only sixteen to the next meeting.[17] In the next few days, the Executives purged a non-attending colleague and admitted to the General Committee three captains of sailing vessels who might be helpful if the dreaded federal orders came for assaults against the Vigilance Committee. The vigilantes also captured a new group of exiles to send out on the next steamer.[18]

On Monday, July 21, the mail steamer puffed away from the dock with its usual complement of passengers, miscellaneous cargo, gold, and mail. It carried four new exiles to its first stop at the mouth of the bay—all Broderick men. On the same ship departed Executive Samuel T. Thompson, a vigilante vice president who had been regretfully released by his colleagues. Excitable auctioneer Thomas J. L. Smiley replaced him in the vice presidency.[19] In a letter sent by the steamer, one disgruntled local citizen voiced an increasingly common opinion "about the Vigilance Committee—It is a mercantile Insurrection its head is in Front Street & its Tail is every where. . . . It commenced in a Spirit of Vengeance & after Two months the end is not yet. . . . It is time the Committee was dispersed & the Tramp of Armed Foreigners no longer heard or Seen in our Streets. . . . I for one am sick of it."[20]

On the evening of July 22, as the mail steamer left the heads for the open sea, the Executives called for closing arguments in the Terry trial. The original eight indictments had been collapsed into seven: resisting arrest by the Committee, assaulting Hopkins with intent to kill, three separate attacks on individuals, and allowing the escape of a man who had defrauded the infant Sanchez heirs, Terry's former clients.[21] Prosecutor Smiley spoke first. Although his speech remains unpublished, he later recalled, "I started off with a few remarks about the solemnity of the occasion . . . and branched off in a manner which took his [Terry's] breath away. I said, 'Gentlemen, in trying Judge Terry, you are trying yourselves. If he is wrong, you are right; and if he is right, you are wrong.'"[22]

Then Terry rose to his own defense. He knew that he was speaking for his life. The judge had prepared a written statement at the Executives' request, but Smiley's assertion galvanized an extemporaneous speech. After flattering the Executives' "noble" goals and acknowledging their shared abhorrence of ballot-box stuffing, he highlighted their main difference: "whether the end justifies the means." Turning to the specific counts against him, Terry denied that Hopkins had had a warrant, and pointed out that the vigilante was a complete stranger who "committed a fierce and violent assault on me, attempted to wrest a gun from my hands, with the . . . evident intention of taking my life." Terry explained that he had only joined the Law and Order Party in opposition to the vigilantes at the request of "gentlemen of undoubted character," and with the governor's assurance that federal arms would be forthcoming. Finding himself deceived, and "misled as to our power to raise funds . . . I was about retiring, defeated and dispirited from the field, when

I unfortunately became involved in the only collision which occurred during the whole campaign." His actions had resulted from his sworn judicial duty to uphold the law and all those protected by it. "You," he addressed the Executives, "although you may feel assured that you are right, must see that I could not, with any regard to principle or my oath of office, side with you."[23]

Next Terry criticized the Executives' secret procedures. Although he had received copies "of the testimony of a large number of witnesses," he had not been allowed to confront the witnesses against him directly. This skewed system facilitated perjured testimony. He specifically warned the Executives against one of his known enemies who had appeared before them, and cautioned them against being swayed "by the blood-thirsty appeals of a prostituted press." At least one such newspaper had identified "the greatest of my crimes . . . [as] having been born in the south."[24]

Then Terry turned to the Executives directly. Knowing none of them, he harbored no personal animosity, but he was astonished at Smiley's just-completed speech with its appeal "to the basest human nature" by claiming, "if I were right, your acts were wrong." If the Executives followed this reasoning, they would be "unworthy to sit in judgment upon the vilest criminal." But, he countered, the Executives were known "as honest and good citizens," so he could count on them to disregard Smiley's words.[25]

Finally, Terry reviewed the other counts against him. Four alleged attacks dating from 1850 to 1853 he clarified and dismissed, identifying the sum of these ancient allegations as an attempt to sway community feeling and "to compass my ruin as far as possible." His few past altercations simply proved him to be the consummate southerner, one who would "promptly resent a personal affront." Then Terry corrected the totally twisted assertion that he had defrauded the Sanchez heirs when, in fact, he had restored some of their patrimony. Most importantly, despite the most diligent searches, the vigilantes could find no flaw in his behavior without going back at least three years, before his marriage and fatherhood. "I feel proud of the fact," he concluded, "that here, in California where character is held so cheap, . . . where public officers—especially judicial officers—are so frequently accused of bribery, corruption, and malfeasance in office, . . . no charge has been made, no facts testified to by a single witness, calculated to throw a stain on my integrity as a Judge, or my honor as a gentleman."[26]

With the words of their own values ringing in their ears, the Executives sent Terry back to his cell and began to discuss his fate. They took an oath "never to divulge the votes taken in our verdicts rendered in the trial of David S. Terry to any living being outside this room. So help us God."[27] Tempers flared as the arguments lengthened. When the number needed to convict Terry was reduced from two-thirds (twenty-four of thirty-seven) to three-fifths (twenty-two of thirty-seven), the bickering Executives finally agreed on a verdict. Terry was found guilty of resisting arrest by Hopkins and his posse, guilty of the first long-ago attack, and not guilty of another attack, with the last three counts dropped from the record. The Sanchez heirs were not even mentioned. However, the Executives still could not agree on whether Terry had assaulted Hopkins with *intent to kill*.[28] After nine continuous hours in session, the bleary-eyed Executives decided that they would meet again that evening.[29] They donned their hats and slipped out into the thin, gray dawn to the sound of screeching gulls. Morning newspapers were just appearing, containing a telegram stating, "Hopkins is finally pronounced well by his physicians."[30]

Simultaneously, a frightening rumor rocketed through San Francisco: the navy was preparing to attack! All during the night, while the Executives debated Terry's fate, the naval crews stationed at Benecia and Mare Island were putting their warships in fighting order and loading the ships' guns with ball and grapeshot.[31] Quartermaster Kibbe disingenuously speculated to the governor that the action had been prompted by Captain Farragut's recent offer to the superintendent of the Mint to take aboard all the government's gold bullion for safekeeping. Others claimed that the navy had received false information that the vigilantes were about to attack government installations.[32] No one publicly mentioned possible leaks of debates about Terry's fate.

At 7:30 that evening, thirty-six Executives gathered in an anxious city. After resolving a few trivial matters, they returned to the question of Terry's assault on Hopkins with intent to kill. After much inconclusive argument, exasperated French Executive Jules David moved that if "after this third ballot is taken . . . and no verdict is rendered, a Committee of Compromise" would have to make the decision. Under this pressure, the Executives decided that Terry had lacked murderous intent. Smiley, the defeated prosecutor, moved that "when D. S. Terry places in the hands of the Secretary all papers belonging to . . . his trial, then Mrs. Terry be admitted to see him on the former basis of her admission." After drawing up the summary of charges and their verdicts, the Executives finally went home.[33]

They still had to sentence Terry. Three men assumed this task: the two "attorneys," Smiley and Truett, and former Hong Kong merchant (now private investigator) Charles V. Gillespie.[34] With Hopkins recovering, Terry could not be hanged for murder. Having recalled their schooner *Exact* from the hunt for McGowan, they could potentially use it to deport Terry, but where? "There were many suggestions as to what to do with him—some thought we ought to put him on a barren island in the Pacific Ocean and let him starve," recalled a vigilante captain.[35] This plan, however, was rejected as a death sentence. President Coleman later explained the

Executives' conundrum. If Terry was deported to the East, he would gather public sentiment and would probably return, providing "an excuse for others to follow; and the shield extended over him would have extended over others."[36] Executive Gillespie of the sentencing committee predicted a darker outcome. "If he had been sent away, he would have come right back, and if we had undertaken to take him again, there would have been civil war."[37] A pro-hanging Executive later remarked, "The man Hopkins did not die, and that was the most unfortunate thing that ever happened."[38]

Emphasizing the drawbacks of returning exiles, Edward Bulger was back. The Executives had exiled him to Hawaii on the bark *Yankee* under Captain James Smith in the first round of deportations on June 5. In Honolulu, the unsavory Bulger had been repudiated by the American consul. Unable to find work, he faced starvation if he stayed. So he sneaked aboard the *Yankee* as it departed on its return trip across the Pacific. Warned of his pending arrival by the newsboat standing by at Fort Point, vigilantes seized Bulger before the *Yankee* docked and carried him to "the long, low, lead-colored brick building on Sacramento street."[39] As the *New York Times* later reported, "It was deemed certain that Bulger would at once be executed, as a warning to others of the expatriated."[40] Soon a terrified Bulger faced furious Executives. President Coleman asked him, "Are you aware that the sentence of death is hanging over you . . . [because you returned] to this state against the express will and warning of this Committee?" Bulger insisted that he had never been warned. He was removed to his cell, and the Executives decided to "inquire into the truth of his statement" to determine whether he would live or die.[41]

Troubles mounted. That night, Hugh Breen recorded in his diary:

> July 24th Thursday night 11 o'clock. Another murder probably committed today: a man by the name of Joe Hethington [Hetherington] shot a Dr Randall in the St Nicholas Bar Room, a dispute about some property.—He's in the hands of the Vigilance Committee—The Dr will not possibly live as He was shot in the brain & the ball remains there—if he dies there will be another execution by the Vigilance Committee. This Hethington shot a Dr Baldwin some time previous about squatting on his Lot and was tried by the regular courts and as a matter of course was acquitted. This time the chances are against Him.[42]

As the story emerged, Joseph Hetherington, a wealthy Englishman of violent passions, had loaned well-known cheapskate Dr. Andrew Randall some $20,000 to $30,000 secured by valuable city property. Randall, a former assembly member and a major San Francisco landowner, insisted that he did not have to repay the money because of a defect in the mortgage or note. He then left town. When Randall returned, the two ran into each other at the St. Nicholas Hotel. The doctor shot first, but Hetherington proved the better aim. San Francisco policeman Isaiah Lees immediately seized Hetherington but willingly turned him over to his friends the vigilantes, who hauled the Englishman to Fort Gunnybags.[43] Hetherington joined Terry, Brace, Green, and Bulger in vigilante captivity. Who would hang?

While news of the latest killing buzzed around them, Terry's three-man sentencing subcommittee finally reached a conclusion. Although the judge had been fairly convicted, they decided that "the usual punishments" did not apply. Therefore, they declared, "David S. Terry [must] be discharged."[44] An Executive later remarked, "During his [Terry's] long trial the committee all got worked out. Some wanted to hang him and some did not. It would have been much the best thing to have allowed him to leave the State, but we could not get a majority of the committee to do it. Those were very trying times. These things are easy enough to start, but it is hard to control them."[45]

16
Blood Lust

Controlling their followers became the Executives' paramount goal. By established Committee procedure, the Delegates had to approve Executive decisions. At 11:00 the next morning, six Executives faced a hundred Delegates eager to hear the results of Terry's trial.[1] After everyone took a sacred oath of secrecy, Executives Smiley and then Ward spent almost nine hours reading the entire trial transcript aloud. Smiley finished by announcing the Executives' decision to the remaining ninety-five men: they had agreed to let Terry go. Shocked, the Delegates refused. Then they decided to vote on each count separately. They supported the Executives on Terry's guilt in "resistance to arrest" by a vote of ninety-three to two. Likewise, they supported the Executives' "not guilty" verdict in all but one other indictment and agreed to strike them out. But when they addressed the second count, of "guilty of assault on S. A. Hopkins," arguments raged about whether or not Terry had attempted murder. Hours later, the Delegates voted that "all after the word 'guilty' . . . be stricken out so that this verdict shall read 'guilty.'" And since Terry was "guilty," they wanted to punish him. By 12:30 a.m., they had been dickering for more than thirteen hours. Exhausted, President Coleman scheduled another Delegate meeting for 3:00 the coming afternoon and adjourned the assembly.[2]

Someone resorted to private vengeance. Later that night, a lone man crept into Terry's $30,000 state-of-the-art Lone Star Flour Mill near Stockton. Several area farmers had piled grain there, ready for processing. By morning, all that remained was ashes.[3]

Back in San Francisco, as a new day broke, the Executives returned to managing their other captives. At their morning meeting, they pursued the Pueblo Papers investigation; they allowed an attorney to visit Hetherington in his cell under the watchful eye of the Surveillance Committee; and they brought Edward Bulger in for trial. Upon his deportation, they learned, the timorous Bulger had been "so anxious to get out of the hands of the Committee . . . that he tumbled himself on board the *Yankee* without taking time to climb over the side . . . and sneaked away forward."[4] Bulger pled not guilty to "violating and disregarding the decrees of the Committee" because, he claimed, no one had warned him he would be hanged if he returned. "[M]uch excited," he "turned to . . . [an unnamed Executive] and said, 'Don't you remember that when you came to my cell I asked you to read to me a letter which I had just received from my Mother—the contents so affected me that I cried like a child?' You went away from my cell without reading me any sentence whatsoever." As the memory surfaced, the Executive "brought his fist down on the table and exclaimed that he did remember the incident." Clancey Dempster recalled, "We were all very much relieved and the man's life was saved."[5] The Executives promptly decided to bring Bulger's reprieve before the Delegates.

At 3:00 that afternoon, ninety-five Delegates assembled. Two new attendees were allowed to enter, but not allowed to vote in "The People versus Terry" because they had not heard the transcript of trial. Once again, the Delegates refused to support the Executives' verdict of guilty and release of Terry. They also sharply questioned how their verdicts, and those of the Executives, had "been made public on the streets." The Executives could not explain the leak, but placated the Delegates by explaining how they had decided not to hang Bulger. On this matter, the Delegates agreed.[6]

The Bulger decision quickly became common knowledge, and newspapers published harsh reactions. Several pro-vigilante papers demanded that the returned deportee be hanged as the "only means of enforcing the decrees of the Committee."[7] Executive Secretary Bluxome had to rush to press with a letter explaining the verdict: that "the reading of . . . [Bulger's] sentence was omitted," and his reappearance in San Francisco grew from his "desire to return to the Committee, to obtain from them their permission to proceed to New York." Bulger would again be deported. However, any other returning exiles "will suffer the penalty of death," Bluxome insisted.[8]

That evening, the harried Executives met again. They began to probe the source of their breach of secrecy and eventually determined that one of their own colleagues had mistakenly communicated Delegates' votes to a man he mistook for one of the Delegates. He was severely censured but allowed to remain an Executive.[9] Next, they created another new committee to deal with Alfred Green and the Pueblo Papers. Finally, they turned to the trial of Joseph Hetherington. Now formally charged with shooting Dr. Randall, Hetherington pled not guilty, claiming that his action was in self-defense. As witnesses testified for and against him, the news arrived that Randall had just died.[10] Executive Dows later observed that Hetherington had killed "with deliberation, but in other respects he was a good citizen, and never molested anybody. He was not a thief or a rough character."[11] Reaching a decision was hard, and the hour was late. The tired Executives disbanded for the evening, their work no longer a secret.

Melancholy mechanic Hugh Breen had heard all the rumors. That night, he wrote in his diary:

> July 26th Saturday night 10 o'clock. Dr Randall the man that was shot by Hethington [sic] is dead. He died at 9 o'clock this morning. He remained insensible to the last. He is to be interred tomorrow evening. I expect Hethington's fate is sealed—there is another man called Philander Brace in the hands of the Committee who tis said committed two murders one was Col West at the mission and the other His companion in crime when flying from Justice. The other man He shot was named Marion—they [sic] people say or rather tis rumoured that they will hang this Brace an[d] Hethington at one and the same time.[12]

On Sunday morning, in an unusual meeting that conflicted with church services, thirty-one Executives faced a full agenda. They reaffirmed Executive secrecy, issued another strong request for monetary contributions from the Delegates, and allowed four vigilantes to resign because they had been threatened with firing from the U.S. Mint.[13] Wanting to quit, they set up a committee to plan for adjournment.[14]

In order to adjourn, the Executives had to dispose of their remaining prisoners in a manner that the Delegates would accept. They began alternating trials, seeking to placate the Delegates, who would meet that evening to reconsider Terry's fate. First, they returned to Hetherington's trial and heard final witnesses. Executive Smiley, Hetherington's defense attorney, read his client's statement. When an easy agreement eluded the Executives, at 3:00 p.m. without reaching a verdict, the Executives returned to the long-delayed trial of Philander Brace.[15] After hearing more inconclusive testimony about Brace, at 5:30 p.m. the frustrated Executives abandoned Brace's trial and resumed that of Hetherington. They heard the closing statements by the "attorneys" as Smiley opened for the defense and Jules David closed for the prosecution. The long day of difficult trials finally came to an end as the Executives reached a single decision: "Joseph Hetherington having been found guilty of the crime of murder upon the person of Dr. A. Randall . . . is hereby sentenced to death by hanging at such time as will be decided upon by the Executive Committee." Moments later, 106 Delegates gathered. The entire surviving *Minutes* for this meeting read: "Verdict and sentence in case of Joseph Hetherington concurred in."[16]

Smiley, who had defended Hetherington, could barely conceal his disappointment. Later he characterized Hetherington as "a man of great culture, one who was cut out for a parson, in my opinion. He had a strong religious undercurrent in his inner man. I knew him very well." Smiley added that he "would not have been hung in ordinary times. . . . In ordinary times he would not perhaps have been punished."[17]

These were not ordinary times. That same Sunday, while the Executives were deliberating life or death for their fellow citizens in secret session, San Francisco was in an uproar. At Calvary Presbyterian Church, its nationally celebrated pastor, Dr. William Scott, had chosen that morning to preach an anti-vigilante sermon. Scott, enticed to move to San Francisco late in 1854 from his prominent New Orleans parish, had long privately objected to the Vigilance Committee. Alone among the city's Protestant clergy, he had refused to preach in the vigilantes' favor in late May, when Casey and Cora were hanged. Immediately after the seizure of Terry and the Law and Order forces, Scott had again wished to speak out, but he had been dissuaded by his eleven-member church board, nine of whom were active vigilantes. The forty-two-year-old Scott usually saw sweet-faced William Tell Coleman, ten years his junior, sitting up front every Sunday in the personal pew Coleman had purchased for $1,000.[18] But this Sunday, with the Executives conspicuously absent and growing rumors that Terry, Hetherington, Brace, and Green were on trial for their lives, Scott could no longer remain silent.

From his pulpit, the pastor delivered a stirring "Discourse for the Times." He began by upbraiding the general community for its "human depravity," and condemned the frequent public executions as "brutalizing and degrading." A father of eight, he also condemned the transience of life in California, "the absence of family ties," the local fascination with gold, and a people too self-absorbed to "perform the duties of good citizens in upholding the laws of the country." His voice rising to a crescendo, he asked if California was to have only two historical chapters, "gold and blood, and blood and gold? Are we to read of nothing but corruption, fraud and bankruptcy, of arrests and trials and executions—and then again of assassinations and robbery, of murder and hanging. . . . [until] in their innocent plays . . . [our children are] to frighten one another with threats of a Vigilance Committee . . . ?" Leading up to a stirring biblical conclusion, he thundered that "the stream of blood" will never be stayed "while men take the law into their own hands, and while the fierce brutal passions are excited under the pretext of supporting the laws, and revenge is mingled with the maintenance of justice." His sermon riveted the congregation and appeared a few days later as an eight-page, 12½-cent pamphlet in a run of three thousand copies.[19]

The pilloried Executives had to react. That same Sunday night, they had learned that the mail steamer *Sonora* would be arriving shortly from the East, probably with the long-dreaded federal directives. To bolster their precarious position, the Executives rushed to the *Bulletin* with a private letter stolen from the U.S. mails that they had been holding since mid-June. Written by California Militia commander Volney Howard, it suggested that a federal writ of habeas corpus be obtained for Terry as a witness in Durkee's piracy trial, which would either gain Terry's release or force a vigilante clash with federal officials.[20]

The Executives' action backfired. When the letter appeared in print on Monday, public opinion exploded. "[S]uch outrages on the sanctity of private correspondence have never before disgraced any civilized community," a Stockton paper editorialized. "The robber of the mail usually hides his head from the light of day . . . [rather than boast of] such acts . . . in the columns of a public press." The editorial also complained about "one of the many eaves-dropping affairs which have disgusted our people for the last two months," a conversation between "an influential gentleman" and federal judge Matthew Hall McAllister. "What do our people think," it concluded, of this "boasted system of espionage which . . . would disgrace the veriest despotism of Europe"?[21] Interior counties had also tired of receiving fugitives from the vigilantes. For example, when Butte County residents complained about the Committee's exiles and the unconstitutionality of vigilante processes, the *Bulletin* sneered, "Self-preservation is the first law of nature. We are not bound to suffer ourselves to be preyed upon by rogues; we are entitled to drive them away, let who will suffer."[22] Vigilante prestige, the foundation of their public support, dropped even lower.

Isolated inside their fort, the Executives plowed ahead. They notified Hetherington of his impending execution and then faced a grim treasurer's report. Despite some small collections from the public and a loan of $900 ($100 from each of nine different Executives), they had just over $200 cash on hand, a balance of $688.40, and more than $2,000 in approved outstanding debts. Resuming the trial of young Philander Brace, they heard several affidavits read and finally concluded, based largely on his alleged character, "Verdict guilty on first count. Verdict not guilty on second count. Verdict on third count withdrawn. Verdict guilty as accessory in fourth count." That evening, they decided that Brace, too, must hang.[23]

When the Executives called Brace in to inform him of his death sentence, he at first did not believe them. After he was returned to his cell, his mutterings became audible to Alfred Green, who was confined next door. "They say they are going to hang me tomorrow, and that I must prepare for death, but I guess they are only trying to frighten me," Brace muttered. After stewing awhile, he called to his guard and asked to see Executives Coleman, Dows, Aaron Burns, and William Tillinghast. The men came promptly, and Coleman assured Brace of the truth of the sentence. "Brace then drew himself up to his full height, and with flashing eye and outstretched arm" pointed to each of the Executives in turn. "I accuse you before the bar of our Lord Jesus Christ of being a murderer. . . . Nay more, I accuse you of being double murderers; you murder me, and you murder the Constitution and laws of my country." He then named witnesses never called who would have exonerated him. Green, who lived out by the mission, who had been friends with the late West, and who knew one of Brace's potential defense witnesses, called to Dows, the Executive closest to his own cell. "It is my belief that Brace had nothing to do with the killing of West," he whispered. "Green, keep your mouth shut," hissed Dows. "These are critical times, and it may come your turn next." Green then heard Coleman's final statement to Brace: "Prepare for death; you will be hung tomorrow."[24]

Now it was Green's turn to comprehend the seriousness of his situation. Calling to a guard, he proposed to accompany two Executives to his house to retrieve the Pueblo Papers if the Committee would pay him $25,000. In return, Green promised not to negotiate with other "parties adverse to such claims, such as Limantour" and the Philadelphia group who held the Santillán claim. He offered to raise the money himself, "being aware that the Peter Smith claimants [including Broderick] will contribute largely." If the documents were not found to be genuine, he would surrender them to the city, but requested that his own forged order that had deceived Tiburcio Vasquez be returned to him. The eager Executives initially decided to contact "property holders and citizens" to raise the money demanded by Green, but refused to release his forged order without Vasquez's approval.[25]

After reaching this agreement, the Executives turned to long-delayed issues. They cleaned up some annoying business details and responded to Cornelia Terry's almost constant presence since she had been allowed back in to see her still-captive husband four days earlier. They passed a resolution that "No ladies will be allowed to remain in this building after 9 o'clock in the evening."[26] Then, at 11:00 p.m., the Executives again faced the Delegates. The eighty-one men present heard not a word about the Pueblo Papers, but were presented instead with life-and-death decisions. They confirmed they Executives' verdict on Brace and his sentence of death. They also approved hanging him and Hetherington together the following afternoon. Then the condemned men were brought in one at a time and allowed to make a statement. "Brace after hearing his sentence asked, 'Is that all?'" Coleman "answered affirmatively. Brace then replied, 'Then I am ready.'" Hetherington asked to see a minister, but first to see his friend and real estate attorney Henry H. Haight to settle his affairs. This request was denied.[27] Both men were returned to their separate cells for their final night on earth.

The condemned men prepared for death. Hetherington spent all night writing feverishly, trying to put his business in order from memory. Brace, meantime, became aggravated, and one of the Committee arrived and offered to "take a drink together." When Brace drank, he became "a raving maniac." He was sedated and led away to the dark chamber under the stairs where Yankee Sullivan had bled to death.[28]

Outside the fort that night of July 28, Hugh Breen recorded:

> The only talk you hear on the streets is about the horrors of our modern Inquisition, for tis nothing more or less as we outsiders know nothing of what transpires within, not even the members of the Vigilance Committee generally . . . [who] blindly obey their orders, no matter how terrible. The public knows nothing whatever until immediately before the execution of the sentence and then only by rumour until they actually behold the fearful preparations to hurl a fellow being into eternity—So if that is not a modern inquisition I don't know what is.[29]

The gravity of the situation even gave some of the Executives second thoughts. Although they had agreed to hang two more victims, only nineteen men appeared the following morning to refine their plans. This stump of a committee approved an appropriate outdoor site for the execution, since Executive Miers Truett's brother Henry, who was not a Committee member, had objected to their swinging bodies out of the building he partially owned.[30] Carpenters quickly converged on the chosen site with some pre-framed timbers. Under the careful supervision of three men, including John Durkee, who was out on parole pending his piracy trial, the workers raised a platform eight feet square and more than ten feet high, with two gallows frames and a trap door. Ropes with nooses followed.[31]

Gallows construction and the massing of troops at Fort Gunnybags signaled that the hanging would begin. On that beautiful sun-drenched July 29, thousands gathered as the Committee's troops cordoned off the streets, pointing a cannon down each avenue that led to the hangman's tree. Owners of nearby houses rented out space at windows and on rooftops for a dollar a head. Three overloaded structures thunderously collapsed, though no one was seriously injured. A bridge on

Commercial Street also caved in, plunging men into the mud. Onlookers jeered. Even as other buildings sagged, the crowd stayed put. Some men shouted catcalls and ribald jests; the head of the vigilante militia rode slowly along the edge of the crowd, threatening arrests to ensure a respectful silence. The crowd gradually settled down.[32]

Inside the fort, the execution process began. Dr. Cole visited each of the prisoners to check, ironically enough, on their well-being. Hetherington he found "somewhat depressed, yet . . . making an effort to conceal that fact."[33] A *Bulletin* reporter appeared some three hours before Hetherington would swing, finding him still "engaged in writing . . . cool, calm and undisturbed." Hetherington denied that he had committed any crime, as Dr. Randall had fired first, and his own "first shot and the Doctor's second were at the same instant." Born in Carlyle, England, Hetherington estimated his age at thirty-four; he had lived a long time in St. Louis, and in California since 1849. His net worth—much of it in real estate—he estimated "at about $50,000 [some $17.2 million in twenty-first-century dollars] . . . [but] for want of possession of his papers, which he has been unable to get, cannot be settled properly." He urged the reporter to publish his remarks on the scaffold "literally as delivered."[34]

Brace suffered through the night, giving no such interview. The *Bulletin* later described him as a handsome young man who had impressed people with his scholarly education, which it demeaned as "perverted talent."[35] In his long captivity, Brace had previously entertained Dr. Cole (who checked the prisoners daily) by showing how he could slip his hands in and out of his handcuffs, getting free without being detected. Claiming that he had been "born a thief . . . created a thief in his mother's womb," he never confessed to murder. On the morning of his execution, the sympathetic physician gave Brace some brandy.[36] One of the other vigilantes later recalled that Chief of Police W. E. B. Andrews also gave Brace some liquor, after which Miers Truett tried to quiet the raving Brace with valerian.[37] (Valerian can act as a sedative, but it can also cause a paradoxical reaction, intensifying the effect of other drugs, including alcohol.)[38] Executive Smiley later reported that a guard had relayed Brace's request for some whiskey, which Smiley approved. "It was not down [his throat] two seconds before he burst into a flame and commenced singing out, 'Hetherington, in less than an hour you and I will be in hell, and the boys will be singing in the streets.'"[39] Just before his execution, Brace got another shot of brandy from the unsuspecting Dr. Cole.[40]

Terry also felt the pressure of the impending execution. According to a rumor, the judge had been given until 4:00 that day to resign his office, or he, too, would mount the scaffold. Hetherington and Brace were to hang at 5:00. With this latest

As tensions rose, this pro-vigilante illustration emphasized the Committee's all-American patriotism with a giant flag floating over Fort Gunnybags, unrealistically attached to the Monument Company bell. Hetherington and Brace hang below the scaffold, their heads covered with white hoods, as their executioners withdraw. *Courtesy of the Bancroft Library.*

attempt to frighten Terry into resigning, one observer said, "they were dealing with the wrong man."[41]

All eyes in San Francisco were now focused on the scaffold. In midmorning, about eighteen hundred uniformed vigilante soldiers massed in formation in the increasingly oppressive heat. As one vigilante later observed, "we were all the afternoon hanging these men."[42] The Executives first gathered at Fort Gunnybags and learned that they were more than $1,000 in the red before mounting carriages that would take them to the hanging.[43] Young Brace, in the well-guarded first carriage, and Hetherington, in the second, arrived and were conducted up the wooden stairs to the platform by a vigilante executioner who was strangely dressed in a long black muslin robe and cap that he had pushed back on his head, revealing his face. He bound their legs, loosened their collars, and slipped the nooses around their necks. Hetherington, given permission to speak, recounted in a low, clear voice that he had received absolution that morning, was an innocent man (giving the details of the shooting), and was prepared to meet his maker. His solemn speech

This more realistic contemporary image shows a sagging building (on the center right) weighed down by the gaping crowd, while only one man, directly below the scaffold, respectfully removes his hat as Hetherington and Brace prepare to swing. *Courtesy of the California History Room, California State Library, Sacramento.*

was continually interrupted by a delirious Brace, who blasphemed, swore, and condemned the Committee as murderers. Appalled by the display, a clergyman stuffed a handkerchief in Brace's mouth, but he spat it out and raved on. As Brace paused, Hetherington noted that he had not had a fair trial; no jury on earth would have convicted him. Then Brace blurted out that he wished to be hanged with Terry on one side and Hetherington on the other, like the Savior between two thieves. The hangman quickly drew white caps over the eyes of the condemned. Hetherington cried out, "God bless you all! God bless you all! God bless Mr. Fletcher Haight! I wish I could have seen Mr. Henry Haight before I died."[44] A guard struck the bell on the top of Fort Gunnybags, and the bodies dropped. Brace writhed and struggled for a few minutes; Hetherington died motionless. After twisting there for forty minutes, their bodies were removed to the coroner's office.[45]

Once more, San Franciscans coped with a formal lynching. That evening, thousands of people paraded past the open coffins, viewing the strangled dead in their execution garb. A few days later, the Executives gave Hetherington's pistol to real estate lawyer Fletcher M. Haight. Late in 1857, Fletcher wrote to his son, Henry Haight (later governor of California), that Hetherington's land had been sold for taxes. Effusive diarist Hugh Breen, who had been pouring out his heart daily, scratched only this on July 29: "Hethington and Brace was Executed this evening at 6 o'clock."[46] He never wrote another entry.

17
Release

San Franciscans reacted feelingly to the ugly deaths of Hetherington and Brace. "There is a great stillness pervading today," noted diarist Denis Oliver the day after the hanging.[1] Quartermaster Kibbe wrote to Governor Johnson, "This community seems more indignant to-day in regard to the Vigilance Committee than ever before."[2] Vigilance Committee member and newspaper editor William Rhodes dispensed with his usual editorial, writing, "[W]e have no heart to comment on the terrible fate of the two felons." Acquainted with Terry since their boyhood in Texas and a secret witness for his defense, Rhodes added meaningfully, "Truly do we hope that these may be the last executions for crime in our community, for many years to come."[3] Even some Executives felt shaken. For a day and a half after the hanging, only nineteen or twenty men reported, instead of the recent cluster of thirty or so. The few in attendance conducted routine business, facing their enduring lack of funds and discussing the Pueblo Papers. They considered pugilist Christopher Lilly's request to be stricken from the Black List. He was later exonerated and so notified by a published card from "33 Secretary." Meanwhile, the Executives had agreed to return the loaned muskets with a vote of thanks. Not until the afternoon of July 31 did thirty-one Executives finally appear to prepare to meet an intransigent Board of Delegates that evening.[4]

Once again, the Executives faced hostile Committee members. They had a tough sell to make: although Terry had been duly convicted, he could neither be deported nor be executed. Consequently, the Executives allowed only seventy-nine of the ninety-two Delegates attending to vote, limiting the franchise to those who had heard the hours of Terry testimony read. Although Clancey Dempster later solemnly affirmed that "[p]ower to initiate measures was not bestowed on them [the Delegates]," the times had changed.[5] The angry Delegates, who had some ten weeks earlier solemnly sworn "to act with the Vigilance Committee and second in full all their actions as expressed through their executive Committee," now told the Executives what to do.[6] Specifically, they demanded:

> That the Executive [Committee] concurring, Judge Terry be banished from this state at the shortest possible notice under the usual penalty [of death if he returned].
>
> Moved and carried—That the Terry motion be referred back to the Executive Committee for their action.
>
> Moved and carried—In case the Executive Committee do not concur with the Board of Delegates in this action—
>
> Resolved, that the Executive Committee be respectfully requested to meet and act in joint convention with this body during and until the trial of David S. Terry is wholly concluded.[7]

So the Terry case went back to the Executives.

As public sentiment shifted, speculation grew about the potential repercussions of San Francisco's vigilantism. William Tecumseh Sherman wrote to his brother describing the latest events. He noted that the naval sloop-of-war *John Adams* was lurking in the bay to prevent Terry's banishment. Sherman added that the vigilantes "may yet hang Terry to save themselves the consequences of his return to the Bench. If there is not an entire revolution and withdrawal from the Union, then all these acts of violence must come up before our courts."[8] Alfred Green, caged in Fort Gunnybags along with Terry, had heard a similar rumor from the vigilantes' Grand Marshal, Charles Doane, who said that "the Committee had gone too far; that there was no retracing their steps, and that they would have to separate the State of California and the Pacific Coast from the general government."[9] The national government's reaction to the Committee remained a mystery. Although the *Sonora* had docked with the eastern mail not long after the latest hanging, once again it carried no federal instructions.

Even inside the Executive Committee, the vigilantes' problematic actions took their toll. Vice President J. W. Brittan believed a rumor that Sheriff Scannell and the Law and Order Party planned to arrest the Executives one by one as they went home. He therefore carried his cocked pistol in his pocket one night, believing that "these parties had no right to arrest him, and he should defend himself to the utmost . . . [even though] blood would be shed." No one molested him, but when he got home, he could not sleep, comparing his own position to Terry's attack by vigilantes. "He made up his mind that if he had been in Terry's place, he would have done as Terry did, and from that moment he determined that Terry should be free."[10]

The pressure of worsening public opinion weighed heavily on the Executives as they struggled to wind up their business. In the interim before the next Delegate assembly, they repeated the warning to all their current captives except Terry and Green that they must depart on the August 5 steamer. Although Charles Gallagher, one of Broderick's chief lieutenants and Casey's executor, had also been tapped for exile, the Executives formally reversed their decision and never deported him. They also accepted the wavering Brittan's resignation from the vice presidency. Elected to replace him as second vice president was former steamboat captain James D. Farwell, who had tried to lecture Commodore Farragut on the vigilantes' power.[11] Faced with dwindling attendance, the Executives also voted that "hereafter eleven members of Executive Committee constitute a quorum except in Terry case and making new arrests."[12] They would soon forget about the exceptions.

If the Delegates could be persuaded to release Terry and the few remaining blacklisted prisoners could be exiled, the only remaining captive would be Alfred Green. Therefore, a subcommittee of three Executives—Smiley, Dows, and David—began intensive negotiations with Green for the Pueblo Papers. As Green later reported, if he turned over the documents, the Executives had "bound themselves to pay me $25,000 cash upon delivery of the papers, and $75,000 contingent upon the Vigilance Committee's obtaining control of the government, which they expected to do at the next election."[13] The next day, the three Executives escorted Green back to his ranch. As their carriage pulled up, his sister and pregnant wife, who had not seen or heard from him in weeks, fell upon him, weeping. Green called to his eldest brother, whom the vigilantes had let out on parole on July 15, to produce the papers. His brother left immediately for a coal mine that the Greens owned some four or five miles down the coast, where he had hidden the papers the night of the raid.[14]

Then Green learned the full story of the vigilantes' actions. His tall, stately seventy-five-year-old mother came out and, drawing herself up to her full height, said, "'Alfred, my son, you had an honest father, and during his long life there was never a word of reproach brought against his name. I would sooner see you dead and buried than to have you come forth with any stain upon your name or character.' From the manner in which she spoke," Green added, " I judged that some wrongs had been perpetrated during my incarceration."[15]

The scope of destruction became obvious as Green walked through the garden gate. The ground had been entirely dug up, the garden ruined. "I asked who did this." "The Vigilantes," his mother answered, "crowds of them." The ruffians had been there every day, not just digging up the garden but tearing up all the carpets and floors of the house. They threatened the women, "some saying to them, 'You have these papers on your person. Give them up, or we will strip you naked and take them from you.'" They claimed that only surrendering the papers would save Alfred from execution.[16]

Tensions mounted. While David, Dows, and Smiley waited around for the Pueblo Papers, Green's mother showed her son the editorials that had been printed about him, "accusing me of almost every crime that a bad man is capable of committing." Then his brother arrived with an old-fashioned mahogany case. Pointing to it, Green told the Executives, "[H]ere are the papers. Don't touch them."[17]

The incredulous Executives reacted angrily. Green reported, "Tom Smiley was the first to answer. Said he, 'How is this, Mr. Green? Did you not make a contract with us to deliver over those papers upon payment of $25,000 and contingent, and you to have your liberty also? Do you mean to keep your contract or not?' at the same time he and the others [were] putting their hands upon their pistols." Unarmed, and surrounded by the unarmed women, Green exploded, "Do you call this a contract? Your Committee come out here, and arrest me in the dead of night, and carry me a prisoner to your fort, and keep me for weeks, and I know nothing of what is happening outside." Yes, he had made an agreement, but "when I consider that that bargain was made by me in ignorance of what transpired during my incarceration . . . the outrages . . . the fearful lies they have had published about me and my family, I would have let the flesh rot upon my bones before I would have deigned to make any kind of a bargain with you.'" He would give up the papers only if "the Committee pass [and publish] a resolution that there is nothing against me or any member of my family, and let it be signed by the proper officers."[18]

What Green understood all too well was that in an era when deals were done "on a handshake," a man's reputation helped gauge his monetary worth. A contemporary businessman explained, "Mercantile bills are an exceedingly difficult kind of security to understand. . . . The 'credit' of a person—that is, the reliance which may be placed on his pecuniary fidelity—is a different thing from his property. No doubt, other things being equal, a rich man is more likely to pay than a poor man, but on the other hand there are many men not of much wealth who are trusted in the market, 'as a matter of business.'"[19] These mercantile bills were a sort of IOU brought to a bank that would "discount" them, giving the borrower their face value minus an interest charge. Borrowers had to repay the full value of the note by the date stated on it, or it could be renewed for an additional interest charge. Typically, borrowers—or those to whom they gave the notes as payment—had to endorse these documents to indicate their readiness to repay in the event of a default.[20] Only honorable men could engage in this business. Green needed public redemption. He demanded reimprisonment.

Dispirited, the Executives and Green returned to Fort Gunnybags to face their unrelieved difficulties. After Green was dumped back into his cell, the other Executives heard about the poor conduct of their police officers and their use of "improper language to the females of the [Green] family." They promised an internal investigation.[21] Preparing for another Delegate meeting two days later, just after the August 5 steamer's departure, the Executives admitted a fully recovered Sterling Hopkins to their chambers. Hopkins requested "the privilege of an interview with David S. Terry ... to arrange ... a money compromise" to the Terry impasse. The horrified Executives refused this dishonorable offer. Shortly thereafter, ninety-nine Delegates reported to their meeting, which Coleman chaired. In the first order of business, the Delegates backed an Executive decision to reprimand and discharge a vigilante who had aided a ruffian in escaping the city police. Second, each of the attending Executives presented his individual opinion on the Terry case. On a call for a vote to reconsider the Delegates' earlier sentence of banishment for Terry, the motion failed, thirty-nine noes to thirty-six yeses.[22] The following page in the *Minutes* is blank.[23] We can only imagine the issues discussed, the passion expended. Hours later, the meeting closed inconclusively.

The meeting resumed the next day. The weather was "excessively hot."[24] Only eighty-nine reported to the stifling committee rooms that evening. The Executives, having done the math from the previous tally, allowed seven new handpicked men to vote, their "having this day read the [Terry trial] testimony."[25] As Coleman later recalled, with "the First Vice President [Smiley] in the chair," the Delegates found "the Executive[s] firm and unchanged," resulting in "a long discussion."[26]

Facing an armed General Committee of thousands, the Executives could not simply win on an up-and-down vote. For their own safety, they had to convince their followers of the rightness of their conclusions. Inside the vigilantes' fort, the rancorous debate apparently lasted six hours. Additional information is scarce, but as a disgruntled French newspaper subsequently spouted, the Executives relied on the kinds of "tricks so frequent among politicians." Specifically, they decided to "close the doors at eight o'clock precisely, not to be opened again the same evening ... to influence some by promises; frightening others by fabricating stories of the enormous expenses of sending away into banishment and the transportation of the prisoner; fatiguing the unhappy; working in secret to deceive those who did not understand English." Around 1:30 a.m., the Executives "adroitly proposed the following question to be submitted to a vote of the Delegates: 'In the hands of whom, of the Executive or the Delegates, should rest the sentence to be applied to Judge Terry?' This new question [was] innocently adopted by the honest French Delegates, not suspecting that it was ... a snare for them." The vote favored the Executives, forty-four to thirty-six.[27]

Within minutes, ten Executives gathered in their own chambers. Executive Aaron Burns had to be rousted out of his bed to make up the eleven-man quorum.[28] With Smiley presiding, N. O. Arrington moved "[t]hat D. S. Terry is brought before this body and that the sentence in his case be read to him and that he be forthwith discharged. At 2.15 am David S. Terry was released from custody."[29]

Sturdy defense attorney Miers Truett, one of the eleven, hurried to the prison to release the judge. As the two men strode past the almost empty line of cells, Terry murmured to the last remaining inmate, "Good-bye Mr. Green." Shortly thereafter, Green recalled, "the vigilantes arrived in the building in great numbers. I heard a great commotion on the floor underneath, also on the second floor around where I was." Everyone was discussing Terry, and Green caught these words: "'They have let Terry go!' 'If Terry is allowed to go, why should they keep Green?'"[30] His hopes rose.

Terry's ordeal was not yet over. As Truett led the judge through the labyrinthine Fort Gunnybags, the powerful young Executive caught sight of some four to six hundred angry vigilantes, forewarned by leaks or rumors, prowling outside the main Sacramento Street entrance. Fearing the "danger of Terry's being attacked," Truett quietly smuggled the judge through the Executives' private entrance and "to the house of his friend, [D. W.] Perley," where Cornelia Terry was waiting. Then Truett went home for some much-needed sleep. He was soon awakened by vigilantes Isaac Bluxome Jr. ("33 Secretary") and 7th Division captain and former fire chief George Hossefross. The two warned Truett of the growing crowd outside Fort Gunnybags. They cautioned that he had better "get Terry out of town before daylight . . . [or] he might be assassinated."[31] By now, "about a thousand men [are] hunting for Terry," said Bluxome.[32]

For the sake of his own honor, Truett had to protect Terry. Although Bluxome and Hossefross "had brought a large squad of men with them" for that purpose, Truett balked at trusting them. Out loud, he reasoned that a crowd would attract attention, and that they had better split up. The so-called protective guard dispersed to various points throughout the night-black city as the vigilante leaders went back to Perley's house, where they "found Terry and many of his friends still up, conversing," drinking champagne and enjoying the kind of food Terry had gone without for those seven long weeks.[33] The judge must have been startled by the sudden reappearance of his former captors. Bluxome knew that Terry hated him "like the devil," but he nonetheless offered his own room as a hiding place, saying, "they will not hunt you there."[34] Perley refused to trust Bluxome. Terry, remembering that Truett had kept his promise to protect him from the mob at the armory during his initial capture, turned to his former "defense counsel" for advice. At Truett's suggestion, decoy groups of Terry's supporters scattered in various directions while Truett conducted Terry to the nearby Broadway Wharf. Some of Terry's friends had hired a small boat there to take him to the *John Adams*.[35] Anyone trying to capture Terry now would have to face the guns of the U.S. Navy.

As dawn broke, a furious crowd two to three thousand strong massed at Fort Gunnybags. Someone tried to ring the bell to call the vigilantes to arms, but the Executives had muzzled the clapper.[36] Truett remembered vigilantes "in the rooms and outside, . . . very much excited, and demanding to know why Terry had been discharged, and particularly why he had been discharged in such a manner."[37] Another Executive observed that Terry's release "nearly broke up the Committee."[38]

In his thin-walled cell, Green heard the commotion. He recalled the Executives "addressing distinct and separate bodies. The general line of the speakers . . . [attempted] to pacify the dissatisfied members of the mass of the Vigilance Committee," the only time any Executives had communicated directly with the general members rather than working through the Delegates. "I could hear statements to the effect that a U. S. man of war had drawn up, that they had to let Terry go or they would have been bombarded, and advising the members to be calm, to exercise discretion and patience, and other remarks to that effect," he added.[39] Observing the tense scene, Truett felt completely justified in his actions of the previous night.[40]

The fallout continued. At 11:00 a.m., some nine hours after Terry walked free, eleven Executives had to face angry, incredulous colleagues. Amidst furious denunciations, four Executives filed a formal letter of protest.[41] That afternoon, Thomas Sim King, the editor of the *Evening Bulletin*, who had long libeled Terry, snarled that "the Executive Committee have taken action which . . . [is] criminal, unwise, and weak. . . . They no longer represent the feeling of our community."[42] An accompanying article called on "the betrayed members of the body to reorganize themselves and elect an executive body of tried men, fewer in number, but with stout hearts and clean hands. . . . No more secret execution committees must exist."[43] Catholic merchant Denis Oliver excitedly reported that some vigilantes "threaten to hang their own members that let him go. . . . The Law & Order party are in great glee."[44]

The vigilantes' long campaign to destroy Terry's character had backfired. An anonymous letter in the *Bulletin* asked if the freed judge was the same "*criminal* that hundreds and thousands of the Vigilants have spent their money and their time, and sacrificed their hours of rest in guarding for the last six weeks." What had happened to the Executive Committee? "They could hang poor Brace for the commission of a crime two years ago, and *transport* a large number for wrongs done before the Committee was formed, and why should they not do the same by this *judge*, who makes his *decisions* with cold steel, in hot blood?"[45] Other, similar letters poured in. A few days later, one vigilante personally wrote to the Executives, citing the Terry debacle, and resigned.[46] At Grand Marshal Doane's insistence, the departing vigilante was formally dismissed with disgrace.[47]

The vigilantes' opposition celebrated just as ardently. The day after Terry's release, men and women piled onto the federal sloop-of-war *John Adams* all day long to congratulate the judge "on his escape from the den on Sacramento street." That afternoon, an excited crowd gathered along the Pacific Street Wharf to see Terry take the regular 4:00 p.m. steamer, the *Helen Hensley*, back to Sacramento, accompanied by almost three hundred personal friends who had also booked passage. Cornelia Terry, accompanied by friends, also waited on the upriver steamer for her husband. Navy sailors from the *John Adams* lowered a boat and, with the judge sitting tall in their midst, rowed him out some two hundred yards to put him aboard the *Hensley* as it puffed alongside. Supporters crowded around Terry, some of them in tears. When Terry appeared on the hurricane deck, a mighty cheer went up from the crowd on the wharf, echoed by his friends on board. As the steamer passed the *John Adams*, its crew mounted the rigging, waving their caps as naval officers stood with their heads uncovered. The *Adams* fired a salute, and received three rousing cheers from the throng aboard the steamer, which dipped its flags.[48] (Boutwell later disingenuously explained to Farragut that this signal was to inform Terry's "friends that the Judge had departed, so that they might know the fact without coming off to the ship to ascertain it.")[49] Farther out on the bay, the federal revenue cutter *Marcy* gave a three-gun salute, repaid by wild cheering from the *Hensley*. As the steamer paddled up toward Benecia, the thirty members of San Francisco's newly energized Young Men's Democratic Club on board, wearing their white satin badges, honored Terry with a badge of his own. Three cheers sped the steamer on from Benecia. It was almost 2:00 a.m. when the *Helen Hensley* rounded the bend in the American River and its passengers saw Sacramento lit in a blaze of fire. "All along the levee, from the steamboat landing to a couple of squares beyond, were stationed double files of firemen, dressed in their red shirts, and carrying in their hands brilliant torches," a reporter marveled. The fire companies had set tar barrels alight all along the landing, shooting up red, blue, and green flames. As the steamer chugged slowly toward the dock, "artillery was booming out its deep-toned welcome, and rockets were traversing the heavens in every direction, and breaking in beautiful coruscations of light and color." The crew returned the salute by vigorously ringing the *Hensley*'s bell, answered by more "artillery, rockets, and the excited cheers of the multitude at the landing." As the boat slowly swung around to the pier, the crowd caught sight of Judge Terry on the forward upper deck. Wild, spontaneous shouts echoed across the dark water.[50]

Sacramento gave Terry a hero's welcome. As soon as the gangplank was lowered, a jubilant crowd rushed on board and bore the judge on their shoulders to an open carriage drawn by four matched bay horses, accompanied by outriders, and lit by firemen with torches. A parade two thousand strong wound through the city streets as ladies threw bouquets and men shouted out their welcome. At the Orleans Hotel, beneath a candle-lit transparency reading "David S. Terry, Welcome Home! Law Is Mighty and Will Prevail!" Terry heard a short welcoming speech, then mounted the newly constructed speakers' platform. Looking out over the flames and flowers, he acknowledged the emotional impact of this "earnest and unexpected reception.... I have only performed a duty prompted by a love and veneration for the Constitution," he insisted. Despite the vigilantes' best efforts, Terry's reputation, his most sacred possession, had remained untarnished. Well aware of this fact, he expressed his strongest gratitude for "the esteem of those whose good opinion is dearer to me than life." Terry continued his brief remarks, then again thanked his supporters. After more cheers and showers of blossoms, the crowd heard five other speakers and finally departed, satisfied, at 4:00 a.m.[51] Citizens of Terry's home in Stockton echoed this ebullient welcome on the evening of August 16.[52]

While interior citizens cheered Terry, in San Francisco the Executives were dealing with the continuing negative fallout. In hopes of exoneration, the vigilante leaders decided to print twenty-five hundred copies of Terry's transcript of trial to show the judge as he really was. They authorized an expenditure of $300 for this purpose despite their increasingly dismal finances. By August 9, the balance sheet was anything but balanced: "Audited bills unpaid $1867.83. Cash on hand about $50.00." The Executives curtailed other expenses and began selling membership certificates to any member in good standing for $2.50, urging "all who can afford to pay more . . . to do so."[53] As knowledge spread of the details of Terry's escape from Fort Gunnybags, the Executive Committee twice had to defend Miers Truett against internal accusations of treason. They finally decided to hold a limited adjournment on August 21, just after the departure of the next steamer. After that, they would meet only three times weekly "until otherwise ordered," or when they were driven by other nagging unfinished business, including the fate of men still on the Black List and of pueblo advocate Alfred A. Green.[54]

18
A False Finale

Most pressing after the Terry debacle, the Executives had to justify their continued existence by securing the Pueblo Papers. Just hours after Terry was released, Executives David, Dows, and Smiley had gone to Green's cell and inquired "on what terms I would deliver up the archives," Green recalled. Green demanded "$50,000 . . . for I am going to take all the members [of my family] out of the country, for I will not live in a country that will not protect its citizens.'"[1] Unwilling to pay that much for the documents, the Executives discussed several alternatives. On August 10, to sweeten their proffered deal, they formally pardoned all the Green brothers except Alfred.[2] Unfortunately, an anonymous letter appeared in the *Bulletin* the next day claiming that James King of William had been on the point of publishing an exposé about San Francisco real estate when he was shot. The letter promised revelations that would doom the legitimacy of the Pueblo Papers.[3] The startled Executives pressured Green, and some "threatened to hang him. Others held that we could not, as he had not been guilty of murder," remembered Clancey Dempster.[4] Within another day or two, Green had secured the required published resolution about himself and his family's honor, and was set at liberty. One of his brothers brought the papers to the Executives, but only on September 12—a full month later—did the Executives grant their Green committee "the power to act as they saw fit."[5] The subcommittee paid Green $12,500 for the Pueblo Papers—half the promised amount, but, they claimed, it was all they could afford. They also alerted his creditors. Thus, when Green collected the cash, "a party of unscrupulous men, in connection with some of them who were in the Vigilance Committee, and in league with the land sharks outside, seized upon four or five thousand dollars of the money, under a pretended legal order, and carried it off,"

Green complained. Later, the debts ascribed to Green were set aside, he added, but all the same, "the land sharks got the money."[6] He would need to find another way to recoup his finances.

While the Executives had dealt with their most pressing land business in secret, public events had been set in motion to meet the long-standing vigilante goal of a regime change in San Francisco. During the long, leaky debate about Terry's sentence, the *Bulletin* had issued a call for "A Reform Party." Citing concern for "the future well-being of the state," the article declared, *"The men we need in office are the men who do not seek it."*[7] The power-hungry Executives were thus publicly repudiated. On August 8, with San Francisco still reeling from the jolt of Terry's release, the *Bulletin* had followed up by announcing a "great Mass Meeting" to be held in three days, aimed at political reform. The paper also printed an anonymous letter demanding a new state constitution that would leave "no room for such an illegal body as the Vigilance Committee."[8] There would be no easy political shoo-in for current vigilante Executives.

Given the shock of recent events, the new mass meeting began hesitantly. Voicing the views of many of the city's elite, Ira P. Rankin, who had also chaired the July 14 mass meeting (which had demanded that all elected officials resign), opened by observing, "I doubt the propriety of the movement at the present time [although] I most fully endorse the platform." Then he introduced the meeting's officers, including Frederick A. Woodworth, a land claimant under the Pueblo Papers, who had been number 4 in the 1851 Committee and was the brother of Selim E. Woodworth, its much-respected former president.[9] Reading a prepared speech, Woodworth outlined the usual complaint of San Francisco's alleged "violence, crime, and corruption." Claiming reform failure by the Whigs, Democrats, and American Party (Know-Nothings), he denied any interest in "interfering with the nominations of [national] President or Vice President," failing entirely to mention state officials, who had already set in motion San Francisco electoral reforms. Woodworth called for a "victory over ... our oppressors, and ... a Revolution that shall never go backward," promising that this crusade could be "carried, if you [interior sections] desire it, into all parts of the state."[10] The vigilantes' legal adviser promptly responded by offering a newly formed reform party—the Republicans! In the subsequent confusion, someone offered a resolution sustaining the current vigilantes.[11] "The effect was magical," recorded the partisan *Bulletin*. This motion carried with a thundering "aye," and the few succeeding "nays" "brought forth a universal burst of laughter as the miserable minority ... quietly slunk away" or pretended they had not spoken. At least this time there were no arrests by vigilante "police."[12] A motion for an Executive Committee on nominations failed initially, but after much debate, it was adopted. Its numbers were set at twenty-one, but three of the men proposed were rejected and replaced by others in attendance. Chairman Rankin closed the gathering by averring that, although he had signed the call for the meeting, "he did not wish to be considered as one of the projectors of the movement."[13] Among all this confusion, San Francisco's People's Party had been born.

The Democrats immediately convened their own city nominating convention, demanding men of unimpeachable character to "take the wind out of the People's party, which has just sprung to life," noted Denis Oliver. Their selections—including at least two secretly active vigilantes—included none of the old Broderick operatives.[14]

Inside their fort, the uneasy Executives formally prepared to disband. Debating the date of their final parade, they alternated between August 18, before the next mail steamer would leave, and August 21, after its departure. They settled on the latter date, ensuring that news of any disturbances would not be reported immediately in the East. However, when they approached the Delegates for their decision, the Delegates chose August 18.[15]

The anxious Executives felt some relief when the eastern mail arrived on August 14 with letters saying that there would be no federal intervention.[16] This East Coast decision making had taken months. Easterners had first learned of San Francisco's vigilantes on June 14, a month after Casey shot King. Committee actions had gained new notoriety on July 28, when the *New York Times* briefly reported Terry's arrest, and the U.S. Senate passed a resolution calling for information from President Pierce on "the self-styled Vigilance Committee in California."[17] Pierce had waited a full month to respond to Governor Johnson's June 19 request for federal arms, but his July 19 letter was not published in the *New York Times* until August 9. Only then did the eastern public read that Pierce had refused to supply any weapons. An accompanying letter from the secretary of state, New Yorker William Marcy, acknowledged the effect of the tremendous time lag between the two coasts: "The president will not allow himself to believe that the prevalence of rash counsels and lawless violence still continues in San Francisco," Marcy had written on July 19. Pierce trusted that by the time their communications were received, "the citizens . . . will already have assumed their obedience to the laws."[18]

President's Pierce's avowed belief in San Franciscans' speedy return to the status quo must have received a nasty jolt when the California news of July 21 arrived in New York on August 14, just as the Executives in San Francisco were planning their grand finale. That day, the front page of the *New York Times* carried large-type subheadings: "Vigilance Committee Still in Session" and "Trial of Judge Terry in

Progress." In this article, the pro-vigilante *Times* correspondent, "F. W. R.," claimed, "Nine-tenths of the people throughout the State acknowledge the necessity of [the Vigilance Committee's] action, and stand ready to give material aid if necessary." Furthermore, "the Governor has ceased all opposition to the people's tribunal," he claimed. The writer elaborated on Hopkins's stabbing, described the ongoing search for Judge Edward McGowan, and reported the arrest of "38 persons . . . about half of them . . . [with] sailing orders for this steamer." Among those arrested was "Alfred A. Green," kidnapped from his home because of the Pueblo Papers, who was also incorrectly reported as being accused of murder. "Nobody doubts, who knows the winning ways of the Committee, that the papers will be forthcoming," the correspondent wrote. Four lines of type announced Philander Brace's conviction, and that "he will be hung." Hetherington received no mention. The correspondent disparaged San Francisco's halting new government under the Consolidation Bill, embroidered the report of official misconduct, and concluded with items including Californians' response to the presidential nominations.[19]

Given the earlier arrival of another government steamboat in New Orleans, the news of Terry's continuing incarceration had already sped out to Harris County, Texas (today's Houston and environs). From there, Cornelia Terry's sister wrote on August 8, "You cannot imagine what an excitement our little town is thrown in. Yours & cousin Dave's letters [which Cornelia saw published on July 2 in California] have been copied in all our papers" and received widespread approval. "Cousin Frank [David Terry's older brother] is almost like a mad man—he says if cousin Dave dies, one hundred men die for him. . . . He is not the only one, who will die for him, if necessary. It will be the sadest [*sic*] day for the San Franciscans that ever dawned—if one hair of his head is touched."[20]

Unaware of growing concerns in the East, the Executives planned their final parade in San Francisco.[21] It was to be a magnificent affair. Vigilante military companies threw themselves into preparations. Company D, for example, opened a subscription book to defray expenses, and mandated that each member wear "Black clothes & Glazed Caps, [and] White Gloves" for the occasion.[22] Unimpressed, Denis Oliver recorded in his diary, "The vigilance committee are making great preparation for having a grand Military Parade through the City next Monday. The Traitors are thinking of Disbanding."[23]

While the Vigilance Committee was winding down in San Francisco, events continued to unfold on the East Coast. Governor Johnson's emissaries, after being exposed to yellow fever in Cuba leading to their quarantine in New York, finally arrived in Washington, D.C., to present the governor's pleas for federal arms to President Pierce.[24] The vigilantes' emissary called just after they left, creating confusion in the sectionally divided cabinet and the White House.²⁵ On August 29, Senator Sam Houston, already famous as a leader in the Texas Revolution, rose in Congress "to present a memorial . . . for the purpose of asking [federal] intervention in behalf of the Hon. David S. Terry." The Texas legislature had demanded that he do so, and had sent a companion memorial to President Pierce. After three other senators attested to Terry's high moral character, and one tried to affirm the loyalty of the Vigilance Committee to the Union despite rumors to the contrary, the Senate referred the whole matter to its Judiciary Committee.²⁶ As far as they knew, Terry was still in captivity, on trial for his life.

On the West Coast, completely oblivious to this mushrooming debate, the Executives directed their closing pageant. On August 18, the Vigilance Committee appeared with all the pomp of a genuine finale. Companies of vigilantes (estimated at 2,700–5,000 men, depending on the political leanings of the reporter) marched to parade position on that chilly gray morning, with regimental banners flying. The popular 1851 Executives (not part of the current Committee) rolled out in carriages at the beginning of the mile-long display, followed by the 1856 Committee's young president, William Tell Coleman, on a white horse and Grand Marshal Charles Doane on a black one (perhaps for easier escape in a disturbance). To the music of spirited bands, other mounted Executives and Committee leaders followed, then cavalry, infantry, captured California Militia cannons, the French Legion, German committeemen, and additional American vigilantes. Following the artillery came a float depicting Fort Gunnybags, decorated with five guns of small caliber. The spectacle wound back and forth through the hushed crowds packed into downtown San Francisco. "I never in my life saw so many persons together," proudly wrote vigilante police chief R. B. Wallace.²⁷ All along the route, women threw bouquets, which were crushed under the horses' hooves. As Coleman passed underneath a floral wreath on Stockton Street, a woman released a cord so that the wreath dropped over his head and rested on his shoulders as he waved triumphantly. Another division captain noted that until this final showing, the general public had not been "acquainted with our strength; they underestimated it."²⁸ A public farewell address promised to revive the organization, "if it were necessary, to protect its members against violence or malicious prosecution on account of the action of the committee."²⁹

Returning to their fort immediately after the parade, the relieved Executives "noticed with the utmost pleasure the unanimity of feeling and correctness of deportment displayed this day." They also requested that Grand Marshal Doane compliment the officers and men under his command for "the proficiency of their military evolutions and of the zeal they have at all times evinced in the performance

A San Francisco artist captured the grandeur of the vigilantes' final parade (starting with the Committee of 1851 on the left) and the huge throng of observers it attracted. *Courtesy of the Bancroft Library.*

of their arduous duties." They remembered to issue a French translation three days later. Finally, they commended the police department for its many "valuable services"—services that had not yet concluded.[30]

While the public and the General Committee retired, well satisfied at this assumed conclusion of the vigilantes' activity, the Executives continued meeting. As Executive Manrow noted, "We kept the organization together as a sort of self-protection after we disbanded." This included "a military force of about three to four hundred [men] ... pickets ... and spies ... and a guard always at hand." They retained the daily password for admission.[31] In fact, noted a contemporary historian, the Committee "was never formally dissolved."[32]

With the vigilantes' local efforts supposedly ended, Coleman was ready to return east on the August 20 steamer. The *Alta* had already advertised a new company with a Wall Street address: "Coleman's CALIFORNIA LINE! New York and San Francisco ... every Californian [is invited] to ship by it."[33] Commerce had often distracted Coleman, even during the active life of the Committee. As another Executive later recalled, "Coleman did not attend fully to his [vigilante] business and frequently he had the Vice President in the chair, most of the time, in fact.

James D. Farwell and Thomas J. L. Smiley were the Vice Presidents."[34] Decades later, Coleman rationalized that Smiley had become sufficiently organized and "wanted to lead. I was willing so far as it was safe," although "many others were not." He added, "I became worn and feared illness, and didn't in the least fear any rivalry. I had no desire or personal ambition."[35] When he packed his bags, Coleman probably included the elegant certificate awarded to him by his fellow Executives.[36] Before leaving, the vigilante president wrote a page-long letter to Governor J. Neely Johnson, formerly his "particular friend," lamenting that he had not had time to visit Johnson in Sacramento before his departure. Although the Vigilance Committee had wrecked Johnson's California political career, Coleman disingenuously referred only to three months of differences about "the local politics of this place." He added, "I feel assured that if you could have been really more correctly informed on the true state of things here . . . you as an individual would have agreed with them," meaning the vigilantes. Oddly, he did not write "us." Coleman suggested that they "bury the hatchet" and meet as friends "in the spring . . . when I return with my family."[37] Johnson's response, if any, was not recorded.

As Coleman sailed for the East, the remaining Executives removed the gunnybags and threw open their fort to a curious public for three days. Throngs viewed the artwork donated to the Committee, including a bust of James King of William made from a cast just after his death; the prison cells with air holes bored into the floor; captured California Militia muskets hanging from the walls and ceiling; several shiny cannons; Terry's rifle; embroidered banners; the ropes with which four men had been hanged; and the Bible on which members took their solemn oaths. Flowers sent by sympathetic ladies perfumed the air. Each of the divisions had its own display, and they vied with each other in grandeur. The sword donated to the Company D commander "was almost encased in wreaths of roses." The 23rd Division displayed beautifully sewn American, German, French, and English flags. The 5th Division, or Coleman Guards, showed off their arms, including the whale harpoon "borne on . . . the taking of the jail . . . by the old salt who knew so well how to use it." The partially opened "patent ballot box" drew an admiring crowd. Respectable ladies—reportedly more than 2,860 of them—got preference upon entering with their parties, and one man whose sick wife had stayed home complained that he could not get in at all despite the extended hours.[38] But not everyone was enthralled. As Denis Oliver noted, "The vigilance committee through [sic] their Rooms or Prison open to the public with a box at the Door to receive contributions to defray part of their expenses. I will not go near there. They give a Ball at the Musical Hall tonight to raise funds."[39] Admission cost five dollars.[40]

The Executives needed the money. The day before the parade, they learned that they had spent $29,826.56 to date; held audited bills of more than $1,400 that had been approved but remained unpaid; and possessed less than $150 in the kitty.[41] A three-man Executive Finance Committee solicited more donations; others sold the old "George Law" muskets to members for $1.25 each. Executive and merchant-auctioneer Smiley auctioned off memorabilia, including "lumber, part composing the scaffolding of Brace and Hetherington, and part of the cells of Casey and Cora," as well as "mattresses, furniture, utensils, and arms." From this last effort they realized only five or six hundred dollars.[42]

As the Executives tried to clear their debts, the still-powerful Democrats gathered to elect delegates to the party's nominating convention. Thanks to Broderick's acting as a "spoiler," Gwin's seat had been vacant since 1855. And since senators were elected by state legislatures at the time, and the Democrats were the only statewide political party, these men, in effect, would be able to choose two U.S. senators in January 1857. Everyone knew that David Broderick coveted a senatorial position. For three months, the vigilantes had tried hard to break Broderick's power by attacking his followers. They had succeeded in gutting his organization in San Francisco, but they could not get rid of the man himself. On election night, as Broderick supporter and fellow Catholic Denis Oliver recorded in his diary, "The Democrats held a primary election in various Districts for Delegates to go to Sacramento. . . . The friends of Mr. Broderick were successful."[43]

Most of California's residents resumed their accustomed routines. David Terry returned to the California Supreme Court with enhanced stature due to his captivity.[44] The day the court opened, he was awarded "a magnificent silver pitcher . . . [inscribed to] 'Hon. D. S. Terry, from the ladies of San Francisco, who admire his courage, honor his patriotism, and take the highest pride in his heroic resistance to tyranny—August 26, 1856.'"[45] Meanwhile, a number of dogged Executives continued meeting—twenty-one on August 25 and 26, seventeen on August 27.[46] Then their wall of secrecy crumbled. On August 28, the unfriendly *Herald* published a list of names, "kindly furnished us by a friend, who is one of the 'knowing ones.'" It began with "Wm. T. Coleman, President . . . Isaac Bluxome, (33), Secretary . . . Thos. J. L. Smiley, Prosecuting Attorney," and so on. A "Recapitulation" immediately followed: "Merchants, 22; Merchants' Clerks, 2; Ex-bankers, 1; Merchandise Brokers, 2; Assayers, 1; Wharfingers [wharf supervisors], 2; Steamboat Captains, 1; Stevadores [*sic*], 1; Searcher of Records, 1; Real Estate Agents, 2; Builders, 1; Machinists, 1; Blacksmiths, 1; Total, 40."[47] Although the names of a few Executives were missing, all but one of those listed had in fact served actively as Executives or as heads of key subcommittees. For a group that had relied on the protection of secrecy, this list was stunningly accurate.

That same day, the steamer *Golden Age* arrived in San Francisco, twenty-three days out of New York, with unsettling reports of the increasingly negative views in the East. The anti-vigilante *San Francisco Herald* hailed the news and highlighted a letter published in New York by deportee J. R. Molony, the chief prosecution witness in John Durkee's upcoming piracy trial. From exile, Molony outlined the events of his capture and imprisonment: the handcuffing and hiding; the failed writ of habeas corpus; the fruitless pressure on him to serve as a witness against David Terry; and, finally, his forced departure on the mail steamer of July 5, leaving his wife behind and large debts uncollected. When his Executive escort insisted that he sign a letter stating his "desire" to leave, Molony refused, until two friends on board guaranteed him that signing under duress would not abrogate his constitutional rights. Molony had demanded that the Executives explain the charges against him. "'We are not here to answer any questions,' was the answer, and they walked away," he reported.[48] News also arrived of another deportee's letter published in New Orleans, stating that any man condemned by the Vigilance Committee "had to quit the city at the sacrifice of his property and his business, or be the means of shedding the blood of hundreds of innocent men, by inaugurating a[n armed] conflict."[49] Reading this and other news, Denis Oliver succinctly reported that "all the Eastern Newspapers are out against the vigilance committee."[50] Particularly given the bicoastal nature of most merchant-Executives' business dealings, their work was far from over.

19
Pirates and Payback

Of more immediate concern than adverse eastern opinion, the Executives had to weather the federal piracy trial of their members who had attacked the *Julia*. On September 1, the U.S. Circuit Court for Northern California opened with Judge Matthew Hall McAllister (earlier buttonholed by deportee Charles Duane, the former fire captain, on the inbound steamer) and Judge Ogden Hoffman on the bench. McAllister revealed his strong anti-vigilante bias in his charge to the grand jury that "anybody engaged in . . . outrages against the United States [including stealing letters from the U.S. mail] must be considered as a principal in them." He then gave the standard demand for secrecy, which was promptly ignored.[1] Simultaneously, in their covert meeting, the Executives proposed "publishing a full and complete History of the Origin and Doings of the Committee of Vigilance together with such testimony and facts as may be in the hands of the Executive Committee" to raise money and stimulate (they hoped) positive testimony.[2] Faced with their need for secrecy, the motion failed. This proposal was never raised again.

The new federal grand jury soon indicted vigilantes John Durkee and Charles Rand for piracy in the attack on the *Julia*. The accused submitted to arrest and were locked in the county jail because Judge McAllister refused to set bail, although eight Executives had volunteered to be their bondsmen.[3] After all, Durkee had been elevated to deputy director of vigilante police less than two weeks earlier, in the shakeup that followed the revelation of the Green women's mistreatment.[4] Locked in James Casey's old cell in the county jail, Durkee heard a rumor that Boutwell's sloop *John Adams* had docked nearby in order to hang him from the yardarm in the event of a conviction. If that were to be attempted, Durkee confidently put his faith in Committee intervention.[5]

Durkee knew his fellow vigilantes. Upon hearing about his incarceration, some men rushed up to the roof of Fort Gunnybags and began ringing the Monument bell. Confused vigilante militia rushed to the now-unfortified building, wondering whom to attack. The alarmed Executives dispersed their followers, set a new guard on the bell, and personally called on Judge McAllister to renew the request for bail for their men. The judge remained adamant.[6] "It was with utmost difficulty that I prevailed on the committee not to attack the jail and rescue the men from the U.S. Marshal," wrote Durkee's defense attorney, Joseph Bryant Crockett, a few days later.[7] Clashes with federal authorities must be avoided at all costs.

Alarmed by the ferocity of their rank and file, twenty-seven Executives met that night to plan their next action, but the *Minutes* are silent on the outcome.[8] The next day, the *Herald* published a rumor that a motion to rescue Durkee and Rand had been supported by Charles Doane, the Grand Marshal, and Executives George Ward, William Rogers, Thomas J. L. Smiley, Jules David, James Dows, Charles V. Gillespie, Isaac Bluxome Jr., John Manrow, and Alfred Tubbs.[9] Nothing happened. The grand jury then indicted two additional vigilantes for piracy. The alerted Executives promptly commanded these men "to absent themselves from the city for a short time, their expenses to be paid by the Committee of Vigilance."[10] They were never apprehended. The Executives also carefully examined the list of available jurors and directed that notices be posted so that members could identify those unfriendly to the Committee and report their names "to the Executive Committee in writing as soon as possible."[11]

Sure enough, vigilante considerations controlled the jury selection. Denis Oliver was called to jury duty, but reported that he "would not be accepted as a Juror because I am predisposed against the vigilance committee."[12] The judges also banned members of the Young Men's Democratic Club from the jury, as well as sworn vigilantes.[13] For once, vigilante secrecy paid off when the first name drawn "was a member of the committee," a relieved Durkee later remembered.[14] He served. Outside the Committee, who knew?

Emotions ran high as the September 5 steamer prepared to leave the dock. Writing for the outgoing mail, defense attorney Crockett called the charge of "piracy ... preposterous ... [and] a pretext for producing a collision between the committee & the U.S. authorities." Were such a clash to occur, it would "result in a revolution throughout the state ... [and] a repudiation by this state of the federal authority."[15] Publicly echoing Crockett's thoughts, William Rhodes, an active vigilante and the proprietor of the *True Californian*, editorialized that no force "which the State of California can concentrate at San Francisco, including all the aid she can expect from the Federal authorities, will be sufficient to harm a single hair of the heads of

Durkee and Rand." Rhodes emphasized that "six thousand men, now in this city, fully armed . . . would spill the last drop of their blood, and dissipate the last cent of their fortunes, before they would permit either one of these gentlemen . . . to be incarcerated in a dungeon, or swung from a scaffold. . . . The attempt to do so, will be a signal for bloodier days than Paris ever saw."[16] Executive Dows, having just resigned as vigilante treasurer (he was replaced by French Executive Jules David), boarded the outgoing steamer for New York. On board, Dows angrily announced to his shipmates that if the vigilantes were convicted, "Judge McAllister and the Jury, and the United States Marshal would be hung out of the windows of the Court House." Furthermore, he sneered, should the federal government try to intervene, the vigilantes intended to "take the United States Mint, Mare Island, Navy Yard, Fort Point, and all the United States vessels lying in the harbor."[17]

Quietly watching developments, Captain Farragut wrote to the secretary of the navy in the outgoing mail. He first expressed gratification that "the Department approves of my course in the past, and equally so that it found no fault with Commander Boutwell," as both had striven "to procure the release of Judge Terry." He also informed the secretary that, although the vigilantes had ceased public drilling, "the men retain their arms, and stand ready to answer a call to arms at any moment. Within a few days past they have issued an order, through the daily papers, to Supervisor J. D. Musgrove, to leave the state forever."[18] Mapmaker Musgrove's successful disappearance had tipped the Executives' hand. Their prolonged existence was now a secret to no one.

Further revealing the Executives' ongoing activities, two new vigilante exiles departed on the September 5 steamer. James "Liverpool Jack" Thompson, blacklisted since June 9, had been warned to leave on August 20 or face execution. He had gone into hiding, but was soon tracked and captured. When he was brought before the Executives, their death threat proved hollow. Thompson told them that he would leave if he could get a sailor's berth on a ship for China, and the cash-strapped Executives willingly let him try. In the end, they had to pay to ship him to Panama. Another new exile, John Stephens, was simultaneously shipped out because he had assaulted "a member of this Committee of Vigilance and a messenger of the 23d Company" while on an official errand. In this case, the Executives sent Stephens a disingenuous letter stating that his "prayer [to leave] had been granted upon the especial condition that you never return under penalty of <u>death</u>."[19]

The departing steamer not only bore the most recent vigilante exiles, it also carried copies of *Trial of David S. Terry by the Committee of Vigilance, San Francisco*, which had been hurriedly published by the Executives. Locally, the seventy-five-page booklet seemed to be having the desired effect on public opinion. As a Sacramento paper noted, "almost everyone we have conversed with this morning has read it." As a result, approval rose for the Executives' decision to release Terry. However, Terry's much-blackened reputation also improved. As the article continued, "[H]owever much prejudice... [must exist] against Terry, all must admit that his bearing and deportment, during his confinement, was that of a brave, fearless, and honorable gentleman, who, believing he was guilty of no crime, trusted his case to the generosity and magnanimity of his judges." Terry glowed "in a more favorable, and we believe a truer light, before his fellow-citizens," rendering them "ashamed of the wrongful thirst for vengeance upon him which they harbored in moments of excitement and passion."[20] The Executives also hoped for a favorable response in Congress, where they knew that lengthy petitions from Texas had been received "asking legislative action in behalf of Judge Terry."[21]

As the steamer churned away, tensions rose over the vigilante piracy case. When the trial started on September 8, the "court house & the avenues leading to it were packed & jammed as full as they could be," mostly with pro-vigilance men, reported defense attorney Crockett.[22] Durkee was the first to go to trial; the outcome in his case would govern that of Rand. The prosecution called several witnesses who came when they were summoned. Then they got to James R. Molony. Three times, the deputy marshal went to the door and called out Molony's name. Three times, no one responded. Molony, of course, was in New York, where he had been exiled by the vigilantes, precisely so that he could not testify in this case. The court then heard several witnesses in Durkee's defense. Diminutive, fiery Executive George Ward, the last defense witness, testified that the arms received from the schooner *Julia* had been sent away from the Vigilance Committee rooms the same day they were received. They had been captured only for self-protection and were never used, he insisted. (Only the attack on the *Julia* was before the court. The simultaneous boarding of the *Mariposa*, with its cargo of Sharps rifles bought by Terry and actively employed by the vigilantes, never came up.) As long as the governor's Proclamation of Insurrection was in effect, Ward claimed, it was unreasonable to expect the return of state arms to Quartermaster Kibbe. The vigilantes still retained them. However, Ward pledged "to deliver them up at the proper time."[23]

As the trial wore on, Judge McAllister faced a quandary. Although he despised the vigilantes, he had to protect the dignity of his court. He faced essentially the same problem that had confronted Governor Johnson, William Tecumseh Sherman, and Commander Boutwell. If Durkee were to be convicted of piracy, could the sentence be enforced in the face of the vigilantes' armed strength? Both he and Judge Hoffman wrote to General Wool, informing the commander that the marshal had insufficient forces "to ensure the safe-keeping of the prisoners, or command respect for the process of the court" in the face of hostile crowds both inside and outside the courtroom. Would Wool be willing to provide aid? Ever consistent, Wool refused.[24]

Late on September 11, Durkee's trial ended with wordy summations from the prosecution and the defense. Then McAllister gave the all-important charge to the jury, essentially dictating the trial's outcome. In a surprising about-face, he followed the argument of the defense. If the vigilantes had taken the arms for their own use, he instructed, Durkee must be found guilty. However, if the arms had been taken only to prevent their being used against the defendants, the verdict should be not guilty. Departing the courtroom, the jury returned within three minutes. As Crockett promptly wrote to his wife, the vigilantes "were acquitted by the jury. The verdict was received with a shout by the crowd, and the prisoners were carried out of the room by the people in the wildest excitement." An exhausted Crockett, who had just delivered his lengthy summation, went home to bed, only to be awakened shortly by "a brass band" and "tremendous cheers. . . . Everybody is sick of the continued agitation, except a few hot-headed & reckless men on each side, who will speedily relapse into their original insignificance," he optimistically—and unrealistically—concluded.[25]

While the piracy verdict took one burden off the Executives, they retained a lingering fear of federal retaliation, and they still had to pay their bills. Invoices for previous services kept rolling in, including one for guns and ammunition for a total of $122. This bill was marked "Objected to."[26] Another man submitted a bill "For bringing Maloney [*sic*: Molony] as a prisoner in my carriage to Comm. Rooms," noting, "This bill has been before presented for $10 & audited for $5—but never paid."[27] On September 11, even the previously compliant Pacific Mail Steamship Company presented the Executives with a bill for the June 5 deportation of their first exiles: Charles Duane, William Mulligan, and William "Wooley" Kearney.[28]

The Executives then attempted some moneymaking schemes, but with uneven results. Sales of the Terry trial booklet slowly generated income: $500 by September 9, and another $650 by October 7.[29] By mid-September, sales of printed membership certificates had brought in some money, but they also caused spiteful repercussions: James N. Olney and J. L. Polk, both active vigilantes, were accused of mishandling funds.[30] Olney, who as captain of the Citizens' Guard and Deputy Grand Marshal had engineered many arrests, was cashiered, and a week later was given a final payment of $100.[31] Polk, in turn, accused Smiley of fraud, although the Executives cleared Smiley and declared that Polk "was [the] guilty one." Polk was expelled from the Committee, and he was reported as a defaulter on blackboards within Fort Gunnybags.[32] Meanwhile, overenthusiastic vigilante H. Channing Beals placed an advertisement in two September 8 morning papers. "Vigilantes Ahoy!" read the ad, which promised that men with two sponsors among the (supposedly secret) current Committee had the right to join by application for the sum of five dollars.[33] That afternoon, angry Executives confronted Beals and sent notices to the *Alta California* and the *Chronicle* stating that the ad was "unauthorized" and that any future communication should bear "the seal of this body."[34]

The only other Committee recourse was to slash expenses. On September 12, new treasurer Jules David recommended that "all the employees of the Committee of Vigilance" be discharged, "except the following: 2 policemen, 2 Sergeant At-Arms and Mr. H. C. Beals."[35] (Kept on salary for five more months, Beals was allowed to continue printing and selling properly authorized certificates well into the following year.)[36] The Executives had already sold the "patent ballot box" with its sliding panels to a member for $4,000, with $500 paid up front and the remainder due in $500 increments as soon "as the same should be collected by public exhibition of the said Box throughout the State." Unfortunately, the expected throngs did not turn out to view this artifact despite an Executive-generated certificate testifying to its genuineness. On September 16, the purchaser had to beg off from his second payment and was compelled to return the box.[37]

In late September, eastern news arrived by steamer that threw the city into renewed turmoil. President Pierce had changed his mind. Calling Congress into an extra and extraordinary session, the president had forced passage of the Army Appropriations Bill. Thanks largely to the pressure put on Congress by pro-Terry Texans, the bill contained a provision to use some of these new military appropriations to provide Governor Johnson with federal arms. Before sending the weapons, however, Pierce had decided to poll his sectionally divided cabinet. The president encountered strong opposition from Secretary of War Jefferson Davis of Mississippi (later president of the Confederacy), who balked at sending federal troops or weapons to fight in one of the sovereign states.[38] Although the prospect of an actual government attack remained uncertain, the Executives warned their police to avoid arresting men "on the coasters of the bay," whose waters were under federal jurisdiction.[39]

A second jolt came with the simultaneous arrival by steamer of copies of the *Presbyterian*, a religious paper printed at Philadelphia. It contained a letter written by the Reverend William A. Scott of San Francisco's Calvary Church, titled "The Church and Lynch Law," that was highly critical of the vigilantes, This nationally prominent minister had avoided expressing his anti-vigilante views since the explosive reaction to his July sermon "A Discourse for the Times." Now, Scott explained, his continuing silence on the Committee's activities had put him in

An elaborate personalized certificate could be bought by any Vigilance Committee member in good standing to commemorate participation in the exciting organization and help reduce its outstanding debts. Gorham Blake, number 5337, bought his too late to receive a document signed by Committee president William Tell Coleman and had to be content with the signature of the vice president, Thomas J. L. Smiley, instead. Other signatories (who had previously signed with Coleman) included Secretary Isaac Bluxome Jr., Grand Marshal Charles Doane, and Deputy Treasurer William Meyer. Treasurer Jules David, a Frenchman and a Jew, was not allowed to sign.
Courtesy of the California History Room, California State Library, Sacramento.

the false position of seeming acquiescence. Since the Committee had supposedly disbanded and tempers had allegedly cooled, he "came out fully and honestly with his views, and so expressed them, that they might be received here [in San Francisco] after the people had settled calmly down to reflect and reason."[40]

Scott had badly misjudged the emotions of his adopted city. Tempers flared. A young assayer of the U.S. Mint immediately publicized his intention to speak against Dr. Scott and the Army Appropriations Bill. His boss, however, warned him that if he spoke publicly, even under a pseudonym, he would be fired from the Mint.[41] Then, just before the Calvary Church opened for worship on Sunday, October 6, someone hung Reverend Scott in effigy from a lamppost across the street. Disgusted San Franciscans blamed the Committee for this anonymous shocking act. In response, the Executive members of Scott's congregation crowded Calvary's pews, along with numerous anti-vigilance citizens who thought his church might otherwise be deserted. The perpetrators were never caught.[42]

The Executives, meanwhile, were dealing with problems related to the deportees. They had explicitly retained the right to banish whomever they saw fit, and to punish any returning exiles. On October 3, they instructed the chief of police "to arrest J. R. Maloney [sic] or any other person banished on his return," and to publish a list of persons exiled.[43] Anyone caught would be hanged. Two days later, they learned that Martin Gallagher, deported on June 5, was back in San Francisco. Vigilante police could not find him, so the Executives grilled the master of the bark *Glencoe*, which had brought Gallagher back to San Francisco. The captain "stated that he did not bring Martin Gallagher but that he had brought a man from the [Hawaiian] Islands named Wilson [Hunt] who was placed on board by the U.S. Consul." This particular passenger "left his vessel in a boat as soon as he had dropped his anchor."[44] The Executives soon learned that Gallagher, who as a boatman was familiar with ships, hard work, and the sea, had been able to work his way to Puget Sound on the *Glencoe*. From there he shipped to San Francisco to get his wife, and the wife and two children of fellow exile Bill Lewis, who was waiting for them in Callao, Peru. Dodging vigilante police, Gallagher escorted the small, anxious group to safety there.[45]

The banished took their own actions against the vigilantes. A nasty shock greeted William Tell Coleman when he stepped off the Atlantic steamer in New York in mid-September, after leaving San Francisco on August 20. He was immediately arrested for kidnapping. J. R. Molony had filed the complaint. Pointing out that Coleman, "the leader of the Committee," was "very wealthy," Molony sought $100,000 in damages and requested that Coleman's bail be set at $100,000. The court, however, halved that amount, and the vigilante president was soon out on bail.[46] The Executives learned of this development only when the eastern mail steamer docked on October 14. Then, penning his own reaction to this news, the vigilantes' current director of police, R. B. Wallace, responded to his mother's concern about reports of anti-vigilante arrests in the East. He counseled her to "have no fear for my safety in the event of my visiting New York," and assured her that his enemies were like "cur dogs." If attacked, "I would shoot one as quickly as the other."[47] In the meantime, the Executives formed a new subcommittee "to examine evidence against Maloney [sic] and compile a sketch of his case and most prominent bad acts and forward this to Wm. T. Coleman." Clancey Dempster, the son of missionaries, moved that "Wm. T. Coleman be informed that the Executive Committee recognize the suit commenced against him by J. R. Maloney [sic] is an attack upon the entire Committee of Vigilance and [we] will be prepared to act as if each member were personally in jeopardy."[48] In San Francisco, the Executives' expenses continued to mount.

20
Politics and Property

Despite the continuing setbacks, the remaining Executives clung tenaciously to their goals: political power over San Francisco and ownership of its land. Realizing that they might lose control of both, they began by maneuvering committed vigilantes onto the People's Ticket for the election of November 1856, held statewide in conjunction with the national presidential race. The candidates included Grand Marshal Charles Doane for San Francisco sheriff, Executive Richard M. Jessup for state assembly, and *two* vigilantes for city police chief: James Curtis, formerly head of the vigilantes' police, and the current deputy director of police, exonerated pirate John L. Durkee.[1] Neither Curtis nor Durkee would step aside.

Under political pressure, Committee solidarity frayed further. Dr. R. Beverly Cole, the vigilantes' head physician, strongly believed that the Executives' political involvement had "compromised the dignity of the Committee," detracted from its important service, and created suspicion "in the minds of the community at large ... as to their real purpose and aims." Therefore, Cole had "consented, much against my will, to accept a nomination for Mayor [on the moribund Know-Nothing ticket] as against what was recognized as the Vigilance Committee ticket, without any earthly hope of success."[2] Shortly thereafter, the Executives received a petition requesting Cole's appointment as surgeon general of the Committee. They returned the paper to the young doctor without comment and a week later voted "[t]hat members of the Committee be requested to decline nominations upon tickets opposed to the People's Ticket."[3] Cole's name disappeared from the *Minutes*.

The old animosity toward the vigilantes returned in the feverish election season. Once again, Justice David S. Terry became a political lightning rod. Although

Terry was not up for reelection to the state supreme court until 1859, a newspaper article passed from San Francisco's *American* to the *Alta* to the *Sacramento Daily Union* called upon the judge to tender his "resignation to the Governor, previous to the coming election," for having "openly abjured the party that elected" him, the Know-Nothings. Given that most of the 1855 Know-Nothings had scattered to other parties, Terry's return to the Democrats was hardly unique. Nonetheless, the article insisted that under the circumstances, a man of "such high-toned and honorable feelings" could hardly retain his seat.[4] Unsurprisingly, Terry ignored the renewed suggestion that he resign.

While the Executives acted in secret, the Committee's opponents also organized for the coming election. Northern Democrats held their first public meeting on October 7, when Denis Oliver and friends touted Broderick as "our choice, for US senator."[5] With both senatorial seats up for election in 1856, "The Political Cauldron is almost overflowing. Politics are the all absorbing topic," wrote Oliver.[6] On primary election day, "I was very busy electioneering from 11 to 3," he added. "The struggle was between the Federal office holders [Gwin's and Senator John B. Weller's "Chiv" Democrats] and Mr. Broderick. The Broderick ticket carried every one of the 12 Districts. . . . It was a great triumph. . . . [I]t was the most exciting primary election ever held in this City." Oliver himself was rewarded for his diligence with a nomination to the state assembly on October 20. He accepted reluctantly, urged by David Broderick and others. Soon, the nominating committee of the People's Party contacted Oliver about his views on current issues. He refused to take a stand but told them "I would go for what I considered the best interest of the city."[7] Oliver would lose in the November 4 election.

In the meantime, Oliver participated in the drive to save the anti-vigilante *Herald*, which came up for auction in a sheriff's sale in early October. The brother of a former proprietor bought it for $1,500, given that "there was little disposition to bid on it, both on account of the mortgages and friendly feelings toward its present proprietors," reported a Sacramento paper.[8] Friends of the newspaper began a subscription list and canvassed San Francisco for sympathetic supporters, raising some $10,000 by October 29 to ensure the paper's continuance.[9]

The Executives, meanwhile, had not been so fortunate in their own financial efforts. They had turned again to the Chinese for money, as they had in July, thanking them in mid-October "for liberal donations to the Committee."[10] The same day that the Executives tapped the ever-vulnerable Chinese, they incurred a new, unavoidable expense in connection with slowly developing San Francisco real estate controversies. They hired Alabama native Samuel W. Inge, federal assistant counsel and a former federal land commissioner, promising him $2,500 if he would prosecute pueblo suits all the way to the U.S. Supreme Court if necessary. Then they released to him their hard-won Pueblo Papers.[11]

Perhaps to placate previously alienated southerners, the Executives announced Inge's secret hiring in an advertised appeal "To the Public" published four days before the election. Signed by Jules David, George Ward, and T. J. L. Smiley, this appeal also revealed for the first time that the Vigilance Committee had "purchased from Alfred A. Green for the sum of $12,500, the Pueblo Papers (which establish beyond doubt the City's rights against all adverse claims) . . . [bought] by the Committee solely for the public good." The Executive signatories suggested a one-half percent tax on the assessed valuation of all those whose titles were threatened by competing claims but were supported by the Pueblo Papers. The Executives stressed that they had "given and will continue to give their service gratuitously" and urged affected property holders to pay promptly when collectors called with written authority bearing the seal of the Committee.[12] The results were not reported.

As election day approached, another major political issue haunted the Executives. The Committee's earlier affront to Governor Johnson was now a threat to vigilante hegemony in San Francisco. For the city's votes to count, the governor would have to lift his Proclamation of Insurrection. He refused to do so without the return of the captured state arms. If the Executives failed to release them, San Francisco's elections would be voided, and the city's votes toward state offices would not count. Given the perpetual split between San Francisco and the rest of California, virtually all of the Committee's political power would evaporate. Startled at this legal reality, the Executives initially refused the governor's demand for fear that the weapons would be used against them.[13] Once again, William Tecumseh Sherman stepped in to mediate, offering to receive and store the arms "as a mutual friend." Ultimately, however, the Executives decided to surrender the weapons to Quartermaster Kibbe, who had long been requesting them. Kibbe received the arms at 9:00 a.m. on November 3, the day before the election. There was no time to inventory the materials surrendered, some of which were never returned. Nonetheless, on November 3, Governor Johnson lifted his proclamation.[14] San Francisco's votes would count.

The Executives had done what they could to influence the November 4 elections. With the Delegates' approval, they had promulgated lengthy instructions on appropriate electoral behavior to protect the polls. They had explicitly retained the sole right to strike the bell in an emergency, so they set themselves up in rotating shifts in their meeting room all throughout election day and night, while the votes were being counted.[15] While the city awaited the outcome, vigilante police director R. B. Wallace scratched a quick note to his mother for the November 5 mail steamer, which had been delayed several hours to ascertain California's presidential election returns. "Buchanan has carried this state," Wallace reported. "The Peoples Ticket has carried in this city, upholding the Vigilance Committee, and turning out the rowdies who have had sway."[16] In one quick election, the vigilantes had replaced Broderick's machine with their own.

This transition came at some cost. Former director of police W. E. B. Andrews had been badly injured in a melee in the Ninth Ward in which two other vigilantes were involved, including John Durkee, the exonerated pirate.[17] Durkee was in a foul mood, having lost the election for police chief to fellow vigilante James Curtis after poll-side rumors claimed that Durkee had accepted $500 to withdraw from the race. When Durkee was dragged before the Executives to explain himself, others, including Wallace, justified his attack on Andrews as "part of a general row and not meriting the attention of this Committee." Curtis also denied offering any bribes to get Durkee to withdraw.[18] A few days later, Durkee traced the source of the rumor, and bought "one of the largest and heaviest cowhides to be had"—a thick strip of leather some three or four feet long with a sort of handle at one end. When the rumormonger appeared, Durkee pulled "the cowhide from under his coat" and swung it "with all the strength he could command," nearly cutting the other man's coat from his back. After this vicious beating, Durkee turned himself in to his close friend, city police captain Isaiah Lees, a vigilante supporter. After a short stay in the police station, he was released on his own recognizance.[19] A few days later, the Executives banished Durkee "from the service of the Committee of Vigilance" without publicity.[20] Three days afterward, his victim limped before the Executives, complained about Durkee's assault, and demanded that his assailant be ejected from the Committee. Under the circumstances, the Executives tabled his request.[21]

With the 1856 election over and the People's Party in control of San Francisco, the Executives were finally ready to relax. They took their giant bell down from the roof and discharged all their police except Captain Wallace.[22] They were almost ready to adjourn for good when the mail steamer brought more bad news from New York. William Tell Coleman, out on bail after Molony's accusation, had just been rearrested on a complaint of kidnapping by William Mulligan, the former jailer who had recently been deported. Coleman was out again, this time on an additional $25,000 bail.[23] New York police had also arrested other alleged kidnappers, Executives James Dows, Miers Truett, and William Rogers, who were also in the East on business. Charles Duane would soon file his own suits against the lot of them, additionally claiming that he had lost a $60,000 contract to grade a San Francisco street and had been unable to collect money owed him as fire chief due to his deportation by the Committee.[24]

Given their promise to support beleaguered colleagues in the East, the Executives' monetary obligations soared. Truett, Terry's sturdy defender, particularly needed help because he had no large New York business house (as did Coleman). Desperate to return to his business, Truett wanted to get back to San Francisco, despite being under indictment in New York for kidnapping. Consequently, he stowed away in the baggage room of the outbound steamer, but was discovered just as the boat was about to sail. With tongue firmly in cheek, he wrote from New York's Eldridge Street Prison that his accommodations were "very comfortable," and claimed that the experience "will enlarge my information."[25] As his honor slipped, so, by extension, did that of his colleagues. Truett later described the expense of his captivity. "There were three [cases] against me, and I was kept under bail of about $280,000" (more than $5 million in twenty-first-century dollars).[26] He finally located two bondsmen, including Cornelius K. Garrison, the established steamboat magnate and former mayor of San Francisco who had earlier refused to provide free passage for vigilante exiles. Before posting Truett's bail, however, Garrison had called on Charles Duane, one of those suing the Executives. Garrison told Duane "that Truett had asked him to go on his bond, but that he would not do so unless I was willing that he should." Luckily for Truett, Duane had no objection.[27] The Executives later sent Garrison a heartfelt resolution of thanks.[28]

The Executives did what they could to meet these new expenses. Twenty-three of them gathered in San Francisco to approve a motion assessing each member of the Vigilance Committee five dollars to defray the cost of the continuing New York lawsuits. At the same meeting, they discussed Coleman's latest letter from New York regarding the potential of land. While awaiting his kidnapping trials, the vigilante president was pursuing an attorney's advice on real estate fraud. Coleman had enclosed a draft of a legal approach "for examination by members of the Committee."[29] Of course, any more litigation would increase the Committee's expenses.

In volatile San Francisco, money was in increasingly short supply. By late 1856, gold reserves had dwindled; merchandise was stockpiled, and citizens approached for donations increasingly objected to supporting a Committee that had so visibly disbanded. On November 21, with only thirteen members attending, the Executives agreed to refuse any future expenses either for Executives or for members of the General Committee arrested in the East. These resolutions had to be "sent to every absent member of the Executive Committee in the City," by that time more than a dozen men. Shortly thereafter, unable to pay their rent, the Executives considered cramming into a free room over Smiley's store, but reluctantly admitted that they could not fit without moving a partition.[30]

The hard-pressed Executives faced another financial demand when Sterling Hopkins revisited their chambers with his hand outstretched. Having failed to get their permission to demand payment from Terry before the judge's release, in early September Hopkins had returned to the Executives for "personal relief." After tussling with this request for three weeks, they granted him $1,200 "in equal monthly sums commencing September 1, 1856."[31] By February 1857, however, the increasingly cash-strapped Executives lowered the amount to just $150 more, "to be paid in installments of $50.00 per month."[32] Two months later, Hopkins sent a letter, presumably requesting more money. The Executives tabled it. Only then would they finally be rid of him.[33]

Meanwhile, San Franciscans actively tussled over their one remaining asset: land. Passions erupted violently in early December when an "old-fashioned 'squatter riot'" broke out, with "pistols, knives, clubs, bricks, &c" brandished by angry residents, "but thanks to the prompt action of the police, [now headed by vigilante James Curtis, they] were not used." An upcoming lecture on the validity of French merchant José Yves Limantour's claim was labeled an attempt "to frighten people into the buying of the Limantour claim . . . since the purchase of the 'Pueblo title,' or 'Green papers' by the Vigilance Committee" had slashed Limantour's popularity and his income.[34]

Energized by this turbulent controversy, Limantour's downfall soon followed. In early December 1856, Denis Oliver recorded in his diary, "Lamentour [sic] the great Land claimant was arrested by the U. S. Marshal for perjury and I hope he will be punished as he claimed nearly all my Property in his fraudulent claim."[35] Land attorney Samuel W. Inge, hired by the Executives and given the use of the Pueblo Papers, had gone on the attack. Confronting Limantour's secretary in a grand jury session with the "pretend original [Limantour] grant," Inge had demanded, "Did you ever see that paper before?"

"I think I have."

"Is that your writing?"

"It looks like mine."

The secretary quickly added, "I did not know what I was about at the time. I wrote several other papers of the same character, at the request of the same party [Limantour]."

On learning about his secretary's confession, Limantour became "terribly frightened, and . . . asked that a large guard be placed in his cell, evidently fearing that the Vigilance Committee will take him out and hang him," an article reported.[36] Another of Limantour's employees testified to the same deception in front of the U.S. commissioner in late December.[37] The secretary later admitted that he thought he was confessing in front of the Vigilance Committee, not the county grand jury. He consequently feared for his life. Had he known the truth, he claimed, he would have said nothing.[38]

While some San Franciscans celebrated, the Executives had to foot the bill. Denis Oliver jubilantly noted, "Lamentour [sic] is not able to get bail and is in the County Jail, his secretary confessed the fraud. There is great excitement on the streets as the secretary was also arrested as a witness."[39] For the successful litigation, the Executives had to pay "Inge $2500 for costs [from] funds collected to pay costs of suits in New York."[40] Consequently, by the end of 1856, Executive treasurer Jules David had only $1,000 left to forward "to Coleman in New York to defray in part expenses of suit pending against him," which he forwarded with a disheartening explanation of the Committee's lack of funds.[41]

Undaunted, President Coleman, in New York, set in motion a new vigilante business opportunity. In the East, he had seen firsthand the moneymaking opportunities in boosting California. Therefore, on December 1, 1856, he had met with fellow Californians at New York's swanky Metropolitan Hotel to "consider matters of importance to the progress of the State."[42] Coleman complained of seriously reduced emigration: of an expected 25,000 overland emigrants, fewer than 5,000 had arrived in the past year, and these were mostly families of men already present.[43] Coleman wanted more settlers to improve California's commerce. However, he had no intention of including all comers. When he spotted vigilante exiles J. R. Molony, William Mulligan, and John Crowe in the listening crowd, he hastily disbanded the meeting and called another at his office, "confined to those of one sentiment upon the Vigilance Committee issue."[44] At this second meeting, Coleman organized the "New York Committee of Pacific Emigration," adding Oregonians at their request. Harping on a theme then consuming San Francisco's Executives, Coleman disingenuously assured his audience that land "titles were fast being confirmed and now the chief want was good occupants." Attendees at that New York meeting agreed that they would communicate these radiant western opportunities by newspaper, pamphlet, and special agents, and would state "on what terms they will sell lands for farms, vineyards, gardens, town lots to actual settlers." The group also considered starting their own steamship line to provide transportation to this veritable Eden on the West Coast.[45]

Of course, landownership in San Francisco was anything but settled. Action on contested land grants shortly moved to Mexico. Early in 1857, Limantour managed to find a bondsman and left for Mexico.[46] After being paid by the Executives, Inge also headed south to seek additional evidence of Limantour's fraud. With heartening success, Inge located two of the Frenchman's assistants, one of whom "told of the meetings in Mexico when [the late] William A. Richardson, [the late Mexican California governor] Micheltorena, and Limantour were all together," where they signed a predated paper embossed with a seal, knowingly committing fraud.[47]

Alfred A. Green, perpetual advocate of the authenticity of the Pueblo Papers, also went to Mexico. After his run-in with the Vigilance Committee, Green had left the field of battle, but he was lured back by tales from a half-drunk editor. The man told Green that the bank of Palmer, Cook and Company, a financial supporter of the Philadelphia/Santillán claimants, had paid for the publication of lies damning the Pueblo Papers. Having been political friends with PC&C for years, Green felt betrayed. He rushed home and announced to his mother, "I am going to reinstate myself in the good opinion of the people of San Francisco." He therefore went to Mazatlán to "hunt up the original grantee, Father Santillán, force him to acknowledge that the claim was fraudulent, and get what proof I could to overthrow it," Green later wrote.[48] He had known the priest for years because the road from town to Green's home, which he called Ocean House, ran past the mission.[49] However, he needed funds to cover his trip because most of the $12,500 paid him by the Executives for the Pueblo Papers had been seized by "land sharks." Later it would be revealed that David Broderick had bought a piece of Green's land called the "Pavilion property" just southwest of the city. The politico also had obtained half-interest in "the Ocean House property or Green's Rancho" on the western edge of the San Francisco peninsula.[50] Green got the money he needed, and Broderick got another claim to San Francisco's land.

PART IV

A New Era

21
Reputation's Rollercoaster

The state's overall opinion of San Francisco's vigilantes emerged clearly in the 1857 legislature. That January, as ex-Executive Richard Jessup (who had resigned from vigilante leadership) watched helplessly, the assembly selected as chaplain the Reverend Dr. William Scott, who had called the vigilantes a lynch mob. The state senate chose a Catholic, Father Joseph A. Gallagher, who had been vilified by James King of William.[1] The pro-vigilante San Francisco *Globe* soothingly editorialized that these choices had no "direct bearing on the question of Vigilance or anti-Vigilance." Gallagher, it claimed, was "a worthy and beloved pastor" who deserved the senate's compliment, which was additionally "a rebuke to a licentious press." Scott, too, had "many friends and warm admirers, without regard to his private opinions," disingenuously attributing "liberal views and good motives" to the legislators "in the selection of a Catholic and Protestant Chaplain."[2]

Next, the legislature met in joint convention to nominate candidates for U.S. senator, guaranteeing their election. Again the results went directly counter to vigilante preferences. Broderick's partisans successfully maneuvered to make the long-term senator the first choice, and rammed through their favorite for the nomination, promptly followed by his official election and the signing of his commission.[3] For the second Senate position, the clever new U.S. senator struck a backroom deal. As a San Francisco resident soon accurately reported, "the agony is over. David C. Broderick is elected U. S. Senator for the long term (six years) and [former Senator William M.] Gwin for the short term (four years).... One hundred guns from Telegraph Hill for each was given by their respective friends—but Gwin has sold his friends for the sake of being elected. He has signed a contract giving Broderick the entire Federal patronage of California and report says fifty thousand dollars also."[4] In contrast, an anonymous writer claimed that Broderick's election had resulted not from the new senator's own machinations, but from the "violation of great principles by the Vigilance Committee and the reckless attacks upon Mr. Broderick and others, by the *Bulletin* and *Alta*." The writer ascribed the recent political change of heart to "sober second thought," noting that "public sentiment was with the Committee *while the excitement lasted*." Now the people and their newly elected legislature "condemn the whole proceeding. The selection of Broderick is the first fruits of this condemnation, and *not* the result of his personal popularity."[5] The *Globe*'s editor, while printing this view, retaliated that manly sentiments in "defense of the slandered and persecuted" had elevated Broderick, perhaps augmented by "a deeper scheme."[6] Unquestionably Broderick had corralled all the federal patronage, but some readers also understood the last reference to pertain to San Francisco's land. Certainly, the legislature that had elected Broderick to the Senate would never ratify the Van Ness Ordinance, which required legislative approval to take effect. That unlikely action would dispossess all the "Peter Smith" men, including California's newest U.S. senator.

Having won power in San Francisco but lost it at the state level, the Executives reorganized. They "invited" non-attending colleagues to resign. Three left; fifteen new men were nominated; five were elected, and three accepted.[7] Two of these new Executives were particularly concerned with San Francisco real estate. The first, Horace M. Whitmore, was actively challenging the Limantour claim as fraudulent.[8] The second, Frederick A. Woodworth, number 4 in the popular 1851 Committee, a litigant for pueblo land, and most recently active in the People's Party, not only joined the Executive Committee but got its support for statewide office. In mid-February, when a state senator resigned to take up a federal appointment, a pro-vigilante newspaper touted Woodworth's potential as a replacement, representing approval for "the action of the Vigilance Committee."[9] Newly arrived Hubert Howe Bancroft, later the leading historian of the vigilantes, joined known Executives on the published list of Woodworth supporters.[10] Running against a Democrat and a Republican, Woodworth won. Unlike Jessup, he also remained a member of the Executive Committee.

In the 1857 legislature, both Woodworth and Jessup quietly supported the vigilantes. They helped pass a revision of the 1856 San Francisco Consolidation Act, giving the state a new responsibility: "To provide ways and means for the prosecution of the claims, in the name of the city of San Francisco, to the pueblo lands now pending for the same."[11] Thus the state, not the Executives, now had to fund any future litigation based on the Pueblo Papers.

Californians' attention soon turned from the state legislature to international events. Conflict in Central America, the quickest crossing for anyone traveling to or from the state by sea, intruded on public consciousness. Capitalists had been competing for trans-isthmus steamer traffic since 1851. The federally funded mail steamer had begun operations across Panama in 1848; native New Yorker Cornelius Vanderbilt had opened a competing transit across Nicaragua three years later. A varying cast of entrepreneurs on both coasts had slipped in and out of the competing companies as California traffic increased and the financial stakes rose. Former San Franciscan William Walker, now the president of Nicaragua, had complicated matters when in 1856 he summarily transferred Vanderbilt's Nicaraguan transit company to others, including one of his friends, former San Francisco mayor Cornelius Garrison. Vanderbilt fought back. He had become America's first tycoon by exploiting a whole host of nascent business practices: buying and building steamships, negotiating backdoor deals, seeking federal funding, and manipulating the growing New York stock market. Not to be denied, he now instigated a war with Walker in Nicaragua.[12]

Californians waited breathlessly for more information about the crucial Central American crossing. As of the end of December 1856, when Coleman convened his pro-vigilante crowd in New York and vigilante Executives in San Francisco hired Samuel W. Inge to litigate pueblo land titles, the state had received only sketchy tales of the latest fighting on the isthmus. Frustrated, the *Sacramento Daily Union* called Nicaraguan news "most meager and contradictory."[13] Details took time to reach San Francisco, but Walker's Nicaraguan empire was crumbling. As the situation there worsened, Garrison and his partner suspended all sailings from California to Nicaragua. A furious Walker complained about their "weakness and timidity" and called their action "treachery."[14] A New York article linked "the late summary proceedings of the San Francisco Vigilance Committee" with Walker's fight: it suggested that vigilante exiles "will have the satisfaction of dying in a good cause, of which they have not the shadow of a chance at home. Send them down."[15] Prizefighter Christopher Lilly, who had been blacklisted, arrested, and finally released by the Vigilance Committee, indeed went down to Nicaragua. Finally removed from the vigilantes' Black List in August 1856, he left early in 1857, and in March a report arrived that his "schooner had been captured by the Costa Ricans, and he had been sent to Guatemala for trial as a pirate," as a result of which he was shot to death.[16] That same month, Garrison's Pacific Line through Nicaragua formally disbanded.[17] Passengers now bought tickets only for the Panama crossing. By May 1, 1857, William Walker had left Nicaragua. Although "the grey-eyed man of destiny" promised that he would return, the idea he had symbolized of private rule of a sovereign nation began to fade. If any vigilantes had treasured his example in imagining their own "Pacific Republic," they now abandoned this dream.

While these events unfolded on the isthmus, forty men met in San Francisco in April 1857 to follow up on Coleman's New York meeting to propose a new business opportunity. They formally established the California and New York Steamship Company, billed as "a people's line," a code phrase for vigilantes. Their prospectus promised "first-class steamships on the Atlantic and Pacific oceans for the transportation of passengers and freight, &c., between San Francisco and New York, and New Orleans, via Panama, until further developments shall render a change of the route . . . desirable." The company's new directors proposed that travel time between coasts be cut dramatically, encouraging émigrés, to whom they could sell property.[18] Title to land in California, particularly to the all-important San Francisco waterfront, would be crucial to the success of this venture. The organizers announced a capital stock of $1 million, in four thousand shares of $250 each, payable in installments.[19] They approached capital formation with the same technique they had successfully used to fund their recent vigilante activity: personal subscriptions.

This time, collections went poorly. By the end of May, the *Minutes* report, "Treasurer instructed to remit to Mr. Coleman in New York $1000 and inform him of the extreme difficulty attending collections in San Francisco." At the same meeting, the Executives tendered their "[t]hanks to Smiley for liberal and gratuitous proffer of rooms now in use by the Executive Committee."[20] They could no longer afford rent.

To complicate matters for the Executives, Edward McGowan had returned from hiding. The vigilantes had hunted this well-known man-about-town for sixteen months at an estimated cost of $8,000 (roughly $200,000 in modern currency). He was still very much wanted in San Francisco when he appeared in Sacramento in early March 1857.[21] The Executives immediately made plans to arrest him if he came to town. They also instructed assemblyman Richard Jessup, their man in the legislature, to "resist any bill . . . authorizing the change of venue in the trial of Ned McGowan," who was under official indictment as accessory to the murder of James King of William for allegedly loaning James P. Casey a pistol.[22] In Sacramento, legislative debate reminded assemblymen that "the criminal statutes of the Vigilance Committee . . . [stipulated that] no party . . . shall come within the boundary lines of San Francisco, except at the direst peril of his life." Despite an Executive-generated false disclaimer that vigilante penalties no longer applied, the legislature staunchly passed the bill for a change of venue for McGowan's trial. McGowan, some forty pounds lighter thanks to his time on the run, stayed in Sacramento. Vigilante spies continued to watch him. While he waited, McGowan published his book, the colorful *Narrative*, describing his escape and sparing the Committee no insults. The Executives promptly canceled the old general arrest order for their growing nemesis and instead plotted an elaborate scheme for his capture, reactivating the police force and preparing a makeshift cell.[23] They wanted to hang him. A potential split surfaced in the Executive Committee when new Executive Horace M. Whitmore (elected in January) moved that "this Committee be cautioned as to their future actions, but that they have full power to act." Executive John Manrow, who had sat as judge during all the previous vigilante trials, counteracted with a motion that the "committee have same power in relation to exiles should any return."[24]

California's formal legal process temporarily saved McGowan from the vigilantes. He was arrested on May 13, 1857, on a bench warrant from the Seventh District, which covered the area north of the bay.[25] The judge who presided at McGowan's trial at Napa on May 24 later remembered that McGowan had stood accused of "being accessory to a murder—a murder, however, with which he had had no connection."[26] Dr. R. Beverly Cole, formerly the Committee's head physician, supported McGowan. Cole had been repudiated by the Executives when in 1856 he ran for mayor on the Know-Nothing ticket in protest of vigilante meddling in San Francisco's elections. Now he appeared at McGowan's trial with a badly preserved partial cadaver opened to show "the chest, arteries, and general internal appearance." Cole explained to the jury how the festering sponge placed in the wound had actually killed King. His argument proved convincing. At the end of May, McGowan walked free.[27]

Discouraged, the remaining Executives again consulted their Delegates. They called them into session on June 8 and, among other issues, discussed appropriate actions if Edward McGowan were to appear in San Francisco. At the end of the meeting, the Delegates expressed confidence in the decision of the Executives, but endorsed no specific response.[28] The vigilantes' enthusiasm for new executions was waning.

Further complicating Executive activities, land issues were mushrooming as courts returned to the question of whether there had once been a Mexican pueblo at San Francisco. A superior court case pitting a claimant with a pueblo-derived title against a defendant who held titles under both Limantour and Santillán led to a decision in favor of the former.[29] In his successful litigation, the victor's attorney had utilized the "celebrated Pueblo papers, purchased from the Brothers Green by the Vigilance Committee." The newspaper made the specious argument that this lawsuit had helped "to prove the authenticity of these papers."[30] At the same time, the U.S. District Court under McAllister and Hoffman dismissed the federal appeal against the existence of a Mexican pueblo at San Francisco. News arrived from the

East that the U.S. attorney general had declined to contest this decision.[31] Thus, the federal government would no longer stand in the way of the courts' legitimization of claimants under the Pueblo Papers.

Unfortunately for pueblo advocates (including the Executives), the competing Santillán claim, now held by the San Francisco Land Association of Philadelphia, also prevailed in court. The same U.S. District Court that had just dismissed the appeal against the pueblo's existence approved the competing Santillán claim "for several thousands of acres of land between California street and Mission creek."[32] The day after this decision, Alfred Green returned to San Francisco. He had tracked down Father Santillán in Mazatlán, Mexico, and wrung from the priest the admission that, although his grant was dated 1846, the document had really been signed in 1850, well after the Mexican regime had ended.[33] He insisted that the Santillán claim held by McGowan's Philadelphia friends was a fraud.

Although Green was too late to influence the district court's decision on the Santillán matter, he was not about to waste his efforts in Mexico. He turned to the usual method for mobilizing popular support: a mass meeting. On May 2, 1857, San Francisco's citizens gathered, allegedly to fight "for the protection of their interests, and those of the city." At the meeting, which was chaired by San Francisco's mayor, the crowd listened quietly to promises of "important evidence" about Santillán's alleged fraud, procured "with great labor and expense." After a few preliminary resolutions, a pensive Green stood up to speak. "Fellow-citizens of San Francisco," began the former vigilante captive, "[i]t is with a considerable degree of nervousness that I arise to address you, after the stirring events of the past year." Gaining courage, Green outlined the history of the pueblo claim, and explained how he had just met with Father Santillán in Mexico. Insisting that the good father "was deceived and betrayed and made the victim of evil-designing men, some of whom are now living, others have since died," Green briefly outlined the scope of the spurious claims, "not merely around San Francisco . . . [but] from San Diego to the line of Oregon." These frauds, he insisted, had paralyzed the state and dampened emigration, since people could not get legal ownership of land. Like so many of his listeners, Green wanted to increase his personal wealth through real estate with secure title. In closing, he highlighted his greatest concern: "All I ask for myself is the time to show the honesty of my purpose and to vindicate my character before the world."[34] A United States attorney who had just been urged by the crowd to mount a legal appeal against the Philadelphia consortium, and who had also been in Mazatlán, then testified to Green's integrity. The attorney's testimony meant so much to Green that he later included this lawyer's affidavit in his autobiography.[35] With the approval of the meeting, the mayor then appointed a committee of five to raise money to procure further evidence of fraud in grants competing with those of the pueblo in order to present the information to the U.S. district attorney. One of the five appointed was Executive James Dows, back from New York.[36]

Green's improving reputation and the public's acceptance of his speech may have emboldened his brothers. In mid-1857, former vigilante captives John and Daniel Green filed a $50,000 suit against the Committee for kidnapping and personal injury. The pro-vigilante *Alta*, reporting on the case, opined, "If any serious injuries were inflicted during this incarceration, we should suppose they had been amply compensated for by the payment of some $12,000 by the Executive Committee for a quantity of written documents," confusing Alfred Green's Pueblo Papers with personal injuries under litigation. The same article excused kidnapping and incarceration by the vigilantes generally as "absolutely necessary," claiming that the Committee had acted with "utmost caution" and "no degree of wantonness," and that they were "performing the duties which the people demanded of them." The writer blamed the "anti-Vigilance men and presses" for keeping "alive a spirit of discord and dissension," also blaming them for the ongoing New York suits.[37] Fanned by the press, the old rancor lingered.

While the Green brothers' suit awaited a hearing, Limantour's land claim leapt into the news. Very late on August 21, after the steamer had sailed, a loud yell rang out in San Francisco from Limantour's leading witness. He had been stabbed in the chest with his own knife, a wound that allegedly would have proved fatal if not for his thick covering of blankets. Limantour, now back in San Francisco, insisted that outsiders had done the deed. Others accused Limantour's followers or the victim himself. "Limantour offered a reward of $5000 for the discovery of the perpetrators," wrote the local federal prosecutor to his superior, "and the amount has been claimed by Messrs. Northam and Whitmore—agents of the Anti-Limantour property Holders." Whitmore—also a new vigilante Executive—joined his colleague in claiming that the wound was self-inflicted, then began a court action for recovery of the $5,000 reward.[38] After this debacle, Limantour sailed back to Mexico, where he remained permanently.[39]

Later, the disputed Peter Smith titles came before the California Supreme Court, which included Justice Terry. The court reluctantly upheld them, reasoning that rejecting the shaky Peter Smith sales would invalidate *all* the titles traced back to the old Pueblo of San Francisco. Chief Justice Hugh Murray penned the unanimous decision; Terry concurred, because "in questions affecting the title to real estate, it is better that a uniform rule of decision should be established and adhered to" in order to protect large investments in "the most valuable real property in the state." Within a month, Murray was dead, and Terry, as the senior member of the court, moved up to chief justice. Stephen J. Field was appointed to fill the remaining vacancy. A strong advocate of San Francisco's former existence as a pueblo, Field joined in supporting the same decision on rehearing.[40] The Pueblo Papers and the Executives' efforts in seizing them increased in significance.

Any boost to the Committee's prestige resulting from its purchase of the Pueblo Papers was undercut by the actions of San Francisco police chief James Curtis, a well-known Committee member. In early August, Curtis had exercised one of the old vigilante tactics to try to shame sixteen young vagabonds suspected of being petty thieves into leaving the city. None had been indicted or brought to trial. Nonetheless, Curtis locked the boys in the station house and threatened to exhibit them in irons, just as the vigilantes had done with the captured Law and Order militiamen. Several of the prisoners said they would die before being taken out and thus displayed. Some stripped off their shirts to avoid being exhibited, but "they were taken out with coats buttoned closely to the chin," reported the pro-vigilante *Alta*. With the young men handcuffed together in pairs, Curtis paraded them to the Plaza and left them chained to the flagpole for nearly two hours with insulting placards on their backs. Then he marched them back to jail. Even the *Alta* called this exhibit of the innocent "disgusting and revolting in the extreme." The entire Executive-approved Board of Supervisors also condemned Curtis's action as "an offense against public decency . . . and an invasion of [the] right of personal liberty and security."[41]

The vigilantes' prestige slipped further with assaults from another quarter. The respectable reputations that had allowed the Executives to exercise such power were increasingly coming into question. The cause was Judge Edward McGowan. Now at liberty in Sacramento, McGowan had gone on the attack. In late August 1857, he started a Sacramento newspaper, which was originally called the *Phoenix* (a legendary bird believed to have risen from the dead), but was later renamed the *Ubiquitous* (as he called himself while in hiding because he was reported as having been spotted all over the West). In the paper, which he published until June 20, 1858, McGowan aired his own defamatory views and others' corrosive letters about private persons, particularly ex-vigilantes.[42] In an ongoing series about the Executives, for example, he featured the activities of Executive Charles V. Gillespie in Hong Kong. He reported that Gillespie had first defrauded Wetmore and Company, then "ship captains, merchants, Chinese." When Gillespie was caught, McGowan alleged that "his property was confiscated by order of the Governor of Hong Kong." With only slight exaggeration, he claimed that only through American intercession was Gillespie deported rather than hanged.[43] Shortly thereafter, McGowan published

S. A. Hopkins,

HANGMAN,

WHOSE NECK WAS MARKED FOR THE ROPE.

In this drawing with layered meanings, McGowan (also quite an artist) stressed the two actions that earned vigilante Sterling Hopkins lasting notoriety: when he slipped the noose over the neck of James P. Casey, and when he was stabbed in the neck while wrenching Terry's gun away from the retreating judge. *Courtesy of the Bancroft Library.*

a love letter supposedly written by Executive secretary Isaac Bluxome Jr. to one of his "two mistresses, . . . [although he] is at the same time courting a fine young lady, a Miss R., a resident of Bush street. One of his mistresses, Lou. J. . . . is really attached to him," but the other "is down upon him for his unfaithfulness and treachery" and had handed over his letter.[44] If in fact Bluxome had gone courting, he was unsuccessful until 1864, when he finally married.[45] McGowan also featured an article on vigilante policeman and "enthusiastic choker" James Bovee, who had helped capture Molony and Terry: "Bovee is a thief and a highway robber," he wrote, who had "robbed a Mexican of $27.50," as attested to by his accomplice, "now confined on board the prison brig at Sacramento, for grand larceny."[46]

Likewise, McGowan attacked Sterling Hopkins. He branded the Hopkins family generally as "a horde of harlots and rogues," writing that Hopkins "a few years ago . . . acted as *pimp* for [his] own sister." He would allegedly "wait in the neighborhood, 'till the *amour* of his sister had ended, and receive the money she had earned."[47] Lest anyone forget the cause of Hopkins's notoriety, McGowan appropriately illustrated his latest article. Knowing the power of publicity, he thus guaranteed that his old enemies would have a harder time than ever operating unchecked in San Francisco.

Back in May 1856, the young Executives had launched their Vigilance Committee in an enthusiastic burst of self-interested indignation. More than a year later, unable to disband due to lawsuits and debts and faced with slipping prestige, they fought back by returning to city politics. After detailing three Executives to secure "suitable nominations for public office in the next election" through San Francisco's People's Party, they forwarded the names of Executive William Tillinghast for city and county treasurer, former Grand Marshal Charles Doane for sheriff, and Executive Fred Woodworth for judge of elections in the Ninth District.[48] With the editorial urging of the pro-vigilante press, the People's candidates won easily. Tillinghast then tried to resign as an Executive, but it took three weeks before a quorum could be corralled to accept his resignation.[49]

Having finally assembled a quorum after four aborted attempts, twenty-six Executives tried to relieve themselves of ongoing responsibilities. They formally vacated the arrest order for Edward McGowan without attempting to win the Delegates' approval. They elected new member Horace M. Whitmore as treasurer to replace Jules David, who "had left for the East and resigned as treasurer" without informing his colleagues. They authorized Whitmore "to collect $5.00 monthly from each member of the Executive Committee, . . . [retroactive to] Sept. 1, 1857 as an Executive Fund for current expenses." Then the Executives passed a preamble and resolution that extolled the worthiness of the new San Francisco government and lifted the threat of death looming over returning exiles, pending Delegate approval.[50]

Once again, the Delegates refused to cooperate. It took three more meetings over the next nineteen days to wear them down. They did not want to pardon the deportees. During the contentious meetings, Delegate attendance dropped from seventy-four to sixty-six to fifty-nine as votes slowly swung to the Executives' side. Finally, on October 12, 1857, thirty-three men agreed to drop the death penalty for returning exiles; twenty-two objected. A motion to reconsider was voted down fifty-four to five.[51] The Delegates never met again.

22
Seeking Resolution

Four days later, fourteen Executives attended their last regular meeting. They approved an "Address," to "be published in all the morning papers under the seal of the Committee and signed '33 Secretary,'" to accompany their previously approved "preamble and resolution" extolling San Francisco's present good government and announcing the end of the death penalty for returning exiles. With President Coleman still in New York, they took the precaution of empowering Vice President Smiley to call another meeting if necessary.[1]

While the Executives were anxiously trying to wrap up their Committee, the East had crashed into a financial panic. San Francisco received the news of this devastating chain reaction on the November 3 steamer. Back in August, an Ohio bank had collapsed after the entire holdings of the parent company had been embezzled. Other eastern banks, which had also rashly extended credit, immediately slapped strict regulations on their creditors. Holders of commercial paper started selling at ruinous prices. Stock prices plummeted. Eastern bankers waited for salvation in California gold, which for years had propped up the national economy. Then a fifteen-ton load of gold secretly shipped out from the San Francisco Mint went down in a howling hurricane off Havana, Cuba. More than four hundred people drowned, and some $1.8 million in solid gold (more than $8 million in twenty-first-century currency) went to the bottom of the ocean. There would be no redemption. In New York alone, bloated issues of state bank notes and unsecured loans stranded banks with $12 million in liabilities in excess of their available capital. All over America, banks failed. Businesses were bankrupted.[2] The Panic of 1857 set its teeth into the nation.

Some failures were deliberately caused. Vigilante exile J. R. Molony, who was still making trouble for the Executives with his New York lawsuits, had two brothers in the liquor business in New Orleans. In early September, their warehouse, stuffed with some twelve hundred flammable barrels of liquor, burst into flame. Complicating the firefighters' efforts, a second blaze simultaneously struck a bar and restaurant in a distant district. Both fires had been lit by incendiaries.[3] They were never caught. Within the next five weeks, the liquor firm of Molony and Brother joined sixty-four other eastern businesses that had either failed or been suspended.[4] The tragedy rolled westward. In San Francisco, 1857 brought 128 failures, revealing $2,696,865 in liabilities in businesses with only $264,707 in assets.[5]

As the panic deepened, events seemed to be closing in on the beleaguered Executive Committee. The Executives had originally disdained lawyers, but now they badly needed more legal help. The previous summer, they had hired the firm of Cook and Fenner to help fight a personal injury suit filed by brothers John and Daniel Green. Trenor Park, who had always advised them anyway, joined the legal team.[6] In December, they hired another attorney, Delos Lake, who, as a former state judge, had upheld the pueblo title. He had to defend them against another personal injury suit in Downieville, California, filed by James Hennessey, who had been blacklisted but was never caught.[7] In February 1858, the sixteen remaining Executives learned that they owed their attorneys an additional $1,000 for litigation that was still pending.[8] Simultaneously, the state assembly considered a bill allegedly for the suppression of mobs and insurrections, but which really targeted the old Vigilance Committee. It permitted a trial in any county of the state, regardless of where the offense was committed; it removed legal protection against self-incrimination; and it allowed the state to place a lien against "All property, real, personal and mixed" of anyone convicted under the act.[9] Although the act failed to pass, it helped inspire an attack by a crowd on a former vigilante, leaving the victim with "his face, hands, and chest . . . cut and bruised in a horrible manner."[10]

Despite these setbacks, at least one legislative action secretly benefited the harried Executives. Broderick's enemies in California took advantage of the senator's absence in Washington, D.C., to undercut his land claims. The 1858 state legislature finally considered San Francisco's 1855 Van Ness Ordinance, voting to approve revised wording that granted city land titles based on "any conveyance duly made by the [state-authorized] Commissioners of the Funded Debt." This provision cut out the competing Peter Smith claimants (who held title from the city), including Broderick and his supporters.[11] At the same time, revised section 11 read, "Nothing contained in this ordinance shall be construed to prevent the city from continuing to prosecute, to a final determination, her claim . . . for pueblo lands," which would ultimately give the city (not the state) the power to convey titles.[12] Given the destruction wrought by the Panic of 1857, land promised more financial security than ever.

More immediate salvation seemed at hand when news spread of gold on Canada's Fraser River. Throughout the fall and winter of 1857–58, gold-hungry San Franciscans pulled their money out of banks and dashed to the docks to book passage north, hoping for a revival of the "Days of '49." Approximately 6 percent of San Francisco's population departed, and the city's real estate lost 50 percent of its value.[13] To the Executives' relief, Edward McGowan abandoned his vilifying newspaper for a chance to strike it rich in Canada. Just before he embarked, the slandered vigilante Bovee took a shot at him, but missed. Bovee was arrested, but with his intended victim gone, the case was dropped.[14] Executive Miers Truett, out on bail from his kidnapping suits in New York, also rushed to the Fraser River. There he did poorly, got drunk, and took his own potshot at McGowan. He also missed.[15]

On the Fraser River, McGowan encountered an old friend, twenty-nine-year-old Martin Gallagher, and taught him a thing or two about the law. When Gallagher returned to San Francisco in February 1858, he filed a lawsuit against the bark *Yankee*, which had carried him to Hawaii from San Francisco with the first shipment of exiles on June 5, 1856. At the time of his capture, Gallagher had been working as a watchman at the U.S. Customhouse when six armed vigilantes appeared to "arrest" him. Therefore, he could file his suit in the U.S. District Court for Northern California, known to be unfriendly to vigilantes.[16]

All of San Francisco learned more about the secret work of the vigilantes as Gallagher's case came to trial. In court, Gallagher testified that when he was seized and imprisoned by the Vigilance Committee on May 25, 1856, he had been "an American citizen, resident here, and a man of good reputation and fair character, engaged as a night watchman in the Custom House, at a salary of $120 per month."[17] Locked up against his will for several days, "without having had any trial, or being confronted with any accuser or witness against him," he was read a document calling him "a rioter, a disturber of the public peace, a promoter of quarrels at the polls on days of election . . . [and] a bad man." Sentenced to leave the state and facing death if he returned, he was handcuffed, shoved on the *Yankee*, and dumped in Hawaii with nothing but the filthy clothes he was wearing. On the streets there, "he was an object of marked curiosity . . . jeered and insulted," and branded as "the worst of the lot" from San Francisco, accused of being "captain of a band of robbers" with "a hand in killing James King of William." Dogged by this slander, he could not find work, but was saved by a Good Samaritan who supported him for about three months until he could ship out to Puget Sound under an assumed name. From there he had returned briefly to San Francisco in October 1856 for his wife and the family of fellow exile Bill Lewis, and conducted them all to safety in Peru. Only in January 1858 did Gallagher feel that he could return to San Francisco without being hanged by the vigilantes. He therefore charged the *Yankee*'s captain, James Smith, a vigilante, with taking payment to deprive him of his liberty, of property worth $5,000, and of "his office in the Custom house, whereby he sustained damage in the sum of $25,000." Captain Smith was promptly arrested; his vessel was attached, and his bail was set at $8,000. The captain was soon released on his own recognizance to hunt up bondsmen.[18]

No doubt Smith located some of the scattered Executives, fourteen of whom reunited for another special meeting on April 15, 1858, after a seven-week hiatus. Fourteen months earlier, the Executives had paid Captain Smith $225 for transporting Gallagher, Edward Bulger, and William Carr on the *Yankee* in the first cohort of exiles.[19] Now they added the captain's current plight to their monetary obligations and assumed another debt for $250 advanced by Treasurer Whitmore to their team of lawyers. Simmering friction spurred a remodel of their Law Committee and an "earnest appeal" by Smiley and Henry Hale "for aid and unanimity in response to law suits commenced and pending."[20] In another meeting six days later, the energetic Smiley, now the acting president, "suggested . . . selecting one hundred picked men from the body of Delegates and General Committee who could be relied on for aid in money and effort." Tired Executives postponed this action "until more pressing necessity," which never came.[21] As their attorneys stalled most litigation with a variety of legal tactics, the Executives would meet no more that year. However, the events they had spawned so many months earlier had not yet ended.

The next attack came from Martin Gallagher. His suit for $25,000 was first heard in the U.S. District Court for Northern California in late May 1858, with the attorney in Executive employ defending the bark *Yankee* (the ship, not the captain) against him.[22] The taking of testimony continued into late June, when Judge Ogden Hoffman ruled that the vessel itself could not be held responsible for Gallagher's deportation. He had to sue the ship's captain directly. So Gallagher returned to court with a new complaint, alleging that Captain James Smith had conspired with the Vigilance Committee to banish him from San Francisco. The taking of new testimony continued for months.[23]

While Gallagher's case rested, Judge Hoffman returned to the ongoing Limantour suit. In 1858, a newly appointed United States special counsel brought forward a mass of new evidence (including 250 photographs of documents) to contest Limantour's claims to most of San Francisco and to neighboring islands. Luckily for the contesting claimants, in April 1858 a box had been found at the Benecia Armory, containing official Mexican forms different from those used by Limantour, a Mexican governor's account book that did not mention Limantour, and a request for paper with official seals (such as that used by Limantour) that could not be met because the paper had not been printed. Federal attorneys had also gone to Mexico, where they had discovered forged papers slipped into preexisting files. Limantour countered these federal efforts by hiring San Francisco newspaperman John S. Hittell to write a pamphlet outlining the justice of his claims.[24] After more months of testimony, on November 19, 1858, Judge Hoffman rendered a fifty-six-page opinion strongly influenced by the photographs of the seals and paper, denying both of Limantour's claims as thoroughgoing frauds.[25] He echoed the opinion of the U.S. attorney general, who called Limantour's claim "the most stupendous fraud ever perpetrated since the beginning of the world."[26] Limantour had lost, and Executive Whitmore, who represented 225 competing claimants, received $20,000 for three years of labor.[27] Contemporaries later credited him with guaranteeing "that the Limantour Fraud was detected and thwarted."[28]

The Executives then tried to hasten the settlement of other competing claims. Early in 1859, James Dows, Henry Hale, Horace M. Whitmore, and William Tillinghast attended huge mass meetings demanding the overthrow of the Santillán claim, held by the San Francisco Land Association of Philadelphia. Joining Alfred A. Green, who still supported the idea of a pueblo, they had been among some eight thousand signatories of a hastily drawn petition sent to Congress to ask for a private bill overturning this claim, particularly if it was approved by the U.S. Supreme Court. Another meeting promised a future assault on the Peter Smith claimants, of whom Broderick had been one of the most prominent.[29]

In the midst of this commotion, Judge Hoffman returned to Martin Gallagher's damage suit. Two months after throwing out Limantour's claim, he again brought the 1856 vigilantes back into the news. Although Hoffman noted that his own powers extended only over maritime affairs (a federal issue), he still criticized the "investigation, called by them [the Executives] a trial." He blamed the entire 1856 Vigilance Committee for kidnapping and deporting Gallagher, adding that Captain Smith had been a willing participant. Given his limited jurisdiction, he emphasized that "masters and agents of ships should learn, that whatever ... power ... illegal bodies of men may usurp [on land], ... on American vessels on the high seas the laws of the United States are still supreme."[30] He awarded Gallagher $3,000 and costs.[31] An infuriated editor at the *Alta* returned to the old arguments of honor and social class. He attacked Hoffman for ignoring "evidence of the respectable body of gentlemen [the Executive Committee] before whom this notorious individual

[Gallagher] was proven to have been guilty of crimes, enough to condemn him to a punishment provided for the most degraded of felons."[32] Equally stung, Smith decided to appeal.

The Gallagher case thus continued at the Executives' expense. Captain Smith's lawyers, hired by the Executives, brought legal action in the U.S. Circuit Court, Judge McAllister presiding.[33] Soon, sixteen Executives assembled at a special meeting heard from their lawyer that "Judge McAllister would not reverse the decisions of Hoffman giving $3000 damages against the Bark Yankee but was urging appeal to the U.S. Supreme Court," a very expensive undertaking. Rather than make an Executive decision, they authorized their Law Committee "to make arrangements such as they deemed advisable about appeal in case of Gallagher vs. Capt. Smith."[34] At a special meeting a month later, the Executives once again had to face the "matter of indebtedness of the Committee."[35] Burdened by debt, how could they possibly afford more litigation?

No record of the Law Committee's "arrangements" has survived, but as Gallagher's lawsuit paused, he stayed in San Francisco and resumed his usual life. One night in mid-June, after barhopping with friends, he was accosted by saloonkeeper Thomas Roach, who called him back to ask, "What do you have against me?" The two argued. The inebriated, unarmed Gallagher said that he did not want to talk to "no damned mean Irish son of a —— and took two drunken punches at Roach. Instead of backing up, Roach stepped forward and took another blow to the face, then whipped out a knife and slashed Gallagher across the stomach. Former vigilante target John Cooney, who was accompanying Gallagher, later testified that "Gallagher loosened his pants and raised his shirt, and I saw his entrails; Gallagher cried out to Roach, 'Oh, you son of a ——, you called me back to kill me.'" Two days later Gallagher died, leaving a wife and an eight-month-old son. Roach came to trial in mid-August. Yes, he had killed an unarmed drunk, but "Roach always had the reputation of being a peaceable man," witnesses claimed. The jury struggled over the verdict for five hours, but in the end found Roach not guilty.[36]

In the meantime, Molony's case against forty-two vigilantes had come up for jury trial in New York. Cited as *James R. Molony v. James Dows*, it privileged the oldest and best-connected Executive as the main defendant.[37] James Dows, now almost fifty years old, was well known as the brother of a wealthy, famous grain merchant who even had a ship named after him. Given the potential for swaying juries based on the character of the participants, President William Tell Coleman, now thirty-five, had hoped to start with the suits filed by the pugnacious William Mulligan, who had just assaulted a San Francisco vigilante whom he had spotted in New York.[38] Instead, in Molony, Coleman had to face the brother of a former

U.S. representative. Only Executives Coleman and Miers Truett attended the trial, in which James Roby Molony was suing the Executives for $100,000 in damages. In front of the jury, Molony's attorney recapitulated all the facts of those events of 1856: Molony's transporting of the state arms in response to the call of the governor and the orders of his militia commander; the attack on the *Julia*; Molony's initial captivity and release; the pursuit by Hopkins; the attack on the armory; and Molony's subsequent captivity for almost two weeks while he waited for the next steamer, during which time he was imprisoned in a tiny, dark cell, with just room enough "for a cot, and to turn around in," where he was subject to "imprisonment, threats, and fear" to extract more information. Three times he had been handcuffed, the last while being driven in a carriage escorted by a vigilante pistol brigade to the dock in the middle of the night. Shut up in a steamship's stateroom "guarded by a large number of the Committee," Molony had been informed of his banishment and the sentence of death if he ever returned. He had had no opportunity to wind up his business and had been forced to leave his wife behind. In sum, he had suffered great mental and physical injury and had "been degraded and blasted in character and position," and seen his business "broken up and crushed," losing his "property, interests, credit, circumstances, plan, prospects and arrangements; deprived of his home and accustomed means of support, livelihood and occupation, and the future of his life destroyed."[39]

The heavily biased trial proceeded. The judge readily admitted negative remarks about Molony, but negative statements about James Dows and other Committee members were disallowed, despite consistent objections from Molony's counsel. In aid of this effort, the Executives had collected anti-Molony testimony for the defense; any positive testimonials they received were filed without forwarding.[40] Molony's assertion that he had lost thousands of dollars in book debts for lack of his papers was stricken from the record on the basis that "this was special damage and should have been averred in the complaint." Likewise, the judge struck Molony's testimony that he had been forced to leave his wife behind and had to bring her to New York at his own expense. On the other hand, the judge admitted forty-eight pages of testimony that Molony had been a member of the Vigilance Committee of 1851 and had witnessed the hangings and deportations at that time, over the strenuous objections of Molony's counsel that the current complaint had nothing to do with the first Committee.[41]

Coleman informed the remaining Executives of the trial's outcome. At the end of six days of testimony, he gloated in a letter that even though Molony's lawyers had "succeeded to their satisfaction in getting the case in court, . . . we succeeded after a hard fight in getting them out of court completely . . . [for] want of jurisdiction."[42]

This verdict alone shows the weakness in the vigilantes' case. The judge had allowed a week of testimony before basing his decision on what was normally a preliminary finding, which would have eliminated the need for a trial.[43] Coleman, who was no lawyer, continued describing the results as he saw them. He reported that witnesses had proved on the stand that "the V. C. was a revolution—an insurrection & all that <u>which we wanted</u> . . . & therefore no action against its members would hold in a mere <u>civil</u> suit here," eliminating another avenue for New York litigation. Disappointed at the outcome, Molony's lawyers called for a new trial, "which was refused—then they gave notice for an appeal . . . to the Court of Appeals. Meantimes Mr. Maleny [sic] says he will push his other suits [against other Executives] without delay." Coleman closed the letter by warning the Executives "to keep all cases in Califa from Judges, but have juries" try them.[44] Herein lay the threat of Molony's appeal, which would go before an appellate judge, who would simply evaluate the record of *Molony v. Dows* for legal irregularities, of which there were many. In contrast to the trial judge's seven-page opinion, Molony's attorneys had written a twenty-seven-page rebuttal, titled "Remarks on the foregoing Case and Opinion," ending with a two-page list of pro-Molony facts disallowed at trial and specific prejudicial evidence entered against Molony. Someone then had the entire document published.[45] Coleman himself may have funded the publication, because he wanted to have the case "wide spread & discussed fully before any other cases come up," since William Mulligan and Charles Duane had filed similar suits. In the same letter, Coleman complained to the San Francisco Executives about the business he had lost due to his eight days in court on Molony's case. He appreciated Truett's presence, but hated the expense of bringing witnesses "from the West—from Phila. Boston, & all over the country." Therefore, "Truett & myself deemed it best to draw on you at 30 days draft for $5000—which we did & trust you will duly honor," he wrote. Wishing to "drive the scoundrels out of New York & away from any position in which they will be <u>seriously annoying</u>," Coleman requested "$15,000 here & $10,000 in Califa." Recognizing that this amount was a "large sum," he opined that "out of 6000 people [the rough total number of members in the 1856 Committee] at least 1000 will contribute & $25 as p[e]r each of these will make the sum—If that much can be raised now I'll go $1000 of it <u>individually</u> if <u>necessary</u>" despite the sums he had already spent. He urged the California Executives: do "<u>not ask for small</u> amts."[46]

Not until May 2, 1859, when twelve Executives again gathered, did anyone respond to the news from New York. In addition to Coleman's letter, they had since received similar correspondence from Truett and their New York attorney, who had been paid by a "draft on Whitmore for $5000 at 30 days." The new treasurer requested that "each member state the amount he will advance towards payment of the assumption of Mr. Whitmore for $5000" to total this amount.[47] Coleman's suggestion of raising an additional $10,000 was not even discussed. Two more special meetings devised "ways and means" of covering their debts, including a plan to send their Collection Committee out to "call upon [San Francisco] County officers and residents for subscriptions corresponding to [their] salaries."[48] The results were not reported, but most of the small leather-bound collection books still in existence are blank.[49]

23
Irreconcilable Differences

While the Executives labored on in San Francisco, the nation started splitting over the spread of slavery, permitted by the U.S. Supreme Court's 1857 decision in the *Dred Scott* case.[1] President Buchanan had urged Congress to accept Kansas as a slave state on the basis of its pro-slave Lecompton Constitution, making it a test of party loyalty. Freedom-loving Kansans had countered with the Topeka constitution to bring the territory in as a free state. Debate over the dueling Kansas constitutions raged in Washington, D.C., and in California. In Washington, Senator Broderick sided with the "Little Giant," Illinois senator Stephen Douglas, in supporting a free-soil Kansas in direct opposition to the president, the national leader of their Democratic Party.[2] By early 1858, close to four-fifths of California representatives agreed with Broderick.[3] The new senator had clearly matured from a provincial politico into an up-and-coming national statesman.

However, the Chiv Democrats, represented by William Gwin in the U.S. Senate, still held political power in California. The California Supreme Court soon upheld slavery when Justice Peter Burnett issued a bizarre opinion that a slave brought to California had to remain enslaved only because this was "the first case" of its type. "But, in reference to all future cases," Burnett declared, the rules liberating slaves would be enforced and "laid down strictly, according to their true intent and spirit."[4] Vehement protesters blamed Chief Justice David S. Terry, a former slaveholder, who had concurred with Burnett for legal reasons. One journalist moaned that this disgraceful news would go out to the nation on the February 20 mail steamer, calling Burnett "an amiable old gentleman" who had "been dragooned into making an ass of himself by the notoriously incompetent . . . Chief Justice." The writer called for petitions addressed "to these two Supreme Judges, demanding their resignation."[5]

Posing for renowned photographer Matthew Brady, David C. Broderick struck a classic pose, trying to look the gentleman upon his entrance to the U.S. Senate, where the columns above him had been carved by his Irish immigrant father. *Courtesy of the National Archives, photo no. 111-B-4139.*

Tempers had not cooled by 1859, when California's fractious Democratic Party factions held separate conventions. Terry, up for reelection, was deemed unelectable by the Chivs but was invited to speak. To loud applause, he extolled the national Democratic Party and belittled the infant Republicans. He also separated "true" Democrats from Broderick's followers, who, although they claimed to be "Douglas Democrats," actually followed the freed slave, "the Black Douglas [great cheers], whose name is Frederick, not Stephen," he claimed. Having just cut Broderick off from his main national connection and called his faction a pack of abolitionists (a serious insult in those days), Terry exited the platform to "three hearty cheers."[6]

Back in California, Broderick learned about Terry's inflammatory remarks. Taking a seat next to Terry's former law partner in a posh dining room, the senator loudly commented that he had once claimed that Terry was the only honest man on the California Supreme Court, but he now took it all back and wished that the vigilantes had hanged Terry when they had the chance.[7] Terry soon heard about Broderick's insult, and issued a challenge to duel once the election was over.

The men seemed unequal opponents. Broderick had dueled before, and had escaped injury when his opponent's bullet struck his watch. Terry had never fought a duel in his life. The same day Terry sent the challenge, he wrote to Cornelia: "Dearest Neal, I have reason to believe that my affair will be properly settled without a resort to the 'last argument.'"[8] He promised to telegraph "as soon as matters are properly arranged," adding, "Kiss the boys."[9] That telegram never came. The press predicted a Broderick victory. San Francisco's *Morning Call* called Terry "a first-rate shot," but noted that Senator Broderick, who had recently practiced at a shooting gallery, had "fired two hundred shots at the usual distance, and plumped the target every time. He is also a man of firmer nerve than his opponent."[10] Despairing for her husband, Cornelia Terry reserved outbound tickets on the next mail steamer for herself and her three surviving sons. A friend commented on "the intense solicitude Mrs. Terry was experiencing," but "knew she had the fortitude . . . to sustain herself nobly and suffer her grief."[11] A contemporary observer blamed both duelists' recent opposition to the vigilantes for hardening "the high chivalrous position assumed by two men . . . [which] prevented the reconciliation that ought to have been made in all reason."[12]

San Francisco police chief Martin Burke, who had held the same position in the Vigilance Committee, tried to stop the illegal duel. He broke up the first attempt but had to rush back to town "to see that Terry was not insulted on his way to the Courtroom, as I knew that the feeling against him among the members of the Vigilance Committee was [still] very bitter indeed." Burke even placed "three men under arrest whom I found were determined to shoot him on sight." When the police court judge acquitted both duelists on "technical points," the disgusted Burke "determined to take no further part in the proceedings."[13]

The next day, Terry and Broderick, with seconds, surgeons, and seventy-three spectators, met again in a foggy little glen at the far southern end of today's San Francisco. At the shortened count of "Fire—One—Two" (chosen by Broderick), both men fired.[14] Broderick's bullet struck the ground in front of Terry. A split second later, Terry's bullet entered Broderick's body to the right of his heart and lodged in his left side. He had shot Broderick through the lung.

Their seconds hustled both duelists into waiting coaches and left the dueling grounds. Terry returned to his home and family, while Broderick's friends sought a local refuge. Each bump over rough dirt and uneven plank roads jarred the bleeding senator, and his accompanying surgeon gave him chloroform to quiet his pain. They drove him all the way across San Francisco, away from the nearby Ocean House of Alfred A. Green, in which Broderick was half owner. They hurried past Empire Engine House No. 1, full of Broderick's loyal firemen, who would soon name their company after him.[15] They lurched near the hospital, where the Sisters of Mercy would have given tender care to one of the city's most famous Catholics, but didn't stop. Instead they conveyed Broderick to the northern limits of the San Francisco Peninsula, to the house of the man who was later the main heir in Broderick's admittedly forged (but legally sanctioned) will.[16] Three days later, Broderick died.

The shock of Broderick's death reverberated throughout California. The outcome blasted the Chivs' reputation, and northerners became the only "true" California Democrats. Colonel E. D. Baker, who had hung Cora's jury with tales of Belle's devotion, eulogized the dead senator as an advocate of free soil and a fighter "against the despotism of organization and the corruption of power. . . . He was honest, faithful earnest, sincere, generous, and brave; . . . Good friend! True hero! Hail and farewell."[17] Overlooked in the genuine outpouring of regret and indignation, few people realized that Broderick had accomplished something the vigilantes never could do. The night before the illegal duel, Terry had resigned from the California Supreme Court. The following July, he was acquitted of murder and withdrew to his home and a private legal practice. Despite a heated public outcry, no one suggested reorganizing the vigilantes and getting a rope.[18]

The scattered Executives recorded no reaction to the duel nor its outcome. They had met only twice so far that year. In June, thirteen Executives had gathered to reorganize subcommittees and address their perpetual money problems. They had also decided that Coleman should "be corresponded with about New York suits and asked for account of receipts and expenditures," for the first time expecting their president to justify his actions. They decided to hold daily meetings in Clancey Dempster's office. If they did so, they kept no record.[19] The next extant *Minutes*, for Friday, July 8, 1859, read simply: "No quorum."[20] On October 28, almost six weeks after the duel, nine men gathered in Dempster's office, where they refused to compromise with the late Martin Gallagher's heirs on his successful lawsuit. They also appointed three men each to sell the remaining muskets and other property, and to invest any surplus funds in San Francisco bonds. On November 3, 1859, their final *Minutes* state: "that the Finance Committee be instructed to reimburse the bondsmen in the Gallagher case for any amount of damages which they may be subjected to," and "that the Law Committee have full power to act with reference to the Green suit as in their judgment may seem advisable." Only seven dogged Executives had hung on until the end: James Dows, Miers Truett, Clancey Dempster, Henry Hale, Alfred Tubbs, and E. P. Flint, who had participated since the beginning, and Fred Woodworth, who had been added early in 1857.[21] If the Executives held any meetings after that, they kept no record.

Despite the end of their formal organization, the former Executives still had to face lawsuits based on their vigilante days. In mid-June 1859, James Hennessey's case, begun in Downieville, was heard in Sacramento on appeal. The unsympathetic judge there asked why, in 1856, Hennessey had not sought assistance from the sheriff. "If the power of the county is insufficient," the judge noted, "the Governor is required to call out the militia, and if forces of the State should prove insufficient the Federal Government is brought to bear." The judge decided that Hennessey had no case.[22] Undaunted, former fire chief Charles Duane, one of the vigilantes' earliest exiles, returned to San Francisco in 1860 and followed the late Martin Gallagher's lead in order to bring his suit in the sympathetic U.S. District Court for Northern California. Duane sued all the captains whom he had encountered in his 1856 banishment, initially winning a total of $7,000 against two of them. On appeal to the U.S. Supreme Court in 1866, Duane's case was remanded to assess lower damages. In the end, Duane got $50.[23] Also in 1860, a jury heard John Green's complaint of harm suffered while in vigilante captivity. Former Executives appeared to see if Green could identify them. The rubbernecking public got a good look at some of the men who had been their secret rulers, while the newspapers conflated Green's injury suit with the contest for San Francisco land. Testimony frequently focused on the Pueblo Papers, who had them, who knew who had them, who translated them, and "how the Green papers got into the hands of the Vigilance Committee," all testimony exonerating the Executives.[24] In the end, the jury awarded John Green $150, which, because it was less than $200, made him liable for the costs of the trial. The jurors' per diem alone came to $144.[25] Daniel Green dropped his case.

J. R. Molony came back to San Francisco to testify for the Greens. On the witness stand he described the attack on the jail, the execution of Casey and Cora, the capture of state arms from the *Julia*, and his own arrest alongside Justice Terry to spellbound jury members and observers.[26] As the trial ended, he returned to New York to pursue his own goals, knowing that success there in his legal appeal would set an important precedent for other suits against the bicoastal Executives. But on August 19, 1861, Molony died suddenly at his hotel. No cause of death was reported. His legal appeal died with him.[27]

The legitimacy of the Pueblo Papers, now owned by the Executives, also inched toward a legal resolution. The Executives found an ally in California Supreme Court justice Stephen J. Field, who rendered a decision in 1860 that upheld the Van Ness Ordinance and invalidated the Peter Smith titles. To reach this conclusion, which cut out Broderick's heirs and associates, Field reasoned that San Francisco's pueblo lands were held in trust for the public and could not be subject to "seizure and sale under execution" for city debts. Four earlier state supreme court decisions had declared just the opposite.[28] In frustration, the *Alta* asked a frequently recurring question: "Have We a Settled Title among Us?" The answer, it decided, was "no."[29] Field's decision prompted a monster rally (with unidentified sponsors), convened in a hall bedecked with four maps: the Peter Smith tract, painted a bloody red; the "Bolton Santillán [Philadelphia-held] Forgery," in black; the now-defunct "Limantour swindle" (overturned in 1858), in green; and the Van Ness (pueblo) lands, exhibiting the city's "native purity," labeled "San Francisco Redeemed." Among the speakers was Alfred A. Green, who "did not confine himself to the matter before the assemblage, but entered into a lengthy personal defense." He reminded the crowd of his former fact-finding trip to Mexico, adding that he had even traveled to Washington, D.C., to present evidence against the Santillán claim to the U.S. attorney general (who rejected the proffered evidence). Green "claimed a share of the work in sustaining the Van Ness Ordinance," which Field had just upheld, cutting out the Peter Smith men. Finally, Green harped on his most precious theme: "The pueblo must be established in San Francisco."[30] That same year, matters seemed to be moving in a positive direction when the U.S. Supreme Court rejected the Santillán claim, knocking out another major competitor of the pueblo advocates.[31]

The resolution of land titles receded in importance as the nation broke asunder. The election of Republican president Abraham Lincoln in the fall of 1860 guaranteed the secession of the South. Looking back, Judge Harvey S. Brown, one of the original Executives who had helped direct the attack on the jail, declared, "I believe in my inmost soul, that the two Vigilance Committees that we had here in San Francisco had as much to do with the Southern Rebellion as any one thing, . . . because application was made to the Federal Government by the regular authorities in 1856 for aid in suppressing this Committee and it was refused." Consequently, "Southern States had a right to believe . . . that they could overturn state governments without interference from the Federal Government."[32]

During the war, the cohesion of the 1856 Executive Committee shattered. After fighting began in South Carolina, a pro-northern mass meeting accepted the leadership of a Union Committee of Thirty-Four, which included former vigilante Martin J. Burke (the new Committee's Grand Marshal) and ex-Executive Clancey Dempster. They helped constitute a shadowy "Home Guard" to elect pro-Lincoln

Leland Stanford, a former Committee member, as governor of California on the 1861 Republican ticket before disbanding. Politically, long-Democratic California became a Republican state. Some fourteen thousand Californians went to fight for the Union; others joined the City Guard of the local militia to provide Union support at home if necessary.[33] William Tell Coleman, who returned to the Pacific coast in 1864 on behalf of his in-laws' failed bank, stayed in San Francisco for the presidential campaign, which pitted the faltering incumbent Lincoln against "peace Democrat" General George McClellan, who promised conciliation with the South. Coleman joined McClellan's "Broom Rangers" (named after the split brooms they carried), mostly made up of men of Irish descent who embraced the idea of secession and a Pacific Republic.[34] The local Copperheads (southern partisans from the North) also formed a Central Club and elected Coleman President.[35] In the course of the campaign, Coleman "made a speech, in which he made the assertion that he had never voted for the extradition or hanging of any Catholic or Democrat," recalled ex-Executive Oliver Crary. Upon hearing this, Crary "went up to the platform, and holding a paper which Coleman had dictated at the time the Vigilance Committee perpetrated their coup d'etat when Terry was arrested . . . said, 'Coleman, did you dictate this paper?' He said that I was taking unfair advantage in public."[36] In late September, three or four hundred Broom Rangers marched through a pro-Union mass meeting, cheering for McClellan and hissing Lincoln. Shortly thereafter, with the support of the Union League, Martin Burke quieted rowdy Broom Rangers at another public meeting, leading his enlarged police force through a rapidly silencing crowd. He also headed the revived military arm of the 1856 Vigilance Committee, which held weekly meetings and swelled to 3000 volunteers by the time voters reelected Lincoln on November 4.[37] In later years, other Executives belittled Coleman. Smiley, for example, referred to him as "Billy" Coleman.[38] Isaac Bluxome Jr., formerly "33 Secretary," declared that Coleman had once "had the confidence of the whole country, but after he went in with the Broomrangers in politics, and became secesh [a secessionist], the people discarded him."[39]

The war also transformed California politics. Crary insisted that Coleman had returned with the intention of being elected U.S. senator by the state legislature.[40] Indeed, in 1865, as the war wound down, Coleman's name was actually placed in contention before a legislative joint session. He lost by a vote of twenty-six to ninety-two.[41] Simultaneously, the old People's Party disintegrated when its 1865 nominating convention passed a resolution to back only candidates who had "voted for Lincoln and Johnson at the Presidential Election in 1864." All the respectable Democrats deserted it, leaving it weakened beyond revival.[42] The political arm of the Vigilance Committee was gone forever.

24
Lasting Transformations

The war that split the North and South also cemented California more firmly to the East. At first, when war loomed, the old idea of a "Pacific Republic," discussed by the vigilantes, became more widely articulated by the state's elected officials. In his 1860 departure speech, outgoing governor John B. Weller had predicted that if civil war came, California "will not go with the South or the North but here on the shores of the Pacific found a mighty republic which may in the end prove the greatest of all."[1] As the war began and the South seceded, a majority of California's congressional representatives openly favored a Pacific republic.[2] Senator Milton Latham publicly stressed California's unique resources and asked, "Why should we trust to the management of others what we are abundantly able to do ourselves . . . [especially since] the North and South have proved themselves incapable of living in harmony with one another?"[3]

Alarmed by this possibility, the U.S. Congress (by then composed only of the northern states) prioritized improved communication. The process had begun in 1860, before the war, when the pony express had engaged sinewy young men and fast horses to bring the New York mail from the railhead in St. Joseph, Missouri, to San Francisco in thirteen days. When the telegraph was strung to Carson City, Nevada (then in Utah Territory), later that year, news sped across the nation in nine days. In October 1861, only months after the war began, a transcontinental telegraph line began zipping news from New York to San Francisco in hours.[4] No more could private justice be wrought secretly in San Francisco while federal officials back east remained ignorant and uninvolved.

Furthermore, the East needed California gold more than ever to fund the war. When the South seceded, the precious metal went only to the North on previously established steamer lines. Five or six million dollars in gold received every month helped prop up Union government bonds, sold abroad to finance increasingly expensive northern military campaigns.[5] California also sent silver. In October 1859, five tons of silver ore from Nevada's Comstock Lode had arrived in San Francisco, worth $2,500 to $3,000 a ton.[6] By 1862, during the war, silver production yielded $6 million in bullion. That amount doubled in 1863, and rose to $16 million in 1864 before experiencing a rapid decline, although production continued at a reduced rate for years.[7]

Californians benefited from wartime financial transactions. Men who manipulated large silver stock issues backed by small mining claims in the Comstock Lode acquired the largest fortunes. None of the Executives topped the list of the newly wealthy, although former Executive Miers Truett became one of the lesser beneficiaries of the silver boom.[8] Many more Californians prospered when California, alone among the states, remained on the gold standard. The federal government pressed federal "Greenbacks" into circulation, which provided a windfall of an additional 25 to 50 percent for those who insisted on payment in gold but paid debts in these depreciated paper notes.[9] San Francisco bookseller and publisher Hubert Howe Bancroft, later an apologist for the vigilantes, recalled that, from 1860 to 1865, "fortunes were thrust on California merchants, . . . from the depreciation of the currency in which they paid their debts—fortunes which otherwise could never have been accumulated but by generations of successful trade."[10]

This new financial era forced California to abandon its earlier constitutional prohibition of public banks, with far-reaching results. The state legislature of 1862 passed acts that permitted publicly chartered mutual savings banks, which were able to loan money, invest funds, and receive deposits, though they could not create any kind of paper to circulate as money.[11] Two years later, new banking amendments spurred the creation of the Bank of California under head cashier William Ralston. Formerly a secret vigilante supporter, he became the center of a whole new coterie of businessmen and politicos, called "Ralston's Ring," who became San Francisco's new power brokers, supplanting the old merchant-Executives.[12]

The pressing federal need for better transportation and communication with golden California prompted the war's most momentous change: a transcontinental railroad. Before the war, this long-discussed project had stalled in debates over the eastern terminus of the line. Once the South became a separate nation, Congress passed Pacific Railroad bills in 1862 and 1864, establishing a northern terminus for California and its gold. Both the state legislature and the San Francisco city supervisors passed bills in 1864 to support the Central Pacific Railroad, which would build eastward from California.[13] This combined legislation catalyzed the rise of

To ensure that they could control entry into San Francisco without depending on land owned or claimed by former 1856 Executives, the builders of America's first transcontinental railroad ended the journey at the East Bay (see train on right) and provided their own water transportation into the city. *Courtesy of the Bancroft Library.*

four new tycoons, all of whom were former small businessmen from Sacramento. Back in May 1856, a suppliant Collis Huntington, then a moderately wealthy storekeeper, had written to vigilante president William T. Coleman requesting "the Articles by which the San Francisco Committee are governed." Sacramento, too, was considering forming a "Vigilant Committee," and rather than draft its own constitution, it was looking to the City by the Bay to "obtain a copy of your laws."[14] Fellow Sacramento shopkeeper Leland Stanford actually joined San Francisco's Vigilance Committee the day before Terry stabbed Hopkins.[15] By the mid-1860s, these two men, together with colleagues Mark Hopkins and Charles Crocker, had become the "Big Four," daring entrepreneurs who would successfully promote iron rails across America and bind them with a golden spike in 1869. Their financial strength and clever dealing spawned a political system that would rule California for decades despite periodically ardent opposition.

The nascent railroad had an immediate effect on the former Executives and their objectives. It diminished reliance on the Port of San Francisco and extinguished single-minded dependence on its wharves. Even before the railroad's arrival in 1869,

California merchants had turned to eastern suppliers. Out-of-state business agents toured the interior, signing up buyers for goods delivered directly by rail from such places as Chicago and Omaha. Understanding California's power structure, the Big Four chose to terminate their line in Sacramento, their hometown, not in San Francisco, the stronghold of the formerly elite commission merchants-*cum*-vigilante Executives. The giant bay, which had been such a boon to maritime commerce, now became a huge obstacle to be circumvented by a series of railroads along its south shore or crossed by Big Four–owned ferries. Over-speculation in San Francisco lots, stimulated by the promise of iron rails, collapsed.[16] Wealthy William Ralston of the Bank of California decided to enter the transportation race by incorporating a competing internal rail line, the San Francisco and Colorado River Railroad, which would stretch from the bay to San Diego, then swing east to the Colorado River to join another incoming trunk line. Trying to keep up with this new world order, William Tell Coleman joined Ralston's incorporators. The group applied to San Francisco's supervisors for a subsidy, which was soon overturned by voters at the polls. Ralston's line was never built.[17]

The nation as a whole developed a new power structure. Northern victory in the Civil War greatly strengthened all three branches of the national government, a fact not lost on Justice Stephen Field. Elevated from the California Supreme Court to the Supreme Court of the United States in 1863, the clever Field used his increased powers on behalf of the pueblo advocates. In those days, U.S. Supreme Court justices literally "rode circuit," so Field was able to maneuver the pertinent lawsuit into his own federal circuit court in California, where, acting alone by choice, he reaffirmed his own state supreme court decision by deciding that a pueblo had truly existed in San Francisco. Federal attorneys were poised to contest this finding in the U.S. Supreme Court, where Field feared that the pueblo would be revealed as a fraud. Understanding the might of the constitutional separation of powers, Field helped author an act "to quiet the title of the city to all the lands" of the Pueblo of San Francisco introduced into Congress by Broderick's pliable successor, Senator John Conness.[18] Field's gambit worked. When in 1866 Congress passed Conness's act and the president signed it, the federal attempt to disprove the existence of a pueblo at San Francisco collapsed. The United States government, represented by the attorney general in the executive branch, could not try a case in the Supreme Court that the United States government (Congress, in the legislative branch) had just settled. "Upon the acquisition of California [by the U.S.], there was a Mexican Pueblo upon the site of the city," Field insisted in his *Reminiscences*.[19] He was dead wrong. As a former San Francisco judge noted a few years later, "At this time there is no Court, State or national, that pretends that the Alcalde grants [legitimized by

San Francisco's "pueblo" status] have any validity except that bestowed upon them by virtue of the Van Ness Ordinance and subsequent ratification by the Legislature and Congress. That is sufficient now; but meantime a wonderful amount of injustice has occurred in the matter."[20]

Specifically, the lands in question went to wealthy men who had long sought ownership. Executives Coleman, Farwell, Bluxome, and Woodworth, defined by the Van Ness Ordinance as people "in possession," all received clear title. Historian John S. Hittell essentially described the coterie of 1856 Executives when he noted, "The inhabitants were many; the people in possession were few, but they had money, political influence, [and] organization.... Thus a domain which might have been sold for millions of dollars, or given in small lots to ten thousand poor citizens, anxious to secure homes, was bestowed upon a few."[21] Theirs was a pyrrhic victory. With the railroad nearing completion, the old waterfront shrank in importance. Lands in the so-called pueblo "remained nearly stationary, while the growth, the fashion, and the wealth gravitated rapidly to the southward, and to the western addition," much of the area controlled by Ralston. Elegant hotels, homes of wealthy families, "the most fashionable promenades, leading theaters and churches" sprang to life on formerly peripheral lands belonging to a new elite, not former vigilante Executives.[22] Newly confirmed owners therefore rented their "pueblo" land around Portsmouth Square to the Chinese, who usually paid more than twice in rent what white residents offered and provided plenty of cheap labor.[23]

The Civil War not only had affected California, it had altered perceptions all across the nation. Two former San Franciscans had become national heroes. David Farragut—America's first admiral—had successfully led his fleet into heavily mined Mobile Bay lashed to the mast, shouting his famous command, "Damn the torpedoes! Full speed ahead!" Troops commanded by former San Francisco banker William Tecumseh Sherman had made the famous—or notorious—March to the Sea, first taking Atlanta, Georgia and then burning through the heart of the South, destroying everything in their path. The collective impact of the war on the vigilantes was even greater. In 1865, as America totaled up its wartime dead of more than 620,000, very few cared about a minor political kerfuffle in antebellum San Francisco.[24]

This reality came home sharply to transplanted New York journalist Franklin Tuthill, who published a 657-page *History of California* in 1866. He devoted more than a hundred pages to the 1856 Committee and the People's Party, even though he had arrived in San Francisco with his pro-vigilante prejudices after the Vigilance Committee had publicly disbanded. He nonetheless set the canon for future histories: "Law had been used as a machinery for screening villains from punishment . . . and [the vigilantes] set law in an honored seat again. They purified the city. . . . They made the ballot-box sacred once more." He did relate a recurring San Francisco scene in which a former vigilante "met one whom he had not seen for several weeks, and extended his hand in a friendly salutation. 'There's blood on it,' said the old acquaintance, drawing back; 'I don't know you sir.'"[25] Tuthill also acknowledged that contemporary discussions of "the revolution of 1856 in miscellaneous company" could be "unprofitable, and a quarrel-breeder." He also bemoaned that "in the great events that have lately convulsed our country, these local matters, that used to hold the peaceful, law-abiding world breathless, will be forgotten, if the record is much longer delayed."[26] He was right. His book, published by Bancroft, failed to cover its printing costs.[27]

Financially and socially, California was changing. As the railroad built west, poor laborers flocked into California, lured by exaggerated accounts of the state's fabulous wealth. In 1868–69, some 50,000 immigrants arrived and had to weather the droughts of the winters of 1869 and 1870. Crops failed; banks closed; and by January 1870, San Francisco housed some 7,000 desperate people. For the first time in its history, the city saw a meeting for "the establishment of a soup house for the poor."[28] In 1873, a new national panic began slowly rolling west across the nation. In San Francisco, in August 1875, the severely over-leveraged Bank of California closed its doors. Distressed, banker Ralston went for a swim in the bay and drowned.[29] Although the bank reopened a few months later, Californians reacted to the economic disturbances by returning the Democrats to power.[30]

Of greater concern to the former Executives, Union hero William Tecumseh Sherman simultaneously published his *Memoirs*, which denounced the 1856 vigilantes. "As they controlled the press, they wrote their own history, and the world generally gives them the credit of having purged San Francisco of rowdies and roughs," he wrote. He condemned their "dangerous [operating] principle" of secrecy and private justice. Sherman further alleged that once the Committee had seized power, the same rascals "that had infested the City Hall were found in the employment of the 'Vigilantes,'" whose own court was headed by "a Sydney man."[31] James Dows reacted angrily, calling the general "a damned fool," adding that the young Sherman "would have found it a damned sight worse job than walking through Georgia if he had attempted to do anything in opposition to the Committee; we would have strung him up as we would a dog."[32]

Sherman had destroyed the reputations of publicly identified vigilantes to the national reading public. Fortunately for the majority of the Executives, they had been known only by their numbers. To redeem their shrinking status, recognized Executives began to speak out. Sixty-five-year-old Charles V. Gillespie, earlier savaged in McGowan's paper as a cheat and absconder, granted the first full interview in November 1875. His ten-page statement began with the explanation that he had been driven out of the British colony by "Hong Kong fever," not malfeasance, and continued with a description of San Francisco in 1848, its transformation in the gold rush, his participation in the first and second Vigilance Committees, and his varied opinions of some of his fellow Executives, and of Terry. He said not a word about the Pueblo Papers or any anti-vigilante lawsuits.[33]

Gillespie gave this interview to eager publisher-turned-historian Hubert Howe Bancroft, who had begun to promote his series of books on the American West all over the country. Bancroft sensed a money-making opportunity in the vigilantes, a project that could sell thousands of books to former members and sympathizers. He consequently began writing his own version of local vigilantism in 1875, "entitled *Popular Tribunals*, making of it three volumes and then reducing it [to two]. I . . . finished the first writing of it in 1877," he later attested. But he was not yet ready to publish. The second volume dealt almost exclusively with San Francisco's 1856 Committee. In initiating this effort, Bancroft relied largely on newspapers, while acknowledging that they were "not the most reliable testimony upon which to base history." Nonetheless, he tapped the *Bulletin* ("radical on the side of vigilance"), the *Herald* ("the rabid law and order point of view"), and, for "more moderate expression . . . still leaning to the side of vigilance . . . the *Alta California*, the *Sacramento Union*, the *Courier, Chronicle*, and *Town Talk*." All but one of his sources thus took the vigilante point of view. Having determined to his own satisfaction the Committee's outward activities, Bancroft sought the "inner, hidden, and hitherto veiled part."[34]

Probing for the records of a group sworn to secrecy proved a tremendous challenge, even for the persistent Bancroft. He started by sending his agent to speak with former Executives, "these hard-headed, cold-blooded Yankees," without result. "One of them when spoken to . . . drew his finger across his throat significantly saying 'that would be to pay if I told all.'" The Executives "did not want to talk about it, to think about it. It was a horrid night-mare in their memory, and they would rather their children should never know anything about it."[35] Alfred Tubbs, who had remained a loyal Executive from beginning to end, later explained, "When the question of giving the committee papers to Mr. Bancroft first came up, a lawsuit was pending in New York, brought by some man against Mr. Coleman as an outcome of those times, and he did not care to have these things come out. I voted in favor of delivering them [the Committee papers] to Mr. Bancroft," but the majority did not.[36]

At least William Tell Coleman, who was well known as the Committee president, personally cooperated in Bancroft's quest. In 1876, Coleman contacted Bancroft and offered to give him a statement on both Vigilance Committees. The result, a

174-page dictation, became the longest by far of almost three dozen collected by Bancroft on the 1856 vigilantes.[37] The old vigilante president followed the exact order of the 1856 Executive *Minutes*, often quoting items verbatim, including letters more than twenty years old. He redacted material no longer complimentary, editing the Executives' most sensitive record for public exposure. San Francisco land contests, and Alfred Green, got only passing mention.

Bancroft's book was far from complete when disturbances, both local and national, struck again. California suffered a severe drought in the winter of 1876–77; grain crops failed, cattle died, and the supply of gold severely declined. Although the Southern Pacific Railroad completed its line from San Francisco to Los Angeles and on to the Colorado River by April 1877, the expected horde of tourists did not arrive. Many instead attended the national Centennial Exposition in Philadelphia in 1876, and in 1877 sought to avoid the parched, unattractive state of California.[38] Simultaneously, the 1876 presidential election, seemingly won by the Democrats, instead brought in minority Republican Rutherford B. Hayes and the federal Compromise of 1877. This agreement undercut any attempt to bring civil rights to the racist South, ended its military occupation by Union troops, promised federal aid for a southern railroad, and opened the South to northern capital, which could benefit directly from the reduced status of the black population.[39] The status of labor dropped nationwide, and business acquired the upper hand. By 1877 the East was in an uproar as railroad workers rioted in an attempt to maintain their slipping status and wages. A modern historian has identified the late nineteenth century as characterized by "tightened systems of transport and communication, the spread of a market economy . . . [and] the remaking of cultural perceptions."[40] Like the rest of America, California, once so isolated by land and sea, could no longer operate apart from these national trends.

In July of that year, white workingmen rioted in San Francisco. Their special target was the Chinese, who provided cheap labor for California businessmen, many of them former Executives.[41] Fiery Irish immigrant Denis Kearney in his "sandlot speeches" stirred up the unemployed, who disrupted commerce and forced the rich to sell property at a loss. Two hundred of San Francisco's mercantile and industrial elite gathered to demand "the formation of a Vigilance Committee," and elected former Unionist Martin Burke, the old Vigilance Committee and city police chief, to head the meeting. Burke vehemently opposed re-creating the Committee: "we could arrive at the end desired better by keeping within the law," he insisted. He proposed "strengthening the militia" and supporting judges so that they would have "more strength to support the laws." He claimed that the group eventually accepted his view, and then chose an eleven-man executive committee, including himself and Coleman, to enforce it.[42] Coleman told a different story. He later insisted that he was "given charge of the entire movement, with absolute control," and established a system of membership rolls, "a pass-word . . . [and] badges marked 'Committee of Safety'" for men who formed companies of one hundred, selected their own officers, and "reported to me for confirmation."[43] With improved transnational communications, Coleman's request for federal arms and naval support quickly reached Washington, D.C., and earned approval within twenty-four hours. Despite the influx of weapons, however, he armed his followers with six thousand pickaxe handles, which they used to protect the wharves of the Pacific Mail Steamship Company, where workingmen had massed to try to drive off incoming Chinese.[44] Unlike Burke, Coleman sought to avoid, not support, the judicial process. He justified his "pick-handle brigade" by claiming that if "arrests were made, immediate legal action would be taken in behalf of the arrested parties; the *habeas corpus* and jury trials would be brought into play; complications would arise that would give us greater trouble than to meet these forces face to face and treat them effectually on the spot."[45] In this latest vigilante effort, a few men were killed, others wounded, and thousands of dollars' worth of property was destroyed in fights between the pick-handle brigade and hoodlums who rampaged through the Chinese ghetto.[46] Five days after its formation, the new vigilance organization disbanded, earning Coleman the sobriquet "that lion of the Vigilantes" (a name that stuck) from observant author Robert Louis Stevenson, and, in the same paragraph, "the intermittent despot" (which did not).[47] After a few more days, the riots faded. So did the new vigilantes.[48]

25
Secrets

By 1877, vigilantism existed in a different world. Although a Sacramento paper complimented the newest San Francisco vigilantes, commending their prior experience and honorable motivation, it also noted, "The Constitution provides methods by which obnoxious laws and treaties many be altered or abrogated, and constitutional methods of redress are the only ones which law-abiding men can think of employing." Otherwise, actions outside the law could challenge "the very existence of Society in the United States."[1]

Throughout America, society was indeed realigning. After Reconstruction of the South ended in 1877, national interests turned to the country's burgeoning industrial revolution. The public embraced new inventions, which enriched capitalists and proved beneficial to the increasingly educated middle class. Washington Gladden, an early reformer, extolled "[t]he steam-engine, the spinning-jenny, the power-loom, the power-press, the sewing-machine," finding God's design in "all these mechanical devices by which labor is saved and production increased" in a surge toward humanity's "perfect destiny."[2] By the time the last of the vigilantes disbanded, the nation was well entrenched in the "Gilded Age," a name immortalized by Mark Twain in his book by the same name published in 1873.[3] Interestingly enough, it dealt with shady land deals and attempts to entwine the federal government, but its title became a shorthand for an era when the ostentatious wealth of the very rich tended to obscure the increasing poverty of the laboring poor.

As the nation wheeled through kaleidoscopic change, crafting a history acceptable to the members of San Francisco's 1856 Vigilance Committee took years. Bancroft, the first to publish, gradually accumulated more pro-Committee sources. He finally persuaded Isaac Bluxome Jr., the secretary of both committees, to let him have the books and papers from 1851. He later felt that as he wrote at length about the 1851 Committee, members of the 1856 Committee became jealous that their story might not be as well told.[4] But the 1856 papers remained out of his reach.[5]

These records had always been secret. Back in 1856, the idea of publishing the Executive *Minutes* as a potential money-maker had been proposed more than once. At the beginning of July, when the Committee dominated San Francisco and was even more powerful than the governor, the Executives rebuffed the first request to share its secrets. E. Gould Buffum, the pro-vigilante editor of the *Alta California* newspaper, had publicly promised "a history of the stirring events which have recently agitated San Francisco."[6] Without the needed records for evidence, his article never appeared. In August, as the Committee publicly wound down, San Francisco's anti-vigilante *Herald* had sneeringly suggested that the Committee could get $10,000 for its proceedings.[7] Seriously considering this suggestion, on September 1, as the *Minutes* note, the Executives had constituted a "Committee of five . . . on propriety and policy of publishing a full and complete History of the Origin and Doings of the Committee of Vigilance together with such testimony and facts as may be in the hands of the Executive Committee."[8] Then the idea stalled. Devoted Vigilance Committee member William Rhodes, editor of the pro-vigilante but failing newspaper the *Daily True Californian*, approached the Executives in the fall of 1856 with an offer to publish a history of the organization, "provided access would be afforded me to the records of that Body for such information as cannot be elsewhere obtained of an authentic character." They declined his proposal.[9] Much to the Executives' alarm, after their grand "final" parade, Samuel Colville, the publisher of the popular *Colville's San Francisco Directory* listing the city's residents, organizations, and businesses, included a short summary of the Vigilance Committee and the names of all the Executives in his 1856 edition. Luckily, he brought the proofs to the Executives for their approval.[10] They insisted that he continue to protect their identities. Those perusing *Colville's Directory* now read, "Ten days after this sheet was in print, and in the hands of the binder, the compiler received . . . [this] communication" refusing permission to publish the names. As Colville noted, the page could not be changed "without serious loss," so employees painstakingly went through every directory and pasted this explanation over the entry.[11] The Executives pronounced themselves "satisfied with the corrections."[12] Four months later, editor Thomas Sim King of the *Evening Bulletin* newspaper, the Committee's mouthpiece, came before the Executives "asking for all records of Committee in preparation of a publication on the subject of the acts of the Committee of Vigilance." The Executives again refused consent.[13] In the end, the Executives held tight to their secret *Minutes*.

Theodore Hittell, who had been crafting his own history of California since 1870, fared no better. His project got a boost in 1876 when Congress demanded a history of each state in conjunction with the national centennial. The Society of California Pioneers donated $1,372 to aid this effort, and Hittell won a coin toss with his brother, John, to secure this support.[14] Plugging on, he refused to use Bancroft's *Works*, and instead went after primary sources himself, lengthening the time he needed to complete his project.[15]

Bancroft, too, incessantly sought the most sensitive primary sources. At least a dozen of the 1856 vigilante leaders agreed to an interview in 1877, and another half dozen a year later.[16] They expressed a wide variety of views about the old Committee. For example, former Executive George Frink recalled, "The beauty of this [1856] Vigilance Committee was that everything was done with such consideration." He felt that the Executives were "patriots, . . . so that no man could find fault that anything was hastily or ill done."[17] But Executive T. J. L. Smiley, recalling his own efforts on behalf of the Law and Order captives, said, "I saved them from indignities, from insult, from imprisonment, and perhaps from the cart whip, but they gave me the blame of all the indignities they suffered, and for a year or two afterwards they gave me showers of brickbats and insulting words, and to this day bear me a grudge."[18] In contrast, Francis Pinto, eventually head of the 5th Division, reported, "I made many very agreeable acquaintances."[19] John Manrow, the judge for the Committee's murder trials, complained, "It seemed to me a most ridiculous thing for a temporary organization to banish people. Billy Mulligan was banished and came back again, and after shooting fire or six people was shot himself by Hopkins in broad daylight. Another fellow they banished was . . . Charles P. Duane, here yet."[20]

During the interview process, Bancroft discovered that Clancey Dempster held the 1856 Executives' papers, which he still craved. In 1878, he curried favor with the youngest Executive by showing him drafts of *Popular Tribunals*. Dempster responded that he had "read yr. [your] volumes 1 & 2 through the first time, without stopping to make any of the notes you requested." Due to poor eyesight, he could not do more.[21] Four years later, Bancroft submitted his latest draft to William Tell Coleman, who called the manuscript "<u>too important to you</u>, to me, and to <u>our people</u>, to be neglected in anything." The old vigilante president therefore offered to "run over them [the pages] as rapidly as I can, making such notes as suggest themselves to me."[22] Simultaneously, San Francisco land issues returned to the news when the Philadelphia consortium that held the Santillán claim tried unsuccessfully to get a private bill through Congress to grant it title.[23] The touchy topic of San Francisco land ownership therefore remained unexpressed.

Bancroft's work on the 1856 Vigilance Committee finally reached fruition in 1887 with the publication of the second volume of *Popular Tribunals*. He had briefly secured the loan of the *Minutes*, but was forbidden to keep it for his library. He therefore rushed through the writing of this volume, making no citations, but creating hasty references to the *Minutes*, such as in "a special session held at four o'clock on Wednesday the 4th of June, the following motion made by Mr. Truett . . . carried."[24] He dedicated this volume to "William T. Coleman, Chief of the Greatest Popular Tribunal the World has ever Witnessed."[25] It is the only one of Bancroft's works to include a dedication of any kind.

In his account of San Francisco's 1856 Vigilance Committee, Bancroft created a saga of good and evil. Of the vigilantes, he wrote, "During all that wild, tumultuous time the Executive[s] sat in their chamber and directed every movement. Invisible, omnipotent, and omniscient, their powers and intelligence bordered on that of the deity."[26] He also blackened the reputations of anyone in the opposition. Terry, he wrote, "had come to San Francisco for the express purpose of precipitating a bloody collision between the Committee and the state authorities, . . . finally to resort to the use of a deadly weapon upon a man who was seeking to do him no harm."[27] Bancroft dismissed J. R. Molony with this remark: "Mr. Maloney [sic] deserved the thanks of a grateful posterity for dying so soon. Courts are more uncertain than death."[28] He included an entire chapter on "The Honorable Edward McGowan," so scurrilous that McGowan sued the Bancroft History Company in 1889 for $50,000 in damages and retained David S. Terry to represent him. This lawsuit apparently died with Terry later that year.[29] In short, according to Bancroft, the Executives were heroes, their enemies were villains, and the results of their Committee were honesty, economy, and political virtue. No connection existed between vigilantism and contested property.

In the East, reviewers panned Bancroft's book. The *New York Times* complained, "The firm grasp of his subject, characteristic of the able historian, is in his work conspicuous by its absence." The writer did credit Bancroft with providing "a large amount of information" but denounced his use of "a large amount of his personal opinions," and suggested that the "gathered facts" needed "a clear, terse, and straightforward discussion of them as would have made their lessons general." This reviewer also pinpointed the self-interest of San Francisco's 1856 Executives. Quoting Smiley, who said, "I have seen at one time, . . . not less than five men . . . taking their turn at guard, not one of whom was worth less than half a million dollars," the reviewer asked, "Why should not a rich man have patriotism and exercise self-denial when his interest in the welfare of the State is so much greater, pecuniarily, than that of the poor man, whose services he seems to expect for nothing? There being neither honor nor profit in acting as a common soldier in the Vigilance ranks, Mr. Smiley's remark would have been much stronger had he said: 'I have seen at one time five men not having a pecuniary interest in San Francisco to the extent of over 50 cents on guard, defending the right from pure love of right.'"[30] Bancroft's lavish acclaim had not convincingly redeemed the vigilantes.

Theodore Hittell, still working on his history, no doubt read reviews such as this. In his deliberate way, he strove to be as professional as Bancroft was not. The first of his two "centennial" volumes on California's Spanish and Mexican eras appeared in 1885; the last two volumes of his massive *History of California* appeared only in 1897. Volume 3 covered the gold rush, both of San Francisco's Vigilance Committees, and the Workingmen's riots, including some 200 pages (out of 980) on the 1856 Committee. Volume 4, issuing the same year, contained about a hundred pages more of political events, some related to the Vigilance Committee, a fact carefully disguised by their placement. To demonstrate his professional use of the historical method, Hittell cited his sources. He somehow obtained the Executive *Minutes* and cited it repeatedly throughout volume 3.[31] Writing history with such careful attention to detail required that he keep the *Minutes* beside him as he wrote, but, like Bancroft, he had to return the original. So, risking death, he made a copy.

Theodore Hittell's bias toward the 1856 vigilantes was better hidden than that of the emotive Bancroft. Despite his insight into the full range of the Executives' motives and actions, Hittell created his own prejudiced twist on the history of San Francisco's 1856 Vigilance Committee. To downplay any hint of Executive property interests and maintain the fiction of their purely inspired political reform, the knowledgeable land lawyer carefully separated information on the two related topics. Hittell discussed the Pueblo Papers in the third chapter of volume 3, but reached discussion of the Committee only in chapters 7 through 14. He also criticized the Peter Smith sales in volume 3, but in a chapter separate from the Vigilance Committee. In volume 4 he discussed the Van Ness Ordinance in two short pages, although he certainly understood its effect in nullifying any titles secured by Peter Smith claimants.[32] Hittell treated politics with the same organizational deftness. Again splitting cause and effect, he disparaged Broderick's election to the U.S. Senate only in volume 4, an event with no apparent connection to the 1856 Committee discussed in volume 3.[33] In case anyone doubted his position, he made his point absolutely clear in concluding almost thirty-five hundred pages of California history. He praised the "genuine Californian character . . . of men who . . . face danger with intrepidity"; who experience great shifts in fortune

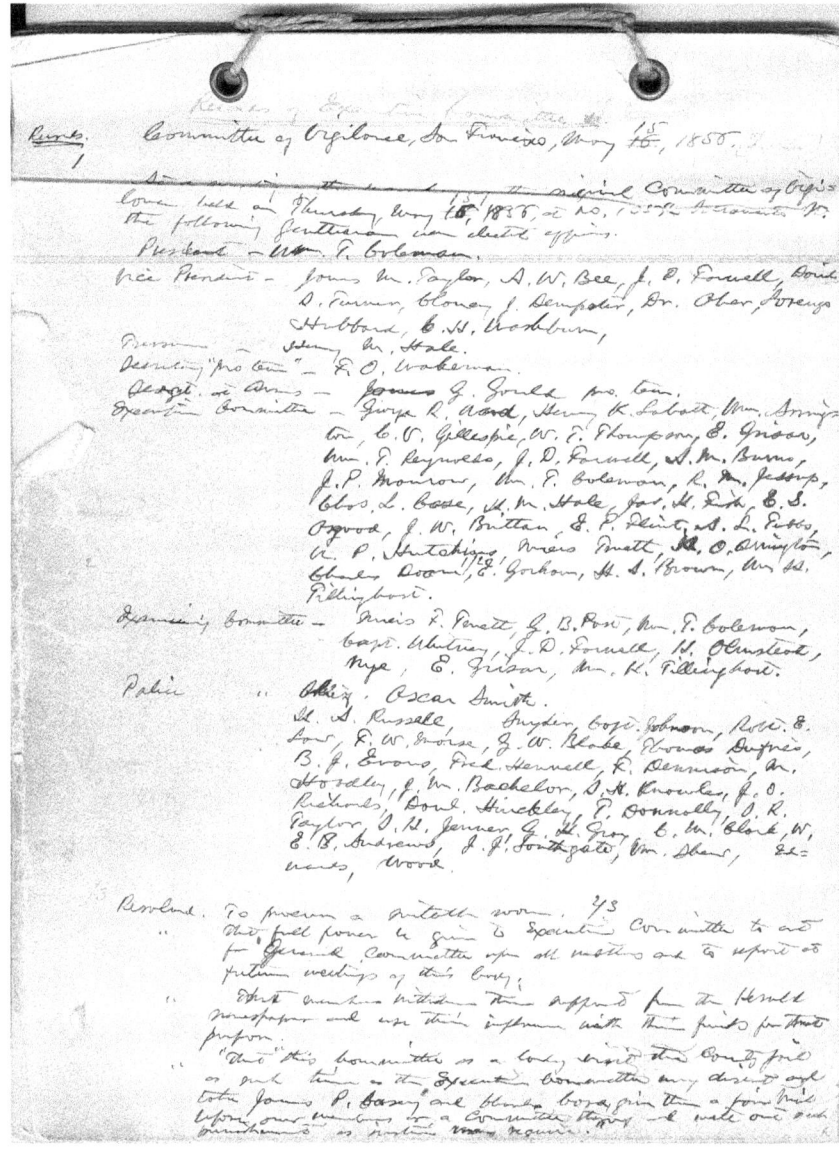

Theodore Hittell's copy of the Executive *Minutes* reveals the true scope of actions by San Francisco's 1856 Vigilance Committee, a record its participants strove to hide for the rest of their lives.
Courtesy of the California State Library—Sutro Branch, San Francisco.

"with equanimity"; who possess "worth and strength" and patience and "recognize their own rights, and . . . insist upon and maintain them." The first indicator of this "extraordinary character, was the vigilance committees and particularly that most remarkable and significant one that may be, and generally is, called the great one of 1856."[34]

Both authors made these assessments despite emerging facts to the contrary. In another indication of the changing times, the California legislature of 1877–78 had passed, over the governor's veto, a bill granting Alfred Green $20,000 "for services rendered . . . in establishing the city's [San Francisco's] pueblo title and causing the rejection of the Bolton or Santillan title."[35] Feeling thus redeemed, in 1878 Green had presented Bancroft with his own eighty-six-page autobiography, replete with tales of his personal struggles to get the Pueblo Papers verified, their alleged significance to the city land cases, and his anti-vigilante opinions.[36] Bancroft ignored Green's work completely. In his chapter "The Pueblo Papers," Bancroft only emphasized Green's deceptive acquisition of the papers, the Executives' timely purchase of them (without reimbursing the *californio* whom Green had cheated), and the unsuccessful outcome of the Greens' personal injury lawsuit, ignoring any other legal struggles over land.[37] Hittell, in mentioning the Pueblo Papers, wrote only that "notwithstanding the decisions of the courts to the contrary, there seems never to have been a pueblo . . . at San Francisco; and the Green papers did not and could not prove one. But as Green had succeeded in making the committee believe his papers valuable, it agreed to give him twelve thousand five hundred dollars for them."[38] Somehow, Green bore the fault for the vigilantes' land grab. Yet Hittell had recorded, as far as can be determined, the full Executive discussion of the arrests of the Green brothers, plans for their trial, and the lengthy captivity of Alfred Green, the longest of any vigilante victim.[39] Hittell also disparaged Green's efforts in volume 4, sneering "that it did not appear that Green had ever rendered any service [to the public]; that if he had, it was not to benefit San Francisco, but . . . to spite the Bolton claimants."[40] According to both authors, land contests had not been important to the Committee, and the Executives had remained focused solely on political reform.

The old Executive Committee needed these words to restore their respectability, and to put to rest any doubt about the wisdom of their youthful endeavors. After all, only their superior social status had allowed them to command their troops back in 1856. Some forty years later, everyone agreed that California in the 1850s had been different from the eastern states, but increasing numbers of Americans could not imagine its isolation, its reliance on the steamer schedule, and its unpredictable events. Furthermore, the rest of the nation, to which California was now so well connected, could not see the respectability in swinging men into eternity from the windows of a warehouse. The United States was busily spawning great reform movements, such as Populism, the Social Gospel, and Progressivism. If the old vigilantes did not want to become pariahs, they could never release their *Minutes*, which contained all their names, decisions, and actions.

Furthermore, by the time these histories appeared, the fashion for thousand-page tomes was fading as people enjoyed a host of other diversions. Americans, both men and women, were embracing a more athletic, outdoor life, including roller skating and bicycling, and watching exciting spectator sports such as baseball. The wordy histories by Bancroft and Hittell now had to compete with popular novels of the 1890s, including Arthur Conan Doyle's *Adventures of Sherlock Holmes*, Robert Louis Stevenson's *Dr. Jekyll and Mr. Hyde*, and Frank Baum's *The Wizard of Oz*.[41] In 1903, just six years after Hittell's work on the Vigilance Committee appeared, the first automobile bound for the East Coast chugged out of San Francisco, arriving in Vermont after nine weeks on the road (only six of them actually spent driving).[42] A new age had dawned.

The popularity of short original newspaper articles had also increased, led by technological changes in the speed of information obtained by telegraph and telephone, printed up by high-speed ("lightning") presses. The first central telephone exchange had opened in 1878, and by the early 1890s networks had spread to most urban areas. Newspaper publishers increasingly issued evening editions in order to entertain those traveling home from work or shopping by streetcar. Sunday newspapers, with colorful supplements highlighting separate topics such as sports and entertainment, expanded to fill the leisure of those working six days a week in offices or factories, which were increasingly lit by kerosene, gas, and finally, electricity.[43] The growing popularity of human-interest stories found an example in San Francisco's *Alta California*, which in 1884 published a series of articles authored by Edward McGowan about life "In the Fifties." Some thirty years after he published his *Narrative*, McGowan had forgiven the old vigilantes. In a free-wheeling interview, he chose William Tell Coleman as one of San Francisco's two most successful merchants, lauding the head of the Committee that would have hanged him. McGowan extolled Coleman as "a grand man in more than merchandizing. His word is mighty in the [Merchants'] Exchange; it is influential in [the] community.... And his generosity is as noted as his great business qualities are distinguished."[44]

Furthermore, the sanitized version of the 1856 San Francisco Vigilance Committee fit well into the myth of the West then promulgated in dime novels and in the thoughtful academic interpretation by Frederick Jackson Turner. In the mythic story, California was the ultimate destination for those who went west to find individual opportunity and bring civilization to a savage place. To achieve this laudable end, rough justice was sometimes required, but, in the end, it provided safety and prosperity for all. As the nation industrialized, Americans treasured this view, and accepted the idea of the West as a "safety valve" for disaffected eastern labor. Of course, the disaffected had to be controlled. Thus, the published cover-up of the 1856 Vigilance Committee fed these notions and satisfied national cravings, as well as protected the participants.[45]

The selective preservation of key records also helped further this laudatory view of San Francisco's 1856 Committee. Many important files from that period have gone missing, particularly those related to land. Documents for both of Limantour's claims to the Bay Area were forwarded to Washington, D.C., in 1856. Those pertaining to his island claim still exist; those regarding San Francisco real estate have disappeared.[46] Most of the Santillán papers found their way into Bancroft's library, but correspondence between San Franciscans and the organizers of the San Francisco Land Association of Philadelphia, which bought this grant, is scarce. Records of the spurious pueblo at San Francisco are also compromised. Lawyer John Dwinelle, in aid of the original land litigation, published most of the Pueblo Papers in 1867 as *The Colonial History of San Francisco*. However, he substituted the 1858 Van Ness Ordinance for the 1855 original, which can be found only in newspapers today.[47] But by the turn of the twentieth century, very few people cared.

In the twenty-first century, America is still dealing with vigilantism. Vigilantes periodically patrol along the U.S.-Mexican border, and an armed group of states-rights advocates continues to defend a Nevada rancher who will not pay his federal grazing fees. His son launched a vigilante takeover of the Malheur National Wildlife Refuge in southeastern Oregon in January 2016 with occupiers from all over the country. Local residents asked the vigilantes to leave. They refused. Oregon's governor requested federal intervention, but for weeks the FBI held back. Eventually some vigilantes were arrested; one was killed when he resisted. As the standoff drew to a close, County Sheriff David Ward, who had had several terse conversations with the vigilantes, spoke out: "[T]his has been tearing our community apart. It's time for everybody in this illegal occupation to move on. It doesn't have to be bloodshed in our community. [If] we have issues with the way things are going in our government, we have a responsibility as citizens to act on them in an appropriate manner. We don't arm up. We don't arm up and rebel. We work through appropriate channels. This can't happen anymore. It can't happen in America and it can't happen in Harney County."[48]

Can it? The world needs reminders of what really happened in 1856 and needs to consider the results. There is a fine line between secrecy and forgetting. Due to their true agenda, the Executives had to keep their secrets, and, in the end, became forgotten. A few artifacts serve as casual reminders: the Monument bell at the office of the Society of California Pioneers; two of the vigilantes' unused cartridges left over from the attack on the jail in the Oakland Public Museum.[49] A dedicatory plaque on a building deep in San Francisco's current financial district, not far from Sherman's old office, still standing near Chinatown, tells those who stop to read it that here was "Fort Gunnybags." Yet most people have never heard of the men who formed America's largest vigilante committee. Their violent deeds pale beside more recent horrors; the question of San Francisco's ownership has long been resolved. But the Committee's activities, couched in its secret *Minutes*, deserve to be remembered as a valuable, cautionary tale. Vigilantism, by its nature, does not last, and there are going to be second thoughts. People have to decide, as did the sheriff of Harney County, whether or not these things should happen in America.

Notes

Preface and Acknowledgments

1. "Steamers," *San Francisco Daily Herald* [hereafter *Daily Herald*], June 5, 1856.
2. [Dillon], "T. H. Hittell Papers," underlining in the original.
3. Culberson, *Vigilantism*, 1–12.
4. *Statutes of California, Passed at the Seventh Legislative Session, Begun on the Seventh Day of January and Ended on the Twenty-First Day of April, One Thousand Eight Hundred and Fifty-Six, at the City of Sacramento* (Sacramento: James Allen, 1856), 150.
5. Bancroft, *History of California*, 6:758.
6. Special thanks go to the creators of the California Digital Newspaper Collection, cdnc.ucr.edu.

Introduction

1. Hittell, *A History of the City of San Francisco*, 113.
2. Dwinelle, *The Colonial History of San Francisco*, 204, 329, 331; *Colville's San Francisco Directory*, 241; Soulé, Gihon, and Nisbet, *Annals of San Francisco*, 548, 798, Decker, *Fortunes and Failures*, maps 3 (199) and 4 (208); Hittell, *History of California*, 3:370–73.
3. Bancroft, *Popular Tribunals*, 2:365.
4. Ibid., 369.
5. "The Place in History of the California Pioneers," 13, 16–18.
6. McGowan, *Narrative*; [Gray], *Judges and Criminals*.
7. Royce, *California*, 365–66, 394.
8. Williams, *History of the San Francisco Committee of Vigilance of 1851*, 18, 473.
9. Scherer, *"The Lion of the Vigilantes,"* jacket copy.
10. Lotchin, *San Francisco*.
11. Brown, *Strain of Violence*, 134.
12. Ibid., 358 n. 4.
13. Decker, *Fortunes and Failures*.
14. Senkewicz, *Vigilantes in Gold Rush San Francisco*, 212.

15. Ibid., 189.
16. Mullen, *Let Justice Be Done*.
17. Ethington, *The Public City*.
18. Jolly, "Inventing the City."
19. Robinson, *Land in California*, 229–45.
20. Fritz, *Federal Justice in California*, 180–209.
21. Johnson, *José Yves Limantour v. The United States*.
22. Bancroft, *Popular Tribunals*, 2:94.

1. Unstable Ground

1. *McElroy's Philadelphia Directory for 1855*, 65, 76, 106, 107, 122, 181, 276, 320, 413.
2. San Francisco Land Association, *Articles of Association and Agreement*, 5, 16, 223.
3. Ibid., 6–9, quote from 6.
4. Johnson, *José Yves Limantour v. The United States*, 29–35.
5. Dwinelle, *The Colonial History of San Francisco*, especially 49–59.
6. Scherer, "The Lion of the Vigilantes," 22; Bancroft, *Chronicles of the Builders of the Commonwealth*, 1:390, 303–26, quote from 315. Birthdate from Phelps, *Contemporary Biography of California's Representative Men*, 272.
7. "Auction Sales," *Daily Alta California*, May 9, 1856.
8. Coleman, "Statement," 161.
9. Bancroft, *Chronicles of the Builders of the Commonwealth*, 1:385.
10. Soulé, Gihon, and Nisbet, *Annals of San Francisco*, 798.
11. Green, "Life and Adventures of a 47er of California," 25.
12. Hittell, *History of California*, 3:336.
13. "An Imitator of Sam Patch," *Wide West*, March 29, 1857.
14. Truett, "Statement," 1.
15. Garnett, *Papers of the San Francisco Committee of Vigilance of 1851*, pts. 1 and 2; Williams, *Papers of the San Francisco Committee of Vigilance of 1851*, pt. 3.
16. George Wilkes of the *National Police Gazette*, quoted in Mullen, *Let Justice Be Done*, 88–89. See also ibid., 141–14, 172–75, 230–40 on fires.
17. Williams, *Papers of the San Francisco Committee of Vigilance of 1851*, pt. 3, 178, 643–44.
18. Tuthill, *History of California*, 404.
19. "Coleman, William Tell," in Johnson and Malone, *Dictionary of American Biography*, 295; "Shipment of Treasure, May 5," *Sacramento Daily Union*, May 7, 1856.
20. Hittell, *A History of the City of San Francisco*, 357; "The Pacific Street Wharf Company," *Daily Alta California*, March 30, 1851; Kemble, *The Panama Route*, 136–37.
21. Bancroft, *History of California*, 6:660–61.
22. Williams, *David C. Broderick*, 3–25; Lynch, *A Senator of the Fifties*, 30–36, 39; Bancroft, *History of California*, 6:660.
23. Duane, *Against the Vigilantes*, 53; Lynch, *A Senator of the Fifties*, 49–54.
24. Lynch, *A Senator of the Fifties*, 69.
25. Frink, "Vigilance Committee," 10.
26. Lynch, *A Senator of the Fifties*, 69–70.
27. Burke, "The San Francisco Police," 14.
28. Ryckman, "Vigilance Committee," 2–3.

29. Hittell, *History of California*, 3:399–401; Soulé, Gihon, and Nisbet, *Annals of San Francisco*, 371–74.
30. Hittell, *A History of the City of San Francisco*, 313. See also Hittell, *History of California*, 3:373, 416; "Extending the City Front" and "Memorial to the Legislature," both *Daily Alta California*, January 27, 1852.
31. Hittell, *A History of the City of San Francisco*, 313, 315. See also Hittell, *History of California*, 3:416–18.
32. Hittell, *History of California*, 3:421–22.
33. "Speech of Alderman Carter," *Daily Alta California*, April 13, 1854; "Alderman Carter's Resolution—The Real Issue," ibid., April 18, 1854; "Common Council," ibid., May 12, 1854; "Serious Squatter Outrage," *Sacramento Daily Union* quoting the *Evening News*, June 6, 1854; "Land Titles—Anarchy in San Francisco," *Sacramento Daily Union*, June 10, 1854.
34. Hittell, *History of California*, 3:684–85.
35. "People's Organization," *Daily Alta California*, June 10, 1854; "Wednesday Morning," *Daily Alta California*, June 7, 1854.

2. Feisty Editor, Contentious Elections

1. Taylor, *Seven Years' Street Preaching*, 249–51.
2. Hittell, *History of California*, 3:443; Williams, *History of the San Francisco Committee of Vigilance of 1851*, 188 n. 3, 197–98.
3. Williams, *Papers of the San Francisco Committee of Vigilance of 1851*, pt. 3, 644.
4. Hittell, *A History of the City of San Francisco*, 216–17.
5. Ibid., 228.
6. Tuthill, *History of California*, 407.
7. Sherman, *Memoirs*, 113–14.
8. Hittell, *A History of the City of San Francisco*, 230. For Daniel Page and W. T. Coleman, see Bancroft, *Chronicles of the Builders of the Commonwealth*, 1:390–91.
9. Sherman quoted in Clarke, *William Tecumseh Sherman*, 107, 109, 113.
10. Soulé, Gihon, and Nisbet, *Annals of San Francisco*, 372–74; Dempster, "The Vigilance Committee of 1856," 31; [O'Meara], *The Vigilance Committee of 1856*, 35.
11. Hittell, *History of California*, 3:465–66.
12. "The State Sale," *Daily Alta California*, August 18, 1854; [O'Meara], *The Vigilance Committee of 1856*, 35, who misidentifies the auctioneer as R. D. Sinton. See *Colville's San Francisco Directory*, 202.
13. Dempster, "The Vigilance Committee of 1856," 31–34.
14. Hittell, *A History of the City of San Francisco*, 243.
15. [Gray], *Judges and Criminals*, 18–19.
16. Jolly, "Inventing the City," 265.
17. Coon, "Annals of San Francisco," 5.
18. Thomas, *Between Two Empires*, 9–11, 28–32, 37.
19. Hittell, *History of California*, 4:146–48; Thomas, *Between Two Empires*, 102–4; Hittell, *A History of the City of San Francisco*, 312–13; Bancroft, *History of California*, 6:697.
20. Senkewicz, *Vigilantes in Gold Rush San Francisco*, 165; Myers, *San Francisco's Reign of Terror*, 75; Bancroft, *History of California*, 4:688–90, quote from 689–90; Carr, *The World and William Walker*, 90–91.

21. Holt, *Political Parties and American Political Development*, 136–37; "Grand Flare Up in the Ninth Ward K. N. Council," *New York Times*, August 30, 1856; Witcover, *Party of the People*, 196; Nichols, *The Stakes of Power*, 55–57; Holt, *The Political Crisis of the 1850s*, 166–70.
22. Summers, *The Plundering Generation*, 66.
23. Later (and accepted) wording in Dwinelle, *The Colonial History of San Francisco*, 216–19; "lost," 286. Original wording: "Common Council," *Daily Alta California*, June 20, 1855.
24. "The Charter Election," *Daily Alta California*, May 29, 1855, emphasis added.
25. "Complete Election Returns," *Daily Alta California*, May 30, 1855.
26. Hittell, *History of California*, 4:172, 184–85.
27. Duane, *Against the Vigilantes*, 104; "Through Wells, Fargo & Co's Express," *Sacramento Daily Union*, August 23, 1855; "The Riot Cases," *Daily Alta California*, August 25, 1855; "Recovering," *Sacramento Daily Union*, September 12, 1855; [O'Meara], *The Vigilance Committee of 1856*, 25, 27, quote from 25.
28. Pinto, "Historical Facts and Incidents," 179.
29. Dows, "Statement," 6.
30. Watkins, "Statement," 14.
31. "Complete Election Returns," *Daily Alta California*, May 30, 1855; Hittell, *A History of the City of San Francisco*, 293.
32. "Affairs on the Pacific Side," *Sacramento Daily Union*, September 29, 1854; Bancroft, *History of California*, 4:693–94.
33. "County Affairs," *Daily Alta California*, September 22, 1855.
34. "Gross Election Frauds," *Sacramento Daily Union*, September 8, 1855, quoting *Times and Transcript*, emphasis in the original.
35. "Election Frauds," *Sacramento Daily Union*, September 29, 1854. One of those allegedly stuffing for Garrison on the "Bogus Legislature" (Broderick) ticket was M. Burke, presumably Martin Burke, later vigilante police chief.
36. "Murder of Gen. Richardson," *Daily Alta California*, November 18, 1855; [O'Meara], *The Vigilance Committee of 1856*, 14; quote from "The Recent Tragedy," *Daily Alta California*, November 19, 1855; "Coroner's Inquest on the Body of General William H. Richardson," *Daily Alta California*, November 19, 1855.
37. "The Mystery Unravelled: Why Gen. Richardson Was Murdered," *Daily Alta California*, November 21, 1855. See also "More about Richardson Murder," ibid., November 22, 1855. Her name appears as Arrabella on her tombstone in the Mission Dolores cemetery in San Francisco.
38. "Examination of Haggert for an Attempt to Bribe Mulligan the Jailer," *Daily Alta California*, November 24, 1855.
39. [Editorial], *Evening Bulletin*, November 20, 1855, emphasis in the original. In this formal era, calling William Mulligan "Billy" further diminished him.
40. "Law Report," *Daily Alta California*, January 16, 1856.
41. [Editorial], *Evening Bulletin*, January 17, 1856.

3. Land and Newsprint

1. Green, "Life and Adventures of a 47er of California," 37–38.
2. "Santillán and M'Garrahan," *New York Times*, April 11, 1882.

3. San Francisco Land Association, *Articles of Association and Agreement*, 4.
4. *Report to Accompany Bill S. 215: The Committee on Private Land-Claims, to Whom Were Referred a Memorial of the San Francisco Land Association of Philadelphia, and Also a Bill (S.215) Relative to the Santillan Grant, a Private Land-Claim in the State of California*, Report no. 457, 44th Congress, 1st sess., July 10, 1876, 1.
5. *Colville's San Francisco Directory*, xxxvi–xxxvii; Johnson, *Jose Yves Limantour v. The United States*, 7–43; Bolton and Barron Land Case, 338 N.D. 81 Bd., 3, in Documents Relating to Ownership of the Lands of Mission Dolores.
6. "Death of Capt. Richardson," *Evening Bulletin*, April 21, 1856. William A. Richardson should not be confused with William H. Richardson, shot by Cora.
7. Johnson, *José Yves Limantour v. The United States*, 42.
8. *Colville's San Francisco Directory*, xxxvi–xxxvii.
9. Coon, "Annals of San Francisco," 13.
10. Tubbs, "Recollections of Events in California," 6.
11. "The Lost Archives," *Daily Herald*, May 5, 1856. See also Green, "Life and Adventures of a 47er of California," 38–41; "Lecture on the Pueblo Title," *Wide West*, April 20, 1856; "Pueblo Title," *Evening Bulletin*, April 19, 1856.
12. [Editorial], *Evening Bulletin*, April 5, 1856.
13. [James King of William], "The Spirit of the Morning Papers," *Evening Bulletin*, April 12, 1856.
14. [James King of William], "The County Hospital," *Evening Bulletin*, April 12, 1856.
15. Ellen Ewing Sherman, quoted in McAllister, *Ellen Ewing*, 145.
16. Oliver diary, entry for April 15, 1856.
17. [James King of William], "The Rev. Father Gallagher," *Evening Bulletin*, April 17, 1856.
18. [James King of William], "The Spirit of the Morning Papers," *Evening Bulletin*, April 18, 1856, emphasis in the original.
19. Kemble, *A History of California Newspapers*, 111, 123–24, 115, 98, 109, 111–12, 151, 114, quote from 124.
20. Stillman, "Statement," 3.
21. See *Evening Bulletin*, December 6, 1855, January 7, 1856. On dueling, see Spierenburg, *Men and Violence*, especially 7–11.
22. Bancroft, *Popular Tribunals*, 2:35–37.
23. Green, "Life and Adventures of a 47er of California," 40, 42–43.
24. "The Parties," *Evening Bulletin*, May 14, 1856.
25. Manrow, "Statement."
26. [Gray], *Judges and Criminals*, 22.
27. Hittell, *History of California*, 3:483.
28. "Shooting Affray," *Daily Herald*, May 15, 1856.
29. Ibid.
30. Frink, "Vigilance Committee," 1–5.
31. "An Important Page in California's History," *Wide West*, May 25, 1856.
32. "Grand Flare Up in the Ninth Ward K. N. Council," *New York Times*, August 30, 1856.
33. Coleman, "Statement."
34. Tuthill, *History of California*, 404.
35. Coleman, "Statement," 34–35.

36. Ibid.
37. Farwell, "Statement," 3–4, 13.
38. Bluxome, "Statement," 16.
39. Williams, *History of the San Francisco Committee of Vigilance of 1851*, 192, 225 n. 53.
40. Bluxome, "Statement," 19.
41. Dempster to Bancroft; Daughters of the American Revolution, *California Census of 1852*, 10 vols. (Piedmont, Calif.: Daughters of the American Revolution, Genealogical Records Committee, 1934–35), 6:153.

4. Under Attack

1. *Colville's San Francisco Directory*, 138–39, 164, 1.
2. Clawson, *Constructing Brotherhood*.
3. Burke, "The San Francisco Police," 2.
4. Dempster, "The Vigilance Committee of 1856," 47–48.
5. "San Francisco Committee of Vigilance of 1856 Roster."
6. Coleman, "Statement," 131, 40, 42; underlining in the original.
7. Pinto, "Historical Facts and Incidents," 169.
8. San Francisco Vigilance Committee of 1856, *Executive Minutes* [hereafter *Minutes*], May 15, 1856.
9. "Topics of the Day," *Daily Herald*, May 16, 1856.
10. Frink, "Vigilance Committee," 7–8.
11. "Topics of the Day," *Daily Herald*, May 16, 1856.
12. "The Felon Case," *Evening Bulletin*, May 16, 1856.
13. Kemble, *A History of California Newspapers*, 113.
14. Oliver diary, entry for May 15, 1856.
15. "The Excitement Yesterday," *Daily Herald*, May 16, 1856.
16. Cole, "Statement," 1–4; Lyman, "The Sponge"; Francis T. Gardener, "Notes, Biog[raphical] Materials about R. B. Cole," Richard Beverly Cole Papers, box 2, item 128, 2; "Forms of Application for Enrollment," San Francisco Committee of Vigilance Records, box 5, folder 1-H; *Minutes*, June 12, 1856. However, in his statement (p. 4), Cole claims that his number was 252, not 253, as shown on the certificates. No. 252 was claimed by William H. Miller. See San Francisco Committee of Vigilance Records [HL], box 6, folder 3-T.
17. R. B. Wallace to Father, August 19, 1856, Wallace Letters, folder 7.
18. Pinto, "Historical Facts and Incidents," 193.
19. *Minutes*, May 15, 1856.
20. "Law and Order," *Daily Herald*, May 17, 1856.
21. William T. Sherman to Turner, quoted in Clarke, *William Tecumseh Sherman*, 207.
22. Sherman to Turner, quoted ibid., 210.
23. Quoted ibid., 207. The weight refers to the size of the ball shot by the cannon.
24. "Marion Rifles," *Evening Bulletin*, May 30, 1856.
25. Frink, "Vigilance Committee," 9.
26. Coleman, "San Francisco Vigilance Committees," 140.
27. Sherman, *Memoirs*, 122; William T. Sherman to Turner, quoted in Clarke, *William Tecumseh Sherman*, 211.
28. McGowan, *Narrative*, 20.

29. Pinto, "Historical Facts and Incidents," 170.
30. [O'Meara], *The Vigilance Committee of 1856*, 17–18. See also Crary, "Statement," 9; Wooley, "Vigilance Committee of 1856," 5; Durkee, "Statement," 3; MacDonald, "Recollections of Early Days in California," 2; Frink, "Vigilance Committee," 8.
31. [O'Meara], *The Vigilance Committee of 1856*, 17; Crary, "Statement," 9.
32. Burke, "San Francisco Police," 5.
33. Olney, "Vigilance Committee," 14.
34. Pinto, "Historical Facts and Incidents," 193.
35. *Minutes*, May 16, 17, 1856; "The Excitement in San Francisco," *New York Times*, June 16, 1856; "The Arms of the Vigilance Committee," *Daily Herald*, May 19, 1856.
36. Crary, "Statement," 9.
37. Tubbs, "Recollections of Events in California," 22.
38. Burns, "Statement," 5.
39. *Minutes*, May 17, 1856.
40. *Minutes*, May 18, 1856.
41. Dempster, "The Vigilance Committee of 1856," 48.
42. Pinto, "Historical Facts and Incidents," 170–71. His division rank is listed in the *Minutes* of May 21.
43. Ibid., 171.
44. "The Events of Sunday," *Sacramento Daily Union*, May 21, 1856; Tuthill, *The History of California*, 440.
45. Tubbs, "Recollections of Events in California," 14.
46. "A Day of Action," *Wide West*, May 25, 1856.
47. Coleman, "Statement," 61–62.
48. "Movements of the Vigilance Committee," *Daily Herald*, May 19, 1856.
49. *Minutes*, May 18, 1856.
50. Watkins, "Statement," 12; Wooley, "Vigilance Committee of 1856."
51. Frink, "Vigilance Committee," 11.
52. *Minutes*, May 18, 1856.
53. "Sentence of Rodman M. Backus," *Sacramento Daily Union*, May 3, 1856.
54. McAllister, "Statement," 149.
55. "Affairs in California," *New York Times*, July 17, 1856.
56. "A Day of Action," *Wide West*, May 25, 1856.
57. Wooley, "Vigilance Committee of 1856"; Pinto, "Historical Facts and Incidents," 172.
58. "Movements of the Vigilance Committee," *Daily Herald*, May 19, 1856.

5. In Secret Tribunal

1. Watkins, "Statement," 21–22.
2. Phelps, *Contemporary Biography of California's Representative Men*, 407–8.
3. *Minutes*, May 20, 1856. See also "Mode of Trial," *Daily Herald*, May 22, 1856.
4. "John P. Manrow," *Daily Alta California*, December 14, 1885; Manrow, "Statement," 4.
5. Manrow, "Statement," 6.
6. Smiley, "Statement," 7.
7. *Minutes*, May 19, 20, 1856.
8. Smiley, "Statement," 8.

9. Watkins, "Statement," 13.
10. *Minutes*, May 20, 1856. According to Bancroft, "All testimony was taken down in writing and is now before me. Guilt in both cases was conclusive . . . Cora was convicted by a bare majority; Casey by a unanimous verdict." *Popular Tribunals*, 2:233. The transcript of the trial has not been located, if it still exists.
11. *Minutes*, May 19, 1856.
12. Sherman to Turner, n.d., contained in a letter from Ellen Ewing Sherman to her father, Thomas Ewing, May 18, 1856, quoted in Clarke, *William Tecumseh Sherman*, 215.
13. *Minutes*, May 21, 1856.
14. Ibid. The city and county were coterminous; hence the San Francisco County sheriff essentially also represented the city.
15. Tuthill, *History of California*, 441.
16. "Funeral of Mr. King," *Daily Herald*, May 22, 1856.
17. *Minutes*, May 22, 1856.
18. Oliver diary, entry for May 22, 1856.
19. *Minutes*, May 18, 22, 1856.
20. DeArment, *Knights of the Green Cloth*, 26–32.
21. Watkins, "Statement," 16. See also Burns, "Statement," 3; [Gray], *Judges and Criminals*, 32.
22. Tuthill, *History of California*, 444; *Minutes*, May 22, 1856.
23. Watkins, "Statement," 16, 17.
24. [O'Meara], *The Vigilance Committee of 1856*, 29.
25. "Funeral Procession of James King of William," *Wide West*, June 8, 1856. See also [Dillon], "T. H. Hittell Papers," 2.
26. Doten, *Journals*, 1:278.
27. "Execution of James P. Casey & Charles Cora" (broadside), printed by *Town Talk*, attached to Mortimer J. Smith to Father, June 5, 1856.
28. "A Week of Woe," *Wide West*, May 25, 1856.
29. [O'Meara], *The Vigilance Committee of 1856*, 29. See also Oliver diary, entry for June 21, 1856.
30. Watkins, "Statement," 18–19; underlining in original.
31. [Gray], *Judges and Criminals*, 33.
32. Doten, *Journals*, 1:278.
33. "Topics of the Day," *Daily Herald*, May 30, 1856 (reprint).
34. "Coroner's Inquest upon the Bodies of Cora and Casey," *Daily Herald*, May 24, 1856.
35. "The Events of Yesterday," *Daily Herald*, May 22, 1856.
36. "Outrage," *Daily Herald*, May 24, 1856.
37. "Thursday, May 22," *Sacramento Daily Union*, May 26, 1856. See also "The Bodies," *Daily Herald*, May 24, 1856.
38. "Funeral of Cora," *Daily Herald*, May 25, 1856.
39. "The Funeral of James P. Casey," *Daily Herald*, May 26, 1856.
40. "Funeral of Casey," *Evening Bulletin*, May 24, 1856.
41. Duane, *Against the Vigilantes*, 126.
42. [Gray], *Judges and Criminals*, 34; headstone, Mission Dolores cemetery, San Francisco.
43. Numerous legal historians have recognized this American quality. For example, see Friedman, *Law in America*, especially 3–19.

44. Coleman, "Statement," 134.
45. E. H. Howard to Gentlemen, May 23, 1856, San Francisco Committee of Vigilance Records [HL], box 1.

6. The Black List

1. *Minutes*, May 23, 1856.
2. Dempster, "The Vigilance Committee of 1856," 1.
3. These letters are in San Francisco Committee of Vigilance Records [HL], boxes 2 and 3.
4. *Minutes*, May 20, 1856.
5. [O'Meara], *The Vigilance Committee of 1856*, 47–49.
6. Watkins, "Statement," 1–2.
7. *Minutes*, May 25, 1856. The *Minutes* for May 27 do not reflect this intention, but Hittell's copy for that and the next several days is rather brief. It is likely that he omitted information.
8. "More Arrests," *Daily Herald*, May 27, 1856.
9. Burns, "Statement," 3–4.
10. "More Arrests"; Green, "Life and Adventures of a 47er of California," 50.
11. *Minutes*, May 27, 1856.
12. *Minutes*, May 24, 26, 1856. This is probably Captain Edgar Wakeman, chief of water police in the Committee of 1851. See Williams, *History of the San Francisco Committee of Vigilance of 1851*, 196–97.
13. Gorn, *The Manly Art*, 69; Hughes, *The Fatal Shore*, 160, 267–70, 385–459; Macintyre, *Concise History of Australia*, 70–71.
14. Hughes, *The Fatal Shore*, 212; "One who knows" to "Sir or who [sic] it may concern," San Francisco Committee of Vigilance Records [HL], box 3; "An Item of History," *Evening Bulletin*, May 29, 1856.
15. Gammie, "Pugilists and Politicians," 276; Miller, *Emigrants and Exiles*, 280–82.
16. Gorn, *The Manly Art*, 70–97; Gammie, "Pugilists and Politicians," 269–83.
17. Gammie, "Pugilists and Politicians," 287–88; Pinto, "Historical Facts and Incidents," 180–81; Huggins, "Continuation of the Annals of San Francisco"; Rogers, "Statement," 1.
18. Frink, "Vigilance Committee," 13; Coleman, "Statement," 75–76.
19. Dempster, "The Vigilance Committee of 1856," 57.
20. Hughes, *The Fatal Shore*, 456–82, 577–78.
21. Cole, "Statement," 34.
22. Oliver diary, entry for May 28, 1856.
23. "Another Important Arrest—A Rich Disclosure of the Ballot-Box Stuffing Trade—Recovery of a Mysterious Box," *Daily Alta California*, May 30, 1856.
24. *Minutes*, May 29, 1856.
25. Hittell, *A History of the City of San Francisco*, 248.
26. "Proceedings at a Meeting Held at the City of San Francisco in the State of California on Tuesday the Twenty-Seventh of May, 1856," Johnson Papers, folder 10.
27. Sherman, *Memoirs*, 125.
28. "Our Rulers," *Daily Herald*, May 28, 1856.
29. Sherman, *Memoirs*, 125. Wool favored the North; Davis, obviously, preferred the South.
30. Kemble, *A History of California Newspapers*, 101; Carr, *The World and William Walker*, 105–11, quote from 110.

31. Ibid., 9–150; "Walker, William," in Johnson and Malone, *Dictionary of American Biography*, 10:363–64.
32. Stiles, *The First Tycoon*, 274–76.
33. "Farragut, David Glasgow," in Johnson and Malone, *Dictionary of American Biography*, 3:286–91; "Naval," *Daily Herald*, May 22, 1856. Quote from Sherman, *Memoirs*, 126, emphasis in the original.
34. Sherman, *Memoirs*, 127.
35. *Minutes*, May 30, 1856; "Affairs Yesterday," *Daily Herald*, May 31, 1856.
36. "Card from General Sherman," *Daily Herald*, May 31, 1856.
37. Cole, "Statement," 17–18.

7. Arresting Developments

1. Oliver diary, entry for May 31, 1856.
2. [Gray], *Judges and Criminals*, 89. See also "To the Public," *Evening Bulletin*, May 28, 1856.
3. Doten, *Journals*, 1:280.
4. Emily Mary Sullevan [sic] to James [Sullivan], May 29, 1856, San Francisco Committee of Vigilance of 1856 Papers [BL].
5. "Inquest on the Body of Sullivan," *Daily Herald*, June 2, 1856.
6. M. Hoadley to Wm. S. King [sic], n.d., Milo Hoadley Papers.
7. *Minutes*, May 31, 1856.
8. Matilda Heron to My Dear Friend, March 3, 1855, Correspondence and Papers, Relating Mainly to Edward McGowan, item 3, San Francisco Committee of Vigilance of 1856 Papers [BL].
9. *Minutes*, May 31, 1856.
10. McGowan, *Narrative*, vi–vii, emphasis in the original.
11. Ibid., vi–vii, 26, 34–36.
12. "40 Sergt at Arms" affidavit, June 14, 1856, San Francisco Committee of Vigilance Records [HL], box 3; Lazar Joseph affidavit, June 10, 1856, ibid.; L. Joseph to the Members of the Executive Committee, June 10, 1856, Papers Relating to the San Francisco Committee of Vigilance [BL].
13. McGowan, *Narrative*, 23–26.
14. *Minutes*, May 21, 1856; "Action of the Grand Jury," *Daily Herald*, May 22, 1856; Watkins, "Statement," 5; "Report: Investigation of County Affairs for the Term Ending June 1, 1856," San Francisco Committee of Vigilance Records [HL], box 1, folder 4. The now-known vigilantes were Executive J. W. Brittan; Charles H. Gough, #2601; and William Sherman (not William Tecumseh Sherman), #1232.
15. "Outrage on Major Roman," *Daily Herald*, May 27, 1856.
16. *Minutes*, May 24, 1856.
17. "Domiciliary Visits," *Daily Herald*, May 25, 1856.
18. "Executive Committee," *Daily Herald*, May 27, 1856; letter signed "By Order of the Committee," *Evening Bulletin*, May 28, 1856.
19. Receipts, "V.C. to Washington Restaurant," May 26–June 5, 1856, San Francisco Committee of Vigilance Records [HL], box 8. See http://www.measuringworth.com/ for the value of commodities.
20. McGowan, *Narrative*, 27.
21. *Minutes*, May 30, 31, 1856.

22. Smiley, "Statement," 15.
23. "Circular, 1854," San Francisco Land Association, Circular, Preambles and Resolutions, Forms for Proposals, Etc.
24. *Minutes*, May 29, 1856.
25. "Affairs Yesterday," *Daily Herald*, May 31, 1856; "McGowan," *Evening Bulletin*, May 30, 1856. See also *Minutes*, May 29, June 1, 1856.
26. *Minutes*, May 28, 29, June 6, 1856.
27. McGowan, *Narrative*, 35–50.
28. *Minutes*, June 2, 1856.
29. *Minutes*, May 30, 1856.
30. *Minutes*, June 1, 1856; Duane, *Against the Vigilantes*, 13–16, 22; Stout, *The Liberators*, 64–65; "Topics of the Day," *Daily Herald*, June 2, 1856.
31. Duane, *Against the Vigilantes*, 129–30; "Arrest of Charles P. Duane," *Daily Herald*, June 2, 1856.
32. Oliver diary, entry for June 3, 1856.
33. "Mass Meeting," *Daily Herald*, June 2, 1856.
34. *Minutes*, June 2, 1856.
35. "More Muskets" and "Receiver of Stolen Goods as Bad as the Thief," both *Evening Bulletin*, June 2, 1856.
36. *Minutes*, May 31, 1856.
37. "The Presidio Elections Last Fall; The Confession of Frances Murray, alias Yankee Sullivan," *Evening Bulletin*, June 3, 1856. Historian Philip Ethington credits this article for an immediate surge in vigilante enrollments. Ethington, *The Public City*, 124.
38. W. T. Sherman to Wm. C. Kibbe, June 2, 1856, Vigilance Committee Records [CSL], folder 3.
39. "Mass Meeting on the Plaza," *Daily Herald*, June 3, 1856.
40. *Minutes*, June 2, 3, 1856.
41. Duane, *Against the Vigilantes*, 130–32.
42. J. Neely Johnson to D. Scannell, n.d. [June 1, 1856?], Johnson Papers, folder 11.
43. David Scannell to J. Neely Johnson, June 2, 1856, ibid., folder 12.
44. J. Neely Johnson to William T. Sherman, June 2, 1856, in Johnson, Reports to the Governor, GPI:322.
45. "Militia to Be Called Out," *Evening Bulletin*, June 3, 1856.
46. "Proclamation of the Governor," *Daily Herald*, June 4, 1856.

8. Escalating Tensions

1. "General Orders," *Daily Herald*, June 5, 1856.
2. "News of the Morning," *Evening Bulletin*, June 4, 1856; "Military Movements," *Daily Herald*, June 4, 1856; "City News," *Wide West*, June 5, 1856.
3. J. Neely Johnson to Wm. T. Sherman, June 3, 1856, Johnson Papers, folder 14.
4. "Militia to Be Called Out," *Evening Bulletin*, June 3, 1856.
5. "City News," *Wide West*, June 3, 1856.
6. "Vigilance Bell," *Evening Bulletin*, June 4, 1856.
7. *Minutes*, June 4, 1856.
8. "Treasure Shipped, May 21, 1856," *San Francisco Herald*, May 22, 1856.
9. "Treasure Shipped, June 5, 1856," *San Francisco Herald*, June 6, 1856.

10. Duane, *Against the Vigilantes*, 133–36. See also "Court Proceedings," *Daily Alta California*, March 31, 1858.
11. Tubbs, "Recollections of Events in California," 22.
12. *Minutes*, May 25, 1856.
13. Sherman's letters to his partner from May 20 to July 2 are missing. See Clarke, *William Tecumseh Sherman*, 219; Sherman, *Memoirs*, 127; *Minutes*, June 6, 1856; quote from Tubbs, "Recollections of Events in California," 21.
14. *Minutes*, June 4, 7, 1856. "Interview of the Committee with the Governor," *Daily Herald*, June 9, 1856, lists all the conciliators: J. B. Crockett, E. W. [*sic*: M.] Earl, F. W. Macondray, James V. Thornton, H. S. Foote, James Donahue, M. R. Roberts, John J. Williams, John Sime, Bailie Peyton, and G. W. P. Bissell.
15. Sherman, *Memoirs*, 128.
16. "Interview of the Committee with the Governor," *Daily Herald*, June 9, 1856; *Minutes*, June 4, 1856; Sherman, *Memoirs*, 129–30. See also "The Benecia Conference," *Sacramento Daily Union*, June 11, 1856.
17. W. T. Sherman to Governor Johnson, June 9, 1856, Johnson Papers, folder 22.
18. L. W. Kemp, "Howard, Volney Erskine," Texas State Historical Association, *Handbook of Texas Online*, http://www.tshaonline.org/handbook/online/articles/fho80.
19. "To My Friends in California," *Daily Herald*, June 9, 1856.
20. *Minutes*, June 9, 1856, with notation by T. H. Hittell.
21. Oliver diary, entry for June 6, 1856; "Topics of the Day," *Daily Herald*, June 7, 1856.
22. Robert Mackintosh to Secretary of the Executive Committee, June 7, 1856, San Francisco Committee of Vigilance Records [HL], box 2.
23. *Minutes*, June 6, 7, 8, 1856.
24. Ethington, *The Public City*, 133; *Minutes*, June 9, 1856.
25. "Events of Yesterday," *Daily Alta California*, June 10, 1856.
26. *Minutes*, June 9, 1856.
27. Smiley, "Statement," 15.
28. *Minutes*, June 9, 1856.
29. Ibid.
30. "Visit to the Vigilance Committee Rooms," *Sacramento Daily Union*, August 25, 1856; www.measuringworth.com. See also *Minutes*, June 13, 1856.
31. *Minutes*, June 9, 10, 1856.
32. Kovács, *The History of the Wass de Czege Family*, 164.
33. *Minutes*, June 9–11, 1856, quote from June 10.
34. *Minutes*, June 12, 1856.
35. *Minutes*, June 10, 12, 1856.
36. Receipt "Bought of G. A. Meigs," June 11, 1856, San Francisco Committee of Vigilance Records [HL], box 8; www.measuringworth.com.
37. Olney, "Vigilance Committee," 16–17.
38. Pinto, "Historical Facts and Incidents," 186–87.
39. *Minutes*, June 6, 1856. Those blacklisted were John Crowe, J. W. Bagley, James Hennessey, Wm. Hamilton, John Lawler, Wm. alias Jack McGuire, James Cusick, and Terrence Kelly; the actions were dropped in the cases of Robert Cushing and Ira Cole.
40. Coleman, "Statement," 74.

41. *Proclamation of the Vigilance Committee of San Francisco*, June 9, 1856, available online at Virtual Museum of the City of San Francisco, http://www.sfmuseum.org/hist1/vig56proc.html.
42. *Minutes*, June 12, 1856.
43. [Editorial,] *True Californian*, quoted in "Revolution-Convention," *Sacramento Daily Union*, June 12, 1856.
44. *Minutes*, June 9, 1856.
45. Tuthill, *History of California*, 315–16.
46. J. Neely Johnson to Gen'l W. T. Sherman, June 10, 1856, Johnson Papers, folder 23; J. Neely Johnson to Gen. Kibbe, June 10, 1856, Vigilance Committee Records [CSL], folder 8; J. Neely Johnson to Judge Terry, June 10, 1856, Johnson Papers, folder 24.
47. [J. N. Johnson] to Messrs. Terry, Douglass, Rowe, and Whitman, June 16, 1856, Johnson Papers, folder 29.
48. Smith, *The Sharps Rifle*, 9–16.
49. V. E. Howard to J. Neely Johnson, June 16, 1856, Johnson Papers, folder 30. See also William Kibbe to David S. Terry, September 3, 1856, Vigilance Committee Records [CSL], folder 68.

9. Rumors and Revelations

1. "Affairs of Yesterday," *Daily Herald*, June 12, 1856; "Passing Events in San Francisco," *Sacramento Daily Union*, June 14, 1856. See also Davis, *History of Political Conventions in California*, 43.
2. "Meeting of the Sympathizers," *Daily Herald*, June 13, 1856.
3. Breen diary, entry for June 13, 1856. Punctuation and capitalization added for clarity throughout.
4. *Minutes*, June 14, 1856.
5. "The Patent Ballot-Box," *New York Times*, July 15, 1856; *Minutes*, June 14, 1856.
6. *Minutes*, June 12, 1856.
7. *Minutes*, June 14, 1856.
8. *Minutes*, June 15, 1856.
9. *Minutes*, June 9, 1856.
10. *Minutes*, June 17, 1856.
11. "Abstract from Records of Court," San Francisco Committee of Vigilance Records [HL], box 1, folder 5.
12. *Minutes*, June 6–11, 1856; George Brown to the Committee on Evidence, May 27, 1856, Papers Relating to the San Francisco Committee of Vigilance [BL]; Wm. Lindop to the Executive, June 15, 1856, San Francisco Committee of Vigilance Records [HL], box 2; "People v. Smyth Clark," May 12, June 17, 1856, ibid.; T. H. Phillips to James Dows, June 16, 1856, ibid.; J. V. Diller to Executives, n.d., ibid.; Rogers [signature cut off] to EC, June 5, 1856, ibid.; Thomas Maguire to EC of C of V, July 28, 1856, ibid.; *Minutes*, June 10, 1856. Those newly blacklisted were Smyth Clark, George James, James Musgrove, Thomas Maguire, Christopher Lilly, Liverpool Jack (alias James Thompson), Jim Burke (alias Activity), Philander Brace, Chris Dowdigan, Michael T. O'Connor, Jack Barmor, Tom Mulloy and Sophie McInnes (his "woman"), Jack Lamb, Robert McMahon, Jack Story, Tom Cunningham, and John Nugent of Police (not the newspaper editor of the same name).

13. New York Court of Common Pleas, *Molony against Dows*, 25.
14. "News of the Morning," *Evening Bulletin*, June 4, 1856.
15. *Minutes*, June 16, 17, 1856.
16. "Affairs Yesterday—Another Arrest," *Daily Herald*, June 18, 1856.
17. *Minutes*, June 18, 19, 1856; "Daguerreotyping the Prisoners," *Daily Herald*, June 21, 1856.
18. "The Constitutional Convention," *Wide West*, June 15, 1856.
19. *Minutes*, June 11, 1856.
20. Coleman, "Statement," 103–9.
21. Ibid., 79–80.
22. Dempster, "The Vigilance Committee of 1856," 54.
23. *New York Herald*, quoted in [San Francisco] *Daily Herald*, August 29, 1856.
24. Oliver diary, entry for June 15, 1856.
25. Carr, *The World and William Walker*, 174–83; "Topics of the Day," *Daily Herald*, June 16, 1856; "Probable Suspension of Diplomatic Intercourse with England," *New York Times*, June 18, 1856.
26. *Minutes*, June 15, 1856.
27. *Minutes*, June 18, 1856.
28. J. Neely Johnson to Franklin Pierce, June 19, 1856, printed as "The Vigilance Committee of California and the Administration," *New York Times*, August 9, 1856.
29. "Requisition on the General Government," *Sacramento Daily Union*, June 20, 1856.
30. Alonzo Phelps, "Squire P. Dewey," in *Contemporary Biography of California's Representative Men*, 266.
31. F. D. Callendar to J. Neely Johnson, June 18, 1856, Johnson Papers, folder 33.
32. Isaac Wistar to Governor Johnson, June 18, 1856, Johnson Papers, folder 32.
33. "The Vigilance Suit in San Francisco," *Sacramento Daily Union*, July 20, 1860.
34. *Minutes*, June 20, 1856.
35. C. E. Wetmore to Gentlemen of the Vigilance Committee, June 20, 1856, San Francisco Committee of Vigilance of 1856 Papers [BL].
36. Breen diary, entries for June 16, 17, 20, 1856.
37. *Minutes*, June 20, 1856.
38. Durkee, "Statement," 3–4.

10. Vigilante Blood

1. Testimony of John Mannix, quoted in Gordan, *Authorized by No Law*, Appendix, 59–61, abstracted from report of trial in the *Evening Bulletin*, September 12, 1856.
2. Transcript of testimony in "Trial of United States v. John L. Durkee," in Gordan, *Authorized by No Law*, 59–60.
3. John M. Gray statement, June 21, 1856, San Francisco Committee of Vigilance Records [HL], box 2; *Minutes*, June 21, 1856.
4. "Events of Yesterday," *Daily Alta California*, June 22, 1856.
5. John Phillips to the Executive Committee, June 24, 1856, San Francisco Committee of Vigilance Records [HL], box 2; R. B. Wallace to Chairman, Police Committee, June 16, 1856, ibid.
6. *Minutes*, June 22, 1856.
7. Sterling Hopkins testimony, in *Trial of David S. Terry*, 20; Hamilton Bowie testimony, ibid., 34–35.

8. Bowie testimony, ibid., 34.
9. H. A Russell testimony, ibid., 7.
10. Various testimony, ibid.; quotes from James S. Bovee testimony, 8.
11. Testimony of Joseph Capprise and James Dunlevy, ibid., 11–12, 32–33, quotes from Dunlevy. All artistic renditions and most written accounts fail to note that two men had hold of Terry's rifle, the second being Joseph Capprise. Later accounts armed Terry with a Bowie knife, a large, ponderous weapon that probably would have severed Hopkins's head from his body. Terry's nephew, who in later years lived with his uncle, reported that Terry carried a small sheath knife. See John Wharton Terry, "David S. Terry: Notes Prepared for Mr. Klette," Terry Papers [SUL], 6.
12. *Minutes*, June 21, 1856.
13. Pinto, "Historical Facts and Incidents," 198.
14. Cole, "Statement," 12; Olney, "Vigilance Committee," 11–12.
15. Ayres, "Personal Recollections of the Vigilance Committee," 174.
16. Pinto, "Historical Facts and Incidents," 198–99.
17. Frink, "Vigilance Committee," 15–16.
18. Pinto, "Historical Facts and Incidents," 198–99.
19. Ayres, "Personal Recollections," 174.
20. [Gray], *Judges and Criminals*, 59.
21. Dempster, "The Vigilance Committee of 1856," 8.
22. *Minutes*, June 21, 1856.
23. Volney E. Howard to William T. Coleman and others styling themselves the Vigilance Committee, June 21, 1856, quoted in Bancroft, *Popular Tribunals*, 2: 404.
24. "To His Excellency, J. Neely Johnson, Governor of the State of California," *Daily Herald*, June 25, 1856.
25. J. R. West, "Statement of the Arms . . . Taken by the Vigilance Committee," November 25, 1856, Vigilance Committee Records [CSL], folder 76.
26. R. P. Ashe's testimony, in *Trial of David S. Terry*, 36. See also Truett, "Statement," 4.
27. William Tecumseh Sherman to Henry Smith Turner, July 2, 1856, quoted in Clarke, *William Tecumseh Sherman*, 223.
28. *Minutes*, June 21, 1856.
29. R. P. Ashe's testimony, in *Trial of David S. Terry*, 36.
30. Rogers, "Statement," 12.
31. *Minutes*, June 21, 1856; Hittell, *History of California*, 3:571.
32. Watkins, "Statement," 19.
33. Smiley, "Statement," 8.
34. *Minutes*, June 21, 22, 1856; "Result of the Military Election Yesterday," *Evening Bulletin*, April 11, 1856.
35. [Gray], *Judges and Criminals*, 63.
36. [Brief History], Vigilance Committee Records [CSL], folder 70.
37. Ibid.
38. *Minutes*, June 25, 1856.
39. Gillespie, "Vigilance Committee," 9.
40. Smiley, "Statement," 8–9.
41. "Card from the Jackson Guards," *Daily Herald*, June 27, 1856.
42. [Gray], *Judges and Criminals*, 63.

43. "Card from the Jackson Guards." See also Coleman, "Statement," 94–96; Watkins, "Statement," 19; Dows, "Statement," 10; *Minutes*, June 25, 1856.
44. "Arms Captured," *Daily* [? (name cut off)], Scott Papers, box 8.
45. Coleman, "Statement," 97.
46. Rogers, "Statement," 13.
47. Coleman, "Statement," 92–94.

11. Unintended Consequences

1. [O'Meara], *The Vigilance Committee of 1856*, 40–41.
2. Breen diary, entry for June 21, 1856.
3. *Minutes*, June 21, 1856.
4. "Topics of the Day," *Daily Herald*, June 22, 1856.
5. "More Bloodshed," *Daily* [? (name cut off)], Scott Papers, box 8.
6. Cole, "Statement," 7, 12–14.
7. *Minutes*, June 22, 1856.
8. "Card from Doctor Pigne Dupuytren," *Daily Herald*, July 14, 1856; Cole testimony, in *Trial of David S. Terry*, 18; *Minutes*, June 21, 1856; 680 Secry [H. Channing Beals] to [Investigating Committee], n.d., San Francisco Committee of Vigilance Records [HL], box 2.
9. William Kibbe to Judge Creanor, June 21, 1856, Vigilance Committee Records [CSL], folder 14.
10. William Kibbe to J. Neely Johnson, June 21, 1856, ibid., folder 15.
11. Qr. Mr. & Adjt. Genl. Cal. [William Kibbe] to the Executive Committee, June 21, 1856, Johnson Papers, folder 40.
12. Olney, "Vigilance Committee," 23–24.
13. *Minutes*, June 22, 1856.
14. Ibid.
15. McAllister, *Ellen Ewing*, 151.
16. *Minutes*, June 22, 1856.
17. Hittell, *History of California*, 3:575–76.
18. Coleman, "Statement," 98.
19. *Minutes*, June 22, 1856.
20. Smiley, "Statement," 9.
21. *Minutes*, June 22, 1856; Tubbs, "Recollections of Events in California," 16.
22. "New York's 'Favorite Son,'" *Evening Bulletin*, June 25, 1856.
23. *Minutes*, June 21, 1856.
24. *Minutes*, June 22, 1856.
25. Ryckman, "Vigilance Committee," 18.
26. Hall, *The Terry-Broderick Duel*, 31.
27. Cecil Harper Jr., "Runnels, Hardin Richard," *Handbook of Texas Online*, http://www.tshaonline.org/handbook/online/articles/fru13.
28. "Judge Terry's Letter," *Sacramento Daily Union*, July 4, 1856, reprinted from the *Herald* and *Sun* of July 2, 1856. See also "The Crivellari and Related Families," http://wc.rootsweb.ancestry.com/cgi-bin/igm.cgi?op=DESC&db=imccriv&id=I4018; Kenneth W. Hobbs, "Terry, David Smith," *Handbook of Texas Online*, https://www.tshaonline.org/handbook/online/articles/fte29; Terry's Texas Rangers, http://www.keathleywebs.com/terrysrangers/.

29. "Topics of the Day," *Daily Herald*, July 1, 1856; Kenneth W. Hobbs, "Terry, Benjamin Franklin," *Handbook of Texas Online*, http://www.tshaonline.org/handbook/online/articles/fte28; Hobbs, "Terry, David Smith," ibid., http://www.tshaonline.org/handbook/online/articles/fte29. Quote from "Topics of the Day."
30. David S. Terry to My Dear Cousin [Cornelia Runnels], November 7, 1851, Terry Papers [HL], box 1, folder TE 124.
31. Ibid.
32. Ibid.
33. "Topics of the Day," *Daily Herald*, July 1, 1856; *Trial of David Terry*, 56.
34. David S. Terry to Dear Cousin [Cornelia Runnels], October 7, 1851, Terry Papers [HL], box 1, folder TE 123.
35. David S. Terry to My Dear Cousin [Cornelia Runnels], November 7, 1851, ibid., folder TE 124.
36. David S. Terry to Cousin [Cornelia Runnels], April 16, 1852, ibid., folder TE 125.
37. David S. Terry to Cousin [Cornelia Runnels], May 1, 1852, ibid., folder TE 127.
38. Ophilia Runnels to Cornelia Runnels Terry, November 25, 1853, ibid., folder TE 57.
39. Frank D. Terry tombstone, Stockton Rural Cemetery, Stockton, Calif.
40. Cornelia Runnels Terry tombstone, Stockton Rural Cemetery.
41. *Minutes*, June 23, 1856.
42. *Minutes*, June 25, 1856.
43. *Minutes*, June 23, 1856.
44. D. S. Terry to the Executive Committee, June 24 [*sic*: 23], 1856, San Francisco Committee of Vigilance of 1856 Papers [BL].
45. *Minutes*, June 23, 1856; "Demand for the Release of Mr. Moloney," *Daily Herald*, June 24, 1856.
46. Pinto, "Historical Facts and Incidents," 201.
47. Qr. Mr. & Adjt. General Cal. [Kibbe] to J. Neely Johnson, June 24, 1856, Vigilance Committee Records [CSL], folder 18.
48. *Minutes*, June 23, 1856.
49. *Minutes*, June 24, 1856.
50. 3147, 6th Div. to the Executives of the Vigilance Committee, June 26, 1856, San Francisco Committee of Vigilance Records [HL], box 1.
51. Thomas N. Cazneau to Gen. W.C. Kibbe, June 26, 1856, Vigilance Committee Records [CSL], folder 22.
52. *Minutes*, June 26, 1856.
53. *Minutes*, June 23, 1856.
54. *Minutes*, June 26, 1856.
55. Cole, "Statement," 16–17.

12. Mounting Opposition

1. *Minutes*, June 24, 1856; "Wetting the Sand Bags," *Evening Bulletin*, June 25, 1856; "Extension of Fort Gunny-bags," *Daily Herald*, June 29, 1856; "The Vigilance Committee," *Wide West*, June 29, 1856.
2. *Minutes*, June 26, 1856.
3. Tubbs, "Recollections of Events in California."
4. *Minutes*, June 26, 1856.

5. Ibid.
6. Ibid.
7. Breen diary, entry for June 27, 1856.
8. *Minutes*, June 27, 1856.
9. Ibid.
10. Farwell, "Statement," 23.
11. *Minutes*, June 27, 1856.
12. *Minutes*, June 26, 1856.
13. *Trial of David S. Terry*, 4–7. For Capprise's effort, see 11.
14. *Minutes*, June 27, 1856.
15. David S. Terry to Capt. E. B. Boutwell, June 28, 1856, in *Message of the President of the United States in Compliance with a Resolution of the Senate of the 28th Ultimo, Calling for Information Respecting Any Correspondence or Proceedings in Relation to the Self-Styled Vigilance Committee in California*, United States, Senate, Ex. Doc. No. 101, 34th Congress, 1st sess., 27, emphasis in the original.
16. J. Neely Johnson to Cmdr. E. B. Boutwell, June 27, 1856, Vigilance Committee Records [CSL], folder 24.
17. E. B. Boutwell to Governor, June 29, 1856, Vigilance Committee Records [CSL], folder 27.
18. "Marine Intelligence," *Daily Herald*, June 17, 1856.
19. *Minutes*, June 28, 1856.
20. [O'Meara], *The Vigilance Committee of 1856*, 41–42.
21. Farwell, "Statement," 19–20.
22. Olney, "Vigilance Committee," 21.
23. Farwell, "Statement," 19–20.
24. Tubbs, "Recollections of Events in California," 18.
25. Gillespie, "Vigilance Committee," 9.
26. *Minutes*, June 28, 1856.
27. Farwell, "Statement," 20–22.
28. D. G. Farragut to J. C. Dobbin, June 30, 1856, in Farragut, *The Life of David Glasgow Farragut*, 172–73.
29. D. G. Farragut to E. B. Boutwell, July 1, 1856, ibid., 179–80.
30. *Minutes*, June 29, 1856.
31. *Minutes*, June 30, July 1, 1856.
32. 680 Secy [H. Channing Beals] in re James George (237), n.d., San Francisco Committee of Vigilance Records [HL], box 2, underlining in the original.
33. E. T. Mennomy and Towsend Bagley testimony, n.d., San Francisco Committee of Vigilance Records [HL], box 2; nos. 225, 226, 235, 263, 270, 296 to Headquarters, V.C., July 17, 1856, ibid.
34. "The Work of Purification Commenced," *Daily Herald*, July 1, 1856.
35. "Judge Shattuck's Opinion on the Case of Judge Terry," *Daily Herald*, June 27, 1856. A copy of the broadside is held by the Huntington Library.
36. David S. Terry to Captain E. B. Boutwell, June 28, 1856, in *Message of the President . . . in Relation to the Self-Styled Vigilance Committee in California*, 27.
37. E. B. Boutwell to the Executive Committee of Vigilance, June 28, 1856, Vigilance Committee Records [CSL], folder 26.

38. *Minutes*, June 28, 1856.
39. "The Charge of Piracy against J. L. Durkee," *Sacramento Daily Union*, July 2, 1856.
40. Oliver diary, entry for June 27, 1856.
41. "The Safety of the People Is the Highest Law," *Evening Bulletin*, June 23, 1856.
42. "A Card," *Daily Herald*, June 27, 1856, emphasis in the original.
43. *Minutes*, June 30, July 1, 1856.
44. Burns, "Statement," 5.
45. Smiley, "Statement," 10–11.
46. Farwell, "Statement," 22.
47. Dempster, "The Vigilance Committee of 1856," 10–11.
48. Wm. C. Kibbe to J. Neely Johnson, June 30, 1856, Vigilance Committee Records [CSL], folder 29.
49. J. Neely Johnson to W. C. Kibbe, June 30, 1856, ibid., folder 30.
50. J. R. West to J. Neely Johnson, June 30, 1856, Johnson Papers, folder 47.
51. Wm. C. Kibbe to J. Neely Johnson, June 30, 1856, Vigilance Committee Records [CSL], folder 29.
52. Cornelia Terry to Gentlemen, July 1, 1856, Terry Papers [HL], box 1, folder TE 104.
53. [Untitled], *Daily Herald*, June 30, 1856.
54. "Terry's Trial—Well?," *Evening Bulletin*, June 26, 1856.
55. C. D. Tucker to [Cornelia Terry], June 29, 1856, Terry Papers [HL], box 1, folder TE 251.

13. Sectional Strife

1. "Charles P. Duane's Attempt to Return on the John L. Stephens," quoted from the *San Francisco Bulletin* in the *Sacramento Daily Union*, July 3, 1856.
2. Gordan, *Authorized by No Law*, 4–6.
3. "Charles P. Duane's Attempt to Return on the John L. Stephens." See also Duane, *Against the Vigilantes*, 142–47.
4. Stillman, "Statement," 5.
5. "Charles P. Duane's Attempt to Return on the John L. Stephens."
6. Bancroft, *History of California*, 6:700–701.
7. "Topics of the Day," *Daily Herald*, July 2, 1856.
8. Nevins, *Ordeal of the Union*, 2:472–79.
9. Ibid., 438–39; Charles Sumner, "The Crime against Kansas," in *Appendix to the Congressional Globe*, 34th Cong., 1st sess., May 19, 1856, 529–31.
10. Nevins, *Ordeal of the Union*, 2:441–46; Richards, *The Slave Power*, 195–97; Leonard, *The Power of the Press*, 84–85; Puleo, *The Caning*.
11. "The Attack on Senator Sumner," *Wide West*, July 6, 1856.
12. "Topics of the Day," *Daily Herald*, July 2, 1856.
13. Tubbs, "Recollections of Events in California," 15.
14. "Topics of the Day," *Daily Herald*, July 1, 1856.
15. Shafter, *The Life, Diary and Letters*, 182, entry for July 3, 1856.
16. D. G. Farragut to Farwell and Case, July 1, 1856, in Farragut, *The Life of David Glasgow Farragut*, 178–79.
17. E. B. Boutwell to Capt. D. G. Farragut, July 2, 1856, quoted ibid., 180–81.
18. D. G. Farragut to E. B. Boutwell, July 2, 1856, quoted ibid., 182–83.

19. D. G. Farragut to J. C. Dobbin, July 2, 1856, quoted ibid., 174–76.
20. Wm. M. Hoge (?), Thompson Campbell, Thos. W. Sutherland, W. H. French, P. Bequette, Walter M. Rockland, Jas. C. L. Wadsworth, Wm. Bouthwell, and Henry B. Truett to the Executive Committee, July 2, 1856, San Francisco Committee of Vigilance of 1856 Papers [BL].
21. New York Court of Common Pleas, *Molony against Dows*, 35.
22. "Molony, Richard Sheppard," *Biographical Directory of the United States Congress*, http://bioguide.congress.gov/scripts/biodisplay.pl?index=M000846.
23. *Minutes*, July 4, 1856.
24. "Mrs. Terry's Letter," *Sacramento Daily Union*, July 4, 1856, reprinted from the *Herald* and *Sun* of July 2, 1856.
25. "Judge Terry's Letter," ibid.
26. No. 2871 [Edward David Jones] to the Executive Committee, June 11, 1856, San Francisco Committee of Vigilance Records [HL], box 2.
27. *Minutes*, June 13, 19, 1856; No. 2871 to Executive Committee, June 11, 1856.
28. "A Peep at the Interior of the Bastille," *Daily Herald*, August 29, 1856.
29. [O'Meara], *The Vigilance Committee of 1856*, 50.
30. "J. R. Moloney [sic]," *Daily Herald*, August 2, 1856.
31. *Minutes*, July 5, 11, 12, 1856.
32. *Minutes*, July 19, 1856.
33. *Minutes*, July 22, 1856.

14. A New Agenda

1. Crary, "Statement," 11.
2. Pinto, "Historical Facts and Incidents," 193.
3. "The Consolidation Act, and Our New Officials," *Evening Bulletin*, July 1, 1856.
4. "County Affairs," *Evening Bulletin*, July 8, 1856.
5. *Minutes*, June 30, July 9, 1856. Those thanked were Col. Isaac Williams of Rancho Chino, William Workman of Rancho Puente, Thomas Martin of Santa Barbara, and Abel Stearns of Los Angeles.
6. McGowan, *Narrative*, 53–112.
7. Receipt, J. D. Farwell bought of J. D. Farwell, July 10, 1856, San Francisco Committee of Vigilance Records [HL], box 8; www.measuringworth.com.
8. "Later from Southern California," *Evening Bulletin*, July 19, 1856.
9. McGowan, *Narrative*, 140–57; *Minutes*, July 30, 1856.
10. *Minutes*, May 25, 1856.
11. *Minutes*, July 11, 1856.
12. The complete list: Michael Brannigan, James W. Stillman, Christopher Lilly, J. D. Musgrove, Jim Burke alias Activity, John Cooney, J. P. [sic: Patrick J.] Hickey, *Minutes*, July 6, 1856; James Thompson alias Liverpool Jack, *Minutes*, July 7, 1856. Hickey was involved in a "squatter fight" with Colonel George H. Howard of the 7th Division. See *Minutes*, August 16, September 10, 1856.
13. *Minutes*, July 20, 1856.
14. "Another Arrest," *San Joaquin Republican*, July 13, 1856; "Official Evidence of the Death of Chris Lilly and ____ Yates," *Marysville Daily Herald*, November 10, 1857.

15. *Minutes*, July 10, 1856.
16. T. G. Phillips to James Dows, June 19, 1856, San Francisco Committee of Vigilance Records [HL], box 2.
17. J. V. Diller affidavit, n.d., ibid.
18. "News from California," *New York Times*, September 29, 1856; "The Report of the Board of Examiners," *Daily Alta California*, August 14, 1858.
19. *Minutes*, July 9, 1856.
20. Oliver diary, entry for July 11, 1856.
21. *Minutes*, July 11, 1856.
22. *Minutes*, July 11, 14, 1856, quote from July 14.
23. *Minutes*, July 15, 1856.
24. Oliver diary, entry for July 12, 1856.
25. Z. Z. to Editor of the Herald, *Daily Herald*, July 14, 1856.
26. *Minutes*, July 12, 1856; see, for example, "Official Corruption," *Daily Alta California*, July 13, 1856.
27. Coleman, "Statement," 120–21.
28. Hittell, *History of California*, 3:619.
29. *Minutes*, July 13, 1856.
30. Green, "Life and Adventures of a 47er of California," 44, 45.
31. "More Domiciliary Visits," *Daily Herald*, July 15, 1856.
32. *Minutes*, July 14, 1856.
33. Green, "Life and Adventures of a 47er of California," 48–49.
34. Ibid., 46–49.
35. *Minutes*, July 14, 1856.
36. Ibid.; "Mr. Pelton's Reply," *Daily Herald*, July 15, 1856.
37. "The Meeting Last Evening," *Daily Herald*, July 15, 1856. Those imprisoned were John Manning, Thomas Rooney, S. S. O'Reilly, Jim Godfrey, Michael Hayes, J. T. Dickson, Pat Flay, M. C. Cartellon, Benj. Cook, M. Dalton, S. McCready no. 5281, Jacob Ritchie, J. W. Auld(?), and John Brady. Godfrey was released at his wife's request. See *Minutes*, July 14, 1856.
38. D. G. Farragut to J. C. Dobbin, July 17, 1856, in Farragut, *The Life of David Glasgow Farragut*, 184–85.
39. William C. Kibbe to J. Neely Johnson, July 15, 1856, Vigilance Committee Records [CSL], folder 41.
40. *Minutes*, July 15, 16, 1856.
41. Oliver diary, entry for July 14, 1856.
42. "Arrival of Steamer Golden Age," *Daily Herald*, July 15, 1856; Nevins, *Ordeal of the Union*, 2:467, 456–58, 469–70; Carr, *The World and William Walker*, 193; Doten, *Journals*, entry for July 15, 1856, 1:298–99; Breen diary, entry for July 15, 1856.
43. *Minutes*, July 19, 1856.
44. In copying the *Minutes*, Hittell completely skipped p. 294. *Minutes* exist only for the 11:00 a.m. meeting (p. 293) and 7:30 p.m. meeting (p. 295) on Monday, July 21, 1856. The 2:00 p.m. meeting has no record.
45. [O'Meara], *The Vigilance Committee of 1856*, 54–55, 12–13.
46. Dows, "Statement," 7.

47. Manrow, "Statement," 7.
48. Ryckman, "Vigilance Committee," 19–20.
49. [O'Meara], *The Vigilance Committee of 1856*, 55–56.

15. Trying Times

1. *Minutes*, July 14, 1856. Vasquez—not the outlaw of the same name—had been officially appointed by California's Mexican government as guardian of the Pueblo Papers.
2. *Minutes*, July 14, 15, 16, 1856, emphasis added.
3. *Minutes*, June 3, 7, 9, 13, 1856, quote from June 13.
4. "Horrible Murder at the Mission Dolores—Great Excitement—Determination to Lynch the Murderers," *Daily Alta California*, June 4, 1855.
5. "Tragical Death of Marion the Murderer," *Daily Alta California*, June 6, 1855.
6. Thomas S. Miller/ One of the Committee of Vigilance/ No. 1520 to Gentlemen, May 27, 1856, San Francisco Committee of Vigilance Records [HL], box 1.
7. Pinto, "Historical Facts and Incidents," 205.
8. "Abstract from Records of Court," San Francisco Committee of Vigilance Records [HL], box 1, folder 5.
9. 1794 to Gent[lemen], June 12, 1856, San Francisco Committee of Vigilance Records [HL], box 2.
10. Pinto, "Historical Facts and Incidents," 205; *Minutes*, June 19, 1856; Cole, "Statement," 8.
11. *Minutes*, July 13, 1856.
12. *Minutes*, July 17, 1856.
13. *Minutes*, July 11, 1856.
14. Bluxome, "Statement," 19–20.
15. Dows, "Statement," 8–9.
16. *Minutes*, July 16, 1856.
17. *Minutes*, July 18, 1856.
18. *Minutes*, July 18, 19, 20, 21, 1856.
19. *Minutes*, May 18, 1856.
20. E. A. Scott to Daughter (C. T. Hubbell), July 20, 1856, 2–4.
21. *Trial of David S. Terry*, 3. The *Minutes* of July 22, 1856, provides a slightly different list.
22. Smiley, "Statement," 10.
23. *Trial of David S. Terry*, 24–25.
24. Ibid., 25–26.
25. Ibid., 26.
26. Ibid., 26–28.
27. Dempster, "The Vigilance Committee of 1856," 11.
28. *Minutes*, July 22, 1856.
29. Ibid.
30. [Untitled], *San Joaquin Republican*, July 24, 1856.
31. "City News," *Wide West*, July 27, 1856; "Two Weeks Later from California," *New York Times*, August 30, 1856.
32. William C. Kibbe to J. Neely Johnson, July 24, 1856, Vigilance Committee Records [CSL], folder 47.
33. *Minutes*, July 23, 1856.

34. *Minutes*, July 24, 1856.
35. Pinto, "Historical Facts and Incidents," 204.
36. Coleman, "Statement," 116.
37. Gillespie, "Vigilance Committee," 10.
38. Crary, "Statement," 6.
39. "Return of Bulger," *San Joaquin Republican*, July 27, 1856.
40. "Two Weeks Later from California," *New York Times*, August 30, 1856.
41. *Minutes*, July 24, 1856.
42. Breen diary, entry for July 24, 1856. Breen consistently spelled Hetherington's name as "Hethington," but it has not been corrected here.
43. *Minutes*, July 24, 1856; [O'Meara], *The Vigilance Committee of 1856*, 31–32; "The Shooting of Dr. Randall," *San Joaquin Republican*, July 26, 1856; "Two Weeks Later from California," *New York Times*, August 30, 1856; Ayres, "Personal Recollections," 175; Tuthill, *History of California*, 487; Hittell, *History of California*, 3:610.
44. *Minutes*, July 24, 1856.
45. Tubbs, "Recollections of Events in California," 17.

16. Blood Lust

1. *Minutes*, July 24, 1856.
2. *Minutes*, July 25, 1856.
3. "Flouring Mill," *Sacramento Daily Union*, December 21, 1854; "Mill Burnt," *Daily Alta California*, July 26, 1856; "Brief Glances," *Daily Alta California*, July 28, 1856.
4. "A Parting Chat with Billy Mulligan," *Sacramento Daily Union*, June 11, 1856.
5. Dempster, "The Vigilance Committee of 1856," 13–14.
6. *Minutes*, July 26, 1856.
7. "What Is to Be Done with Bulger?," *Sacramento Daily Union*, July 28, 1856.
8. "Sentence of Bulger," *Evening Bulletin*, July 28, 1856.
9. *Minutes*, July 27, 1856.
10. *Minutes*, July 26, 1856.
11. Dows, "Statement," 9.
12. Breen diary, entry for July 26, 1856.
13. "Truth, Every Word of It," *San Joaquin Republican*, July 31, 1856.
14. *Minutes*, July 27, 1856.
15. Ibid.
16. Ibid.
17. Smiley, "Statement," 12.
18. Drury, *William Anderson Scott*, 160–86.
19. Scott, *A Discourse for the Times*.
20. "Letter from Gen. Howard to B. W. Leigh," *Evening Bulletin*, July 28, 1856.
21. "Shamelessness of the Inquisitors," *San Joaquin Republican*, August 4, 1856.
22. "Ship the Rogues and Save the Country," *Evening Bulletin*, August 6, 1856.
23. *Minutes*, July 28, 1856.
24. Green, "Life and Adventures of a 47er of California," 52–54.
25. *Minutes*, July 28, 31, 1856.
26. *Minutes*, July 28, 1856.
27. Ibid.

28. Green, "Life and Adventures of a 47er of California," 56, 54.
29. Breen diary, entry for July 28, 1856.
30. *Minutes*, July 29, 1856.
31. "Execution of Hetherington & Brace by the Vigilance Committee," *True Californian*, July 30, 1856; [Gray], *Judges and Criminals*, 99–100; "Execution of Joseph Hetherington and Philander Brace," *Evening Bulletin*, July 30, 1856.
32. "Execution of Hetherington & Brace by the Vigilance Committee"; [Gray], *Judges and Criminals*, 80–84, 99–100; "Execution of Joseph Hetherington and Philander Brace."
33. Cole, "Statement," 8.
34. "Interview with Hetherington," *Evening Bulletin*, July 29, 1856; www.measuringworth.com.
35. "Execution of Joseph Hetherington and Philander Brace," *Bulletin*, July 30, 1856.
36. Cole, "Statement," 8–9.
37. Durkee "Statement," 7.
38. "Valerian," University of Maryland Medical Center, http://www.umm.edu/altmed/articles/valerian-000279.htm.
39. Smiley, "Statement," 12–13.
40. Cole, "Statement," 9.
41. W. C. Kibbe to J. Neely Johnson, July 30, 1856, Vigilance Committee Records [CSL], folder 50.
42. Frink, "Vigilance Committee," 21.
43. *Minutes*, July 29, 1856.
44. "Execution of Hetherington and Brace by the Vigilance Committee."
45. Ibid.; Crary, "Statement," 8; "Execution of Joseph Hetherington and Philander Brace"; [O'Meara], *The Vigilance Committee of 1856*, 33–34; Hittell, *History of California*, 3:612–15; "Two Weeks Later from California," *New York Times*, August 30, 1856.
46. "Inquest on the Bodies of Hetherington and Brace," *Daily Herald*, August 2, 1856; "Coroner's Inquest," *San Joaquin Republican*, August 3, 1856; *Minutes*, August 2, 1856; F. M. Haight to Henry [Haight], December 19, 1857, Henry Haight Papers; Breen diary, entry for July 29, 1856.

17. Release

1. Oliver diary, entry for July 30, 1856.
2. W. C. Kibbe to J. Neely Johnson, July 30, 1856, Vigilance Committee Records [CSL], folder 50.
3. "Remarks," *True Californian*, July 30, 1856.
4. *Minutes*, July 30, 31, August 3, 1856; "Christopher Lilly," *Daily Herald*, August 6, 1856.
5. Dempster, "The Vigilance Committee of 1856," 59.
6. "San Francisco Committee of Vigilance of 1856 Roster."
7. *Minutes*, July 31, 1856.
8. W. T. Sherman to My Dear Brother [John Sherman], August 3, 1856, quoted in Thorndike, *The Sherman Letters*, 60.
9. Green, "Life and Adventures of a 47er of California," 60.
10. Frink, "Vigilance Committee," 16–17.
11. *Minutes*, August 1, 1856.
12. *Minutes*, August 2, 1856.

13. Green, "Life and Adventures of a 47er of California," 62.
14. Ibid., 62–63, 65; *Minutes*, July 15, 1856.
15. *Minutes*, July 14, 1856; Green, "Life and Adventures of a 47er of California," 62–64.
16. Green, "Life and Adventures of a 47er of California," 64–65.
17. Ibid., 64–66.
18. Ibid., 66–68; *Minutes*, August 10, 1856. For amount, see also *Minutes* of July 28, 30, 31, 1856.
19. Nathan Trotter, quoted in Tooker, *Nathan Trotter*, 179.
20. Lamoreaux, *Insider Lending*, 1–2.
21. *Minutes*, August 3, 1856.
22. *Minutes*, August 5, 1856.
23. Page number 358 in the original is provided, but it has no entry.
24. Oliver diary, entry for August 6, 1856.
25. *Minutes*, August 6, 1856. They were C. H. Gough, W. O. Smith, R. B. Hampton, R. Lewis, C. D. Cushman, D. W. C. Thompson, and Samuel Soulé.
26. Coleman, "Statement," 124.
27. "Unpardonable Outrage! Gross Political Fraud and Trickery among the Reformers . . . Translated from the *Echo du Pacifique*," *Daily Herald*, August 13, 1856. This translation is a letter from "866, Vigilant," who has not been identified. The vote is reported in *Minutes*, August 6, 1856. The time comes from "Charges against Judge Terry," *Evening Bulletin*, August 7, 1856. The newspaper got the news before Terry did.
28. Frink, "Vigilance Committee," 18.
29. *Minutes*, August 7, 1856.
30. Green, "Life and Adventures of a 47er of California," 61.
31. Truett, "Statement," 4–5.
32. Bluxome, "Statement," 18.
33. Truett, "Statement," 4–6.
34. Bluxome, "Statement," 18.
35. Truett, "Statement," 4–6.
36. "Repudiation of the Executive Committee; Vigilantism in Trouble," *San Joaquin Republican*, August 9, 1856.
37. Truett, "Statement," 6.
38. Frink, "Vigilance Committee," 18.
39. Green, "Life and Adventures of a 47er of California," 61.
40. Truett, "Statement," 6.
41. *Minutes*, August 7, 1856.
42. "The First False Step," *Evening Bulletin*, August 7, 1856.
43. "Dereliction of Duty—What Must Be Done?," *Evening Bulletin*, August 7, 1856.
44. Oliver diary, entry for August 7, 1856.
45. "Is It All a Dream?," *Evening Bulletin*, August 8, 1856, emphasis in the original.
46. No. 2795 to Sir, August 11, 1856, San Francisco Committee of Vigilance Records [HL], box 1.
47. *Minutes*, August 14, 1856.
48. "Release of Judge Terry" and "The Trip to Benecia," *Daily Herald*, August 8, 1856.
49. D. G. Farragut to J. C. Dobbin, August 19, 1856, in Farragut, *The Life of David Glasgow Farragut*, 187–88.

50. "Release of Judge Terry" and "The Trip to Benecia"; "Reception of Judge Terry in Sacramento," *Daily Herald*, August 9, 1856.
51. "Release of Judge Terry" and "The Trip to Benecia"; "Reception of Judge Terry in Sacramento"; "The Grand Reception Fizzle at Sacramento," *Evening Bulletin*, August 11, 1856.
52. "Reception of Judge Terry at Stockton," *Daily Herald*, August 20, 1856.
53. *Minutes*, August 5–9, 1856.
54. *Minutes*, August 8, 9, 1856. On Truett, see also *Minutes*, August 16, 1856.

18. A False Finale

1. Green, "Life and Adventures of a 47er of California," 61–62.
2. *Minutes*, August 8, 9, 10, 1856.
3. "Corruption in High Places—An Expose of Pueblo Titles," *Evening Bulletin*, August 11, 1856.
4. Dempster, "The Vigilance Committee of 1856," 2.
5. *Minutes*, September 12, 1856.
6. Green, "Life and Adventures of a 47er of California," 68–69.
7. "A Reform Party," *Evening Bulletin*, August 6, 1856, emphasis in the original.
8. "Terry and the Vigilance Committee," *Evening Bulletin*, August 8, 1856.
9. "Legal Intelligence," *Evening Bulletin*, May 17, 1856. Woodworth had sued another man who got his land from Limantour and successors. The jury ruled in favor of Woodworth, but an appeal was likely.
10. "Mass Meeting of the People," *Daily Alta California*, August 12, 1856.
11. "By the State Telegraph Line," *Sacramento Daily Union*, August 12, 1856.
12. "Unanimity on One Point," *Evening Bulletin*, August 12, 1856.
13. "Mass Meeting of the People," *Daily Alta California*, August 12, 1856.
14. Oliver diary, entry for August 11, 1856; "Convention of the Democracy," *Daily Herald*, August 12, 1856; "The Democratic Primary Election Today," *Daily Herald*, August 23, 1856. Identified vigilantes are G. B. Post, #58, and S. J. Ashley, #4414. See Applications for Membership, San Francisco Committee of Vigilance Records [HL], box 4, folder 1-A, and box 5, folder 9-P.
15. *Minutes*, August 8, 13, 1856.
16. For Marcy's original, see W. L. Marcy to J. Neely Johnson, July 19, 1856, Johnson Papers, folder 56.
17. "The News by the Illinois," *New York Times*, July 28, 1856; *Message of the President of the United States . . . in Relation to the Self-Styled Vigilance Committee in California*.
18. "The Vigilance Committee of California and the Administration," *New York Times*, August 9, 1856. On Marcy, see Spencer, *The Victor and the Spoils*, 365–75.
19. "Two Weeks Later from California," *New York Times*, August 14, 1856.
20. Sister [Mary Sessums] to Sister [Cornelia Runnels Terry], August 8, 1856, Terry Papers [HL], box 1, folder TE 66, underlining in the original.
21. *Minutes*, August 17, 1856.
22. [Untitled], August 16, [1856], San Francisco Committee of Vigilance Records [HL], box 1.
23. Oliver diary, entry for August 16, 1856.
24. R. Augustus Thompson [and F. Forman] to J. Neely Johnson, July 20, 1856, Johnson Papers, folder 57.
25. Phelps, *Contemporary Biography of California's Representative Men*, 266–67.

26. "San Francisco Vigilance Committee," *Congressional Globe*, 34th Cong., 2nd sess., August 29, 1856, 69–70.
27. R. B. Wallace to Father, August 19, 1856, Wallace Letters, folder 7, underlining in the original. See also [Gray], *Judges and Criminals*, 93–94.
28. Olney, "Vigilance Committee," 21; "Arrival of the George Law," *New York Times*, September 15, 1856.
29. Hittell, *A History of the City of San Francisco*, 260.
30. *Minutes*, August 18, 21, 1856.
31. Manrow, "Statement," 11.
32. Hittell, *A History of the City of San Francisco*, 260.
33. "Coleman's CALIFORNIA LINE!," *Daily Alta California*, August 15, 1856.
34. Burns, "Statement," 6.
35. Coleman, "Statement," 124 1/2. Although Bancroft crossed out Coleman's words, writing above them in the third person, the original is clearly legible.
36. *Minutes*, August 19, 1856.
37. William T. Coleman to J. Neely Johnson, August 20, 1856, Johnson Papers, folder 65, underlining in the original.
38. *Minutes*, August 22, 1856; "Visit to the Vigilance Committee Rooms," *Sacramento Daily Union*, August 25, 1856; "Exhibition of Chamber of Horrors" and "Fort Gunny-Bags by Moonlight," both *Daily Herald*, August 22, 1856; Tuthill, *History of California*, 505; "The Rooms of the Vigilance Committee," in "Scrapbook of Clippings," San Francisco Committee of Vigilance of 1856 Papers [BL].
39. Oliver diary, entry for August 21, 1856.
40. "A Grand Ball of the Stranglers!," *Daily Herald*, August 21, 1856.
41. *Minutes*, August 17, 1856.
42. Crary, "Statement," 12; Frink, "Vigilance Committee," 9; *Minutes*, August 25, 1856; quote from Bancroft, *Popular Tribunals*, 2:544–45.
43. Oliver diary, entry for August 23, 1856.
44. "The July Term of the Supreme Court," *Daily Herald*, August 22, 1856.
45. "San Francisco Letter, *Sacramento Daily Union*, September 1, 1856.
46. *Minutes*, August 25, 26, 27, 1856.
47. "Executive Committee," *Daily Herald*, August 28, 1856.
48. "A Peep at the Interior of the Bastille," *Daily Herald*, August 29, 1856.
49. [Untitled], *New York Times*, July 31, 1856.
50. Oliver diary, entry for August 28, 1856.

19. Pirates and Payback

1. "Topics of the Day," *Daily Herald*, September 2, 1856.
2. *Minutes*, September 1, 1856.
3. *Minutes*, September 2, 1856.
4. *Minutes*, August 16, 1856.
5. Durkee, "Statement," 6.
6. *Minutes*, September 3, 1856.
7. J. B. C. [Joseph Bryant Crockett] to My Dear Wife, September 19, 1856, Crockett Papers.
8. *Minutes*, September 4, 1856. Only the date and time of the meeting and the number present (27) were recorded.

9. "Rumors Last Night," *Daily Herald*, September 5, 1856. A. L. Tubbs was reported as "H. Tubbs."
10. *Minutes*, September 5, 1856.
11. *Minutes*, September 8, 1856.
12. Oliver diary, entry for September 11, 1856.
13. Tuthill, *History of California*, 508; Gordan, *Authorized by No Law*, 50.
14. Durkee, "Statement," 7.
15. J. B. C. [Joseph Bryant Crockett] to My Dear Wife, September 4, 1856, Crockett Papers.
16. "The Prospect Ahead," *True Californian*, September 5, 1856.
17. New York Court of Common Pleas, *Molony against Dows*, 28.
18. D. G. Farragut to J. C. Dobbin, September 2, 1856, in Farragut, *The Life of David Glasgow Farragut*, 190–91.
19. *Minutes*, August 28, September 3, 4, 5, 1856; quote from 33 Secretary [not Bluxome's hand] to John Stephens, September 5, 1856, San Francisco Committee of Vigilance Miscellany [CHS], MS 51/4, underlining in the original.
20. "The Terry Case," *Sacramento Daily Union*, September 4, 1856.
21. "Congressional Proceedings—Extra Session—Passage of the Army Bill," *Daily Alta California*, September 30, 1856.
22. J. B. C. [Joseph Bryant Crockett] to My Dear Wife, September 19, 1856.
23. "Law Intelligence—U.S. Circuit Court," *Daily Herald*, September 12, 1856.
24. Gordan, *Authorized by No Law*, 50–51, quote from 50.
25. J. B. C. [Joseph Bryant Crockett] to My Dear Wife, September 19, 1856, underlining in the original.
26. Charles Curry, dealer in Guns, Rifles [etc.], San Francisco Committee of Vigilance Records [HL], box 8.
27. Committee of Vigilance to Edward Ryan, August 29, 1856, ibid.
28. *Minutes*, September 11, 1856.
29. *Minutes*, August 23, September 9, October 7, 1856.
30. *Minutes*, September 16, 1856.
31. *Minutes*, September 23, 1856.
32. *Minutes*, September 26, 1856.
33. "Vigilantes Ahoy!," *Daily Alta California*, September 8, 1856.
34. *Minutes*, September 8, 1856.
35. *Minutes*, September 12, 1856.
36. *Minutes*, February 13, 1857.
37. *Minutes*, September 2, 7, 16, 1856, quote from September 2.
38. "Letter from Washington," *Daily Alta California*, September 30, 1856; "Domestic Intelligence," *Sacramento Daily Union*, September 30, 1856.
39. *Minutes*, October 21, 1856.
40. "In Regard to the Obnoxious Letter," *Morning Globe*, October 6, 1856.
41. "The Federal Government and the Vigilance Committee—Those Secret Instructions," *Daily California Chronicle*, October 6, 1856, capitalization as in the original.
42. "Dr. Scott and His Opponents—The Doctor Hung in Effigy—A Short Review of the Matter" and "Dr. Scott Is Really Doing Good for What Little Evil His Letter May Have Done!," both *Morning Globe*, October 6, 1856; "Topics of the Day," *Daily Herald*, October 6, 1856.
43. *Minutes*, October 3, 1856.

44. *Minutes*, October 7, 1856.
45. Bancroft, *Popular Tribunals*, 2:595.
46. "Arrest of the Head of the Vigilance Committee," *New York Times*, September 19, 1856.
47. R. B. Wallace to Mother, November 5, 1856, Wallace Letters, folder 7.
48. *Minutes*, October 17, 1856.

20. Politics and Property

1. "People's Ticket," *Daily Herald*, September 12, 1856.
2. Cole, "Statement," 21.
3. *Minutes*, October 7, 14, 1856.
4. "Hugh C. Murray," *Sacramento Daily Union*, September 27, 1856.
5. Oliver, diary entry for October 7, 1856.
6. Ibid., entry for October 28, 1856.
7. Ibid., entries for October 10, 11, 20, 24, 27, 1856.
8. "Resume of San Francisco News," *Sacramento Daily Union*, October 3, 1856.
9. Oliver diary, entry for October 29, 1856.
10. *Minutes*, October 14, 1856.
11. Ibid.
12. "To the Public," *Daily Alta California*, October 31, 1856.
13. *Minutes*, October 7, 14, 21, 1856.
14. Clarke, *William Tecumseh Sherman*, 252–53; J. Neely Johnson proclamation of November 3, 1856, Johnson Papers, folder 78; quote from W. T. Sherman to Governor Johnson, October 29, 1856, ibid, folder 71; William C. Kibbe to the Executive Committee, October 15, 1856, Vigilance Committee Records [CSL], folder 71; *Minutes*, November 3, 1856; J. Neely Johnson to William C. Kibbe, December 17, 1856, ibid., folder 73; George R. Ward to Gen. W. C. Kibbe, December 20, 1856, ibid., folder 74.
15. *Minutes*, October 28, November 3, 1856.
16. R. B. Wallace to Mother, November 5, 1856, Wallace Letters, folder 7, underlining in the original.
17. 2187 M. M. Lewis to Executive Committee, n.d., San Francisco Committee of Vigilance Records [HL], box 2; R. B. Wallace to Chairman, Police Committee, June 16, 1856, ibid.; John Phillips to Executive Committee, June 24, 1856, ibid.; *Minutes*, November 5, 1856.
18. *Minutes*, November 5, 1856.
19. "The San Francisco Cowhiding Affair," *Sacramento Daily Union*, November 10, 1856.
20. *Minutes*, November 11, 1856.
21. *Minutes*, November 14, 1856.
22. *Minutes*, November 7, 11, 1856.
23. "Rearrest of the President of the Vigilance Committee," *New York Times*, October 21, 1856.
24. Duane, *Against the Vigilantes*, 36–37; Hittell, *History of California*, 3:642; New York Court of Common Pleas, *Molony against Dows*, 13.
25. "Myres [sic] F. Truett, Esq.," *Daily Alta California*, March 29, 1857. See also Duane, *Against the Vigilantes*, 149.
26. Truett, "Statement," 7. For amount, see www.westegg.com/inflation/ and www.measuringworth.com.
27. Duane, *Against the Vigilantes*, 149.

28. *Minutes*, June 26, 1857.
29. *Minutes*, November 15, 1856.
30. Bancroft, *Literary Industries*, 148; *Minutes*, November 21, 28, December 5, 1856.
31. *Minutes*, September 2, 26, 1856.
32. *Minutes*, February 13, 1857.
33. *Minutes*, April 17, 1856.
34. "San Francisco Correspondence," *Sacramento Daily Union*, December 8, 1856.
35. Oliver diary, entry for December 10, 1856.
36. "Complete Expose of the Limantour Fraud—Confession of Emile Letanneur, His Secretary," *Sacramento Daily Union*, December 13, 1856.
37. "Testimony in the Limantour Case," *Daily Alta California*, December 31, 1856.
38. Johnson, *José Yves Limantour v. The United States*, 47–48.
39. Oliver diary, entry for December 12, 1856.
40. *Minutes*, December 12, 1856.
41. *Minutes*, December 12, 17, 1856.
42. "Letter from New York," *Daily Alta California*, January 5, 1857.
43. "Important Movement of Californians in New York," *Daily Alta California*, December 31, 1856.
44. "Letter from New York," *Daily Alta California*, January 5, 1857.
45. "Important Movement of Californians in New York," *Daily Alta California*, December 31, 1856.
46. Johnson, *José Yves Limantour v. The United States*, 73.
47. Ibid., 47–48.
48. Green, "Life and Adventures of a 47er of California," 69–70.
49. Barry and Patten, *Men and Memories of San Francisco*, 227.
50. *People v. John A. McGlynn, et al.*, 1862, California Supreme Court Case 9459, Transcript File no. 3494, California State Archives, Sacramento, 35, 36.

21. Reputation's Rollercoaster

1. *Minutes*, January 9, 1857; "Action of the Legislature . . . Threats of the Enemies of San Francisco . . . Will They Be Carried Out," *Daily Globe*, January 10, 1857.
2. "Action of the Legislature . . . Threats of the Enemies."
3. Hittell, *A History of the City of San Francisco*, 298.
4. John G. Hyatt to Dr. C. M. Hitchcock, January 20, 1859 [1856; typescript in error], Manuscript Collections, California State Library, box 11, June 19 [*sic*: January 20], 1856.
5. "Why Mr. Broderick Was Chosen—A View Different from That Taken by the Globe," *Daily Globe*, January 10, 1857, emphasis in the original.
6. "The Reply to Amador—The Bulletin and Mr. Broderick," *Daily Globe*, January 10, 1857.
7. *Minutes*, May 15, June 14, 1856, January 30, February 6, 1857.
8. Northam, Dictation, 6. See *Minutes*, July 28, 31, 1856.
9. "The Election for State Senator," *Wide West*, February 22, 1857.
10. "Senatorial Nomination," *Wide West*, February 22, 1857.
11. "Laws of California," *Sacramento Daily Union*, April 23, 1857.
12. Carr, *The World and William Walker*, 101–2, 241–42; Heintz, *San Francisco's Mayors*, 20–22; Kemble, *The Panama Route*, 66–67; Stiles, *The First Tycoon*, 150, 228–83; [Untitled], *Daily Alta California*, October 7, 1854; May, *Manifest Destiny's Underworld*, 175–77, 359

n. 13; McGuinness, *Path of Empire*, 125, 1–2; "Profitable Idleness" and "Arming Themselves," both *Wide West*, May 4, 1856.
13. "The Nicaragua News," *Sacramento Daily Union*, December 22, 1856.
14. Quoted in Dando-Collins, *Tycoons' War*, 317.
15. "The Position of the Filibusters," *Wide West*, January 18, 1857, reprinted from the *New York Herald*.
16. *Minutes*, August 3, 1856; "News of the Week," *Wide West*, March 8, 1857.
17. Kemble, *The Panama Route*, 75.
18. "A New Steamship Scheme," *Wide West*, April 19, 1857.
19. "California and New York Steamship Company," *Daily Alta California*, April 18, 1857. See also advertisement in *Wide West*, May 17, 1857.
20. *Minutes*, May 22, 1857.
21. "Who Pays the Piper," *Daily Herald*, August 27, 1856; www.measuringworth.com.
22. *Minutes*, March 1, 2, 1857.
23. *Minutes*, April 17, 24, May 1, 15, June 3, 8, 1857.
24. *Minutes*, January 30, May 1, 1857.
25. "Arrested at Last," *Wide West*, May 17, 1857.
26. Shuck, *History of the Bench and Bar*, 380.
27. "Napa City Correspondence," *California Chronicle*, May 30, 1857.
28. *Minutes*, June 8, 1857.
29. Court Proceedings, March 21, 1857, "Topics of the Day," *Daily Herald*, April 4, 1857. The case when heard in Superior Court was reported as *Jesse D. Carr v. Burdett, et al.* William Hart bought Carr's interest. "Burdett" was probably a misspelling, because when the case was heard on appeal by the California Supreme Court, it had become *Hart vs. Burnett, et al.*, 15 Cal. 530.
30. "Court Proceedings," *Daily Alta California*, March 28, 1857.
31. "Court Proceedings," *Daily Alta California*, March 30, 1857. By statute, McAllister also served on the District Court when it decided land cases. See Fritz, *Federal Justice in California*, 135.
32. "Meeting of Settlers Opposing the Bolton & Barron Claim," *Daily Alta California*, May 3, 1857.
33. James R. Bolton, Claim for Mission Dolores, U.S. Court for the Northern District of California, land case 338 N.D. 81 Bd., 725–33.
34. "Meeting of Settlers Opposing the Bolton & Barron Claim."
35. Green, "Life and Adventures of a 47er of California," 84–85. The attorney was Louis Blanding.
36. "Resume of San Francisco's News," *Sacramento Daily Union*, May 5, 1857.
37. "Suits against the Vigilance Committee," *Daily Alta California*, July 17, 1857.
38. Peter Della Torre to J. S. Black, September 4, 1857, quoted in Johnson, *José Yves Limantour v. The United States*, 56; "Another Claim for the $5000," *Daily Alta California*, August 26, 1857.
39. Johnson, *José Yves Limantour v. The United States*, 73.
40. *Welch v. Sullivan et al.*, 8 Cal. 165 (1857), in H. Toler Booraem, ed., *Reports of Cases Determined in the Supreme Court, State of California*, 2nd ed., vol. 8 (San Francisco: Sumner Whitney and A. L. Bancroft and Company, 1875), 511–12. See also "Supreme Court Decisions," *Daily Alta California*, September 8, 1857.
41. "City Items," *Daily Alta California*, August 11, 1857.

42. Kemble, *A History of California Newspapers*, 268, 271.
43. "McGowan's Lives of the Stranglers!!! The Life of C. V. Gillespie," *Phoenix*, October 18, 1857. For a more reliable but basically similar historical account, see Smith, "The Gillespie Brothers," 25–26.
44. "33 Secretary!," *Ubiquitous*, February 28, 1858.
45. Phelps, *Contemporary Biography of California's Representative Men*, 271.
46. "Policeman J. Bovee," *Phoenix*, October 25, 1857.
47. "Sterling A. Hopkins," *Ubiquitous*, March 21, 1858, emphasis in the original.
48. *Minutes*, June 26, 1857.
49. "People's Nominations" and "Only a Week," both *Daily Alta California*, August 26, 1857; *Minutes*, September 22, 1857.
50. *Minutes*, September 22, 1857.
51. *Minutes*, September 24, October 5, 12, 1857.

22. Seeking Resolution

1. *Minutes*, October 16, 1857.
2. Kinder, *Ship of Gold in the Deep Blue Sea*, 16–75; Kemble, *The Panama Route*, 142; Cross, *Financing an Empire*, 230.
3. "Two Disastrous Fires in New Orleans," *Sacramento Daily Union*, October 3, 1857.
4. "Eastern Failures and Suspensions," *Sacramento Daily Union*, November 19, 1857.
5. Cross, *Financing an Empire*, 230, 234.
6. *Minutes*, July 24, August 7, 1857.
7. *Minutes*, December 18, 1857; Fritz, "Politics and the Courts," 156; "The Courts," *Sacramento Daily Union*, September 13, 1859.
8. *Minutes*, February 23, 1858.
9. "Mr. Lee's Anti-Vigilance Bill," *Sacramento Daily Union*, February 15, 1858; "Mr. Lee's Anti-Vigilance Bill," *Sacramento Daily Union*, February 16, 1858, quote from the latter.
10. "From Our Evening Edition of Yesterday," *Daily Alta California*, February 16, 1858.
11. Dwinelle, *The Colonial History of San Francisco*, 217.
12. "The Van Ness Ordinance," *Daily Alta California*, March 5, 1858; Dwinelle, *The Colonial History of San Francisco*, 218.
13. Cross, *Financing an Empire*, 236.
14. "By the State Telegraph Line," *Sacramento Daily Union*, June 30, 1858.
15. Hauka, *McGowan's War*, 75.
16. "Court Proceedings," *Daily Alta California*, March 31, 1858.
17. "San Francisco News," *Sacramento Daily Union*, March 31, 1858.
18. "Court Proceedings," *Daily Alta California*, March 31, 1858.
19. *Minutes*, February 27, 1857.
20. *Minutes*, April 15, 1858.
21. *Minutes*, April 21, 1858.
22. "By the State Telegraph Line," *Sacramento Daily Union*, May 22, 1858.
23. "By the State Telegraph Line," *Sacramento Daily Union*, June 30, 1858; "Court Proceedings," *Daily Alta California*, August 27, 1858.
24. Fritz, *Federal Justice in California*, 165–66; Johnson, *José Yves Limantour v. The United States*, 53–63.

25. Fritz, *Federal Justice in California*, 167–70; Johnson, *José Yves Limantour v. The United States*, 53–63.
26. J. S. Black to Chairman of Senate Judiciary Committee, April 22, 1858, in United States, House of Representatives, *Expenditures on Account of Private Land Claims in California*, Message of the President of the United States, Ex. Doc. No. 84, 36th Congress, 1st sess., House of Representatives, May 22, 1860, 5.
27. Northam, Dictation, 6. See *Minutes*, July 28, 31, 1856.
28. Barry and Patten, *Men and Memories of San Francisco*, 230.
29. "The Santillán Land Swindle," *Daily Alta California*, February 1, 1859; "City Items," *Daily Alta California*, February 3, 1859; "The Memorial to Congress in the Santillán Case," *Daily Alta California*, February 5, 1859.
30. "Court Proceedings," *Daily Alta California*, January 19, 1859.
31. Ibid.
32. "Judge Hoffman's Decision in the Gallagher Case," *Daily Alta California*, January 19, 1859.
33. "Gallagher Suit Appealed," *Sacramento Daily Union*, January 22, 1859; "By the State Line," *Sacramento Daily Union*, April 6, 1859; "By Telegraph to the Union," *Sacramento Daily Union*, April 14, 1859.
34. *Minutes*, January 26, 1859; see also "By the State Telegraph Line," *Sacramento Daily Union*, May 22, 1858.
35. *Minutes*, February 28, 1859.
36. "The Recent Death of Martin Gallagher," *Sacramento Daily Union*, June 19, 1859; "The Killing of Martin Gallagher," *Sacramento Daily Union*, June 20, 1859; "Court Proceedings," *Daily Alta California*, August 18, 1859; "Acquittal of Thomas Roach," *Daily Alta California*, August 19, 1859. Quotes from "Killing" and "Court Proceedings."
37. 8 Abb. Pr. 316 (N.Y. Common Pleas 1859); see New York Court of Common Pleas, *Molony against Dows*.
38. "Law Intelligence," *New York Times*, September 27, 1858.
39. New York Court of Common Pleas, *Molony against Dows*, 6–11, 27–28, 30, 40.
40. *Minutes*, February 27, 1857.
41. New York Court of Common Pleas, *Molony against Dows*, 13–14, 27–28, 30, 45–50, 54–102, 139.
42. Wm. T. Coleman to James Dows, T. J. L. Smiley, C. J. Dempster, and Henry M. Hale, April 5, 1859, San Francisco Committee of Vigilance of 1856 Papers [BL], underlining in the original.
43. Thanks to the Hon. Betty Dawson, retired judge of the Fifth California District Courts of Appeal, for this insight.
44. Coleman to Dows, Smiley, Dempster, and Hale.
45. New York Court of Common Pleas, *Molony against Dows*, 105–11, 113–40.
46. Coleman to Dows, Smiley, Dempster, and Hale.
47. *Minutes*, May 2, 1859.
48. *Minutes*, May 6, 9, 1859.
49. San Francisco Committee of Vigilance Records [HL], box 9.

23. Irreconcilable Differences

1. In short, the justices had declared the 1820 Missouri Compromise unconstitutional, invalidating the law that prohibited slavery in the northern part of the old Louisiana

Purchase. Therefore, all territories could become slave states, regardless of their geographical location. Congress also lost the right to legislate regarding slavery, and all African Americans—slave or free—were denied U.S. citizenship. For the most thorough treatment, see Fehrenbacher, *The Dred Scott Case*.

2. "Speech of Hon. David C. Broderick, of California, against the Admission of Kansas," *Daily Alta California*, May 1, 1858; *Appendix to the Congressional Globe*, 35th Cong., 1st sess., March 22, 1858, 193–201.
3. "Our Sacramento Correspondence," *Daily Alta California*, February 13, 1858.
4. "Supreme Court Decisions" and "The Archy Case," both *Sacramento Daily Union*, February 12, 1858.
5. "The Supreme Court Decision in the Case of Archy, the Slave," *Daily Alta California*, February 14, 1858; "That Decision," *Sacramento Daily Union*, February 16, 1858; "The Archy Decision," *Sacramento Daily Union*, February 25, 1858; "Our Supreme Bench," *Daily Alta California*, February 20, 1858.
6. "Democratic Lecompton Convention," *Sacramento Daily Union*, June 25, 1859, brackets in the original.
7. Exactly what was said was variously reported. See "News of the Morning" and "By the State Telegraph Line," both *Sacramento Daily Union*, June 28, 1859; "The Broderick and Perley Difficulty," *Daily Alta California*, July 1, 1859; "The Duel," *Daily Alta California*, September 14, 1859; "Challenge of D. W. Perley to Senator Broderick—Correspondence between the Parties—Note of E. J. C. Kewen," *Sacramento Daily Union*, July 1, 1859.
8. Charles Duane, quoted in "The Broderick-Smith Duel, 1852," in Shuck, *History of the Bench and Bar*, 232–33.
9. D. S. Terry to Neal, September 9, 1859, Terry Papers [HL].
10. "Dead Shot," *Morning Call*, September 12, 1859.
11. Frank Langdon to Judge [David S. Terry], September 14, 1859, Terry Papers [HL].
12. MacDonald, "Recollections of Early Days in California," 5–6.
13. Burke, "San Francisco Police," 15–18.
14. Ayers, *Gold and Sunshine*, 173; "The Broderick and Terry Duel: The Dueling Correspondence from the *San Francisco Herald*, Sept. 17," *New York Times*, October 4, 1859; J[ohn] W[harton] T[erry] to Dumas Malone, September 17, 1934, David S. Terry Papers [SUL], 13; Williams, *David C. Broderick*, 238.
15. *People v. McGlynn*, 36, 40.
16. Oscar T. Shuck, "The Great Broderick Will Case," in *History of the Bench and Bar*, 209–12.
17. Blair and Tarshis, *Lincoln's Constant Ally*, 195–200, quote on 199–200.
18. See "Acquittal of Judge Terry," *Sacramento Daily Union*, July 9, 1860, which also quotes the San Francisco *Times*, *Bulletin*, and *Morning Call*.
19. *Minutes*, June 24, 1859.
20. *Minutes*, July 8, 1859.
21. *Minutes*, October 28, November 3, 1859. Flint had taken leave "for reasons beyond his control" on May 23, 1856, but returned on February 6, 1857. See *Minutes* for those dates.
22. "The Courts," *Sacramento Daily Union*, September 13, 1859. The judge was John H. McKune.
23. "Court Proceedings," *Daily Alta California*, August 15, 1862; "The Duane Case," *Sacramento Daily Union*, reprinted from the *San Francisco Call*, October 31, 1863; "News of the Morning," *Sacramento Daily Union*, August 23, 1864; *Pearson v. Duane*, 71 U.S. 605 (1867); Fritz, *Federal Justice*, 83.

24. "Vigilance Committee Case," *Sacramento Daily Union*, July 21, 1860.
25. "Vigilance Trial in San Francisco," *Sacramento Daily Union*, July 23, 1860.
26. "The Vigilance Suit in San Francisco: The Pueblo Titles," *Sacramento Daily Union*, July 20, 1860.
27. "Bets in San Francisco," *Sacramento Daily Union*, October 18, 1860; "The Late James R. Molony of California," *New York Times*, October 26, 1866.
28. *Hart v. Burnett*, 15 Cal. 530 (1860).
29. "Have We a Settled Title among Us?," *Daily Alta California*, June 25, 1860.
30. "Mammoth Meeting at the Pavilion," *Daily Alta California*, June 29, 1860.
31. Hittell, *A History of the City of San Francisco*, 319–20.
32. Brown, "Early Days," 19.
33. Robert J. Chandler, "Vigilante Rebirth: The Civil War Union League," *Argonaut* 3, no. 1 (1992): 16; "Statistics of California, 1864," *Sacramento Daily Union*, January 2, 1865; Davis, "The 'Home Guard' of 1861"; Hittell, *History of California*, 4:290.
34. "Meeting of Page, Bacon & Co.'s Creditors," *Sacramento Daily Union*, August 24, 1864; "By Telegraph to the Union," *Sacramento Daily Union*, September 26, 1864.
35. "By Telegraph to the Union," *Sacramento Daily Union*, September 26, 1864.
36. Crary, "Statement," 11.
37. "Union Demonstration," *Sacramento Daily Union*, September 24, 1864; Chandler, "Vigilante Rebirth," 14–15.
38. Smiley, "Statement," 11.
39. Bluxome, "Statement," 19.
40. Crary, "Statement," 11.
41. "Statistics of California, 1865," *Sacramento Daily Union*, January 1, 1866.
42. Coon, "Annals of San Francisco," 27.

24. Lasting Transformations

1. Quoted in Melendy and Gilbert, *The Governors of California*, 87–88.
2. Hittell, *A History of the City of San Francisco*, 331.
3. Quoted in Thomas, *Between Two Empires*, 229.
4. Kennedy, *The Contest for California*, 100, 143–44, 230–40, 275, 285.
5. Cross, *Financing an Empire*, 360.
6. David et al., "Some California Dates of 1859," 28.
7. Hittell, *A History of the City of San Francisco*, 333–51.
8. Cross, *Financing an Empire*, 255, 238; Lewis, *The Silver Kings*; John H. Burke, "The Bonanza Suits of 1877," in Shuck, *History of the Bench and Bar*, 96.
9. Bancroft, *Literary Industries*, 165.
10. Ibid., 154–55.
11. Cross, *Financing an Empire*, 245–46.
12. Ibid., 245–46, 262–70; Lavender, *Nothing Seemed Impossible*, 178–82, 208–16, 239–42.
13. "Statistics of California—1864," *Sacramento Daily Union*, January 2, 1865.
14. C. P. Huntington to W. T. Coleman, May 25, 1856, San Francisco Committee of Vigilance of 1856 Papers [BL].
15. L. Stanford, "Form of Application for Enrollment," San Francisco Committee of Vigilance Records [HL], box 6, folder 2.

16. Hittell, *Commerce and Industries*, 22–26; Hittell, *A History of the City of San Francisco*, 373–75.
17. Lavender, *Nothing Seemed Impossible*, 351–53.
18. *Hart v. Burnett*; Denning, "A Fragile Machine," 37; Fritz, "Politics and the Courts," 155; Field, *Personal Reminiscences*, 140–52. The bill is *An Act to Quiet the Title to Certain Lands within the Corporate Limits of the City of San Francisco*, March 8, 1866 (14 Stat 4).
19. Field, *Personal Reminiscences*, 136.
20. Brown, "Early Days," 15–16.
21. Hittell, *A History of the City of San Francisco*, 364.
22. Ibid., 322–23, 373–75.
23. Tubbs, "Recollections of Events in California," 10.
24. McPherson, *Battle Cry of Freedom*, 755–76, 808–11, 854.
25. Tuthill, *History of California*, 512.
26. Ibid., 517.
27. Bancroft, *Literary Industries*, 174.
28. Cross, *Financing an Empire*, 364–67.
29. Lavender, *Nothing Seemed Impossible*, 348–85.
30. Hittell, *History of California*, 4:566.
31. Sherman, *Memoirs*, 131–32.
32. Dows, "Statement," 8.
33. Gillespie, "Vigilance Committee," dated November 1875. Age calculated from 1852 Census.
34. Bancroft, *Literary Industries*, 655–56.
35. Ibid., 657–58.
36. Tubbs, "Recollections of Events in California," 18.
37. Coleman, "Vigilance Committee, 1856."
38. Hittell, *History of California*, 4:594.
39. Trachtenberg, *The Incorporation of America*, 76–77.
40. Ibid., 3.
41. Saxton, *The Indispensable Enemy*, 113–17.
42. Burke, "San Francisco Police," 11–12.
43. Coleman, "San Francisco Vigilance Committees," 146.
44. Hittell, *History of California*, 4:596–97.
45. Coleman, "San Francisco Vigilance Committees," 147.
46. Hittell, *History of California*, 4:598; "The Hoodlum Riots," *Pacific Appeal*, July 28, 1877.
47. Stevenson, *The Wrecker*, 142.
48. Coleman, "San Francisco Vigilance Committees," 147–48.

25. Secrets

1. "The Riots in San Francisco," *Sacramento Daily Union*, July 27, 1877.
2. Gladden, *Working People and Their Employers*, 14–15.
3. Mark Twain and Charles Dudley Warner, *The Gilded Age* (Hartford, Conn.: American Publishing Company, 1873).
4. Bancroft, *Literary Industries*, 659–61. The massive compilation of the 1851 papers came from Williams, *Papers of the San Francisco Committee of Vigilance of 1851*, pt. 3.

5. Bancroft, *Literary Industries*, 659-61.
6. "History of Events," *San Joaquin Republican*, July 1, 1856.
7. "Topics of the Day," *Daily Herald*, August 18, 1856.
8. *Minutes*, September 1, 1856.
9. Kemble, *A History of California Newspapers*, 124; quote from William H. Rhodes to The Hon. Executive Committee . . . , October 13, 1856, San Francisco Committee of Vigilance of 1856 Papers [BL].
10. *Minutes*, October 10, 1856.
11. *Colville's San Francisco Directory*, 226.
12. *Minutes*, October 17, 1856.
13. *Minutes*, February 13, 1857.
14. Dillon, "Introduction," xlviii.
15. Oak, *"Literary Industries" in a New Light*, 20-21.
16. All are located in the Bancroft Library. At least five have no dates.
17. Frink, "Vigilance Committee," 22.
18. Smiley, "Statement," 9-10.
19. Pinto, "Historical Facts and Incidents," 193.
20. Manrow, "Statement," 8.
21. Dempster to Bancroft.
22. Wm. T. Coleman to Mr. Bancroft, March 8, 1882, San Francisco Committee of Vigilance of 1856 Papers [BL], underlining in the original.
23. Hittell, *History of California*, 4:237-39; "Santillan and M'Garrahan," *New York Times*, April 11, 1882.
24. Bancroft, *Popular Tribunals*, 2:304.
25. Ibid., dedication page.
26. Ibid., 396.
27. Ibid., 467.
28. Ibid., 614.
29. Ibid., 244-66; "Will Sue the History Company," Los Angeles *Herald*, September 2, 1889.
30. "The Second Vigilance Committee," *New York Times*, October 23, 1887.
31. For citations, see, for example, Hittell, *History of California*, 3:557-79.
32. Ibid., 3:379-402, 4:237-39.
33. Ibid., 4:201-11, 3:639-45.
34. Ibid., 4:719.
35. Ibid., 4:591.
36. Green, "Life and Adventures of a 47er of California," title page.
37. Bancroft, *Popular Tribunals*, 2:513-25.
38. Hittell, *History of California*, 3:619.
39. *Minutes*, July 13-October 14, 1856.
40. Hittell, *History of California*, 4:592.
41. Schlereth, *Victorian America*, 220-25, 210.
42. White, *American Vignettes*, 147-50.
43. Schlereth, *Victorian America*, 182-88, 115-16.
44. "In the Fifties," *Alta California*, November 16, 1884. See also "Ned McGowan," *Alta California*, October 13, 1884; "In the Fifties," *Alta California*, October 19, 1884.
45. Literature on the myth of the West is voluminous and growing. For a succinct version, see Smith, *Virgin Land*, especially 36-38, 201-9, 250-59.

46. Johnson, *José Yves Limantour v. The United States*, 2, 77.
47. Dwinelle, *The Colonial History of San Francisco*, 216–19.
48. "Roses and Raspberries" [editorial], Corvallis *Gazette-Times*, January 29, 2016.
49. "Lell Hawley Woolley," the Virtual Museum of the City of San Francisco, http://www.sfmuseum.org/hist6/woolley.html.

Bibliography

Ayers, James J. *Gold and Sunshine: Reminiscences of Early California.* Boston: Richard G. Badger, 1922.
Ayres, William O. "Personal Recollections of the Vigilance Committee." *Overland Monthly* 8, no. 44 (August 1886): 160–76.
Bancroft, Hubert Howe. *Chronicles of the Builders of the Commonwealth: Historical Character Study.* 7 vols. San Francisco: History Company, 1891–92.
———. *History of California.* 7 vols. San Francisco: History Company, 1884–90.
———. *Literary Industries.* San Francisco: History Company, 1890.
———. *Popular Tribunals.* 2 vols. San Francisco: History Company, 1887.
Barry, T. A., and B. A. Patten. *Men and Memories of San Francisco in the Spring of '50.* San Francisco: A. L. Bancroft and Company, 1873.
Blair, Harry C., and Rebecca Tarshis. *Lincoln's Constant Ally: The Life of Colonel Edward D. Baker.* Portland: Oregon Historical Society, 1960.
Bluxome, Isaac, Jr. "Statement," n.d. BANC MSS C-D 179. Bancroft Library, University of California, Berkeley.
Booraem, H. Toler, ed. *Reports of Cases Determined in the Supreme Court, State of California.* 2nd ed., vol. 8. San Francisco: Sumner Whitney and A. L. Bancroft and Company, 1875.
Breen, Hugh. Diary. In author's possession.
Brown, Harvey S. "Early Days of California," 1878. Recorded by Ora Oak. BANC MSS C-D 54. Bancroft Library, University of California, Berkeley.
Brown, Richard Maxwell. *Strain of Violence: Historical Studies of American Violence and Vigilantism.* New York: Oxford University Press, 1975.
Burke, Martin J. "The San Francisco Police," 1887. BANC MSS C-D 322. Bancroft Library, University of California, Berkeley.
Burns, Aaron M. "Statement . . . on Vigilance Committees in San Francisco," 1877. BANC MSS C-D 202. Bancroft Library, University of California, Berkeley.
Carr, Albert Z. *The World and William Walker.* New York: Harper and Row, 1963.

Caughey, John Walton. *Hubert Howe Bancroft: Historian of the West*. Berkeley: University of California Press, 1946.

Chandler, Robert J. "Vigilante Rebirth: The Civil War Union League." *Argonaut* 3, no. 1 (Winter 1992): 10–18.

Clark, Harry. *A Venture in History: The Production, Publication, and Sale of the Works of Hubert Howe Bancroft*. Berkeley: University of California Press, 1973.

Clarke, Dwight L. *William Tecumseh Sherman: Gold Rush Banker*. San Francisco: California Historical Society, 1969.

Clawson, Mary Ann. *Constructing Brotherhood: Class, Gender, and Fraternalism*. Princeton, N.J.: Princeton University Press, 1989.

Cole, Richard Beverly. Papers. MSS 20-4. Archives and Special Collections, University of California, San Francisco.

———. "Statement... on Vigilance Committees in San Francisco," 1877. BANC MSS C-D 180. Bancroft Library, University of California, Berkeley.

Coleman, William T. "San Francisco Vigilance Committees." *Century Magazine* 43, no. 1 (November 1891): 133–50.

———. "Statement." In William Tell Coleman Statements: And Other Material, 1870–1893. Assembled in preparing biography for Hubert Howe Bancroft, *Chronicles of the Builders of the Commonwealth: Historical Character Study*. BANC MSS C-D 755. Bancroft Library, University of California, Berkeley.

———. "Vigilance Committee, 1856," ca. 1880. BANC MSS C-D 181. Bancroft Library, University of California, Berkeley.

Colville's San Francisco Directory. Vol. 1: *For the Year Commencing October, 1856*. San Francisco: Samuel Colville, 1856.

Coon, H. P. "Annals of San Francisco," n.d. BANC MSS C-D 182. Bancroft Library, University of California, Berkeley.

Crary, Oliver B. "Statement on Vigilance Committees in San Francisco," 1877. BANC MSS C-D 183. Bancroft Library, University of California, Berkeley.

Crockett, Joseph Bryant, Papers, 1848–1879. BANC MSS C-B 896. Bancroft Library, University of California, Berkeley.

Cross, Ira B. *Financing an Empire: History of Banking in California*. Chicago: S. J. Clarke, 1927.

Culberson, William C. *Vigilantism: Political History of Private Power in America*. New York: Praeger, 1990.

Dando-Collins, Stephen. *Tycoons' War: How Cornelius Vanderbilt Invaded a Country to Overthrow America's Most Famous Military Adventurer*. Philadelphia: Da Capo Press, 2008.

David, Mrs. Harold, Mrs. Oliver Kehrlein, Miss Dolores Cadell, and Edgar M. Kahn, comps. "Some California Dates of 1859." *California Historical Quarterly* 38, no. 1 (March 1959): 25–29.

Davis, Horace. "The 'Home Guard' of 1861." In *The Pacific Ocean in History*, edited by H. Morse Stephens and Herbert E. Bolton, 363–72. New York: Macmillan Company, 1917.

Davis, Winfield J. *History of Political Conventions in California, 1849–1892*. Sacramento: California State Library, 1893.

DeArment, Robert K. *Knights of the Green Cloth: The Saga of the Frontier Gamblers*. Norman: University of Oklahoma Press, 1982.

Decker, Peter R. *Fortunes and Failures: White-Collar Mobility in Nineteenth-Century San Francisco.* Cambridge, Mass.: Harvard University Press, 1978.

Dempster, C. J., to H. H. Bancroft, October 20, 1878. BANC MSS C-D 599. Bancroft Library, University of California, Berkeley.

Dempster, Clancey John. "The Vigilance Committee of 1856," n.d. BANC MSS C-D 184. Bancroft Library, University of California, Berkeley.

Denning, Robert. "A Fragile Machine: California Senator John Conness." *California History* 85, no. 4 (September 2008): 26–49, 71–73.

Dillon, Richard H. "Introduction." In John S. Hittell, *A History of the City of San Francisco, and Incidentally of the State of California.* Reprint. Berkeley, Calif.: Berkeley Hills Books, 2000.

[Dillon, Richard H.]. "T. H. Hittell Papers." *Sutro Library Notes* 2, no. 3 (Spring 1957): 2–3.

Documents Relating to Ownership of the Lands of Mission Dolores, San Francisco, 1857–1866. BANC MSS 90/161 c. Bancroft Library, University of California, Berkeley.

Doten, Alfred. *The Journals of Alfred Doten, 1849–1903.* Edited by Walter Van Tilburg Clark. 3 vols. Reno: University of Nevada Press, 1973.

Dows, James. "Statement . . . on Vigilance Committees in San Francisco," 1877. BANC MSS C-D 185. Bancroft Library, University of California, Berkeley.

Drury, Clifford Merrill. *William Anderson Scott, "No Ordinary Man."* Glendale, Calif.: Arthur H. Clark, 1967.

Duane, Charles P. *Against the Vigilantes: The Recollections of Dutch Charley Duane.* Edited and with an introduction and notes by John Boessenecker. Norman: University of Oklahoma Press, 1999.

Durkee, John L. "Statement . . . on Vigilance Committees in San Francisco," 1878. BANC MSS C-D 186. Bancroft Library, University of California, Berkeley.

Dwinelle, John W. *The Colonial History of San Francisco.* 4th ed. San Francisco: Towne and Bacon, 1867.

Ethington, Philip J. *The Public City: The Political Construction of Urban Life in San Francisco, 1850–1900.* 1994. Reprint, Berkeley: University of California Press, 2001.

Farragut, Loyall. *The Life of David Glasgow Farragut: First Admiral of the United States Navy, Embodying His Journal and Letters.* New York: D. Appleton and Company, 1879.

Farwell, James D. "Statement . . . on Vigilance Committees in San Francisco," 1878. BANC MSS C-D187. Bancroft Library, University of California, Berkeley.

Fehrenbacher, Don E. *The Dred Scott Case: Its Significance in American Law and Politics.* New York: Oxford University Press, 1978.

Field, Stephen J. *Personal Reminiscences of Early Days in California, with Other Sketches.* [Washington, D.C.]: "Printed for a few friends. Not published,"1893.

Friedman, Lawrence M. *A History of American Law.* 2nd ed. New York: Simon and Schuster, 1985.

———. *Law in America: A Short History.* New York: Modern Library, 2002.

Frink, George W. "Vigilance Committee," n.d. BANC MSS C-D 188. Bancroft Library, University of California, Berkeley.

Fritz, Christian G. *Federal Justice in California: The Court of Ogden Hoffman, 1851–1891.* Lincoln: University of Nebraska Press, 1991.

———. "Politics and the Courts: The Struggle over Land in San Francisco, 1846–1866." *Santa Clara Law Review* 26, no. 1 (1986): 127–64.

Gammie, Peter. "Pugilists and Politicians in Antebellum New York: The Life and Times of Tom Hyer." *New York History* 75, no. 3 (July 1994): 265–96.

Garnett, Porter, ed. *Papers of the San Francisco Committee of Vigilance of 1851*. Pt. 1: *Constitution and List of Members*. Berkeley: University of California Press, 1910.

———. *Papers of the San Francisco Committee of Vigilance of 1851*. Pt. 2: *List of Names Approved by the Committee on Qualification*. Berkeley: University of California Press, 1911.

Gillespie, Charles V. "Vigilance Committee," 1875. BANC MSS C-D 190. Bancroft Library, University of California, Berkeley.

Gladden, Washington. *Working People and Their Employers*. Boston: Lockwood, Brooks, 1876.

Gordan, John D., III. *Authorized by No Law: The San Francisco Committee of Vigilance of 1856 and the United States Circuit Court for the District Court of California*. San Francisco: Ninth Judicial Circuit Historical Society, 1987.

Gorn, Elliott J. *The Manly Art: Bare-Knuckle Prize Fighting in America*. Ithaca, N.Y.: Cornell University Press, 1986.

Gould, Milton S. *A Cast of Hawks: A Rowdy Tale of Greed, Violence, Scandal, and Corruption in the Early Days of San Francisco*. La Jolla, Calif.: Copley Press, 1985.

[Gray, Henry M.] *Judges and Criminals: Shadows of the Past History of the Vigilance Committee of San Francisco, Cal., with the Names of Its Officers*. San Francisco: Printed for the Author, 1858.

Green, Alfred A. "Life and Adventures of a 47er of California," 1878. BANC MSS C-D 94. Bancroft Library, University of California, Berkeley.

Haight, Henry H., Papers, 1846–1885. mss HT 1-457. The Huntington Library, San Marino, Calif.

Hall, Carroll Douglas. *The Terry-Broderick Duel*. San Francisco: Colt Press, 1939.

Hauka, Donald J. *McGowan's War*. Vancouver, B.C.: New Star Books, 2003.

Heintz, William F. *San Francisco's Mayors, 1850–1880: Including a Missing Mayor Discovery*. Woodside, Calif.: Gilbert Richards, 1975.

Hittell, John S. *Commerce and Industries of the Pacific Coast of North America: Comprising the Rise, Progress, Products, Present Condition, and Prospects of the Useful Arts on the Western Side of Our Continent, and Some Account of Its Resources, with Elaborate Treatment of Manufactures; Briefer Consideration of Commerce, Transportation, Agriculture, and Mining; and Mention of Leading Establishments and Prominent Men in Various Departments of Business*. San Francisco: A. L. Bancroft and Company, 1882.

———. *A History of the City of San Francisco, and Incidentally of the State of California*. San Francisco: A. L. Bancroft and Company, 1878. Reprint, with a new introduction by Richard H. Dillon, Berkeley, Calif.: Berkeley Hills Books, 2000.

———. *The Resources of California: Comprising Agriculture, Mining, Geography, Climate, Commerce, Etc., Etc., and the Past and Future Development of the State*. San Francisco: A. Roman, 1863.

———. "Statement," 1882. BANC MSS C-E 198:3. Bancroft Library, University of California, Berkeley.

Hittell, Theodore H. Family Papers, 1869–1922. Collection 1752. California State Library—Sutro Branch, San Francisco.

———. *History of California*. 4 vols. San Francisco: N. J. Stone and Company, 1885–97.

———. "The Place in History of the California Pioneers," n.d. Mss c 979.4 H, California State Library—Sutro Branch, San Francisco.
Hittell Family Papers: Additions, circa 1869–1925. BANC MSS 70/37 c. Bancroft Library, University of California, Berkeley.
Hoadley, Milo, Diary and Related Papers, 1848– [ca. 1856]. BANC MSS C-F 201. Bancroft Library, University of California, Berkeley.
Holt, Michael F. *The Political Crisis of the 1850s*. New York: W. W. Norton and Company, 1978.
———. *Political Parties and American Political Development: From the Age of Jackson to the Age of Lincoln*. Baton Rouge: Louisiana State University Press, 1992.
Huggins, Dorothy H., comp. "Continuation of the Annals of San Francisco." *California Historical Society Quarterly* 16, no. 4 (December 1937): 336-47.
Hughes, Robert. *The Fatal Shore*. New York: Alfred A. Knopf, 1987.
Johnson, Allen, and Dumas Malone, eds. *Dictionary of American Biography*. 22 vols. New York: Charles Scribner's Sons, 1930–58.
Johnson, John Neely. Papers, 1848–1860. BANC MSS C-B 604. Bancroft Library, University of California,
———. Reports to the Governor, 1856–1857. GPI:309–55. California State Archives, Sacramento.
Johnson, Kenneth M. *José Yves Limantour v. The United States*. Los Angeles: Dawson's Book Shop, 1961.
Jolly, Michelle E. "Inventing the City: Gender and Politics of Everyday Life in Gold-Rush San Francisco, 1848–1869." Ph.D. dissertation, University of California, San Diego, 1998.
Kemble, Edward C. *A History of California Newspapers, 1846–1858*. 1858. Edited, annotated, and with a foreword by Helen Harding Bretnor. Los Gatos, Calif.: Talisman Press, 1962.
Kemble, John Haskell. *The Panama Route, 1848–1869*. 1943. Reprint, Columbia: University of South Carolina Press, 1990.
Kennedy, Elijah R. *The Contest for California in 1861: How Colonel E. D. Baker Saved the Pacific States to the Union*. Boston: Houghton Mifflin, 1912.
Kens, Paul. *Justice Stephen Field: Shaping Liberty from the Gold Rush to the Gilded Age*. Lawrence: University Press of Kansas, 1997.
Kinder, Gary. *Ship of Gold in the Deep Blue Sea*. New York: Vintage Books, 1999.
Kovács, András W. *The History of the Wass de Czege Family*. Translated by Ágnes Baricz. Hamburg: Edmund Siemers-Stiftung, 2005.
Lamoreaux, Naomi. *Insider Lending: Banks, Personal Connections, and Economic Development in Industrial New England*. New York: Cambridge University Press, 1996.
Lavender, David. *Nothing Seemed Impossible: William C. Ralston and Early San Francisco*. Palo Alto, Calif.: American West Publishing Company, 1975.
Leonard, Thomas C. *The Power of the Press: The Birth of American Political Reporting*. New York: Oxford University Press, 1986.
Lewis, Oscar. *Silver Kings: The Lives and Times of Mackay, Fair, Flood, and O'Brien, Lords of the Nevada Comstock Lode*. New York: Alfred A. Knopf, 1947.
Lotchin, Roger W. *San Francisco, 1846–1856: From Hamlet to City*. Lincoln: University of Nebraska Press, 1974.
Lyman, George D. "The Sponge." *Annals of Medical History* 10, no. 4 (1928): 467–70.

Lynch, Jeremiah. *A Senator of the Fifties: David C. Broderick, of California.* San Francisco: A. M. Robertson, 1911.

MacDonald, James M. "Recollections of Early Days in California: A Dictation," [1886?]. Typescript. BANC MSS C-D 302. Bancroft Library, University of California, Berkeley.

Macintyre, Stuart. *A Concise History of Australia.* Cambridge: Cambridge University Press, 1999.

Manrow, John P. "Statement... on Vigilance Committees in San Francisco," 1878. BANC MSS C-D 192. Bancroft Library, University of California, Berkeley.

May, Robert E. *Manifest Destiny's Underworld: Filibustering in Antebellum America.* Chapel Hill: University of North Carolina Press, 2002.

McAllister, Anna. *Ellen Ewing, Wife of General Sherman.* New York: Benziger Brothers, 1936.

McAllister, Hall. "Statement... on Vigilance Committees in San Francisco," 1877. BANC MSS C-D 202. Bancroft Library, University of California, Berkeley.

McElroy's Philadelphia Directory for 1855. Philadelphia: Edward C. and John Biddle, 1855.

McGowan, Edward. *Narrative of Edward McGowan, Including a Full Account of the Author's Adventures and Perils While Persecuted by the San Francisco Vigilance Committee of 1856.* San Francisco: The author, 1857.

McGuinness, Aims. *Path of Empire: Panama and the California Gold Rush.* Ithaca, N.Y.: Cornell University Press, 2008.

McPherson, James. *Battle Cry of Freedom: The Civil War Era.* New York: Oxford University Press, 1988.

Melendy, H. Brett, and Benjamin F. Gilbert. *The Governors of California: From Peter H. Burnett to Edmund G. Brown.* Georgetown, Calif.: Talisman Press, 1965.

Miller, Kerby A. *Emigrants and Exiles: Ireland and the Irish Exodus to North America.* New York: Oxford University Press, 1985.

Mills, Hazel Emery. "The Emergence of Frances Fuller Victor—Historian." *Oregon Historical Quarterly* 62 (December 1961): 309–36.

Mullen, Kevin J. *Let Justice Be Done: Crime and Politics in Early San Francisco.* Reno: University of Nevada Press, 1989.

Myers, John Myers. *San Francisco's Reign of Terror.* New York: Doubleday and Company, 1966.

Nevins, Allan. *Ordeal of the Union.* 2 vols. New York: Charles Scribner's Sons, 1947.

New York Court of Common Pleas. *James R. Molony, Appellant, against James Dows, Respondent.* [New York : Sackett & Cobb], 1860. BANC F869.S3.9.C6329N4; BANC FILM 3044 (microfilm). Bancroft Library, University of California, Berkeley.

Nichols, Roy F. *The Stakes of Power, 1845–1877.* New York: Hill and Wang, 1961.

Northam, Edward Fernandez. Dictation, 1887. BANC MSS C-D 837. Bancroft Library, University of California, Berkeley.

Oak, Henry L. *"Literary Industries" in a New Light: A Statement on the Authorship of Bancroft's* Native Races *and* History of the Pacific, *with Comments on Those Works and the System by Which They Were Written.* San Francisco: Bacon Printing Company, 1893.

Oliver, Denis J., Diary, 1856. BANC MSS 2007/118 v. 2 (transcription). Bancroft Library, University of California, Berkeley.

Olney, James N. "Vigilance Committee," n.d. BANC MSS C-D 195. Bancroft Library, University of California, Berkeley.

[O'Meara, James (attributed to "A Pioneer California Journalist")]. *The Vigilance Committee of 1856*. San Francisco: James H. Barry, 1887.

Page, Daniel D. Correspondence, 1847–1868. BANC MSS 77/200 c. Bancroft Library, University of California, Berkeley.

Papers Relating to the San Francisco Committee of Vigilance, 1856. BANC MSS 68/164C. Bancroft Library, University of California, Berkeley.

Peterson, Charles S. "Hubert Howe Bancroft: First Western Regionalist." In *Writing Western History: Essays on Major Western Historians*, edited by Richard W. Etulain, 43–70. Reno: University of Nevada Press, 2002.

Phelps, Alonzo. *Contemporary Biography of California's Representative Men*. San Francisco: A. L. Bancroft and Company, 1881.

Pinto, Francis E. "Historical Facts and Incidents Relating to the 1st Regiment of New York Volunteers in the Mexican War: With Reminiscences [sic] of Life in California from 1849–1856 and Operations of the San Francisco Vigilance Committee of 1856," n.d. Photocopy of typescript. BANC MSS 98/90. Bancroft Library, University of California, Berkeley.

Puleo, Stephen. *The Caning: The Assault That Drove America to Civil War*. Yardley, Pa.: Westholme, 2012.

Richards, Leonard L. *The Slave Power: The Free North and Southern Domination, 1780–1860*. Baton Rouge: Louisiana State University Press, 2000.

Robinson, W. W. *Land in California: The Story of Mission Lands, Ranchos, Squatters, Mining Claims, Railroad Grants, Land Scrip, Homesteads*. Berkeley: University of California Press, 1948.

Royce, Josiah. *California: From the Conquest in 1846 to the Second Vigilance Committee in San Francisco—A Study of American Character*. Boston: Houghton, Mifflin, 1886.

Ryckman, Gerritt W. "Vigilance Committee," n.d. BANC MSS C-D 196. Bancroft Library, University of California, Berkeley.

San Francisco Committee of Vigilance Miscellany, 1856 and [undated]. California Historical Society–North Baker Research Library, San Francisco.

San Francisco Committee of Vigilance of 1856, Minutes of the Executive Committee. California State Library—Sutro Branch, San Francisco, Calif.

San Francisco Committee of Vigilance of 1856 Papers, 1853–1882. BANC MSS C-A 78. Bancroft Library, University of California, Berkeley.

"San Francisco Committee of Vigilance of 1856 Roster." BANC MSS C-A 181. Bancroft Library, University of California, Berkeley.

San Francisco Committee of Vigilance Records, 1853–1858. mss Vigilance Committee. The Huntington Library, San Marino, Calif.

San Francisco Land Association. *Articles of Association and Agreement of the San Francisco Land Association, with Proceedings of the Meetings of Stockholders, Decree of Land Commission of California, and By-laws of the Board of Directors*. Philadelphia: Crissy and Markley, 1856.

———. [Circular, Preambles and Resolutions, Forms for Proposals, Etc.], 1856–57. BANC x F869.S3.76.S1642 no.1-6. Bancroft Library, University of California, Berkeley.

Saxton, Alexander. *The Indispensable Enemy: Labor and the Anti-Chinese Movement in California*. Berkeley: University of California Press, 1971.

Scherer, James A. B. *"The Lion of the Vigilantes": William T. Coleman and the Life of Old San Francisco*. Indianapolis: Bobbs-Merrill, 1939.

Schlereth, Thomas J. *Victorian America: Transformations in Everyday Life, 1876–1915*. New York: Harper Perennial, 1991.

Scott, E. A., to Daughter (C. T. Hubbell), July 20, 1856. Box 19. State Library Collection (SLC), California State Library, Sacramento.

Scott, Rev. Dr. [William A.]. *A Discourse for the Times: Delivered in Calvary Church, Sunday, July 27, 1856*. San Francisco: n.p., 1856.

Scott, William A., Papers, 1830–1885. BANC MSS C-B 360. Bancroft Library, University of California, Berkeley.

Senkewicz, Robert M. *Vigilantes in Gold Rush San Francisco*. Stanford, Calif.: Stanford University Press, 1985.

Shafter, Oscar Lovell. *Life, Diary and Letters of Oscar Lovell Shafter, Associate Justice, Supreme Court of California, January 1, 1864, to December 31, 1868*. Edited by Flora Haines Loughead. San Francisco: Blair-Murdock Company, 1915.

Sherman, William Tecumseh. *Memoirs of General William T. Sherman*. New York: D. Appleton and Company, 1875.

Shuck, Oscar T., ed. *History of the Bench and Bar of California: Being Biographies of Many Remarkable Men, a Store of Humorous and Pathetic Recollections, Accounts of Important Legislation and Extraordinary Cases, Comprehending the Judicial History of the State*. Los Angeles: Commercial Printing House, 1901.

Shumate, Albert. *James F. Curtis, Vigilante*. San Francisco: San Francisco Corral of the Westerners, 1988.

Smiley, Thomas J. L. "Statement . . . on Vigilance Committees and Early Times in San Francisco," 1877. BANC MSS C-D 199. Bancroft Library, University of California, Berkeley.

Smith, Carl T. "The Gillespie Brothers—Early Links between Hong Kong and California." *Chung Chi Hsiao Kan (Chung Chi Bulletin)* 47 (1969): 23–28.

Smith, Henry Nash. *Virgin Land: The American West as Symbol and Myth*. 1950. Reissued with a new preface Cambridge, Mass.: Harvard University Press, 1970.

Smith, Mortimer J., to Father, June 5, 1856. BANC MSS 90/69 c. Bancroft Library, University of California, Berkeley.

Smith, Winston O. *The Sharps Rifle: Its History, Development and Operation*. New York: William Morrow and Company, 1943.

Soulé, Frank, John H. Gihon, and James Nisbet. *The Annals of San Francisco: Containing a Summary of the History of the First Discovery, Settlement, Progress, and Present Condition of California, and a Complete History of All the Important Events Connected with Its Great City, to Which Are Added, Biographical Memoirs of Some Prominent Citizens*. New York: D. Appleton and Company, 1855.

Spencer, Ivor Debenham. *The Victor and the Spoils: A Life of William L. Marcy*. Providence, R.I.: Brown University Press, 1959.

Spierenburg, Pieter, ed. *Men and Violence: Gender, Honor, and Rituals in Modern Europe and America*. Columbus: Ohio State University Press, 1998.

Stevenson, Robert Louis. *The Wrecker*. New York: C. Scribner's Sons, 1891.

Stewart, Robert E., Jr., and Mary Frances Stewart. *Adolph Sutro: A Biography*. Berkeley, Calif.: Howell-North, 1962.

Stiles, T. J. *The First Tycoon: The Epic Life of Cornelius Vanderbilt*. New York: Alfred A. Knopf, 2009.
Stillman, J. D. B. "Statement... on Vigilance Committees in San Francisco," 1877. BANC MSS C-D 202. Bancroft Library, University of California, Berkeley.
Stout, Joseph Allen, Jr. *The Liberators: Filibustering Expeditions into Mexico, 1848–1862, and the Last Thrust of Manifest Destiny*. Los Angeles: Westernlore Press, 1973.
Summers, Mark W. *The Plundering Generation: Corruption and the Crisis of the Union, 1849–1861*. New York: Oxford University Press, 1987.
Taylor, William. *Seven Years' Street Preaching in San Francisco, California: Embracing Incidents, Triumphant Death Scenes, Etc.* Edited by W. P. Strickland. New York: Carlton and Porter, 1856.
Terry, David S., Papers. California and Western Manuscript Collection. MO 119, box 7, folder 50. Department of Special Collections, Stanford University Libraries, Stanford, Calif.
Terry, David Smith, Papers, 1849–1933. MS TE-1-259. The Huntington Library, San Marino, Calif.
Thomas, Lately. *Between Two Empires: The Life Story of California's First Senator, William McKendree Gwin*. Boston: Houghton Mifflin, 1969.
Thorndike, Rachel Sherman, ed. *The Sherman Letters: Correspondence between General and Senator Sherman from 1837 to 1891*. New York: Charles Scribner's Sons, 1894.
Tooker, Elva. *Nathan Trotter, Philadelphia Merchant, 1787–1853*. Cambridge, Mass.: Harvard University Press, 1955.
Trachtenberg, Alan. *The Incorporation of America: Culture and Society in the Gilded Age*. New York: Hill and Wang, 1982.
Trial of David S. Terry by the Committee of Vigilance, San Francisco. San Francisco: R. C. Moore and Company, 1856.
Truett, Miers F. "Statement... on Vigilance Committees in San Francisco," 1877. BANC MSS C-D 201. Bancroft Library, University of California, Berkeley.
Tubbs, Alfred L. "Recollections of Events in California," ca. 1887. BANC MSS CC-D 374. Bancroft Library, University of California, Berkeley.
Tuthill, Franklin. *The History of California*. San Francisco: H. H. Bancroft and Company, 1866.
Van Cortlandt, Augustus, to Uncle William, Calaveras County, Calif., June 17, 1856. BANC MSS C-Y 286. S Bancroft Library, University of California, Berkeley.
Vigilance Committee of San Francisco. *Proclamation of the Vigilance Committee of San Francisco, June 9th, 1856*. San Francisco: Hutchings and Company, 1856.
Vigilance Committee Records, 1856. Box 324. California State Library, Sacramento.
Wallace, Robert B., Letters: ALS, 1852–1860. MS Vault 63. California Historical Society–North Baker Research Library, San Francisco.
Watkins, William B. "Statement... on Vigilance Committees in San Francisco," 1878. BANC MSS C-D 203. Bancroft Library, University of California, Berkeley.
White, John I. *American Vignettes: A Collection of Footnotes to History*. Convent Station, N.J.: Travel Vision, 1976.
Williams, David A. *David C. Broderick: A Political Portrait*. San Marino, Calif.: Huntington Library, 1969.
Williams, Mary Floyd. *History of the San Francisco Committee of Vigilance of 1851: A Study of Social Control on the California Frontier in the Days of the Gold Rush*. Berkeley: University of California Press, 1921.

———, ed. *Papers of the San Francisco Committee of Vigilance of 1851*. Pt. 3: *Minutes and Miscellaneous Papers, Financial Accounts and Vouchers*. Berkeley: University of California Press, 1919.

Williams, R. Hal. *The Democratic Party and California Politics, 1880–1896*. Stanford, Calif.: Stanford University Press, 1973.

Witcover, Jules. *Party of the People: A History of the Democrats*. New York: Random House, 2003.

Wooley, Lell Hawley. "Vigilance Committee of 1856." In *California, 1849–1913; or, The Rambling Sketches and Experiences of Sixty-Four Years' Residence in That State*, by L. H. Woolley, 11–12. Oakland, Calif.: De Witt and Snelling, 1913.

Index

Accessory Transit Company, 64
Adams (ship). See *John Adams* (ship)
Adams and Company, 25–26, 130
Adelaide (ship), 60, 71
Aldrich, Daniel, 58
Allemany, Joseph Sadoc, 53–54
Alta California, 36, 38, 44, 54, 132, 180, 185, 196, 201, 202, 209, 219, 227, 231, 237
American Party. *See* Know-Nothings
Andrews, William E. B., 70, 153, 187
Arrington, Nicholas O., 67, 162
Ashe, Richard Porter, 88, 91–96, 101, 103, 110, 124–25
Australia, 19, 60–62

Backus, Rodman, 49
Bacon, Henry D., 41
Bagley, John W., 38–39, 58
Baker, Edward Dickenson, 31–32, 217
Bancroft, Hubert Howe, 7–9, 196, 222, 226–28, 230–34, 236–37
Barron, Eustace, 34
Beals, H. Channing, 179–80
Black List, 58, 70, 85, 157, 165, 197
Bluxome, Isaac, Jr., 41, 43, 147, 162, 173, 176, 203–4, 220, 225, 230–31
Board of Delegates. *See* Delegates
Board of Land Commissioners (U.S.), 4, 15–17, 23, 34, 122

Bolton, James R., 34
Bolton and Barron land claim, 10, 34, 130. *See also* San Francisco Land Association of Philadelphia; Santillán claim
Boutwell, Edward B., 64, 101, 111–14, 121–22, 164, 175, 177–78
Bovee, James, 92, 110–11, 203, 207
Brace, Philander, 138–40, 145, 148–54, 156–57, 163, 169, 173
Breen, Hugh, 83, 89–90, 99, 144, 148, 152, 156
Brittain, J. W., 158
Broderick, David Colbert, 5, 7, 20–22, 26–28, 30, 58, 84–85, 101–2, 132, 136–37, 151, 173, 185, 187, 191, 195–96, 206, 209, 214–17, 219, 234
Brooks, Preston, 120
Brown, Harvey S., 219
Brown, John, 119–20
Brown, Richard Maxwell, 9
Buchanan, James, 135, 187, 214
Buffum, E. Gould, 231
Bulger, Edward, 70, 75–76, 144–45, 147, 208
Bulkhead Bill, 22, 84
Bulletin. See *Evening Bulletin*
Burke, Martin J., 46, 216, 219–20, 228–29, 244n35
Burnett, Peter, 214
Burns, Aaron, 151, 162
Byrne, Henry H., 59, 85

California Blues, 92–94; armory, 93–97
California Chronicle. See *Chronicle*
Calvary Presbyterian Church, 149, 180, 182
Capprise, Joseph, 110, 255n11
Carr, William "Billy," 62, 71, 75–76, 208
Case, Charles, 124
Casey, James P., 30, 38–40, 43, 45, 48–49, 51–59, 64, 68, 76, 88, 101–2, 109–10, 132, 134, 149, 168, 173, 175, 198, 218
Central Street Wharf, 20
Chinese, 84, 125, 185, 202, 225, 228–29
Chivalry wing (Chivs), 21, 27, 30, 185, 214–15, 217
Chronicle, 36, 38, 43, 54, 180, 227
Citizens' Committee. See Committee of Citizens
Citizens Reform, 68
Civil War (U.S.), 7, 25, 221, 224–25
Cole, Richard Beverly, 44, 56, 62, 65, 92, 100, 153, 184, 199, 246n16
Coleman, William Tell, 8, 9, 17–20, 40–41, 43, 45, 48, 51, 57, 71, 79, 80, 84, 86, 95, 98, 129, 132–35, 138, 143–44, 149, 151–52, 161, 170–73, 182–83, 187–88, 190, 197–98, 205, 210–13, 217, 220, 223–25, 229, 232–33, 237. *See also* W. T. Coleman and Company
Coleville, Samuel, 231
Coleville's San Francisco Directory, 231
commissioners of the funded debt, 22, 24–25, 29, 83, 206
Committee of Citizens, 77–78, 107–8, 125
Committee of Thirteen, 28, 40
Comstock Lode, 222
Conness, John, 224
Consolidation Act, 59, 84, 119, 129, 132, 169, 196
Cook and Fenner, 206
Cooney, John, 210, 260n12
Cora, Belle, 31–32, 49, 53, 56–57, 217, 244n37
Cora, Charles, 31–32, 38–39, 43, 49, 51, 53–57, 76, 88, 101–2, 110, 149, 173, 217–18
Court for the Northern District of California, 34
Crary, Oliver, 47, 129, 220
Crescent Engine Company No. 10, 30, 56–57

Crocker, Charles, 223
Crockett, Joseph Bryant, 176, 178–79
Crowe, John, 190
Cunningham, Thomas, 85–86
Cunningham's Wharf, 20
Curtis, James F., 80, 184, 187, 189, 202
Customhouse, 16, 34, 38, 111, 121, 207–8

Daily Alta California. See *Alta California*
Daily California Chronicle. See *Chronicle*
Daily Evening Bulletin. See *Evening Bulletin*
Daily True Californian. See *True Californian*
David, Jules, 70, 143, 149, 159–60, 166, 176–77, 180, 186, 190, 204
Davis, Jefferson, 63, 180, 249n29
Decker, Peter R., 9
Delegates, 11, 52, 58, 71–72, 85–86, 90, 125, 131, 133, 146–49, 151, 157–59, 161, 163, 168, 186, 199, 204, 208
Democrats, northern, 21, 27, 30–31, 58, 84–85, 167–68, 173, 185, 214–15, 217, 226, 228
Democrats, southern. *See* Chivalry wing (Chivs)
Dempster, Clancey, 41, 57–58, 61, 86, 106, 115–16, 147, 157–58, 166, 183, 217–19, 232
Den, Nicholas, 131
Doane, Charles, 46–47, 51, 79, 97, 158, 164, 170, 176, 184, 204
Dobbin, James C., 113
Douglas, Stephen, 122, 214–15
Dows, James, 41, 47, 49, 85, 107, 111–12, 122, 136, 140, 151, 159–60, 166, 176–77, 187, 201, 209–12, 218, 226
Duane, Charles P., 57, 70–72, 75, 118–19, 175, 179, 187–88, 212, 218, 232
Durkee, John L., 84–85, 90, 101, 113–15, 118, 122, 125, 139, 150, 152, 174–79, 184, 187
Dwinelle, John W., 238

Empire Engine Company, 21, 136; Empire Engine House No. 1, 217
Ethington, Philip J., 10, 251n37
Evening Bulletin, 4, 9–10, 26–27, 36, 38–39, 54, 57, 68, 70–72, 75, 81, 86, 102, 115, 117, 119, 129, 133, 150, 153, 163, 166–67, 196, 227, 231

Exact (ship), 131, 143
Executive Committee, 5–11, 42, 44–54, 58–59, 62, 65–70, 72, 75–81, 83–88, 90–91, 94–102, 106–25, 130–52, 157–90, 196–206, 208–13, 222–27, 231–33, 236
Extension Bill. *See* Bulkhead Bill

Farragut, David Glasgow, 64, 86, 111–13, 121–22, 135, 143, 164, 177, 225
Farwell, James D., 41, 110, 112–13, 115, 131, 159, 172, 225
Fayolle, Amédée, 70
Field, Stephen J., 202, 218–19, 224–25
Fillmore, Millard, 135
Flint, Edward P., 218, 274n21
Foote, Henry, 86
Fort Gunnybags, 45–49, 52–56, 59, 64, 71, 78, 80, 85, 91, 94–101, 107, 109–17, 122–23, 133, 135–39, 145, 152–63, 170, 172, 176, 179
Fort Vigilance. *See* Fort Gunnybags
Fraser River. *See* gold rushes
Fremont, John Charles, 15, 135
French, 43, 47–48, 66, 70, 75, 79, 102, 112, 161, 170–71
Frink, George, 40, 232
Fritz, Christian G., 10

Gallagher, Charles, 53–54, 132, 159
Gallagher, Joseph A., 37, 195
Gallagher, Martin, 58–60, 71, 75–76, 182, 207–10, 217–18
Garrison, Cornelius K., 64, 87, 124, 188, 197, 244n35
General Committee, 6, 42–43, 52, 57, 69, 79, 90, 117, 141, 161, 171, 188, 208
Germans, 47, 49, 86, 170
Gillespie, Charles V., 84, 112, 134, 143–44, 176, 202, 226–27
Gladden, Washington, 230
Glencoe (ship), 182
Globe, 54, 195–96
Golden Age (ship), 52–53, 76, 135, 174
gold rushes: California, 9, 18, 234; Fraser River, 207
Green, Alfred A., 5–6, 33, 36–39, 133–34, 138, 145–51, 158–62, 165–69, 186, 191, 200–201, 209, 217–19, 228, 236
Green, Benjamin, 138
Green, Daniel, 138, 201, 206, 218
Green, Henry, 138
Green, John, 138, 201, 206, 218
Green, Mrs. (mother of brothers), 33, 133–34, 159–60
Green, Mrs. (wife of Alfred), 133–34, 159
Green, Robert, 138
Green brothers, 33, 199, 217
Gwin, William McKendree, 4, 27, 30, 111–12, 121, 173, 185, 195–96, 214

Haight, Fletcher M., 156
Haight, Henry H., 152, 156
Hale, Henry M., 208–9, 218
Hawaii, 76, 144, 182, 207–8
Hayes, Rutherford B., 228
Hayes, Thomas, 59, 98
Hays, John Coffee, 103, 115
Helen Hensley (ship), 164
Hennessey, James, 206, 218
Hensley. *See* Helen Hensley (ship)
Herald, 37–38, 43–44, 63, 70–72, 115, 120–23, 173–74, 176, 185, 227, 231
Heron, Matilda, 67
Hetherington, Joseph, 144–50, 157, 169, 173
Hittell, John S., 38, 209, 225, 232
Hittell, Theodore Henry, 7–9, 38, 54, 129, 133, 232, 234, 236–37
Hoffman, Ogden, 10, 114–15, 118, 175, 178, 199, 208–9
Hopkins, Mark, 223
Hopkins, Sterling A., 54–55, 88, 91–94, 99–102, 109–11, 115, 122, 124, 129, 140–43, 161, 169, 189, 203, 211
Hossefross, George, 162
Houston, Samuel, 103, 170
Howard, Volney Erskine, 78, 82, 92, 94–95, 97, 150
Huntington, Collis P., 223
Hyer, Tom, 60–61

Inge, Samuel W., 185–86, 189–91, 197
Irish, 10, 28, 57–58, 60–61, 78–79

Jessup, Richard M., 184, 195–96, 198
John Adams (ship), 64, 101, 111–12, 135, 158, 163–64, 175
John L. Stephens (ship), 76, 118–19
Johnson, Henry J., 59
Johnson, J. Neely, 5, 30, 45–46, 48, 62–64, 67, 72, 75, 77–78, 82–84, 87–88, 90, 100, 111, 116, 157, 168, 172, 178, 180, 186
Johnson, Kenneth M., 10
Jolly, Michelle, 10
Julia (ship), 88, 90–91, 101, 113–14, 124, 175, 178, 211, 218

Kansas, 6, 119–20, 214
Kearney, Denis, 228
Kearney, William "Wooley," 59, 62, 71, 75–76, 179
Kibbe, William, 64, 72, 82, 100, 107, 116, 135, 143, 157, 178, 186
King, Thomas Sim, 38, 40, 57, 81, 163, 231
King of William, James, 4–5, 24–27, 31–32, 36, 38, 44–45, 47, 51–55, 67, 76, 119, 130–31, 140, 166, 168, 172, 195, 198–99, 207
Know-Nothings, 28, 30–31, 37, 40, 49, 60, 67, 80, 135, 167, 184–85, 199; Council No. 1, 28; hall, 40–41
Kossuth, Louis, 79

Lake, Delos, 206
Land Act of 1851, 4, 16, 27
Larkin, Thomas Oliver, 107
Latham, Milton, 221
Law and Order Party, 45, 64, 72, 75–79, 85, 88, 91–98, 100–101, 109–17, 121, 124, 135, 139, 141, 149, 158, 163, 202, 232
Lees, Isaiah Wrigley, 139, 145, 187
Lewis, Bill, 58, 182, 208
Lilly, Christopher, 60, 131–32, 157, 197, 260n12
Limantour, José Yves, 10, 16, 34, 36, 151, 189–91, 201, 208–9
Limantour land claim, 29, 34, 36, 189–90, 196, 201, 208–9, 219, 238
Lincoln, Abraham, 8, 122, 219–20
Lippitt, Francis J., 80

Lotchin, Roger W., 9
Lucas, Turner and Company, 25, 76

Manrow, John P., 51, 136, 171, 176, 199, 232
Marcy (ship), 164
Marcy, William, 168
Marion, John, 139, 148
Marion Rifles, 79
Mariposa (ship), 91, 95, 178
Masonic Order, 24, 54, 96, 113, 115
Masons. *See* Masonic Order
mass meetings, 71–72, 83–84, 132–33, 167–68, 200–201, 209, 219
McAllister, Matthew Hall, 114, 118–19, 150, 175–79, 199, 210, 271n31
McClellan, George, 220
McElroy, Emily. *See* Sullivan, Emily McElroy
McGowan, Edward "Ned," 5, 28, 34, 46, 67–70, 84, 130–31, 143, 169, 198–99, 202–4, 207, 227, 233, 237
McInness, Sophie, 124
McKinnon, Joseph, 136
Merchants' Exchange, 52, 237
Mint, U.S., 16, 25, 34, 143, 148, 177, 182, 205
Minutes, 6–7, 9, 11, 43–44, 51, 76, 110, 138, 149, 161, 176, 184, 198, 217, 228, 231, 233–34, 237, 239
Mission Dolores, 16, 57, 66, 98, 139, 244n37
Molony, James Roby "Reub," 88, 91–96, 99, 106–7, 121–22, 124–25, 174, 178–79, 182–83, 187, 190, 203, 206, 210–12, 218, 233
Molony, Richard Sheppard, 122
Molony and Brother, 206
Monumental Engine Company, 109; bell, 31, 75, 94, 101, 176, 187, 239
Morning Globe. See *Globe*
Mullen, Kevin J., 9
Mulligan, William "Billy," 31, 38, 57–60, 67, 69, 71–72, 75–76, 179, 187, 190, 210, 212, 232, 244n39
Mulloy, Thomas, 124
Murray, Hugh, 107–8, 124, 201–2
Musgrove, John D., 132, 177, 260n12

National Police Gazette, 20
New York Times, 144, 168–69, 233
Nicaragua, 36, 63–64, 87, 132, 197

North, Hampton, 48, 54
Nugent, John (editor), 38, 43
Nugent, John (police officer), 110–11
Nutting, Calvin, 50, 58

Ocean House, 191, 217
Oliver, Denis J., 37, 44, 62, 66, 71, 87, 115, 132, 157, 163, 168–69, 172–74, 176, 185, 189–90
Olney, James N., 179
O'Meara, James, 136
Oregon, 11, 200, 238

Pacific Empire. *See* Pacific Republic
Pacific Mail Steamship Company, 20, 179, 229
Pacific Republic, 86–87, 120, 158, 198, 220–21
Pacific Street Wharf, 45, 67, 164
Page, Carrie, 20
Page, Daniel D., 20, 25, 41
Page and Bacon, 20, 25, 41
Palmer, Cook and Company (PC&C), 26, 28, 34, 36–37, 68–69, 130, 191
Palmer, Joseph C., 15, 26, 28, 34, 69–70
Panama, 50, 53, 64, 76, 124, 131, 177, 197–98
Park, Trenor, 120, 206
Pearson, Robert, 118–19
People's Party, 7, 9–10, 168, 184–85, 187, 196, 204, 220, 225
Perley, D. W., 162
Peter Smith claims, 21–22, 25, 29, 83, 151, 196, 201–2, 206, 209, 219, 234
Peyton, Bailie, 83–84
Phillips, John, 91–92
Pierce, Franklin, 68, 88, 168–70, 180
Pinto, Francis, 44, 47, 80, 94, 129, 139, 232
Polk, J. L., 179
Post, Gabriel B., 40, 76, 266n14
Pueblo Papers, 5–6, 33, 36, 133–34, 138, 146–47, 151, 157, 159–60, 166–69, 186, 189, 191, 196, 199–202, 218–19, 227, 234, 236, 238; lands, 224–25

Ralston, William, 107, 222, 224–26
Rand, Charles, 175, 178
Randall, Andrew, 144–45, 147–48, 153

Randolph, Edmund, 63–64
Rankin, Ira, 167–68
Republican Party, 135, 167, 215, 219–20
Rhodes, William H., 80–81, 157, 176–77, 231
Richardson, William A., 34, 36, 191, 245n6
Richardson, William H., 31, 38, 51, 245n6
Rivas, Patricio, 63–64
Roach, Phillip, 92
Roach, Thomas, 210
Rogers, William, 176, 187
Royce, Josiah, 8
Runnels, Cornelia. *See* Terry, Cornelia Runnels
Russia American Ice Company, 78
Ryan, Arrabella. *See* Cora, Belle
Ryckman, Gerritt, 136–37

Sacramento Daily Union, 88, 185, 197, 227
Sanchez heirs, 102, 141–43
San Francisco Land Association of Philadelphia, 10, 15–16, 26, 34, 69, 130, 156, 191, 200, 209, 232, 238
Santillán, José Prudencio, 16, 33–34, 191, 200
Santillán claim, 16, 29, 33, 36, 130, 151, 200, 209, 219, 232, 236, 238
Scannell, David, 45–49, 52, 59, 72, 158
Scherer, James A. B., 8
Scott, William Anderson, 149, 180, 182, 195
Selover and Sinton, 26, 29
Senkewicz, Robert M., 9
Shafter, Oscar Lovell, 120–21
Shattuck, David O., 22, 83, 113–14
Sherman, Ellen Ewing, 101
Sherman, William Tecumseh, 5, 25, 45, 48, 51, 62–65, 71–72, 75–78, 82, 96, 101, 158, 178, 186, 225–26, 239, 252n13. *See also* Lucas, Turner and Company
Sinton, R. H., 26
Sisters of Mercy, 37, 217
Smiley, Thomas J. L., 84, 97–98, 100, 102, 110, 115, 124, 138, 141–43, 146, 148–49, 159–61, 166, 172–73, 176, 179, 186, 188, 198, 205, 208, 220, 232–34
Smith, James, 76, 144, 208–10
Smith, Peter, 21–22. *See also* Peter Smith claims

Society of California Pioneers, 232, 239
Sonora (ship), 150, 158
Stanford, Leland, 219–20, 223
steamer day, 50, 75
Stephens (ship). *See John L. Stephens* (ship)
Stephens, John, 177
Stevenson, Robert Louis, 229, 237
Sullivan, Emily McElroy, 61, 66
Sullivan, James "Yankee," 57–62, 65–66, 70–71, 88, 101, 152
Sumner, Charles, 120
Sun, 37, 44, 123

Terry, Benjamin Franklin "Frank" (brother), 103–5, 169
Terry, Cornelia Runnels, 102–11, 116–17, 123–24, 143, 151, 162, 164, 168, 216
Terry, David Smith, 6, 11, 30, 67, 72, 78, 82–83, 88, 91–96, 99–124, 129, 138–46, 149–50, 153–54, 156–59, 168–70, 173–74, 177–78, 180, 184–85, 189, 201–3, 214–20, 227, 233, 255n11
Terry, David Smith (son), 106
Terry, Frank Davis (son), 106
Terry, Samuel Langdon, 106
Texas, 67, 88, 103–5, 169–70, 178
33 Secretary, 43, 71, 162, 205, 220. *See also* Bluxome, Isaac, Jr.
Thompson, James "Liverpool Jack," 177, 260n12
Thompson, Samuel T., 141
tide-lots. *See* water lots
Tillinghast, William, 151, 204, 209
Town Talk, 36, 227
True Californian, 81, 176, 231
Truett, Henry B., 122, 152
Truett, Miers, 46, 48–49, 67, 152, 162–65, 187–88, 207, 211–12, 218, 222, 233
Tubbs, Alfred L., 76, 176, 218, 227
Tuthill, Franklin, 225–26

Union Committee of Thirty-Four, 219–20
U.S. Circuit Court for Northern California, 114–15, 118, 175, 210, 224
U.S. District Court for Northern California, 34, 199–200, 207–8, 218

Vanderbilt, Cornelius, 64, 87, 197
Van Ness, James, 29, 40, 45, 48, 62, 119
Van Ness Ordinance, 29–30, 196, 206–7, 219, 225, 234, 238
Vasquez, Tiburcio, 138, 151, 262n1
Vigilance Committee of 1851, 5, 8–9, 19–21, 23–24, 32, 40, 57, 75–76, 167, 170, 196, 211, 230–31
Vigilance Committee of 1856, 5, 8–11, 17, 33, 41, 51–52, 57, 66, 70, 72, 79, 83–84, 91, 97–98, 111, 113, 129, 131, 135, 139, 141, 149–50, 152, 156–57, 160–61, 168–70, 180, 182–83, 186–90, 196–201, 204, 206–7, 209, 216, 218, 220, 225, 227, 230–34, 236, 238–39. *See also* Delegates; Executive Committee; General Committee

Wakeman, Edgar, 60, 71, 249n12
Walker, William, 28, 36, 63–64, 87, 132, 197–98
Wallace, Robert B., 44, 170, 183, 186–87
Wallace Guards, 79
Ward, George, 59, 146, 176, 178, 186
Washington Restaurant and Saloon, 68–69
Wass, Samu (Samuel), 79
water lots, 16–19, 29–30
Weller, John B., 185, 221
Wells, Fargo & Company, 25, 76
West, Joseph B., 138–39, 148
West, Joseph Rodman, 97–98, 102, 116
Whig Party, 135, 167
Whitmore, Horace M., 196, 199, 201, 204, 208–9, 212–13
Wide West, 86
Wilkes, George, 20
Williams, Mary Floyd, 8
Woodworth, Frederick A., 167, 196, 204, 218, 225, 266n9
Woodworth, Selim E., 18, 167
Wool, John Ellis, 63–64, 67, 77–78, 82, 86, 88, 129, 178–79, 249n29
Workingmen's riots, 228–29, 235
W. T. Coleman and Company, 76

Yankee (ship), 76, 144, 147, 207–8, 210
Young Men's Democratic Club, 164, 176

www.ingramcontent.com/pod-product-compliance
Lightning Source LLC
Chambersburg PA
CBHW020744160426
43192CB00006B/238